2004

Vietnam and the American Political Tradition
The Politics of Dissent

This volume of essays is intended to demonstrate how opposition to the war in Vietnam, the military-industrial complex, and the national security state crystallized in a variety of different and often divergent political traditions. Indeed, for many of the figures discussed, dissent was a decidedly conservative act; they felt that the war threatened traditional values, mores, and institutions, even though their definitions of what was sacred differed profoundly. During the course of the Vietnam War, they came to see the foreign policy, which they were supporting with its willingness to invoke the democratic ideal and at the same time tolerate dictatorships in the cause of anticommunism, as morally and politically corrupt. Though most dissenters were liberal – they believed that government had a duty to regulate the economy, help the disadvantaged, and participate in schemes of collective security – all were conservative in that they increasingly came to perceive Cold War liberalism as a radical departure that threatened the fundamental ideals of the republic.

Randall B. Woods is John A. Cooper Distinguished Professor of History at the University of Arkansas. He has written widely on twentieth-century American history, including *Quest for Identity* (2000), *Dawning of the Cold War* (1991), *Changing of the Guard* (1990), and *Fulbright: A Biography* (1995), which won both the Ferrell and Ledbetter Prizes.

Vietnam and the American Political Tradition

The Politics of Dissent

Edited by

RANDALL B. WOODS

University of Arkansas

CAMBRIDGE
UNIVERSITY PRESS

PUBLISHED BY THE PRESS SYNDICATE OF THE UNIVERSITY OF CAMBRIDGE
The Pitt Building, Trumpington Street, Cambridge, United Kingdom

CAMBRIDGE UNIVERSITY PRESS
The Edinburgh Building, Cambridge CB2 2RU, UK
40 West 20th Street, New York, NY 10011-4211, USA
477 Williamstown Road, Port Melbourne, VIC 3207, Australia
Ruiz de Alarcón 13, 28014 Madrid, Spain
Dock House, The Waterfront, Cape Town 8001, South Africa

http://www.cambridge.org

First published 2003

Printed in the United States of America

Typeface Sabon 10/13 pt.   *System* LATEX 2ε   [TB]

A catalog record for this book is available from the British Library.

Library of Congress Cataloging in Publication Data

Vietnam and the American political tradition : the politics of dissent / edited by
Randall B. Woods.
p. cm.
Includes bibliographical references and index.
ISBN 0-521-81148-1 – ISBN 0-521-01000-4 (pb.)
1. Vietnamese Conflict, 1961–1975 – United States.   2. Vietnamese Conflict,
1961–1975 – Protest movements – United States.   3. United States – Politics and
government – 1963–1969.   4. United States – Politics and government – 1969–1974.
I. Woods, Randall Bennett, 1944–
DS558 .V476   2003
959.704'3373–dc21   2002025619

ISBN 0 521 81148 1 hardback
ISBN 0 521 01000 4 paperback

Contents

Contributors

H. W. Brands, *Texas A&M University*

Robert D. Johnson, *Brooklyn College*

Thomas J. Knock, *Southern Methodist University*

Fredrik Logevall, *University of California, Santa Barbara*

Kyle Longley, *Arizona State University*

Frank Ninkovich, *St. John's University*

Donald A. Ritchie, *U.S. Senate*

David F. Schmitz, *Whitman College*

Robert D. Schulzinger, *University of Colorado*

Randall B. Woods, *University of Arkansas*

Introduction

Randall B. Woods

Political and diplomatic history have fallen into disrepute of late. They are, critics proclaim, concerned with power, elites, and white males, both living and dead. The subfields are allegedly subject to "top-down" treatment and largely ignore the inarticulate, disfranchised, and powerless. All of this is true; much work in diplomatic, and to a lesser extent, political history seems repetitive, overly abstract, and unimaginative. And yet, if one reads the *New York Times* or listens to National Public Radio, much of the reporting has to do with politics at home and abroad, and the interaction between nation states. That is so because educated laypeople find such topics not only interesting but important. They do have a point. In the United States, at least, the national political arena is not only where interests project their power but where the people's representatives discuss the nation's values and goals, in the process forging its very identity. The realm of international relations is where national goals, values, and ideologies compete, coexist, conquer, or perish. In the aftermath of the Cold War the threat of religious, ethnic, and tribal conflict has become as important as the danger posed by international warfare. Nevertheless, power is still exercised to a large extent by national governments, both internally and externally. In truth, though, the distinction between culture on the one hand and politics and diplomacy on the other is artificial.

Isolationism has always been a dominant theme in American foreign policy. The nation was born in part out of a desire to separate itself from the evils of European monarchism and colonialism. In the decades that followed the American Revolution, it labored to avoid entanglement in great power rivalries because entanglement might very well have led to conquest by one of those great powers. With the maturing of the U.S.

economy, businessmen, politicians, and diplomats turned their attention
to overseas markets and sources of raw materials. The need to preserve
and advance the nation's economic interests abroad necessitated a more
active foreign policy, but lingering distrust of great power politics and
foreign cultures prompted the United States to eschew long-term alliances
and act largely alone, a stance historians and political scientists have labeled unilateralism. A third major theme in U.S. diplomatic history has
been the notion of American exceptionalism. Throughout its history, the
United States has operated with the conviction that its experience was
unique, that it was destined to be the freest, most productive, most just
society in human history. As the nation was forced to become more active
in world affairs, many took the position that if the United States could not
preserve its splendid isolation, then it must spread the blessings of its civilization to the less fortunate peoples of the world. Finally, in the aftermath
of World War II, the United States seemed to have embraced the notion
of internationalism, that is, that in a world made small by modern communications and threatened by nuclear warfare, the interest of the United
States was inextricably bound up with the interests of all other nations.
It was therefore incumbent on the Republic to surrender a portion of its
national sovereignty within the context of a global collective security organization. In fact, America's commitment to pure internationalism has
always been more theoretical and rhetorical than real. When vital economic and strategic interests have been at stake, the nation has insisted
on retaining its freedom of action.

Knowing these things to be true, many scholars have assumed that the
key to understanding America's attitude toward the rest of the world,
and hence its role in the international community, is to be found in the
dynamics of its own culture rather than in events abroad. Certainly foreign
wars, economic competition, and ideologies have had a profound effect
on America's foreign policies, but the roots of those policies lay in the
prejudices, preconceptions, and practices of the citizenry. Therefore, what
better place to study foreign policy than the Congress of the United States?
That the Executive rather than Congress is constitutionally empowered
to conduct foreign affairs is certainly relevant but does not warrant the
dismissal of the nation's legislature as both a means and an end to the
study of foreign relations. Unfortunately, the executive branch and its
historians have tended to do just that.

The attitudes, interests, and ideologies that were responsible for the
United States' involvement in the First (1941–1954) and Second (1960–
1973) Indochinese Wars may be found in a study of the Congress and

its ongoing if intermittent dialogue with the Executive. So too may be its decision to withdraw from the latter conflict. In general, senators and members of Congress reflect the regional political cultures from whence they come. Despite the ignorance of many of its members and the irrelevance of their rhetoric – or perhaps because of them – Congress mattered. The events of World War II and the early Cold War combined with the perceptions and preoccupations of the various regions, classes, and ethnic groups comprising the United States to produce the activism that led the nation into the war in Vietnam. Those same views and concerns contributed to the emergence of a congressional consensus in behalf of withdrawal. The argument here, of course, is not that Congress was the cause of American intervention and withdrawal but a rich and perhaps unique matrix for examining those causes.

From 1882 until 1941 Laos, Cambodia, and Vietnam comprised French Indochina, France's richest and most important colony. Following France's surrender to Germany in June, 1940, the region was occupied by Japan – either directly or indirectly – until 1945. In 1946, the French returned to Southeast Asia determined to reestablish control in their former possessions.

The war in the Pacific had given a strong fillip to anticolonial movements throughout the area, and Indochina was no exception. Shortly after Japan's surrender in August, 1945, Ho Chi Minh – leader of the Vietminh, a broad-based but communist-led resistance movement – had proclaimed from Hanoi the existence of a new nation, the Democratic Republic of Vietnam (DRV). Over the next year and a half, however, the French, with the help of the British in the south and the Chinese Nationalists in the north, had managed to reestablish themselves firmly in the south and tentatively in the north. In November, 1946, a bitter colonial war erupted between the French and the Vietminh, culminating in 1954 with France's defeat at the battle of Dien Bien Phu. A subsequent peace conference at Geneva provided for the temporary division of the country at the Seventeenth Parallel. The French withdrew from the peninsula but left an anticommunist regime in place in the south – the Republic of Vietnam (RVN) – under emperor Bao Dai and his prime minister, Ngo Dinh Diem. Within a year Diem had ousted Bao Dai and instituted a presidential system with himself as chief executive. Meanwhile, in the north Ho had established the one-party, socialist DRV.

There was no doubt that Ho, one of the original members of the French Communist Party, was a Marxist-Leninist or that the DRV was a totalitarian regime. After both Moscow and Beijing recognized Ho's government

as the legitimate ruler of all of Vietnam in 1950, the United States concluded that the DRV was a Sino-Soviet satellite and that Ho was a puppet of Stalin and Mao Zedong. Throughout the 1950s the Eisenhower
administration poured economic and military aid into Vietnam. Diem
briefly attempted land and constitutional reform, but proved unsuited to
the task of building a social democracy. A devout Catholic and traditional
Mandarin by temperament and philosophy, he distrusted the masses and
had contempt for the give-and-take of democratic politics. Increasingly,
Diem relied on his family and loyal Catholics in the military and civil service to rule a country in which 90 percent of the population was Buddhist.
His brother Ngo Dinh Nhu used the Can Lao Party, the press, and the
state police to persecute and suppress opponents of the regime. As corruption increased and democracy all but disappeared, a rebellion broke
out in the south against the Diem regime. In 1960 the DRV decided to
give formal aid to the newly formed National Liberation Front (NLF),
as the anti-Diemist revolutionaries called themselves. A variety of factors
combined to ensure that President Kennedy would attempt to hold the
line in Southeast Asia. He viewed the conflict in South Vietnam as one of
Soviet leader Nikita Khrushchev's wars of national liberation, a test of his
administration's resolve just as much as Berlin or Cuba. Kennedy and his
advisers had fully accepted the "domino theory," whereby it was assumed
that the fall of one government in a particular region threatened by communism would lead to the fall of all noncommunist governments in that
area. His agreement in 1961 to the neutralization of Laos, a landlocked
nation wracked by communist insurgency, had further strengthened his
resolve to ensure that South Vietnam remained a "free world bastion."
The number of American uniformed personnel would grow from several
hundred when Kennedy assumed office to sixteen thousand by 1963.

Despite American aid, the Diem regime became increasingly isolated
from the masses. Bribes and intimidation by civil servants and military
officials alienated peasant and urban dweller alike. Law 10/59, which
the government had pushed through the rubber-stamp national assembly,
had given Nhu's police and special forces the power to arrest and execute
South Vietnamese citizens for a wide variety of crimes including black
marketeering and the spreading of seditious rumors about the government. By 1963 the nation was teetering on the brink of chaos, with the
Vietcong (the military branch of the NLF) in control of the countryside,
students and intellectuals demonstrating in Saigon and Hue, Buddhist
monks burning themselves in protest, and high-ranking military officers
hatching a variety of coup plots.

Prior to taking office Nixon and Kissinger had stoutly defended America's commitment to South Vietnam. During the 1968 campaign the Republican candidate had consistently blasted Lyndon Johnson for not doing more on the battlefield to pressure the North Vietnamese; he seemed particularly enthralled with bombing. To Nixon, victory depended on "the will to win," and he boasted to Kissinger that unlike Johnson, "I have the will in spades." America's stand in Vietnam was necessary to contain Chinese communist expansion and to allow "free" Asian nations the time to grow strong enough to defend themselves, he had told the voters. Kissinger took the position that early policymakers had exaggerated the importance of Vietnam to the national interest, but once committed, the United States could not afford to back down. The dispatch of hundreds of thousands of American troops had settled the matter, he argued, "for what is involved now is confidence in American promises."

By inauguration day, however, both Richard Nixon and Henry Kissinger were convinced that the war in Vietnam had to be ended. Indeed, during the campaign Nixon had let it be known that he had a "secret plan" to end the conflict in Southeast Asia. But any peace achieved would have to be "peace with honor," and that meant no unilateral withdrawal, no abandonment of the South Vietnamese government then headed by General Nguyen Van Thieu. Nixon had led the attacks on Truman for the loss of China, and like Johnson he feared the political backlash and the deep divisions that would result if it appeared he had "lost" Vietnam. More important, both he and Kissinger believed that it was imperative to deal with China and the Soviet Union from a position of strength rather than weakness.

Indeed, resolution of the conflict in Vietnam had become central to the president's and national security adviser's plan to make the United States the sole arbiter of world affairs. The new Republican administration accepted the implications of NSC-68, that it was necessary to battle communism on every front, but it believed that global containment could be achieved through diplomacy rather than force of arms. In Kissinger's view the Soviet Union and to a lesser extent Communist China were on their way to becoming satiated, status quo powers. If the United States could disarm their fears and appeal to their economic interests, the two communist superpowers might be persuaded to take their places as responsible members of the international community. The opening of communications with Moscow and Beijing and subsequent negotiations would be dangerous and counterproductive, however, if it appeared the United States was being forced out of Southeast Asia by a tiny underdeveloped nation like North Vietnam.

Richard Nixon wanted to end the war in Vietnam then, but prompted by the JCS, Kissinger, and his new military adviser, General Andrew Goodpaster, the president initially believed that he could do so by winning rather than losing. "I refuse to believe," Kissinger declared, "that a little fourth-rate power like North Vietnam doesn't have a breaking point." The North Vietnamese were on the run, Nixon's advisers reported. In 1967, having fought an unsuccessful guerrilla war, the Communists had decided to change tactics. The result had been Tet, a disaster for the VC. This had been followed by NVA offensives in May and August 1968. Both had been turned back, and in the process B-52s had pulverized enemy troop concentrations. The North Vietnamese had withdrawn 40,000 troops from the south and were in Paris negotiating because they had reached a dead end militarily. If Goodpaster and the JCS were correct, the war was virtually won on the battlefield. America could afford to be tough and drive a hard bargain at the negotiating table, the president decided.

Nixon and Kissinger's strategy was to couple great power diplomacy with force in an effort to win an "honorable" peace at the Paris negotiations. As part of this plan, the president was prepared to threaten the very survival of North Vietnam in order to break the enemy's will. Analogizing between his situation and that faced by President Dwight D. Eisenhower in Korea in 1953, Nixon believed that the threat of annihilation could be used just as effectively against Hanoi as it had against Pyongyang. His image as a hard-line anticommunist would make his warnings credible.

For the next two years Richard Nixon attempted to bully and negotiate his way out of the Vietnam quagmire. He simultaneously announced a policy of Vietnamization and began pulling U.S. combat troops out of Vietnam, authorized a U.S.–South Vietnamese invasion of Cambodia in 1970 intended to destroy NVA and VC strongholds, launched a savage bombing of the North, and continued secret peace talks with the communists in Paris. When the dust had settled, America's position in Southeast Asia was worse strategically and politically than when Nixon took the oath of office. The president was only momentarily taken aback. In early 1971, he decided to continue his policy of lashing out at the enemy while backing out of the ring. To appease critics at home, the timetable for American troop withdrawals was accelerated. Over the protests of General Creighton Abrams, U.S. commander in Vietnam, Nixon ordered the removal of 100,000 troops by the end of the year, leaving 175,000 men in Vietnam of whom only 75,000 were combat forces. At the same time, the White House authorized a major ground operation, codenamed Lam Son, against communist sanctuaries in Laos. The president's justification was the same as that for Cambodia – to buy time for Vietnamization by disrupting enemy supply lines.

Nothing worked. The Laotian offensive was turned back with heavy casualties, particularly among South Vietnamese forces. In 1972, the North Vietnamese invaded across the Demilitarized Zone. They were eventually repulsed, but only after inflicting heavy losses on the Army of the Republic of Vietnam (ARVN). Vietnamization coupled with the increasingly active and pervasive antiwar movement in the United States undermined morale among American servicemen in Vietnam. It was clear even to Nixon by the close of 1972 that the United States could not win.

Peace negotiations between Henry Kissinger and North Vietnamese representative Le Duc Tho, conducted intermittently and secretly throughout the Nixon administration's first four years, began in earnest in January 1973. The atmosphere was tense but businesslike. In a matter of days the diplomats has worked out a peace settlement. The United States agreed to withdraw its troops from Vietnam in a specified time period in return for repatriation of American prisoners of war. The Nixon administration was not required to withdraw support from the Thieu government, but NVA troops were free to remain in the south, and the accords granted recognition to the Provisional Revolutionary Government, the political apparatus established by the NLF. President Thieu protested, but to no avail. Nixon quietly let the South Vietnamese leader know that if he did not endorse the accords, the United States would cut off aid. Thieu held out for a time, but then acquiesced. It was just a matter of time until direct American participation in "America's longest war" came to an end.

Nixon had captured the presidency in 1968 by promising "peace with honor." The administration's prolonged disentanglement resulted in an additional 20,553 American battle deaths, bringing the total to more than 58,000. The fighting from 1969 through 1973 took more than 100,000 ARVN and 500,000 NVA and VC lives. The conflict fueled an already alarming inflationary trend in the United States and shook the nation's confidence to its core. America had taken up the burden of world leadership in the wake of World War II believing that it was fighting to save freedom, democracy, and indigenous cultures from the scourge of totalitarianism. It had been confident of its ability to cope with any crisis, make any sacrifice. In Vietnam, however, the United States threatened to destroy what it would save. In its obsession with the Cold War, it ignored the truth that for many peoples, regional rivalries, socioeconomic grievances, and religious differences outweighed strategic and ideological considerations. With Watergate spreading like the proverbial cancer through his presidency, Nixon was increasingly unable to maintain any sort of consensus in behalf of either continued American participation in the war or continued American support for the South Vietnamese.

The internal struggle in Vietnam reached a denouement more quickly and suddenly than most had anticipated. The peace agreements simply made possible a continuation of the war without direct American participation. The North attacked, the South counterattacked, and the Nixon administration bombed NVA sanctuaries in Laos and Cambodia.

Meanwhile, the antiwar movement in Congress, galvanized by Nixon's invasion of Cambodia, reached a climax. From 1970–1972 the House and Senate considered a number of resolutions either limiting or eliminating the president's capacity to make war in Southeast Asia. In the midst of the Watergate scandal, that impetus expanded to include the president's authority to make war in general. The movement to undermine the presidency's war-making powers culminated with congressional passage of the War Powers Act in the fall of 1973. The measure, originally introduced by Senator Jacob Javits of New York, required the president to inform Congress within forty-eight hours of the deployment of American military forces abroad and obligated him to withdraw them in sixty days in the absence of explicit congressional endorsement. As he had promised he would do, Nixon vetoed the War Powers Act, but Congress voted to override on November 7, 1973. The following week the House and Senate endorsed an amendment to the Military Procurement Authorization Act banning the funding of any U.S. military action in any part of Indochina. In the spring of 1975 the North Vietnamese mounted a major offensive, and the ARVN collapsed within a matter of weeks. With South Vietnamese military and civilian officials struggling to be part of the departing American diplomatic contingent, Saigon fell to the NVA and VC on April 30, 1975.

Though they represented very different regions of the country and a variety of political traditions, the influential senators examined in this volume – Albert Gore (D-TN), Frank Church (D-ID), Ernest Gruening (D-AK), J. William Fulbright (D-AS), Mike Mansfield (D-MO), John Sherman Cooper (R-KY), and George McGovern (D-ND) would play a crucial role in destroying the Vietnam consensus that Lyndon Johnson had inherited and that Richard Nixon sought to perpetuate.

Appalled by the carnage in Vietnam, the conversion of hundreds of thousands of sedentary villagers into homeless refugees, and the inability of the United States to raise up and work through any sort of broad-based political system in the South, McGovern, Church, and company turned against the conflict in Southeast Asia. At various times between 1964 and 1967, they arrived at the conclusion that the war in Vietnam was essentially a civil war and that the United States was simply supporting one side against the other. Indeed, they came to argue that the insurgency in the South was chiefly a response to the repressive policies of the government in Saigon and its American ally. International communism was not monolithic and the domino theory was specious. These legislators, most of them former Cold War activists, came to see that in harnessing their obsession with social justice to anticommunism, liberals had turned the Cold War into a missionary crusade which blinded the nation to the political and cultural realities of Southeast Asia. It also made possible an unholy alliance between realpolitikers preoccupied with markets and bases, and emotionally committed to the domino theory, and idealists who wanted to spread the blessings of freedom, democracy and a mixed economy to the less fortunate of the world. Finally, they came to believe, the nation's misguided crusade in Indochina was threatening the very institutions and values that made America. How and why these senators came to these conclusions and the impact of their positions on the war in Vietnam are the subjects of this volume.

Anti-Imperialism in U.S. Foreign Relations

Frank Ninkovich

What role has anti-imperialism played in U.S. foreign relations? While it is safe to say that it has been an important phenomenon, a more precise appraisal of its significance can come only from an historical understanding of its place among the nation's foreign policy traditions. At first sight, it would appear an easy matter to get a handle on this question, if only because the number of such traditions is quite small. Indeed, over the course of the past century, American foreign policy has been faced, broadly speaking, with only two abiding problems: imperialism and power politics. Because Americans have tended, with allowances for occasional lapses, to be opposed to both practices as a matter of principle, the short list of foreign policy paradigms narrows down rather quickly to two contenders: anti-imperialism and opposition to power politics.

Which to choose? Inasmuch as the two world wars and the cold war were great power conflicts, it seems clear that U.S. foreign policy in the twentieth century has been driven largely by geopolitical[1] motives. It would seem fair to conclude, therefore, that anti-imperialism, however prominent on occasion, has on the whole played only a marginal role in the history of U.S. foreign relations. A parallel verdict would appear to be

---

[1] "Geopolitics," as I use it throughout this essay, should not be confused with power politics, realism, or *Realpolitik*. For my purposes, it means, 1) that its practitioners believed great power conflict to be the chief problem of the modern era; and, 2) that great power dynamics now operated on a global stage. By this definition, even Woodrow Wilson, oftentimes described as an idealist, thought geopolitically.

I would like to thank Robert David Johnson for reading an earlier version of this essay and for pointing out a number of serious blunders and mistakes. All remaining errors are mine alone.

in order when evaluating the importance of anti-imperialism as a scholarly theme, for in academic writing geopolitics has clearly enjoyed privileged status among diplomatic historians and among specialists in international relations. QED: great power antagonisms have been the lead story.

While that conclusion is true, as far as it goes, its bluntness fails to convey the complexity of the relationship between anti-imperialism and other foreign policy outlooks. In reviewing the history of U.S. foreign relations, one can discern a rhythmic pattern of alternating anti-imperialist and geopolitical phases in which the rise of one outlook has coincided with the absence of the other. Though it has often played second fiddle to power political concerns over the past century, anti-imperialism has on occasion done a solo turn on center stage. Typically, it has surged to the forefront of political consciousness in periods of great power calm when it seemed plausible to assume that imperialism was the only serious foreign policy problem facing the United States, only to retreat to the margins of policy influence in more tempestuous times.

This tendency to assert itself in times of geopolitical tranquility helps to explain why anti-imperialism has been, first and foremost, a critique of U.S. diplomacy in which foreign policy evils were usually chalked up to internal causes. Perceiving the world in largely positive and nonthreatening terms, its champions were aroused primarily by home-grown dangers to the nation's identity, in contrast to more externally oriented geopolitical thinkers who have been guided by the survival imperative embedded in Ranke's dictum about the primacy of foreign policy. To label anti-imperialism as a fair weather critique suggests that it exists as a counterpoint to the American belief that the natural state of international relations is (or ought to be) characterized by great power cooperation and commercial and cultural internationalism – a dominant outlook that I have elsewhere called "normal internationalism."[2] Although anti-imperialism has been ideologically hostile to relatively peaceful forms of condominium as well as to geopolitics, in functional terms its success has usually depended upon an environment of great power concord.

Unfortunately, the problem of pinning down anti-imperialism's place is complicated by the fact that it has, over time, assumed a number of different and competing guises. Quite apart from the anti-imperialist critiques

---

[2] For the argument that even Wilsonianism enjoys a junior status in relation to a more fundamental world view that I call "normal internationalism," see Frank Ninkovich, *The Wilsonian Century: U.S. Foreign Policy Since 1900* (Chicago: University of Chicago Press, 1999).

that have tended to emerge in periods of great power calm, a more con-servative strain of anti-imperialism has also come into play. This distinct variant first appeared during World War I, when anti-imperialism became part of the Wilsonian critique of traditional power politics. In this assim-ilated form it played a significant role throughout the remainder of the century as part of a more encompassing geopolitical outlook. This house-broken version of anti-imperialism helped to deflect foreign critiques and siphoned away support that otherwise might have gone to more radical domestic enemies of U.S. foreign policy.

As the foregoing comments suggest, great power conflict and impe-rialism have been connected in some rather tangled ways – and that is without taking into account the knotty theoretical issue of which form of explanation, geopolitical or socioeconomic, provides a superior under-standing of U.S. foreign relations. Although the facts are the same for all sides to the debate, it is possible, depending on one's interpretive stance, to claim that *all* of American foreign policy has been either about externally imposed security concerns or about an internally generated pressure for economic expansion that has had imperialist consequences. This theoret-ical conundrum is too perplexing to tackle here, but it deserves mention because it helps to explain a mindset in which political and scholarly anti-imperialists, by conflating or homologizing power politics and impe-rialism, have time and again used their world view to explain the entire spectrum of American foreign policy behavior.

With a full awareness that this topic could fill a number of books that have yet to be written, this essay will merely try to sketch the ways in which anti-imperialist principles and politics have evolved in the history of U.S. foreign relations. In what follows, I will discuss the variously imbricated careers of five different kinds of anti-imperialism: the pre–Civil War cri-tique of republican expansionism; the conservative anti-imperialism of the 1890s; a geopolitical variety that appeared during World War I as an ap-pendage of Wilsonianism; a left-progressive brand that first surfaced dur-ing the war but flowered as a major political force in the 1920s and; most recently, a cultural critique that has accompanied the completion of the decolonization process and the ebbing of cold war tensions in the 1970s.[3]

Just when anti-imperialism and its evil twin were born is a matter of debate. The United States was, of course, a territorially expansionist

[3] My views on the varieties of anti-imperialism have since been restated in *The United States and Imperialism* (Oxford: Blackwell, 2000), especially in chapter 5.

nation since its inception, and that expansion often provoked opposition. For some historians, this expansionist impulse makes for a tale in which foreign policy has operated under the uninterrupted spell of an ideology of Manifest Destiny, even as the society changed from an agrarian to an industrial economy. The validity of this outlook would appear to turn on the proposition that imperialism as a phenomenon, far from being *sui generis*, is but the outcome of an underlying expansionist impulse.[4]

Whatever the merits of that argument, it seems clear that continental expansion was very different from the kind that emerged at the turn of the century. For one thing, a primary motive of overland expansion was agrarian land hunger, which was fed by the continual opening up of new southern and western areas for settlement. Expansion was contiguous, and annexations were followed-up by a process of state-making in which the territories were gradually assimilated into the Union. Thus, while the Mexican War was nothing if not an expansionist adventure, the United States never envisioned (apart from a few hotheads who wanted to annex the entire western hemisphere) ruling the conquered territories as permanent dependencies because that would have gone against the grain of its ante-bellum ideology of republicanism. "It is surely not necessary to insist," said the *New York Morning News* in 1845, "that acquisitions of territory in America, even if accomplished by force of arms, are not to be viewed in the same light as the invasions and conquests of the States of the old world."[5] The aim was, rather, according to the prevailing romantic republican ideology that justified the war, "extending the area of freedom."[6] In this phase of its history, the United States was what Bradford Perkins has called a "republican empire" – a polity unlike the kind envisioned by the expansionists of 1898.[7]

Opposition to the war also differed from fin-de-siècle anti-imperialism. The protests in this case were aimed not at territorial expansion but at

---

4 See e.g., Anders Stephanson, *Manifest Destiny: American Expansionism and the Empire of Right* (New York: Hill and Wang, 1995); Albert K. Weinberg, *Manifest Destiny: A Study of Nationalist Expansionism in American History* (New York: AMS Press, 1979); Michael Hunt, *Ideology and U.S. Foreign Policy* (New Haven: Yale University Press, 1987).

5 Quoted in Frederick Merk, *Manifest Destiny and Mission in American History: A Reinterpretation* (New York: Vintage Books, 1963), p. 25n.

6 See Robert H. Johannsen, *To the Halls of the Montezumas: The Mexican War in the American Imagination* (New York: Oxford University Press, 1985), p. 53.

7 Bradford Perkins, *The Creation of a Republican Empire, 1776–1865*, vol. I, *The Cambridge history of American Foreign Relations*, ed. Warren I. Cohen (New York: Cambridge University Press, 1993).

the unconscionably aggressive way in which the land was being taken. Many northern Whig critics of the Mexican War believed that it was only a matter of time before the United States would dominate the continent without having to resort to war. Because the North-South conflict was dominated by the issue of the expansion of the institution of slavery and not by any disagreements about the propriety of overland expansion as such, the kinds of constitutional questions that would be raised in the 1890s did not come up in this instance. Expansion did on occasion bring the United States into collision with European states – the independence of Texas and the settlement of Oregon in particular raised some potentially explosive issues. But since the problems were essentially hemispheric and well within the tradition of isolation covered by the Monroe Doctrine, the kinds of geopolitical complications associated with fin-de-siècle imperialism failed to arise.

Although it is plausible to conclude from the foregoing that anti-imperialism, both as a strain of thought and a political movement, first emerged only in the 1890s, the concern with national character and identity that would become a leitmotif of anti-imperialist thought had surfaced much earlier. During the Mexican war, antimilitarist voices attacked war-like expansion as harmful to the moral character of the country, while racial anxieties were simultaneously present in vocal objections to an "amalgamation" of "mongrel races."[8] Kindred sentiments emerged in the 1860s and 1870s in response to attempts by the Johnson and Grant administrations to annex the Dominican Republic. As these kinds of complaints suggested, interests, security, and power political complications were less important to the anti-annexationists than identity issues. While overland expansion was traditional, insular expansion was not. "We cannot have colonies, dependencies, subjects, without renouncing the essential conception of democratic institutions," said the *New York Tribune*, when the Johnson administration, pushed by the expansionist Secretary of State William Seward, had first sought to purchase the island.

Race, an issue that would be closely linked to imperialism and anti-imperialism alike, also made an appearance as a powerful rhetorical club wielded by the opponents of annexation. The chief worry about race was its harmful domestic consequences. "However possible it might be for the United States to annex countries inhabited by the Anglo-Saxon race and accustomed to self-government, the incorporation of these

---

[8] John H. Schroeder, *Mr. Polk's War: American Opposition and Dissent, 1846–1848* (Madison: University of Wisconsin Press, 1973), pp. 76, 94–99.

people ... would be but the beginning of years of conflict and anarchy," the American Minister to London told the British.[9] Criticizing the idea of "absorbing semicivilized Catholic states," the liberal Republican E. L. Godkin, editor of *The Nation*, ridiculed the desire to "make citizens of 200,000 ignorant Catholic Spanish Negroes."[10] "We don't want any of those islands just yet, with their mongrel cutthroat races and foreign language and religion," concluded one newspaper.[11] The same kinds of apprehensions were voiced prior to the Civil War when, from time to time, the idea of annexing Cuba or "All Mexico" bubbled to the surface.

The debate over imperialism in the 1890s marks the only occasion in U.S. history in which imperialism and anti-imperialism were *the* leading foreign policy questions. Though the expansionists of 1898 tried to make the case that colonialism was a historical outgrowth of earlier territorial expansion, both sides sensed that a fundamental change in the underlying philosophy of United States foreign relations was in the offing.[12] Given the widely perceived importance of departing from tradition, imperialism became an urgent theme of mass politics as a resurgent Democratic Party, under the leadership of William Jennings Bryan, took up the anti-imperialist standard. Meanwhile, the formation of an Anti-Imperialist League in Boston, backed by a number of disgruntled members of the Republican establishment, suggested the emergence of an epochal split among the foreign policy elite and the breakdown of a long-standing foreign policy consensus.[13]

The annexationists won this particular battle, but they lost the war when the allure of empire faded almost as quickly as it arose. The arguments of the anti-imperialists, though disregarded in 1898, turned out to have greater staying power and, in the decades to come, were incorporated

---

[9] Allen Nevins, *Hamilton Fish: The Inner History of the Grant Administration* (New York: Frederick Ungar, 1957), p. 262.

[10] William M. Armstrong, *E. L. Godkin and American Foreign Policy, 1865–1900* (Westport, Conn.: Greenwood Press, 1957), pp. 114–15.

[11] Quoted in Nevins, *Hamilton Fish*, p. 318.

[12] Robert Beisner, *From the Old Diplomacy to the New*, argues that U.S. foreign affairs went through a "paradigm shift" in the 1890s. Whatever the truth of that claim, of which this author remains skeptical, it is nevertheless evident that participants in the debate *believed* that a momentous change was in the offing.

[13] Indeed, the split within the foreign policy opinion-making elite, as explained in Ernest May's classical study, *American Imperialism: A Speculative Essay* (New York: Atheneum, 1968), created a need to argue fundamentals before the mass public. The people were thus involved to a much greater degree than usual in the contemplation of foreign policy, a point that caught President McKinley's attention when he realized that imperialism was a vote-winning issue.

into two very different outlooks. On the one hand, their equivocal racial beliefs and their warnings about the geopolitical dangers of empire were integrated into the mainstream of U.S. foreign policy, though only as a subsidiary theme in a more comprehensive geopolitical vision. On the other, their concern with identity and national character became part of a more radical anti-imperialist ideology that emerged in full force in the 1920s.

Opponents of annexing the Philippine Islands hoped to turn race to their advantage in the same way that critics of Grant had used racial fears a generation earlier in the Santo Domingo affair. The turn-of-the-century institutionalization of racial segregation in the South and the growing alarm at immigration from southern and eastern Europe showed that race remained an obsession for many Americans. Unfortunately for the anti-imperialists, race no longer constituted a prima facie case against annexation because, undergirded by an ideology of civilization and the powerful allure of shouldering the "white man's burden," it was also used to powerful effect by their expansionist opponents as an argument for empire. Indeed, one of the striking features of the debate is how strenuously both sides played on the theme of Filipino racial inferiority, only to cancel each other out.

The net result of this stalemate would have been all to the good if it had forced the two sides to argue the issues on foreign policy grounds, but, unfortunately for the clarity of the debate, the appropriateness of imperialism qua imperialism was not really at issue. The anti-imperalists were not opposing colonialism as a generic global phenomenon, nor were they averse to America's exercise of quasi-imperial control over various peoples. On the whole, they did little to discredit the good press that European colonialism had received in the United States in the preceding decades. The belief remained that it was a good thing for the Europeans to be doing on behalf of civilization, but it did not follow that it would also be a good policy for the United States to adopt.

While it is true that anti-imperialism was an opposition to *American* imperialism and not to imperialism as such, putting the issue in that manner still exaggerates the division between the two sides. In combination with racialism, the axiomatic belief in the worldwide spread of western civilization justified a kind of imperialism that nearly no one at the time opposed. The anti-imperialist Thomas Wentworth Higginson, for example, praised Commodore Matthew Perry for "having for the first time opened Japan to modern civilization [and for having] left it to work out its own destiny, and become one of the great free nations of the world."[14] In China, meanwhile, the U.S. position at the turn of the century was guaranteed by a treaty signed in 1844 that took away certain sovereign rights of the Chinese. When Secretary of State John Hay in 1899 and 1900 proclaimed the Open Door notes, the United States acted in defense of this imperialist status quo. That it did so in an attempt to forestall the partition of China by the great powers did not mean that it was seeking sovereign independence for the Chinese. The idea of shouldering the "white man's burden" had long exerted a powerful appeal by justifying the forcible transplantation of civilization to undeveloped peoples, so long as it was not done via outright colonialism.

The influence of civilization as ideology was also evident in changing attitudes about America's role in the Caribbean basin. The debate over empire that stretched between 1899 and 1900 focused almost exclusively on the fate of the Philippines. But the annexation of Puerto Rico, which was invaded and occupied by the U.S. army as part of the campaign against Spain's possessions, generated virtually no discussion, much less opposition, even though a generation earlier this step would have been certain to kick up enormous controversy. As far as the Caribbean was concerned, then, imperialism was now an acceptable policy. This acceptance of regional empire was formalized in Cuba in 1902 with the adoption of the Platt Amendment, which turned the island into a protectorate of the United States, and it was further extended in the first two decades of the century when, in the name of civilization, many Caribbean republics were virtually stripped of their sovereignty. American domination became acceptable as the isthmian canal, often justified as a public work of civilization, approached reality and as the need arose to head off the possible spread of European imperialism to the western hemisphere. To be sure, the seizure of the Panama Canal zone from Columbia excited some vocal opposition, but this was mainly on account of objections to the way in which it was acquired.

These ideological blind spots were congenital defects of the early anti-imperialist way of seeing the world. That opponents of empire could simultaneously reject annexation of the Philippines while still accepting imperialism in general, and that they also went along with participation in the diplomacy of imperialism in China while tolerating U.S. domination

[14] Cited in Jim Zwick, ed., "Anti-Imperialism in the United States, 1898–1935," home.ican.net/~fjzwick/ailtexts/twho899.html.

of the Caribbean, suggests an area of broader agreement with their expansionist opponents. In an attempt to explain the appeal of imperialism, Ernest May has argued that "Men of the establishment belonged both to their own country and to a larger Atlantic community."[15] But that was true of many anti-imperialists as well. The key issue that divided pro- and anti-imperialists, then, was the question of how, not whether, the United States would participate in the global project of civilization. The logic was as simple as it was uncomfortable: To the extent that they accepted the ideology of civilization and its reigning evolutionary hierarchies, they also accepted the rightness of imperialism.

Another major theme of the Philippine debate that would resonate in subsequent versions of anti-imperialism was the suspicion of power politics and militarism. Like the argument about civilization, this geopolitical dimension had also been absent a generation earlier. As naval theorist Alfred Thayer Mahan said: "I am an imperialist simply because I am not an isolationist"[16] For people like Theodore Roosevelt and Henry Cabot Lodge, colonial expansion was an integral part of a "Large Policy" that would make the newly industrialized United States a world power every bit the equal of the European states. Obviously, this argument resonated with military interests, who looked forward to ample appropriations for the armed forces. Whereas internal development once blocked any thought of overseas expansion, the Depression of 1893 and newly popular neomercantilist arguments argued strongly for colonial expansion as a way of dealing with overproduction.

In response to the contention of many annexationists that America's adoption of imperialism would certify the nation's status as a great power in a new global order, much of the anti-imperialist counterattack in the 1890s focused on the dangers of world politics. Imperialism, warned steel tycoon Andrew Carnegie, threatened to pull the United States "into the vortex of the Far East."[17] As Robert Beisner has pointed out, the anti-imperialists objected on three counts. First, entanglement in the diplomacy of imperialism would be a violation of American diplomatic tradition (though, strictly speaking, the Monroe Doctrine's principle of noninvolvement did not take into account the possibility of U.S. entanglement

---

[15] May, *American Imperialism*, p. 229.
[16] Quoted in James C. Bradford, ed., *Admirals of the New Steel Navy* (Annapolis, 1990), 42 in Walter McDougall, *Promised Land, Crusader State* (Boston and New York: Houghton Mifflin, 1997), p. 104.
[17] Quoted in Robert Beisner, *Twelve Against Empire: The Anti-Imperialists, 1898–1900* (New York: McGraw-Hill, 1971), p. 177.

in Asian politics). Second, possession of the Philippines would endanger national security because the islands were so far removed from the United States and so close to potentially hostile powers that they could not help but be a strategic liability. Last, a policy of imperialism would have enormous domestic repercussions by creating a large military establishment, imposing the taxes needed to support them, and taking away resources that otherwise might be used to solve pressing domestic problems.[18]

However, this connection between imperialism and power politics needs to be taken with a grain of salt.[19] If one corrects for the desire to score political debating points, it is evident that neither side was much concerned by the prospect of entering the arena of great power rivalry. If imperialists were advocating geopolitics, it was generally in a benign, non-Darwinian sense in which the acquisition of colonies signaled America's arrival not into some vicious den of great power rivalry but rather into a friendly and cooperative circle of elite powers. Imperialism was undertaken in the name of civilization, which was a universal process in which other advanced nations were participating. As an expression of this view, one British imperialist, reminiscing about these years, spoke for many when he said that "we believed that we were laying the basis of a federation of the world."[20] There was plenty of jingoism at work in the war against Spain, to be sure, but among proimperialists one heard surprisingly little in the way of Darwinian anticipation of globe-girdling struggle.

The absence of geopolitical concern among the anti-imperialists was evident in their preoccupation with identity and morality, a feature of the 1890s debate that would later be incorporated into a more radical anti-imperialist ideology. Though the anti-imperialists were not above pointing to the perils of participation in the diplomacy of imperialism as a scare tactic, the chief dangers of empire were believed to come from within. Senator George Hoar (R-MA) put the concern squarely when he described imperialism as "a greater danger than we have encountered since the Pilgrims landed at Plymouth – the danger that we are to be transformed from a republic, founded on the Declaration of Independence, guided by the counsels of Washington, into a vulgar, commonplace empire, founded

---

[18] Beisner, *Twelve Against Empire*, p. 218.
[19] Many diplomatic historians continue to this day to repeat the platitude, though with a different inflection, that American imperialism heralded the nation's rise to world power status.
[20] John Buchan, quoted in Philip Darby, *Three Faces of Imperialism: British and American Approaches to Asia and Africa 1870–1970* (New Haven: Yale University Press, 1987), p. 45.

upon physical force." As Robert Beisner has suggested, the "mugwump" anti-imperialists worried that "the more America departed from her original character, the more it seemed ... that she began to resemble the old nations of Europe."[21]

Though such identity-based arguments tend to be associated with conservative Republican anti-imperialists, they were also prominently on display in the rhetoric of that ostensible insurgent, William Jennings Bryan, when he insisted that "the highest obligation of this nation is to be true to itself." Once it was admitted, the Great Commoner argued, that "some people are capable of self-government and that others are not and that the capable people have a right to seize upon and govern the incapable, you make force – brute force – the only foundation of government and invite the reign of a despot." This kind of essentialist thinking was integral to Populism, which, despite its radical veneer, was in many ways a backward-looking movement that lamented the corruption of the national character under the onslaught of modernity. Thus the war against the Filipinos was widely condemned as evil, a violation of basic American ideals of moral behavior, while imperialism was denounced as un-American, a denial of the national essence.

There is no reason to call into question William Leuchtenburg's judgment, rendered long ago, that "first and last, it was the conservatives who bore the burden of the anti-imperialist campaign."[22] Nevertheless, one detects within the debate a strand of continuity that connected the anti-imperialism of 1898 to the abolitionist past and to the more progressive and radical variety of anti-imperialism that would emerge in the 1920s. Many of the most vocal opponents of empire, having cut their political teeth on pre–Civil War antislavery protest, brought to their campaign the same air of moral urgency that formerly had infused the abolitionist crusade. The kind of self-confident antinomian belief in the correctness of one's own judgment, however flagrantly at odds with the prevailing political fashion, coupled with a highly moral interpretation of foreign policy behavior, would be a leitmotif of subsequent progressive and radical anti-imperialist dissent.

Though its core ideas would live on, anti-imperialism's failure to strike deeper foreign policy roots was due in part to its lack of a coherent

---

[21] Beisner, *Twelve Against Empire*, p. 15.
[22] William E. Leuchtenburg, "Progressivism and Imperialism: The Progressive Movement and American Foreign Policy, 1908–1916," *The Mississippi Valley Historical Review* 39 (June 1952), p. 486.

world view. Whereas the imperialists had a geopolitical program in which civilization, race, and great power cooperation appeared to go hand in hand in creating a new foreign policy identity for the United States, anti-imperialism was chock full of internal tensions and contradictions. For one thing, its frank inegalitarian racism was jarringly inconsistent with the republican philosophy of liberty. Then, too, its acceptance of a global modernizing process pretty much mandated, as a matter of principle, a toleration of imperialism as a legitimate common project of civilization, even as it rather inconsistently claimed an exemption for the United States on the basis of tradition. Civilization also appeared to call for closer and friendlier relations among the great powers, but the anti-imperialists were of two minds on this issue as well. Thus the same Andrew Carnegie who talked about the "vortex" of the Far East could simultaneously talk about the growing peacefulness of great power relations, the social worker Jane Addams could invoke "an international patriotism," and George Hoar could repair to an internationalist standard when accusing the U.S. of committing crimes against civilization.

Once the imperialist impulse waned, anti-imperialism became a program in search of a problem. For the time being, it went into cold storage even as the Filipino rebellion escalated to serious proportions. With the introduction of 100,000 U.S. soldiers into the islands to pacify the rising, there were a host of reasons why opposition to colonialism ought to have grown in intensity. The savagery required to repress the Filipino rebellion, the problem of immigration, the perception of the Philippines as an economic threat, and the emergence of the islands as a strategic liability provided reasons aplenty to rethink the decision for empire. Nevertheless, because the archipelago had been paid for in blood, there was little likelihood of cutting it loose, especially as McKinley was decisively reelected in 1900 and succeeded by the prestige-conscious Theodore Roosevelt following his assassination in the fall of 1901.

More was involved, however, than a stiffening of the Republican Party position. Even as the justice of some of the anti-imperialist arguments became clear, it was also evident that many of their dire predictions about the domestic impact of empire had been exaggerated. Thus, significant segments of the anti-imperialist coalition softened and ultimately defected. Concerned at being allied too closely with a Democratic Party whose domestic positions were anathema, many conservatives in the Anti-Imperialist League, looking for a way out of their bind, began to argue that the Philippines should be transformed into a protectorate on the pattern adopted for Cuba with the Platt amendment. Since this proposal was, politically, patently unworkable, it was simply a token of the dissolution of the anti-imperialist movement as a whole. For the Democrats, too, policy toward the Philippines moved toward the right following Woodrow Wilson's election as president in 1912. Partly to mollify conservative Filipinos who feared popular control, rather than push for independence the administration contented itself with passage of the Jones Bill, which provided significant elements of home rule to the islands while putting off independence into the distant future.

But anti-imperialist themes were soon rekindled by the First World War. This time, a new and more complex pattern emerged in which mugwumpery was pretty much left behind. On the one hand, the kind of racial views and geopolitical arguments that had been shunted aside in the 1890s became part of the mainstream of U.S. foreign policy; on the other, a more radical left-progressive brand of anti-imperialism emerged as a critique of mainstream policy, thereby setting in place a binary pattern that would be visible for the remainder of the century. In Christopher Lasch's terms, the division was between those who believed that the war was a conflict between autocracy and democracy and those who believed that it was the product of rival imperialisms.[23] Until it was wrecked by Woodrow Wilson's compromises at the Paris peace conference, these two discrete elements of anti-imperialism were combined into a working coalition in support of Wilson's "new diplomacy."[24] Thanks to the relative newness of both points of view and the one-size-fits-all ambiguity of Wilsonianism, anti-imperialists cooperated enthusiastically for a time with those who saw the war in geopolitical terms.

The most significant landmark in the assimilation of anti-imperialism was the fifth of Woodrow Wilson's 14 Points, which spoke to the need to deal with colonial rivalries through an impartial adjustment of colonial claims with due attention to "the interests of the populations concerned." Though nearly everyone took the object of this point to be the disposition of the German colonies and not a challenge to the future of colonialism

[23] Christopher Lasch, *The American Liberals and the Russian Revolution* (New York: McGraw-Hill, 1972), pp. x–xi. N. Gordon Levin, Jr. also captured this ideological bifurcation when he argued that "Wilsonian ideology sought essentially to end traditional imperialism and the balance of power." See also N. Gordon Levin, Jr., *Woodrow Wilson and World Politics: America's Response to War and Revolution* (New York: Oxford University Press, 1968), p. 8.

[24] Arno Mayer, in *Wilson vs. Lenin: Political Origins of the New Diplomacy, 1917–1918* (Cleveland: World Publishing Company, 1974) describes the struggle to define war aims as one between the "forces of order" and the "forces of movement." For a time, Wilson enjoyed the support of the latter.

as such, it did in fact harbor a larger anti-imperialist objective. According to some interpretive glosses on Wilson's text, the implication was "that a colonial power acts not as owner of its colonies, but as trustee for the natives and for the interests of the society of nations." Wilson himself made clear that the idea behind mandates was "to build up in as short a time as possible ... a political unit which can take charge of its own affairs."[25] This new kind of colonialism would have to be collegial, because adherence to a generally accepted "code of colonial conduct" meant that the colonial powers would no longer be free to do as they pleased with their possessions.[26]

Still, for the time being the U.S. was more concerned to temper colonialism than to abolish it. If there was any question that Wilson's position on mandates clearly supported the racialist notion of the "white man's burden," his controversial rejection of the Japanese proposal for insertion of the principle of racial equality in the covenant of the League of Nations demonstrated that racial prejudice was still a formidable barrier to a universalization of sovereignty.[27] Nevertheless, the Wilsonian position did at least address one of the conceptual inconsistencies that had hobbled the conservative anti-imperialism of the 1890s when it proposed trusteeship as a via media between great power rivalry and the possibility of anarchical independence.

The suggestion that imperialism ought to be a cooperative self-liquidating project marked a novel and important development in official American thinking about imperialism. In the 1890s, many progressive pro-imperialists, Woodrow Wilson among them, had rather optimistically assumed that imperialism would be a force for great power cooperation. The Taft administration's bumbling attempt to moderate the diplomacy of imperialism in China prior to the war by promoting a great power consortium in lending and railway management was the most prominent attempt to apply that kind of logic to policy. But the long and tangled chain of events that led to the blow-up of 1914 led many in the left-liberal community who had once supported imperialism to change their minds. It seemed clear that the anti-imperialists had been right: The Great War had been caused in part by an imperialist competition for markets and raw

---

[25] Quoted in Thomas Knock, *To End All Wars: Woodrow Wilson and the Quest for a New World Order* (New York: Oxford University Press, 1992), p. 206.

[26] From Charles Seymour, *The Intimate Papers of Colonel House* (Boston and New York: Houghton Mifflin, 128), IV, 195.

[27] Paul Gordon Lauren, "Human Rights in History: Diplomacy and Racial Equality at the Paris Peace Conference," *Diplomatic History* 2 (Summer 1978), pp. 257–78.

materials. For example, Walter Lippmann, an early supporter of Wilsonianism, argued that the war broke out "because Europe had been divided into two groups which clashed again and again over the organization of the backward parts of the world."[28] According to this point of view, while imperialism might be a good and even noble thing for colonizer and colonized, it was also quite dangerous when viewed from the standpoint of great power relations.

This geopolitical distrust of imperialism lay at the heart of one of the nastier disputes at the peace conference. The quarrel had to do with the disposition of China's Shantung province, where Japan, as a reward for participating in the war, insisted on obtaining all the special privileges formerly enjoyed by Germany. Wilson feared that if the old diplomacy of imperialism were simply reinstalled, the powers would be repeating past errors. "There was a lot of combustible material in China and if flames were put to it the fire could not be quenched,"[29] he told the Japanese delegates at Paris. On the other hand, if he refused to comply with Japan's demands, the alternative prospect seemed even worse. Wilson told Ray Stannard Baker that "if Japan went home there was the danger of . . . a return to the old 'balance of power' system in the world, on a greater scale than ever before."[30]

Wilson's cave-in on Shantung in Paris was interpreted by his former liberal and radical supporters as a sign of backsliding, when in fact it was a preview of the hard and unwelcome choice between geopolitical concerns and anti-imperialism that American policy makers would be forced to make quite often in years to come. For the time being, Wilson chose what appeared to be the lesser of two evils, though a more palatable solution was temporarily worked out by the Harding administration in the Washington Conference of 1921–22. The resulting network of treaties promised to do away with the competitive diplomacy of imperialism and replace it with the cooperative Open Door framework. The old limitations on Chinese sovereignty imposed by the treaty port system, extraterritoriality and the treaty tariff, were slated for abolition, but without setting a firm date for their retirement. For the moment, at least, the treaties had

---

[28] Walter Lippmann, *The Stakes of Diplomacy* (New York: Macmillan, 1917), p. 124. For related analysis see also Walter Weyl, *American World Policies* (New York: Macmillan, 1917) pp. 18, 165, 188.
[29] Meeting of Council of Four, in Ray Stannard Baker, *Woodrow Wilson and World Settlement* (Gloucester, MA: Peter Smith, 1960), II, 252.
[30] Meeting of Council of Four, *ibid.*, II, 266.

seemed to kill two birds with one stone in east Asia: imperialism and power politics.

At the same time that this geopolitical tributary of anti-imperialist thought was entering the mainstream of foreign policy, a quite different kind of anti-imperialism emerged that focused critically on the policies of the U.S. government. In contrast to the nascent Wilsonian view, which saw great power conflict as the chief threat to the nation, anti-imperialists tended to believe, in the aftermath of World War I, that the United States faced no tangible security threat. More worrisome to them than external dangers was the possibility that imperialist policies might lead to military domination of American political institutions. When it came to relations with the outside world, they saw the central problem as the imperialist character of American internationalism, of American foreign policy *as a whole*. Obviously, this approach covered far more than colonialism under its definitional umbrella, including also informal empire and economic and cultural control as part of a comprehensive imperialist syndrome.

In the aftermath of World War I, as fear of another world war evaporated almost entirely with the seeming emergence of great power cooperation, this brand of anti-imperialism became the predominant critique of foreign policy. Its rise was attributable in part to the widespread disillusionment among left-liberal supporters with the shape that Wilson's geopolitical internationalism took at the Paris Peace Conference. While Wilson had gone along with imperialism in order to maintain great power harmony, his critics failed to see the necessity for such a move because, on balance, equity outranked fear in the hierarchy of left-liberal concerns. Showing how easily imperialism and geopolitics could be conflated, the economist Thorstein Veblen called the League of Nations "an instrument of realpolitik, created in the image of nineteenth century imperialism."[31] Instead of seeking to create a just world order based on the principle of self-determination, the great powers seemed bent on maintaining a system of imperial territorial arrangements.

With the Philippines no longer a consuming issue for anti-imperialists, American foreign policy in the Caribbean moved to the head of the line as an object of attention. For a variety of reasons, the United States intervened militarily on seventeen separate occasions in the region between 1901 and 1933. To prevent European financial influence from blossoming into political control, Washington instituted a number of customs

---

[31] Quoted in Knock, *To End All Wars*, p. 253.

receiverships. Interventions in Haiti in 1915 and in the Dominican Republic in 1916 resulted in long-term occupations in which the islands were administered by U.S. military government. For a time, war seemed likely with Mexico over issues having to do with legislation arising from the land legislation of the revolutionary constitution of 1917. The Monroe Doctrine, once concerned primarily with preventing European intervention in the western hemisphere, now appeared to have been transformed into a license for the United States to intervene whenever disorder appeared to threaten American interests in the region. Indeed, the tempo of interventionism, originally designed to ward off European dangers, increased even as the external threat to the security of the western hemisphere diminished to the vanishing point.

As Robert David Johnson has shown in a pathbreaking work,[32] antiimperialism as a self-contained political ideology or world view enjoyed considerable cachet in the 1920s. A band of progressives in the Senate, in combination with a burgeoning peace movement, liberals, intellectuals, and some radical voices, created "a bloc more radical, unified, antimilitarist, and anti-imperialist than during the years before American entry into the European war."[33] This coalition exerted considerable pressure on Republican administrations to retreat from Caribbean interventionism. According to Charles de Benedetti, the opposition to the December 1926 intervention in Nicaragua by an anti-imperialist coalition "proved the single most successful antiwar undertaking of the decade."[34]

For these critics, predation against the weak was the last remnant of a diplomacy of imperialism. According to Johnson, the anti-imperialists believed "that the European war had shattered the old order, and that the United States needed to adjust to the new nationalism of the underdeveloped world."[35] Because the progressive anti-imperialists assumed that the United States faced no fundamental threat from the international environment, they felt free to concentrate on criticizing the United States for its transgressions. In this case, though, they went beyond simply dissenting and proposed an alternative to the new and improved version of Dollar Diplomacy then being practiced by the Republican administrations of Calvin Coolidge and Herbert Hoover. In addition to being

[32] Robert David Johnson, *The Peace Progressives and American Foreign Relations* (Cambridge, MA: Harvard University Press, 1995).
[33] *Ibid.*, p. 200.
[34] Charles DeBenedetti, *The Peace Reform in American History* (Bloomington: Indiana University Press, 1980), p. 118.
[35] Johnson, *Peace Progressives*, p. 198.

anti-interventionist in the Caribbean, they opposed the diplomacy of imperialism in the Far East, particularly in China. They also advocated recognition of the Soviet Union as a way of blunting the appeal of Bolshevism in the underdeveloped world. They urged moral and limited economic intervention in aid of nationalist and democratic forces. They endorsed unilateral disarmament, codification of international law, and use of the war debts settlement to nudge the European powers in a more anti-imperialist direction.

While it was primarily an inner-directed ideology, the progressive anti-imperialism of the 1920s moved a long way in the direction of a comprehensive critique of the broader international environment. Captivated by the vision of a world cleansed of both power politics and imperialism, the senators believed, according to Johnson, that "a world of independent, nationalist-minded nations would create a peaceful, economically open world order."[36] One sees here the emergence of a pluralist and relativist point of view in which the uniformitarian logic of civilization is rejected. Implicit, too, is a pluralist view of race and culture that, over time, would become increasingly sympathetic to the aspirations for independence of colonized peoples. Somewhat more problematically, this viewpoint also preached an economic and cultural internationalism whose inexorable pressure for global integration would, more than anything else, work to destroy the very kind of pluralist world that anti-imperialists imagined in their minds' eyes.

The 1920s were also the decade to which the origins of the radical theoretical critique of imperialism, that later in the century would enjoy some political influence and much greater success in the academy, can be traced. Works by Scott Nearing suggested that the basic impulse of U.S. foreign policy resided in the need to expand economically abroad as a way of alleviating the potentially explosive consequences of overproduction at home. Many progressives like John Dewey accepted the thesis of domestic determinants. "The natural movement of business enterprise," Dewey argued, "combined with Anglo-American legalistic notions of contracts and their sanctity, and the international custom which obtains as to the duty of a nation to protect the property of its nationals, suffices to bring about imperialistic undertakings."[37] A more radical position still emerged when

[36] Johnson, *Peace Progressives*, p. 149.
[37] John Dewey, "Imperialism Is Easy," *The New Republic*, 50 (March 23, 1927), home.ican.net/~fjzwick/ailtexts/dewey.html. In Jim Zwick, ed., *Anti-Imperialism in the United States, 1898–1935*, home.ican.net/~fjzwick/ail98-35.html (January 10, 1999).

The Workers Party, which would later become the Communist Party of the United States, played up the kind of interpretation of imperialism only recently articulated by Lenin. For example, in 1925, it declared that "the steps already taken by the United States government in helping capitalists secure a firmer foothold in the Near East, Far East, Latin America and Europe, are only a prelude to more entangling alliances which are bound, sooner rather than later, to draw an army of millions of American workers and farmers 'over there' to fight for the safety and defense of the foreign investments of our employing class."[38] The progressive view would receive its most powerful and sophisticated statement in the 1930s when Charles Beard, in a number of seminal works, critiqued the implications of economic expansionism.

In retrospect, anti-imperialism peaked as a political force during the 1920s, when for a time it became an ideology that included both a critique and a positive program. However, its fortunes changed quickly in the 1930s. As the clouds of great power conflict began to roll in, anti-imperialism took a back seat to domestic economic recovery, and the peace progressives turned increasingly to isolationism. Indeed, given their anti-European sentiments and their anti-interventionism, even the global program of the anti-imperialists in their heyday could be construed as a species of isolationism. Anti-imperialism had been effective in evoking concerns for American identity so long as geopolitical problems did not intrude. But once great power issues came to the fore and foreign policy attention shifted to Germany's attempt to dominate Europe, the anti-imperialist critique was swamped by antiwar concerns.

Anti-imperialism reemerged as a major theme of American foreign policy during the second World War. There were, of course, sound propaganda reasons for the United States to take an anticolonial line. The nation was fighting a Japan that had made significant headway ideologically among the newly conquered peoples of their Asian empire by claiming to be liberating them from white domination. Thus it made good tactical sense for FDR's Secretary of State, Cordell Hull, to announce in 1942 that other colonial powers should follow the example set by the United States in the Philippines and "earnestly favor freedom for all dependent peoples at the earliest date practicable."[39]

---

[38] Jay Lovestone, "A Program of Action." *American Imperialism* (Chicago: Workers Party of America, n.d. [1925]), home.ican.net/~fjzwick/ailtexts/action.html. In Jim Zwick, ed., *Anti-Imperialism in the United States, 1898–1935*, home.ican.net/fjzwick/ail98-35.html (January 10, 1999).

[39] Cited in Robert J. McMahon, *Colonialism and Cold War: The United States and the Struggle for Indonesian Independence, 1945–1949* (Ithaca: Cornell University Press, 1981), p. 55.

But it was the linkage between geopolitics and imperialism in FDR's mind that was the decisive factor in this anti-imperialist turn. FDR's views on the dangers of modern international politics closely paralleled those of his former Commander-in-Chief, Woodrow Wilson. Like Wilson, he was convinced that imperialism as practiced by the European powers had been exploitative and that it was a fertile source of war. He told his son "Don't think for a moment that Americans would be dying in the Pacific tonight, if it hadn't been for the shortsighted greed of the French and the British and the Dutch."[40] At Casablanca in 1942, he confided the following:

[T]he colonial system means war. Exploit the resources of an India, a Burma, a Java; take all the wealth out of those countries, but never put anything back into them, things like education, decent standards of living, minimum health requirements – all you're doing is storing up a kind of trouble that leads to war.[41]

"To deny the objectives of independence," he said on another occasion, "would sow the seeds of another world war."[42]

Just how exactly the continuation of colonialism would foment war was not made clear. Was it simply a matter of avoiding colonial unrest? Or, as seems more likely, did FDR believe that the colonial system, if left in place, would give rise to great power frictions?[43] Inasmuch as any hope for the postwar effectiveness of the United Nations depended on a unanimity of purpose among the great powers, FDR's musings can be interpreted as either a desire to avoid small power disturbances or as a way of defusing potential time bombs among the great powers – or both. In the end, the way in which imperialism made for conflict was as murky as the manner in which the United Nations was supposed to keep the peace.

Despite such ambiguities, FDR made explicit what had been merely implied in the Wilsonian program: decolonization or anti-imperialism was supposed to be a source of cooperation among the great powers. Unlike the 1890s, when many Americans who contemplated a global role for the U.S. believed that a common civilizing mission would hold together the United States, Great Britain, and indeed the entire great power community, New Deal policymakers failed to see how colonialism could be

---

[40] Gary R. Hess, *Vietnam and the United States: Origins and Legacy of War* (Boston: Twayne, 1990), p. 28.

[41] Quoted in William Roger Louis, *Imperialism at Bay: The United States and the Decolonization of the British Empire, 1941–1945* (New York: Oxford University Press, 1978), p. 226.

[42] *Ibid.*, p. 538.

[43] Warren F. Kimball, *The Juggler: Franklin D. Roosevelt as Wartime Statesman* (Princeton, NJ: Princeton University Press, 1991), p. 128.

conducive to great power cooperation. While the defeat of Germany and Japan promised to eliminate the most abrasive geopolitical points of friction, imperialism was the one major issue that might conceivably divide the superpowers. The die-hard imperialist Winston Churchill may have felt differently, but New Dealers believed that anti-imperialism would bring a degree of ideological cohesiveness to nations whose world views were, in so many other respects, worlds apart.

This geopolitically motivated anti-imperialism did not translate into unequivocal support of international egalitarianism. Despite his clear anti-imperialist inclinations, Roosevelt did not advocate immediate independence for all colonized peoples. To be sure, at times he echoed Bryan's egalitarian sentiments, as when he declared that "there never has been, there isn't now and there never will be any race of people of the earth fit to serve as masters over their fellow men ... We believe that any nationality, no matter how small, has the inherent right to its own nationhood."[44] But FDR, like his predecessors, was not a liberal on race. He continued to believe that some peoples suffered from innate inferiority; indeed, some of his racialist notions seem positively bizarre in retrospect, e.g., his belief that the Japanese were handicapped by a skull pattern that was less developed than the Caucasian.[45]

Even if racist thoughts had not been present in Roosevelt's calculations, the less controversial thesis of cultural lag would have suggested the need for a period of tutelage before granting independence. Thus, as William Roger Louis has shown, for FDR and American policy makers the antithesis of imperialism was not immediate independence, but trusteeship. The future of Korea, for example, was supposed to be resolved in the course of a twenty-five year long United Nations trusteeship. This outlook also made it easier to give in to the U.S. Navy's security-based demand to maintain postwar control of the Japanese-mandated islands. As a result, it is hard to find fault with the conclusion of Scott Bills that "Roosevelt was anticolonial in everything he said and in little that he did."[46]

---

[44] Cited in McMahon, *Colonialism and Cold War*, p. 54.
[45] Cited in Christopher Thorne, *Allies of a Kind: The United States, Britain and the War against Japan, 1941–1945* (New York: Oxford University Press, 1978), pp. 8–9.
[46] Scott Bills, *Empire and Cold War: The Roots of US – Third World Antagonism, 1945–1947* (New York: St. Martin's Press, 1990), p. 204. This may be the place to note that the frequent condemnations of U.S. foreign policy for displaying bogus anticolonialist credentials tend to come from those who adhere to a more radical anti-imperialist perspective that defines as imperialist or neocolonial the geopolitical motives that have justified a cautious approach to decolonization.

The same fissure between principle and practice would cleave the foreign policies of FDR's Cold War successors. Although the Second World War finally delegitimized the scientific and ideological racial doctrines that undergirded colonial control, the politics of the Cold War seriously tarnished the gleaming anti-imperialist self-image of U.S. foreign policy. Events were not mentally scripted this way in advance, for leading American policymakers were fully aware of the passion for self-rule that was sweeping through the world and were quite anxious to take advantage of anticolonial sentiment for Cold War geopolitical reasons. "Few individuals understand the intensity and force of the spirit of nationalism that is gripping all peoples of the world today," said President Dwight D. Eisenhower, concluding that "almost any one of the new-born states of the world would far rather embrace Communism or any other form of dictatorship than to acknowledge the political domination of another government even though that brought to each citizen a far high standard of living."[47] "We have to be spokesman for those wanting independence or we will be licked," Eisenhower's Secretary of State, John Foster Dulles, told one congressman. "That is the basic communist strategy."[48]

But the racialist legacy of the belief in civilization continued to exert a powerful influence upon American policymakers as the very same disparaging attitudes formerly sanctioned by scientific racism were effortlessly restated in pejorative cultural terms. Although it had become politically imprudent to voice such views publicly, Eisenhower and Dulles, among others, realized that U.S. foreign policy on the decolonization issue suffered from a deep tension between public pronouncements and private doubts. Thus Dulles rued "the fact that there had been in recent years a tremendous surge in the direction of popular government by peoples who have practically no capacity for self-government and indeed are like children in facing this problem."[49] And while Eisenhower acknowledged that "In this day and time no so-called 'dependent' people can, by force, be kept indefinitely in that position," he nevertheless agreed privately with Churchill about their lack of capacity for self-rule. Churchill "is absolutely right in his contention that a number of these peoples who

[47] DDE to George Humphrey, March 27, 1957, AWF: DDE Diary Series, box 22, Papers of Dwight D. Eisenhower, Dwight D. Eisenhower Presidential Library (hereafter cited as DDE Papers).

[48] Conversation with Congressman Walter Judd, June 24, 1954, John Foster Dulles Papers, Princeton University, telephone conversations memoranda, box 2 (hereafter cited as Dulles papers).

[49] NSC meeting of June [?] 1958, AWF: NSC series, DDE Papers, box 82.

are screaming for independence are not yet equipped to support it," he said.[50]

Racial and cultural uneasiness was undergirded by a geopolitical logic that forced anticolonialism to take back seat when it came into conflict with Cold War imperatives. Again, the built-in tensions were plain to U.S. policy makers. Dulles complained that the U.S. was "in the awkward position of trying to ride two horses – our Western allies with their colonial policy, and the nationalism of Southeastern Asia."[51] Though he made no secret of America's desire "to beat the Communists at their own game and to sponsor nationalism in the independent colonial areas, which was in accordance with our historic tradition," he complained that "we were restrained from doing so by a desire to cooperate with Britain and France in Asia, in Africa and in the Near and Middle East."[52]

The net result of these mixed motives was a mixed record. If decolonization was thought to threaten the stability of a valuable ally, and if there existed the possibility that independence might produce political instability and radicalization, then the U.S. tended to support the metropole. In the case of Indonesia, for example, policymakers were concerned first and foremost with the survival of the Netherlands and its contribution to European recovery and defense. Thus the United States sided initially with the Dutch in their return to Indonesia, despite the emergence on the islands of a powerful nationalist independence movement. Only after the Dutch failed in their efforts at military pacification and their obduracy began to endanger congressional appropriations for the high priority European Recovery Program did the Truman administration begin to pressure The Hague.

Even though Harry S. Truman insisted on including an aggressive civil rights plank in the 1948 Democratic platform, the United States found itself supporting a racist South African government as it imposed a policy of apartheid upon blacks. Here, too, geostrategic Cold War rationales took priority over anticolonial professions. The need for South Africa's strategic minerals, coupled with the regime's fierce anticommunism dictated a policy of American support. The racism of the Afrikaner-dominated regime and its labeling of all advocates of majority rule as communists

---

[50] DDE to General Alfred Gruenther, November 30, 1954, AWF: DDE Diary Series, DDE papers, box 7.

[51] Richard Harkness memoranda on visits with JFD, Dulles Papers, Princeton, additional papers, box 1.

[52] Memo of Dulles conversation with Anthony Eden, 30 April 1954, Dulles papers, subject series box 9.

made it quite uncomfortable for the United States to provide support to Praetoria. Nevertheless, as Thomas Borstelmann has pointed out, even as Soviet propaganda gleefully pointed out the inconsistency between preachment and practice in American policy, "South Africa's ties to Britain and the United States and its fierce anticommunism put it squarely in the Western camp."[53]

The exception that proved the geopolitical rule was the American response to the spectacular Suez Crisis of 1956. Reacting to a combined Anglo-French-Israeli invasion of Egypt in response to Gamal Abdal Nasser's nationalization of the Suez Canal, the United States for the first time in the postwar years sided against London in its disputes with its former colony. After Eisenhower imposed financial sanctions and an oil embargo on his European allies, the French and British sullenly withdrew. The U.S. rationale had less to do with anticolonialism than with cold war fears that standing by would lead to a loss of the third world to Moscow. "How could we possibly support Britain and France if in doing so we lose the whole Arab world!" expostulated Eisenhower. As Peter Hahn has noted, "the overriding American objective during the crisis was containment of the Soviet Union, a strategic imperative, and not satisfaction of Egyptian aspirations.[54] Nevertheless, it was not an easy thing to do. "It was a more difficult decision than Korea," said Dulles. "It is easier to go against your enemies than it is to go against your friends."[55]

The best-known and most disastrous example of the logic in which the primacy of Europe dictated support of colonialism was Indochina. FDR had been particularly critical of French rule there, insisting that they "had done absolutely nothing with the place to improve the lot of the people."[56] But by the time of the Yalta conference with Churchill and Stalin in February, 1945, he had begun to waver in his determination to expel the French. He now conceded that French trusteeship might be acceptable provided that Paris committed itself to preparing the Vietnamese for independence.[57] Even though decolonization was highly desirable in principle,

[53] Thomas Borstelmann, *Apartheid's Reluctant Uncle: The United States and South Africa in the Early Cold War* (New York: Oxford University Press, 1993), p. 109.

[54] Peter L. Hahn, *The United States, Great Britain, and Egypt, 1945–1946: Strategy and Diplomacy in the Early Cold War* (Chapel Hill: University of North Carolina Press, 1991), p. 247.

[55] James Russell Wiggins, Memoranda of discussions with Dulles, 7 December 1956, Dulles papers, additional papers, Princeton, box 2.

[56] Hess, *Vietnam and the United States*, p. 29.

[57] "Introduction," in Andrew J. Rotter, *Light at the End of the Tunnel: A Vietnam War Anthology* (New York: St. Martin's Press, 1991), p. 9.

the United States could exert only so much pressure on the French. Realizing that putting pressure on Paris to withdraw from Vietnam might
fatally weaken a needed ally in western Europe, Truman acquiesced in the
forcible restoration of French rule in the face of stiff military opposition
from the nationalist Vietminh.

The situation in Indochina was complicated by the fact that the independence movement was communist-led. The State Department, its eyes
riveted on the looming struggle with Moscow, concluded of the Vietminh
leader, Ho Chi Minh, that "we cannot afford to assume that Ho is anything but Moscow-directed."[58] Secretary of State Dean Acheson argued in
1949 that the belief that "Ho Chi Minh is as much nationalist as Commie
is irrelevant," arguing that "all Stalinists in colonial areas are nationalists."[59] With the outbreak of the Korean War in June, 1950, a conflict
that was believed to have global ramifications, Indochina assumed even
greater importance to Washington. "The psychological impact of the fall
of Indochina," said the State Department in 1951, "would be taken as
a sign that the force of communism is irresistible and would lead to an
attitude of defeatism."[60] American aid began to trickle to the French
in 1950, but soon the valves were opened wide to an unrestricted flow.
With the decisive defeat of the French garrison at Dien Bien Phu in May,
1954, direct responsibility for keeping Vietnam noncommunist shifted
to the United States. Inevitably, the United States was viewed by many
Vietnamese as filling the colonialist shoes of the departing French, even
though Americans prided themselves on their anticolonial bona fides.

As the Cold War in Europe began to stabilize, American policymakers shifted their gaze toward the third world. President John F. Kennedy
believed that the battlefields in the global conflict for superpower dominance would shift to the underdeveloped nations in the years to come.
Although the hair-raising crises in Berlin and in Cuba had demonstrated
overwhelming public support for the tough cold war positions staked out
by Kennedy, the success of American policy in Europe and a relaxation
of tension with the Soviets led, ironically, to a drying up of support for

---

[58] Quoted in Robert D. Schulzinger, *A Time for War: The United States and Vietnam, 1941–
1975* (New York: Oxford University Press, 1997), p. 33.

[59] Acheson telegram to Hanoi, May 20, 1949, in U.S. Department of State, *Foreign Relations
of the United States, 1949*, Vol. 2, Part 1, *The Far East and Australasia* (Washington, D.C.:
U.S. Government Printing Office, 1975), p. 29.

[60] October, 1951, Department of State background statement, in James W. Mooney and
Thomas R. West, eds., *Vietnam: A History and Anthology* (St. James, NY: Brandywine
Press, 1994), p. 16.

interventionism in Asia. As the American military commitment in South Vietnam escalated throughout the 1960s, so too did the level of protest.

The opposition to the war came from every segment of the ideological spectrum, but a significant fraction of the dissent was based on an anti-imperialist critique of U.S. foreign policy. Anti-imperialism had lain dormant through the early Cold War years, championed only by a small group of African-American activists and some lonely radical critics of the Cold War.[61] In academia, writing about the Cold War in the 1950s was dominated by an orthodox consensus that had the intellectual field to itself in the absence of any radical revisionist challenge. On the whole, radicalism had been successfully repressed by a culturally suffocating cold war ideology and by the McCarthyist mood that dominated politics in the 1950s. However, as Cold War fears diminished in the wake of the successful resolution of the Cuban Missile Crisis in 1962, radicalism suddenly became fashionable again.

As opposition to the war mounted, the various streams of anti-imperialism that had taken diverging courses in the past came together for the occasion as part of a broad anti-imperialist coalition composed of radicals, conservatives, females, blacks, college students, racists, and egalitarians. As in the 1890s, anti-imperialism once again had a generational dimension, though in this case the roles were reversed: the young people were now most prominent among the antis, whereas in the 1890s the older generation had led the opposition. The early and vocal antiwar position of Senator Ernest Gruening, who cut his teeth in the anti-imperialist debates of the 1920s, added an element of historical continuity to anti-imperialist dissent.[62]

As in the 1920s, economic prosperity provided a receptive social milieu for an economic critique. A suddenly chic New Left historiography, a burgeoning body of work that was inspired by the critical conceptual framework outlined in William Appleman Williams's *The Tragedy of American Diplomacy*, tied American interventionism in the third world to an ideology of "open door" imperialism that sought compulsively to assure access to overseas markets and raw materials. The appeal of the New Left critique was due partly to its all-encompassing definition of imperialism, which included colonialism, neocolonialism or "informal empire,"

[61] On African-Americans, see Penny M. Von Eschen , *Race Against Empire: Black Americans and Anticolonialism, 1937–1957* (Ithaca: Cornell University Press, 1997).

[62] Robert David Johnson, *Ernest Gruening and the American Dissenting Tradition* (Cambridge, Mass.: Harvard University Press, 1998).

and even geopolitics. Meanwhile, a strain of popular sympathy for the communist-led resistance in Vietnam was promoted by the radical anti-capitalist views of many of the New Left critics, for whom domestic and foreign policy critiques coincided.

Radical anti-imperialists made common cause in the 1960s with conservatives who refused to accept the geopolitical rationale for intervention. Notable realists like George Kennan, Walter Lippmann, and Hans Morgenthau, who clearly placed a higher priority on East-West concerns than on North-South issues, argued that the U.S. was overextending itself in fighting a war against a people from whom it had little to fear. Even for many confirmed cold warriors, it was clear that the worst was past. Convinced that the geopolitical importance of Vietnam was being vastly exaggerated, Atlanticists within the administration like George Ball argued that Europe, not remote areas of Asia, were more deserving of the nation's support. In the same vein, Senator J. William Fulbright chastised the Johnson administration for its "arrogance of power," suggesting that the nation, blinded by an imperial vision, had lost sight of its proper geopolitical security concerns. When Fulbright suggested to President Lyndon Johnson that the U.S. should withdraw because the Vietnamese were "not our kind of people," he reintroduced the by-now familiar conservative themes of race and culture as part of the anti-imperialist choral chant, even as critics on the left attacked the administration for its racism in Vietnam.[63]

Like their predecessors, the New Left anti-imperialists displayed an absence of fear. The assumption that the world was inherently a benign place was manifest in their contention that the United States was responsible for the onset of the cold war because, in their view, the Soviet Union's overriding interest in regional security meant that it had never presented an objective geopolitical threat. Opponents of the Vietnam war failed to see why the United States should be intervening in an impoverished far-away land that posed no conceivable menace to the United States. The geopolitical standpoint that had become second-nature to much of the foreign policy establishment typically struck them as being an utterly alien world view. In the aftermath of the Cuban missile crisis and the Nuclear Test Ban Treaty of 1963, the urgency of the Cold War and the gravity of the Soviet, or (as was more often the case in the sixties) the Chinese

---

[63] For Fulbright's blend of liberal internationalism, realism, localism, and racialism, see Randall Bennett Woods, *J. William Fulbright, Vietnam, and the Search for a Cold War Foreign Policy* (New York: Cambridge University Press, 1998).

threat, was not at all evident to anti-imperialist critics. As a consequence, questions of identity – the imperial presidency, militarism, the American national character – once again eclipsed national security issues.

For all the appearance of being a foreign policy upheaval, and despite some calls here and there for American withdrawal from Europe and an end to globalism, anti-imperialist opponents of the U.S. presence in Vietnam failed in their more ambitious aim of derailing a geopolitically based Cold War foreign policy. Because it was composed of philosophically warring elements, the coalition was inherently unstable. Though the mass protests had been organized by radicals, many young people had joined in the demonstrations because they saw no compelling reason to fight in Vietnam, and not from any conviction that U.S. policy as a whole was evil. Anti-imperialism also failed to generate much interest or commitment from the foreign policy elite as an alternative to the reigning ideology. Consequently, as the Nixon administration gradually liquidated the Vietnam adventure in the early 1970s, the anti-imperialist tide began to ebb, leaving the field open to an only partly chastened globalism. Indeed, by mid-decade hard-line cold warriors were vocally reasserting themselves. With the election of Ronald Reagan in 1980, the second Cold War was firmly under way.

By this time, decolonization became all but an accomplished fact and was followed not long thereafter by the quite unexpected end of the Cold War. No longer able to feed off the kinds of political issues that were capable of mobilizing dissent, anti-imperialism retreated to the academy, where the protesters of the 1960s became the "tenured radicals" of the 1980s and 1990s, with many of them mellowing over time. For younger scholars operating within academic cloisters, anti-imperialism increasingly took the rarefied form of postmodern cultural critiques that indicted developed societies for having marginalized and relegated to inferiority nonwhite peoples by means of various exclusionary "discourses." Ironically, the intellectual strength of this critique was inversely proportional to its political vibrancy because the attribution of imperialism to vague social and cultural trends made it difficult to fix responsibility on any single political agent. Even though the United States was clearly the chief promoter of global modernization, it appeared to be an agent of broad transnational forces that were difficult to discuss in traditional state-centered terms.

Nevertheless, this rather abstract critique did robustly confront one of the contradictions of anti-imperialist thought that had remained latent up to this point: its tendency to profess a belief in international pluralism while it simultaneously promoted the process of global modernization and cultural change that was chiefly responsible for undermining cultural diversity.[64] But the tension between progress and identity was more easy to state in the abstract than it was to address in practice. Indeed, many of the nations most critical of westernization were torn between the desire to preserve their cultural identities while enjoying at the same time the material benefits of modernity – benefits that could be purchased only at the steep cost of cultural transformation.[65]

On balance, anti-imperialism as a political force has diminished over time. It was at its most intense in the 1890s, when the question of empire was up for debate. It reemerged in a more radical form in the 1920s, when it became a formidable political force with pretensions of becoming the country's reigning foreign policy ideology. And it surfaced once again in the 1960s, this time as part of a larger wave of dissent that rose and fell with the expansion and deescalation of the war in Vietnam. The century-long ebbing of anti-imperialism was a product of a number of intertwined developments. One was exclusion from the corridors of power. As the emergence of fears of world war and global domination by a hostile power became central concerns of the nation's policy elite, all competing perspectives were elbowed aside. Another was assimilation. With the incorporation of important elements of the anti-imperialist outlook into the Wilsonian mainstream and the acceptance of decolonization as a major foreign policy objective, it became difficult to sustain an anti-imperialist critique of U.S. foreign policy, no matter if decolonization was pursued inconsistently and even half-heartedly. Finally, anti-imperialism lost its object. The delegitimation of racism and colonialism after World War II displaced anti-imperialism into the terrain of a cultural critique whose scholasticism defied translation into a foreign policy ideology with mass appeal.

Thus, at the beginning of the third millennium, one can see how it would be possible to conclude that anti-imperialism has reached its historical terminus. The process of decolonization is virtually completed and the trend toward the creation of a modern "global culture" appears to be unstoppable by political means. Moreover, the period of relatively harmonious great power relations that succeeded the cold war has diminished the

[64] For the idea of cultural imperialism as a critique of modernity, see John Tomlinson, *Cultural Imperialism: A Critical Introduction* (Baltimore: Johns Hopkins, 1991).
[65] On the tension between "essentialism" and "epochalism," see Clifford Geertz, *The Interpretation of Cultures* (New York: Basic Books, 1973), pp. 235–54.

competition for markets, resources, and ideological allegiance in the un-developed regions of the earth. All these developments make it less likely than ever that the kind of pluralistically harmonious world anticipated by many anti-imperialists will be created.

But while the utopian vision of anti-imperialism seems more than ever out of reach, its critical dimension is by no means outdated. Imperialism has always been one of the central themes of world history and there is every reason to suppose that it will continue to be a prominent part of the international landscape in the future – indeed, it might even become its dominant feature. Although great power relations are now relatively placid, it is possible that resource scarcity or overproduction might once again stimulate a neomercantilist geopolitics of imperialism. That is not the only possibility, for imperialism has been a problem during even rel-atively benign periods of normal internationalism. If present trends hold, the gap between the wealthy and the poor nations will continue to in-crease. If, as a result, concerns for global equity become more pronounced, as they are likely to do if economic globalization proceeds unevenly, then disturbing questions of domination and its corrosive effects on America's sense of national identity are likely once again to come to the fore.

World War II, Congress, and the Roots of Postwar American Foreign Policy

Randall B. Woods

In *America's Longest War* and subsequent works, historian George Herring has argued that the assumptions that underlay America's decision to wage cold war against the Soviet Union and its allies – namely, the Domino Theory, the Munich analogy, and the notion of a monolithic communist threat – were responsible for U.S. involvement in the Second Indochinese War. He is certainly correct, but the argument can be taken further. At the close of World War II, diplomats and politicians struggled to devise a strategy for confronting and containing the forces of international communism that fit in with traditional foreign policy philosophies and approaches. Given that the three basic themes of twentieth century diplomacy – isolationism, unilateralism, and internationalism – seemed mutually exclusive and that American foreign policy was traditionally as much or more a function of domestic politics and culture as events in the international arena, the task was daunting. Indeed, if America was to present the communist monolith with a noncommunist monolith of sufficient strength and unity, isolationism, unilateralism, and internationalism would have to be modified and harnessed together in support of the cold war. That is precisely what happened; appropriately enough for a nation with a republican form of government, the articulation and reconciliation of cold war imperatives with traditional approaches to foreign affairs took place in the Congress of the United States.

A substantial portion of this essay first appeared in Arnold A. Offner and Theodore A. Wilson, eds., *Victory in Europe 1945: From World War to Cold War* (University Press of Kansas; Lawrence, 2000).

Foreign affairs were, not surprisingly, much on the minds of the United States Congress, particularly the Senate, as World War II drew to a close. Franklin Roosevelt had paid almost as little attention to that body as he had to the State Department in the years following Pearl Harbor. He had bypassed the Senate, relying on executive agreements rather than treaties in the conduct of wartime diplomacy. The president bullied and cajoled Congress into creating dozens of new bureaucracies – the War Production Board, for example – which in effect usurped congressional prerogatives. Although it had made significant gains in the mid-term elections in 1942, the Republican party had been out of power for twelve years. GOP leaders were determined not to let the Democratic party monopolize the peacemaking. That determination was reinforced by the defeat of Thomas Dewey's "me-too" presidential candidacy in 1944. Though Southern Democrats were as offended by the growth of the federal bureaucracy and presidential power as members of the GOP, the Democratic leadership in Congress had little problem arousing partisan sentiment among the rank and file and persuading them to support first Roosevelt and then Truman's diplomatic initiatives. In the wake of the Yalta Conference in February, 1945, then, the halls of Congress rang with debate over America's proper role in the postwar international community. There existed in 1945 three clearly identifiable foreign policy impulses or alternatives around which legislators coalesced: traditional isolationism, or noninterventionism as its defenders referred to it; conservative internationalism; and liberal internationalism. A fourth option, which historian Justus Doenecke has labeled liberal isolationism, existed but was given very little credence in 1945.[1] It is worth noting, however, that that approach provided the foundation for the New Left/revisionist critique of U.S. diplomacy that was to play such an important role in American intellectual and political life during the 1960s.

There were those in Congress who refused to acknowledge that World War II had forever changed the world and the role that America would be able to play in it. Hardcore isolationists had come to terms with the fact that German, Italian, and Japanese facism constituted an authentic threat to American interests and that war had been necessary. But as they turned their eyes to the future in 1945, they continued to see Britain rather than the Soviet Union as the primary threat to U.S. independence and sovereignty. The isolationists were staunchly anticommunist,

[1] Justus D. Doenecke, *Not to the Swift: The Old Isolationists in the Cold War Era* (Lewisburg, PA: Bucknell University Press, 1979) p. 27.

but they believed that Europe was a European problem. They feared that the Europeans, particularly the British, would once again attempt to use the United States as a cat's paw, expending American blood and treasure to maintain a continental balance of power – "perpetual war for perpetual peace," to use Harry Elmer Barnes's phrase. They insisted that internationalism, and, specifically, the administration's campaign in behalf of a collective security organization, was simply a mask for a policy of realpolitik conducted exclusively by the executive. This new activism would allegedly bankrupt the nation, destroy free enterprise and lead to the creation of a police state.

The personification of isolationism, or noninterventionism, was Robert A. Taft. The junior senator from Ohio was the eldest but not the favorite son of William Howard Taft. He worshipped his father, who much preferred Robert's handsome, outgoing, athletic younger brother, Charles, to the dour, intense young man that Robert became. Following his graduation from Harvard Law School, he returned to Cincinnati to a career in law and politics. The embodiment of Republican orthodoxy, Taft rose through the ranks to occupy a seat in the Senate and became a regular challenger for the presidency from 1940 through 1952.

Taft shared his father's reverence for the Constitution. The greatest threat facing the United States in the late 1930s, he believed, was not disintegration of the international order, but growth in executive authority. The primary reason he opposed an active foreign policy was that such a course inevitably augmented the power of the executive. Congressional acquiescence in Rooseveltian "internationalism," which he saw as merely a desire by the president for complete freedom of action in foreign policymaking, was a threat to the balance of power within the federal system and to the liberties of the people. In 1939 he tried to cut funds for the Export-Import Bank, which he said "could finance a European war without Congress knowing anything about it." As early as January, 1942, Taft was complaining about the postwar expectations of what he referred to as the "war crowd." He railed against Republicans such as Wendell Willkie, Thomas E. Dewey, and the other members of the eastern establishment who wanted to "out-intervention" the Democratic interventionists. The GOP should no more do this than it should try to "out–New Deal" the New Dealers.[2]

---

[2] See Geoffrey Matthews, "Robert A. Taft, the Constitution and American Foreign Policy, 1939–53," *Journal of Contemporary History*: 17; no. 3 (July, 1982), pp. 507–22 and James T. Patterson, "Alternatives to Globalism: Robert A. Taft and American Foreign Policy, 1939–1945, *The Historian*: 36; no. 4 (August, 1974), pp. 670–88.

Not surprisingly the Roosevelt administration feared and resented Taft's "loyal opposition" during World War II. Citing considerations of national security, Cordell Hull, Dean Acheson, Henry Wallace, and others insisted that he "get on the team." Taft would not. As a matter of general principle, he proclaimed, there could be no doubt that criticism of the administration in time of war was essential to the maintenance of democratic government. "The duties imposed by the Constitution on Senators and Congressmen certainly require that they do not grant to the President every power that is requested . . . they require that they exercise their own judgment on questions of appropriations to determine whether the projects recommended have a real necessity for the success of the war," he told a reporter.[3]

Some of his opponents attributed his hypercriticism to obtuseness. Dean Acheson once accused the senator of being a "re-examinist," "like farmers who pull up their crops each morning to see how they had done during the night."[4] Others gave him credit for being bright but insisted that he was virtually devoid of a social conscience. Taft, however, regarded himself as the true guardian of conservatism, the most humanitarian of all doctrines because of its emphasis on individual liberty.

Taft's commitment to congressional independence was rooted not only in his background and education but in a broader philosophy that encompassed the conservative Republicans's commitment to the putative halcyon days of yesteryear. The GOP's attachment to the nineteenth century political and economic system as perceived by conservatives dictated its posture on foreign policy. It aligned Republicans against big government and a strong executive, which they feared would result in dictatorship and destroy political and civil freedom; against large-scale expenditures, which would allow the government to impose "socialist" controls over prices, wages, and the free enterprise system; and against high taxation, which crushed the initiative of the private sector.

Yet, as political scientist John Spanier and others have pointed out, internationalism in the 1940s, even more than the New Deal, required all of these things – a powerful government capable of negotiating with other powerful governments; a strong president who could act decisively and vigorously; and huge outflows of cash to sustain military establishments

---

[3] Quoted in Richard E. Darilek, *A Loyal Opposition in Time of War: The Republican Party and the Politics of Foreign Policy from Pearl Harbor to Yalta* (Westport, CT: Greenwood Press, 1976), p. 28.

[4] *Ibid.*

and finance foreign aid. In that sense, orthodox Republican philosophy seemed to make active participation in world affairs incompatible with the preservation of political democracy and free enterprise. Thus did the Taft Republicans oppose the view put forward by the British government and American internationalists – that Europe was vital to American security; and that both Great Britain and the nations of the Continent, devastated by the war, had to be nursed back to health and strength by the United States.[5]

These views prompted Taft to become the most articulate and effective opponent in the United States of Anglo-American efforts to create an interdependent world economy – multilateralism. "The Capital is full of plans of all kinds," the Ohioan told a group gathered to celebrate William McKinley's 100 birthday in January, 1943. "Every economic panacea any long-haired crank ever thought of is being dusted off and incorporated in a magnificent collection of glittering landscapes supposed to lead to Utopia. Nearly every one of them rests on the huge expenditure of Government without telling us where the money is coming from, when we already face a debt of over $200 billion."[6] In the spring of 1944 he specifically attacked the proposed International Monetary Fund and International Bank for Reconstruction and Development. Both institutions were based on the fallacious assumption that underlay all administration foreign policies, namely "that American money and American charity shall solve every problem."[7]

Committed to the notion that America was and could continue to be economically and strategically self-sufficient, Taft opposed foreign aid in the immediate postwar period, and he voted against ratification of the charter of the North Atlantic Treaty Organization (NATO). As a staunch anticommunist, the junior senator from Ohio did vote for the Truman Doctrine, but only reluctantly. He was careful to observe at the time that "I do not regard this as a commitment to any similar policy in any other section of the world." America should "withdraw as soon as normal economic conditions are restored."[8]

---

[5] John Spanier, *The Truman-MacArthur Controversy and the Korean War* (Cambridge, MA: Belknap Press, 1959) pp. 158–59.

[6] Sidney. M. Shalett, "Stettinius Calls lend-lease vital," *New York Times*, January 30, 1943, p. 5.

[7] Address of Robert A. Taft to War Veterans Club of Ohio, May 6, 1944, box 802, R. Taft Papers, Library of Congress.

[8] James T. Patterson, *Mr. Republican: a Biography of Robert A. Taft* (Boston, MA: Houghton Mifflin, 1972), p. 371.

Taft stood in the wings and cheered on Senator Joseph McCarthy of Wisconsin as he conducted his anticommunist witch hunt during the early 1950s. Taft did so because he saw the campaign against alleged subversives as helpful to the Republican cause. But in supporting McCarthy, Taft acted only partly out of political opportunism. Because McCarthyism represented a variety of isolationism, it buttressed Taft's views on foreign policy. If the real threat to American security came from traitors within, there was no need for alliances, foreign aid, or the United Nations.

Taft also sympathized with the Asia Firsters in his party, those politicians who eschewed engagement in Europe but advocated an aggressive policy in Asia, especially in opposition to communism. He supported U.S. participation in the Korean War and in so doing acknowledged that America had legitimate economic and strategic interests in the Pacific as well as the Caribbean. But that was as far as he would go.

During his campaign for the Republican presidential nomination in 1952, Taft articulated an approach to foreign affairs that Spanier has labeled unilateralism. First, Taft proposed that the United States should withdraw from the United Nations and enter no "entangling alliances" such as NATO. Second, America should stress Asia over Europe, although Taft and his supporters believed that the United States should rely for defense of its interests in the area on island bases and anticommunist allies. Indeed, the third mainstay of the unilateralist position was that the United States should never become bogged down in a war on the Asian land mass. America's resources were limited and the world was full of nations willing to use the United States for its own purposes.[9]

Robert Taft, however, spoke for only one sector, perhaps the more orthodox, of the conservative community. World War II converted a number of former isolationists into conservative internationalists. Japan's attack on Pearl Harbor destroyed the myth of impregnability that the America First movement had worked so assiduously to disseminate in the early 1940s. The Atlantic and Pacific were not great barriers protecting "Fortress America" from attack, as the isolationists had argued, but rather were highways across which hostile ships and airplanes could move and assault the Western Hemisphere. Led by Time-Life publisher Henry Luce, old America Firsters decided that if America could not hide from the rest of the world, it must control it. They would support foreign aid, alliances, and a massive military budget, but not out of any Wilsonian desire to improve the lot of other members of the global village. These nationalists

[9] Spanier, *Truman-MacArthur Controversy*, pp. 156–59.

sought not to save the world, but to safeguard American strategic and economic interests by creating and dominating interlocking spheres of influence.

Arthur H. Vandenberg of Michigan, who succeeded to the chair of the Senate Foreign Relations Committee when the Republicans won control of Congress in 1946, was the leader of these conservative nationalists. Vandenberg shared most of Taft's conservative attitudes toward the Constitution, the role of the federal government in society, the budget, free enterprise, and individual liberty, and he was a thoroughgoing nationalist in foreign affairs. But he became convinced in 1945 and 1946 that the United States could not return to the past and that the best way to preserve the status quo in a dangerous world was to dominate that world.

Interestingly, despite his interwar isolationism, Vandenberg had begun public life as a disciple of Theodore Roosevelt, and his conversion to conservative internationalism at the close of World War II does not now appear as surprising as it did then. But it was no less powerful for that. Vandenberg was an overachiever who emerged from a working class background – his father ran a boarding house and made harnessess – to work his way through the University of Michigan in the waning years of the nineteenth century. Following graduation, he became a journalist. While editor of the *Grand Rapids Herald*, he endorsed the Open Door policy, annexation of the Philippines, and the Roosevelt Corollary to the Monroe Doctrine. During the years prior to America's entry into World War I, Vandenberg was an outspoken interventionist, branding pacifists and noninterventionists as cowards. He supported membership in the League of Nations and during the Red Scare of 1919 proved himself to be as ardent a Bolshevik-baiter as any person in America.[10]

First elected to Congress in 1928, Vandenberg supported the presidential policies of both Calvin Coolidge and Herbert Hoover. Though evidencing some of the Midwestern progressives' distrust of Wall Street, the Michigan legislator showed himself to be devoted to the domestic conservative agenda. He opposed the New Deal and joined with members of the conservative American Liberty League in castigating Franklin Roosevelt as a would-be dictator and a stalking horse for the forces of collectivization. From 1939 through 1941 he fought against Roosevelt's interventionist proposals. War would destroy the free enterprise system; lend-lease, he declared, constituted nothing less than the "suicide of the Republic."[11]

[10] Doenecke, *Not to the Swift*, p. 45.
[11] *Ibid.*

After America entered World War II, Vandenberg, like Taft, quickly accommodated himself to the new circumstances. He supported the war effort and paid tribute to the Atlantic Charter. As the war neared its end, however, he turned his gaze not backward to the putative days of economic self-sufficiency and Fortress America but forward to a postwar world filled with danger and uncertainty. As a thoroughgoing nationalist, Vandenberg believed that the United States had legitimate interests abroad. He concluded that with the destruction of the balance of power in Europe and Asia, the United States would have to don the mantle of world leadership. In January, 1945, Vandenberg shocked his colleagues by endorsing membership in a collective security organization: "I do not believe that any nation hereafter can immunize itself by its own exclusive action ..." he told the Senate. "Our oceans have ceased to be moats which automatically protect our ramparts. Flesh and blood now compete unequally with winged steel. War has become an all-consuming juggernaut... I want maximum American cooperation, consistent with legitimate American self-interest, with constitutional process and with collateral events which warrant it, to make the basic idea of Dumbarton Oaks [that is, collective security] succeed."[12]

As a legislator with a huge Polish constituency, however, he was deeply upset by the February, 1945, Yalta settlement regarding Eastern Europe. Vandenberg perceived the Soviet Union as head of an international communist conspiracy bent on ruling the world. As historian Justus Doenecke has pointed out, he was much more concerned as a delegate to the San Francisco Conference during the spring of 1945 with curbing Russian ambitions and securing the right of nations to act within regional collective security organizations than with fostering international community per se.

Vandenberg's journey from isolationist to conservative internationalist culminated with his dramatic speech to the Senate delivered in February, 1946. "What is Russia up to now?" he asked. After reviewing Soviet activities in the Balkans, in Manchuria, and in Poland, he announced that the world had become divided between two rival ideologies: democracy and communism. Peaceful coexistence was possible only if the United States was as vigorous and firm as the Soviet Union in defending its interests. The United States must establish limits beyond which it would not compromise.[13] The Truman administration responded with Secretary of State

[12] John L. Gaddis, *The United States and the Origins of the Cold War, 1941–1947* (New York: Columbia University Press, 1972) 168.

[13] *Ibid.*, p. 296.

James F. Byrnes Overseas Press Club speech – the second Vandenberg concerto as one reporter dubbed it. Byrnes indirectly denounced Soviet activities in Eastern Europe and promised that henceforward the United States could not and would not permit aggression "by coercion or pressure or by subterfuges such as political infiltration."[14]

Vandenberg's views on foreign policy were determined not only by his nationalism but also by his ambition for both himself and the Republican party. He had closely followed the party line under presidencies from Theodore Roosevelt through Franklin Roosevelt. In late 1945 and early 1946 he sensed that President Truman was politically vulnerable on Yalta specifically and foreign policy in general.[15] Vandenberg and the Republicans came to the conclusion that a hard line toward the Soviets would earn them kudos with the electorate and enable them to recapture control of the White House in 1948. Yet when Truman and Byrnes adopted a confrontational stance toward Moscow in 1946 and 1947, Vandenberg proved to be the epitome of bipartisan cooperation. The former isolationist from Michigan supported the Truman Doctrine and the Marshall Plan in 1947, and U.S. membership in NATO in 1949, not because he wanted to bring the blessings of American civilization to the Greeks and Turks or because he believed that the United States had the duty to promote socioeconomic justice abroad. The purposes of alliances and bases were to establish a Pax Americana that would ensure a stable world and serve America's vested interests. The conservative internationalism that he espoused would remain one of the cornerstones of postwar American foreign policy.

Joining the neoimperialists in pushing for an activist American role in world affairs were Wilsonian internationalists who believed that if the United States had joined the League of Nations and acted in concert with the western democracies after World War I, aggression could have been nipped in the bud. Many of these Wilsonians were veterans of William Allen White's Committee to Defend America by Aiding the Allies formed in 1941 and were supporters of the New Deal who believed that the state

---

[14] Quoted in Randall B. Woods and Howard Jones, *Dawning of the Cold War: The United States' Quest for Order* (Athens, GA: University of Georgia Press, 1991), p. 109.

[15] Public opinion polls indicated that before Potsdam, while Truman was still in his honeymoon period, 87 percent of those questioned approved of the way he was handling his job. A year later with Soviet-American relations strained to the breaking point, that figure had more than halved, dropping to 43 percent. Terry H. Anderson, *The United States, Great Britain, and the Cold War, 1944–1947* (Columbia, MO: University of Missouri Press, 1981), p. 107.

had an obligation to help the less fortunate and to intervene in the private sector to ensure equality of opportunity. Their efforts in behalf of internationalism culminated in the spring of 1945 when the United States led the way in establishing a new collective security organization whose stated goals were to prevent armed aggression and to promote prosperity and human rights throughout the world. When subsequently the UN proved incapable of guaranteeing the political and economic security of Western Europe, these liberal internationalists supported foreign aid and anticommunist alliance systems as mechanisms that would not only protect America from Soviet aggression but bring social justice and economic security first to Europe and then to the less fortunate peoples of the developing world.

Despite his segregationist voting record and his opposition to organized labor, first term Senator J. William Fulbright of Arkansas accurately represented the liberal internationalist philosophy. The junior senator from Arkansas had grown up in Fayetteville, a college community situated in the foothills of the Ozark mountains. Shortly before his graduation from the University of Arkansas in 1924, where he had been active in athletics and campus politics, Fulbright won a Rhodes scholarship. After a full diet of tutorials, rugby, lacrosse, and the Oxford Union, the young Arkansan graduated from Pembroke College with a concentration in modern history. He returned to America and earned a law degree from George Washington University. In 1942, he ran successfully for the House and then for the Senate in 1944.[16]

Fulbright's commitment to internationalism was in part an offshoot of his years at Oxford as a Rhodes scholar. The most important acquaintance he made at Pembroke College was his young tutor, Ronald Buchanan McCallum, whose guidance and instruction were crucial in shaping the young American's intellect and worldview. The two men maintained a close personal and intellectual relationship until McCallum's death in 1973. In 1944, McCallum, a Liberal and an ardent admirer of Woodrow Wilson, published *Public Opinion and the Lost Peace*, in which he challenged the longstanding view of John Maynard Keynes that the peace structure worked out at the Versailles Conference in 1919 was predestined to fail. The concept of the League was sound; the organization had not worked because political figures on both sides of the Atlantic had never been willing to make a true commitment to the principles that

---

[16] See Haynes Johnson and Bernard M. Gwertzman, *Fulbright: The Dissenter* (Garden City, NY: Doubleday, 1966), pp. 17–64.

underlay it and had attempted to use it for their own selfish, political purposes. McCallum concluded his book with an appeal to Americans and
Britons to rediscover and rededicate themselves to the fundamentals of
Wilsonian internationalism, at the core of which was a willingness on the
part of nation states to surrender part of their sovereignty in behalf of the
common good.[17]

Meanwhile, in the United States, first term Congressman J. William
Fulbright, the practicing politician, began to develop and promulgate
his own version of Wilsonian internationalism. In 1943, Fulbright had
coauthored with Senator John Connally of Texas a resolution placing
Congress on record as favoring membership in an international organization dedicated to keeping the peace. Impressed by the subsequent
outpouring of public support for the idea of collective security that followed, the Roosevelt administration boarded the internationalist band-
wagon. The upshot was American leadership in the creation of the
United Nations. No senator was more active in speaking and lobbying for ratification of the UN Charter than the junior senator from
Arkansas.[18]

Central to Fulbright's philosophy was the assumption that there existed
a body of ideas and a constellation of economic and political institutions
that together defined Western civilization, that the United States shared
in these ideals and institutions, and that therefore it had an obligation to
defend them.[19]

Time and again the former Rhodes scholar attempted to demonstrate
that isolationism was merely a facet of old-fashioned nationalism. Those
of his contemporaries who posed as defenders of national sovereignty
were in fact advocating a return to the policies of the interwar period
when the United States refused to acknowledge that its fate was linked
to the fortunes of other democracies. National sovereignty was in fact a
trick, an illusion, especially in the world of airplanes, submarines, and
atomic weapons. Having equated isolationism with obsessive nationalism, Fulbright observed that both led to a narcissistic attitude toward
international affairs. Abnegation, in turn, made possible oppression and

---

[17] George Herbert Gunn, "The Continuing Friendship of James William Fulbright and
Ronald Buchanan McCallum," *South Atlantic Quarterly*: 83; no. 4 (Autumn, 1984),
pp. 417–19.

[18] J. William Fulbright (hereafter JWF) to Edward J. Meeman, March 19, 1945, BCN24,
folder 29, Fulbright Papers, University of Arkansas.

[19] U.S. Congress, Senate, *Congressional Record*, 79th Congress, 1st session, 1945, 91, pt. 3,
p. 2898.

poverty, the twin seeds of war.[20] Horrified by pictures of the destruction wrought by the atomic bombs at Hiroshima and Nagasaki, Fulbright called upon Congress, the nation, and the world to develop a mechanism capable of restraining blood-and-soil nationalism and channeling modern technology into peaceful uses.

What the freshman senator had in mind was an authentic international federation run on democratic principles. In a speech to the American Bar Association in 1945, Fulbright outlined his vision: "The history of government over the centuries, which is largely the chronicle of man's efforts to achieve freedom from the control of arbitrary force, indicate [sic] that only by the collective action of a dominant group can security be obtained."[21] The hope of the world rested with the establishment of a global organization with a collective security mandate and a peace-keeping force sufficient to enforce that mandate. Once the U.N. Charter was ratified, it should be clearly understood that the president through his delegate would have the authority to commit American troops to military action authorized by the Security Council.

Fulbright was an economic as well as a political internationalist; he fully shared the multilateralist views of his friend, Assistant Secretary of State for Economic Affairs, Will Clayton. Unlike Taft who believed that the United States could remain economically self-sufficient and that economic conditions elsewhere in the world had no bearing on American interests, these intellectual heirs of Adam Smith believed that the line between national and international economics was disappearing and that prosperity was infinitely expandable. They looked forward to the creation of an economically interdependent world free of tariffs, preferences, quotas, and exchange controls. To this end Fulbright helped lead the fight in the Senate in 1945 for approval of the Bretton Woods Agreements and in 1946 for passage of the British loan, a $3.5 billion credit designed to rehabilitate Britain's economy and to enable that country to abandon imperial preference and exchange controls.[22]

Fulbright understood the residual strength of traditional isolationism and the implications of conservative internationalism. As early as the

---

[20] U.S. Congress, Senate, *Congressional Record*, 79th Congress, 1st session, 1945, 91, pt. 3, 2899 and U.S. Congress, House, *Congressional Record*, 78th Congress, 1st session, 1943, 8, pt. 9, p. A477.

[21] U.S. Congress, Senate, *Congressional Record*, 79th Congress, 1st session, 1945, 91, pt. 13, pp. A4652–53.

[22] See U.S. Congress, Senate, Committee on Banking and Currency, *Anglo-American Financial Agreement: Hearings*, 79th Congress, 2nd session, 1946.

summer of 1945, he began to express doubts about America's commitment to authentic internationalism. Arkansas's junior senator wondered aloud to the Senate why there was unanimous support for ratification of the U.N. Charter while only weeks before, economic nationalists and neoisolationists had fought vigorously against the Bretton Woods Agreements and the British loan. Could it be, he asked, that they believed that the Charter did not impinge on the nation's sovereignty and that despite its membership in the United Nations, the United States still retained absolute freedom of action?[23]

In the years that followed, Fulbright continued to preach the internationalist creed, but his globalism, unlike Henry Wallaces's, acknowledged the threat posed to the security of Central and Western Europe by Stalinism. He readily admitted that Soviet communism was totalitarian, aggressive, and autarkic. Indeed, like historian Arthur Schlesinger, Senator Hubert Humphrey of Minnesota, and other members of the Americans for Democratic Action (because of his stance on civil rights Fulbright was not a member of this organization, but he was friends and sympathized with most of its founders), Fulbright was an active cold warrior. In the immediate postwar period, he supported the Truman Doctrine, the Marshall Plan and foreign aid in general. During the 1950s he criticized President Dwight David Eisenhower and Secretary of State John Foster Dulles not only for the rigidity of their thinking but also for their lack of imagination in dealing with the communist threat in the developing world and the general ineffectiveness of their policies. As chair of the Senate Foreign Relations Committee, Fulbright was a vigorous supporter of the presidency of John F. Kennedy. In fact, no figure in Washington was more visible in articulating the liberal, activist philosophy that characterized that administration's foreign policies. Effective resistance against the forces of international communism involved not only military strength, he told the Senate, but a willingness to help developing nations "toward the fulfillment of their own highest purposes."[24] America could be truly secure, he seemed to be saying, only in a community of nations whose institutions and values closely resembled its own.

Though it was considered more of a political philosophy and historical interpretation than a viable foreign policy option, and that only by a

---

[23] U.S. Congress, Senate, *Congressional Record*, 79th Congress, 1st session, 1945, vol. 91, pt. 6, pp. 7962–64.
[24] U.S. Congress, Senate, *Congressional Record*, 81st Congress, 1st session, 1951, vol. 97, pt. 1, p. 520–22.

handful of legislators in 1945, a fourth approach – liberal isolationism – manifested itself as World War II came to a close. This perspective did not have as conspicuous a spokesperson as the other three; probably its most influential proponent was Robert M. LaFollette, Jr. "Young Bob," a studious, conscientious public servant authentically dedicated to improving the welfare of his fellow human beings, had succeeded his famous father, Robert M. LaFollete, Sr., in the Senate in 1925. A Progressive from Wisconsin, the younger LaFollette came from a political tradition that viewed Wall Street – that is financiers and corporate executives – as avaricious exploiters of the farmers and artisans of the American heartland. The political and economic systems were controlled absolutely by these plutocrats who set the prices of agricultural commodities and labor at artificially low levels and of manufactured items, especially farm implements, at artificially high levels. The liberal isolationists, who included individuals such as economist-historian Charles Beard and progressive-populist Senator William Langer (R–ND), believed that Wall Street had formed an unholy alliance with British financiers to spread monopoly capitalism abroad and were exploiting the labor and markets of the developing world as well as those of their respective homelands.[25]

The younger La Follette was convinced that wars were caused by imperialism and power politics, that is, the struggle between national corporate elites to dominate various regions of the world. Like his father, who had voted against the Treaty of Versailles, "Young Bob" opposed any peace settlement that perpetuated an unjust status quo or that denied all peoples of the earth the right of self-determination. He opposed American intervention in Nicaragua during the Hoover administration and was an outspoken champion of disarmament during the 1930s. LaFollette supported the Neutrality Acts, pushed for heavy taxation of war profits, and fought tenaciously to keep the United States out of the European conflict.[26] Though he supported the administration after Pearl Harbor, LaFollette expressed grave doubts about the Yalta accords, and he voted against the British loan on the grounds that it would dangerously deplete America's resources.[27]

In essence, LaFollette and the other liberal isolationists believed that America's first priority should be social justice and democracy at home;

[25] Wayne S. Cole, *Roosevelt & the Isolationists, 1932–45* (Lincoln, NB: University of Nebraska Press, 1983), p. 30.

[26] Doenecke, *Not to the Swift*, pp. 27–28.

[27] *Ibid.*, p. 65.

that an activist foreign policy was a diversion from that great objective; and that as long as the political and economic systems were dominated by Wall Street, an activist foreign policy would result in economic exploitation and political oppression overseas. LaFollette was a great defender of the New Deal and even went so far as to advocate nationalization of the railroads and banking system. His desire, like Charles Beard's, was that America construct a social democracy that would stand as an unobtrusive example to the rest of the world.

Building on this tradition, academics, student activists, and a handful of politicians emerged in the 1960s to offer a scathing indictment of the Cold War, U.S. foreign policy, and American society in general. Focusing on the twin evils of discrimination and imperialism, these reformers denied the efficacy of traditional electoral politics and decried established institutions – universities, churches, and government bureaucracies – as inherently corrupt. New Left activists called for the people to resume control of their destinies through direct, "participatory" democracy.[28] By the mid-1960s the great Satan of the New Left had become "corporate liberalism," a phrase coined by Carl Oglesby, president of the Students for a Democratic Society. The term was not new to the movement but Oglesby's linking of it to American foreign policy was. The men who engineered the war in Vietnam "are not moral monsters," he said. "They are all honorable men. They are all liberals." The American corporate machine they oversaw was the "colossus of history," taking the riches of other nations and consuming half of the world's goods. Being decent men, corporate liberals rationalized their rapacity and their policy of counterrevolution with the ideology of anticommunism, defining all revolutions as communist and communism as evil.[29] Isolationism was implicit in the New Left/revisionist indictment. America should dismantle its huge network of bases, disinvest in developing areas, and halt the endless round of military interventions that punctuated U.S. foreign policy during the twentieth century. Without justice and equity at home, an interventionist foreign policy could only be an abomination.

In the years following the Second World War, two of the foreign policy approaches articulated in Congress in 1945 – conservative and liberal internationalism – came together to produce an activism that committed the United States to fighting communism on every front, to use historian

---

[28] Allen J. Matusow, *The Unraveling of America: A History of Liberalism in the 1960s* (New York: Harper and Row, 1984), p. 310.
[29] *Ibid.*, p. 319.

Thomas Paterson's phrase.[30] Conservative anticommunists preoccupied with markets and bases backed by a burgeoning military-industrial complex argued that the only way America could be safe in a hostile world was to dominate that world through a network of alliances and overseas bases, and through possession of the largest nuclear arsenal in the world. Joining them were liberal internationalists, many of whom were domestic reformers, who saw America's welfare as tied to that of the other members of the international community. To a degree they supported alliances and military aid, but in addition, the liberal internationalists wanted to eliminate the social and economic turmoil that they perceived to be a breeding ground for Marxism and an invitation to Soviet imperialism. They wanted to do nothing less than to spread the blessings of liberty, democracy, and free enterprise and to guarantee stability and prosperity to peoples threatened by Communist imperialism. The blending of these two strains led directly to American involvement in Vietnam.

[30] Thomas G. Paterson, *On Every Front: The Making of the Cold War* (New York: Norton, 1979).

The Progressive Dissent: Ernest Gruening and Vietnam

Robert D. Johnson

On August 6, 1964, the seventy-seven-year-old junior senator from
Alaska, Ernest Gruening, delivered a brief address in the Senate cham-
bers. The upper chamber was considering the Tonkin Gulf Resolution,
which President Lyndon Johnson had submitted to obtain approval for
retaliatory air raids against North Vietnam. Though Gruening conceded
the difficulty of rebuffing a presidential request "couched in terms of high
principle and national interest," he dissented from Johnson's approach
for constitutional, historical, and policy reasons. The Alaskan reminded
his colleagues that the aura of increased presidential authority associated
with the Cold War did not absolve senators of their "right and duty"
to express opinions on foreign policy issues, particularly "if those views
embody doubt or dissent." The specifics of Vietnam policy, Gruening
reasoned, made Senate action even more important. He considered the
administration's policy inherently contradictory. Though Johnson had
contended that only the South Vietnamese could win the war, an "inevitable development" of "our steadily increasing involvement" would
be the weakening of the very regime that the president deemed essential
to long-term victory. Regardless of the tactical problems, Gruening could
detect "no threat to our national security" from a Communist victory in
what he perceived as a Vietnamese civil war. Indeed, he claimed, "all [of]
Vietnam is not worth the life of a single American boy." Most important,
the military escalation violated traditional American ideals. Instead of defending freedom and democracy, in Vietnam "we have been supporting
corrupt and unpopular dictatorships which owe their temporary sojourn
in power to our massive support." Instead of embracing anti-imperialism,

the United States had adopted a "wholly misguided" policy of "picking up the burden abandoned by France" in its failed colonial war.[1]

The passionate dissent had little effect among Gruening's colleagues: the resolution sailed through the Senate by a vote of eighty-eight to two. In the White House, however, the Alaskan's outspokenness aroused the President's ire. Johnson privately fumed that the vote proved Gruening was "no good. He's just no good."[2]

In fact, the Alaskan's action should not have surprised Johnson. Gruening's campaign against the war in Vietnam represented only the most controversial aspect of a career characterized by its willingness to challenge mainstream foreign policy. His suggestion that the United States withdraw its troops flowed logically from the anti-imperialist principles he had articulated over the course of four decades as a dissenter. Gruening's ideological consistency, outspoken nature, and involvement with a host of other international issues allowed the senator to position himself as a barometer of anti-imperialist thought in the 1960s Senate. At the most basic level, Gruening saw the United States as a "cradle of revolution," and thus embraced the tradition of American dissent that sought to fashion community – both domestically and internationally – based on principles of liberty, self-determination, and anti-imperialism.

At the same time, Gruening's career also illustrates the frustrations of anti-Vietnam members of the upper chamber. His inability to rally opposition to the conflict significantly altered how the Alaskan approaches his duties as senator. As the war progressed, he became less likely to frame his arguments to woo uncommitted senators, and instead sought to present his case in an intellectually consistent fashion in the hopes of influencing public opinion. Ideologically, his crusade against American involvement in Southeast Asia produced a subtle reconfiguring in Gruening's belief system, intensifying previously submerged elements in his international perspective and prompting him to view the United States itself as the chief obstacle to the fulfillment of his ideals. Gruening's disillusionment, however, also alienated him from his increasingly conservative constituency, and ultimately cost him the Senate seat to which he had aspired for most of his adult life.

---

[1] U.S. Congress, *Congressional Record* [hereafter CR], 88th Congress, 2nd session, 1964, pp. 18413–18414.

[2] Lyndon Baines Johnson, quoted in Michael Beschloss, ed., *Taking Charge: The Johnson White House Tapes, 1963–1964* (New York: Simon and Schuster, 1997), p. 508.

The son of a prominent surgeon and first generation German emigrant, Ernest Gruening was born in New York City in 1887. He attended elite New York City preparatory schools, Harvard, and then Harvard Medical School. His father intended for him to inherit the family's medical practice, but, after receiving his M.D. in 1912, Ernest accepted a position in Boston journalism instead. By the age of thirty, he was managing editor of the *Boston Journal,* where he emerged as a critic of Woodrow Wilson's wartime policies, a betrayal, he contended, of the president's idealistic promise. This disillusioned Wilsonian first came to national prominence in 1921 when he assumed the editorship of *The Nation,* where one of his first tasks was overseeing a series of articles critiquing the U.S. occupation of Haiti. To Gruening, the intervention proved the shortcomings of Wilson's agenda and the folly of employing the military to achieve stability or to promote democracy. More important, he lamented that the intervention tarnished the reputation of the United States as a nation that respected self-determination and the rights of weaker states. After leaving *The Nation* in 1923, Gruening secured a contract to write what he immodestly referred to as "the book," an analysis of the Mexican Revolution. Several years of research in Mexico convinced him that a U.S.–style democracy would not achieve the reforms necessary to bring social and economic justice to Mexican society. His massive study, *Mexico and Its Heritage,* attracted praise from well beyond the anti-imperialist community, establishing him as a leading interpreter of Latin American history and contemporary affairs. It also gave him an opportunity to spell out his emerging anti-imperialist principles in greater detail. The author argued that the United States simply refraining from intervention in the Caribbean Basin would not suffice. Rather, he envisioned anti-imperialists in the United States working with like-minded figures throughout Latin America to create a crossnational alliance committed to reform.[3]

This reputation set the stage for his entrance into government service. In 1934, when Franklin Roosevelt appointed him chief U.S. policymaker for Puerto Rico, Gruening made the transition from critic to administrator. The position afforded an ideal opportunity to translate into practice his belief in the practicality of crossnational, anti-imperialist alliances. Openly aligning himself with reform-minded factions in the Puerto Rican Liberal party, Gruening promoted an economic agenda, which called for the United States to use funds to restructure the island's

---

[3] Ernest Gruening, *Mexico and Its Heritage* (New York: Century Company, 1928).

agricultural economy. In the process, he went well beyond the New Deal reforms then championed by FDR and American liberals. For his economic program had a political agenda. By using government programs to lessen the financial clout of the island's large sugar companies, he intended to weaken Puerto Rico's economic elite, in turn freeing up Puerto Rican politics for reformers whose views he found more compatible. Even more ambitiously, Gruening hoped that Roosevelt would apply his model, a precursor of Point Four and (to a lesser degree) of the Alliance for Progress, elsewhere in his dealings with Latin America.[4]

Gruening's Haitian, Mexican, and Puerto Rican activities had in common a desire to determine the proper nature of the relationship between the United States as a superpower with a revolutionary heritage and weaker nations with an authoritarian heritage intent on achieving political, economic, and social reform. He would retain the basic elements of his dissent – a respect for the potency of nationalism in the underdeveloped world, a call to understand how policy decisions toward one country affected the overall international image of the United States, and a suspicion of using the military to maintain political stability – throughout his public career. Moreover, while he began the 1920s convinced that replicating the U.S. system of government represented the best hope for the nations of the Caribbean Basin, he eventually embraced a more flexible approach which questioned whether political democracy alone would solve the region's deep-seated problems. In its most basic form, this agenda formed an anti-imperialist alternative to Wilsonianism.

Tactically, Gruening's interwar experiences also shaped his later approach to foreign affairs. His Progressive Era idealism led him into a career in journalism and convinced him that the people would repudiate actions, such as the intervention in Haiti, that violated traditional American ideals. Critics of mainstream foreign policy therefore needed to concentrate on bringing facts out into the open – what Gruening termed the "constructive muckraking of American imperialism" – and trust that an aroused public would pressure government officials to reverse their policies. This was not to say that idealists should treat the government as a unified entity. After working alongside anti-imperialist senators such as William Borah (R-ID), George Norris (R-NB), and William King (D-UT), Gruening came to appreciate how the Senate's tolerance of dissenting positions, tradition of

---

[4] Robert David Johnson, "Anti-Imperialism and the Good Neighbour Policy: Ernest Gruening and Puerto Rican Affairs, 1934–1939," *Journal of Latin American Studies*: 29 (1997), pp. 89–110.

unfettered debate, and constitutional mandates to address international
issues could enhance the influence of dissenters beyond their numerical
strength. Given that the New Deal led most American reformers to champion greater presidential power, Gruening's belief that anti-imperialists
could best work through the legislature separated him from his peers. Except for a brief tenure during his stewardship of the PRRA, he correctly
doubted that his views would ever win majority support among executive
branch policymakers.[5]

Finally, Gruening's early experiences revealed the personal characteristics that would reappear later in his career. He once boasted – "at the risk
of being held an incurable optimist and a visionary"– that he could "free
Haiti" with "a hundred thousand dollars." Endowed with this healthy
sense of his own self-worth and a transparent ambition, Gruening wanted
to go beyond simply opposing mainstream policies to affect international
affairs in a positive fashion. Efforts along these lines included his proposal
to pressure Mexico to abolish its army and his 1930s initiatives in Puerto
Rico. But this natural critic always was more confident in detecting the
flaws in U.S. foreign policy than in proposing realistic alternatives, though
he rarely conceded the fact. His tenacity and intellectual self-confidence
drew strong praise from supporters (one admirer labeled him "one of the
most idealistic men he had ever known") but prompted detractors to view
him as arrogant and close-minded. Both sets of perceptions persisted into
the 1960s.[6]

In the short term, his administrative shortcomings, compounded by
the ideological tensions embedded within his program, undermined his
efforts in Puerto Rico, in turn shaking his faith in his anti-imperialist
agenda for the only extended period in his career. He had more pressing problems than an intellectual crisis, however, since in 1939 Roosevelt,
who always proved reluctant to fire his subordinates, reassigned Gruening
to what one national magazine dubbed "the Siberia of the Department."[7]
Gruening reluctantly accepted the gubernatorial position, realizing that he
had no choice if he wanted to continue government service. His newfound

---

[5] Gruening to Oswald Garrison Villard, March 13, 1922, file 1423, Oswald Garrison Villard
Papers, Houghton Library, Harvard University.

[6] Gruening to Roger Baldwin, November 14, 1923, series C, box 327, NAACP Papers,
Library of Congress; Vincent Stillman interview, in report by Special Agent Arthur Hart,
October 20, 1950, New York City, "Re: ERNEST GRUENING, aka Ernest H. Gruening,
Governor of Alaska – Appointee," box 340, President's Secretary's File, Harry Truman
Presidential Library, Independence, Missouri.

[7] *U.S. News & World Report*, April 22, 1949.

pragmatism made him willing to temper his ideological agenda, especially regarding international affairs, in the name of short-term political gain. In the interwar era, for instance, Gruening was known for his sharp anti-militarism. But after World War II and early Cold War defense projects brought a steady flow of federal assistance for Alaskan development initiatives, he altered his opinion. More generally, he highlighted his opposition to communism in the postwar years, championing the Cold War consensus by highlighting the strategic threat to Alaska posed by the USSR. He correctly suspected that doing so would increase defense expenditures in the territory. But, in the process, he lost much of his relevance to debate over the international matters about which he once cared passionately. Then, after Dwight Eisenhower captured the White House in 1952, Republicans won the right to appoint a new governor, this ending Gruening's tenure in Juneau and, apparently, his career in politics.

Although sixty-five years old, Gruening had little intention of retiring from public life, however. But his departure from office noticeably changed how he approached international issues. Beginning in 1953, he threw himself into a new crusade – building public support for Alaskan statehood. Initially, he offered anticommunist sentiments, arguing that statehood would consolidate the U.S. strategic position in the Arctic. But the opposition of the Joint Chiefs of Staff (on the grounds that statehood would deprive the military of the needed bureaucratic flexibility in the area) made Gruening's strategic theories look ridiculous, and he gradually abandoned the reflexive anticommunism of his gubernatorial tenure. Because, in part, he had stressed such arguments for their public relations value, now that they ceased to serve his purposes, he started once again to interpret international affairs in ways outside of the mainstream, bipolar Cold War consensus. It therefore came as little surprise, given his long-standing belief in the fidelity of the American people to anti-imperialism, that he turned to the dissent of his interwar years. In a way, anti-imperialist sentiments were never far beneath the surface, even at the height of his flirtation with the Cold War consensus. In 1954, for instance, he contended that "colonialism is everywhere being re-examined and in transformation" and reasoned that highlighting America's anti-imperialist heritage might serve as the most appropriate way to wage the Cold War. He urged Alaskans to shout "about 'colonialism' at the top of their lungs" as the best means to build public support for statehood. In the process, the former governor returned to his tactical preferences from the 1920s and 1930s. Asserting that "ideas are weapons," he pinned his hopes on an informed public opinion and launched a national lecture tour. Though

Gruening's complaints about the deleterious effects of federal policies on territorial Alaska were a bit far-fetched, the struggle for statehood highlighted his anti-imperialism at just the moment he returned to the national scene, and laid the groundwork for his dissenting activities as senator.[8]

When Congress finally granted Alaska statehood in 1958, Gruening instantly launched a bid for the Senate. He narrowly prevailed in the fall election. His reverence for the upper chamber, first established in the 1920s, had not ebbed in his years away from Washington. In any period, the nature of the institution highlighted two characteristics at which Gruening had long excelled – bureaucratic battling and speechmaking. But he also arrived in Washington just as political and institutional developments were creating a Senate more hospitable to his personality and interests. During the early and middle 1950s, traditional power barons such as Robert Kerr (D-OK) and Richard Russell (D-GA) had set the standard for a body in which senators deferred to senior colleagues and specialized in issues associated with their committee assignments. The Senate, however, became more open and less centralized as the decade progressed, while its ideological character changed after the Democratic sweep in the 1958 elections brought to office not only Gruening but a host of other Northern liberals.[9]

Gruening used this freedom of action to renew his anti-imperialist crusades. Since both the Eisenhower and Kennedy administrations were skeptical of his international viewpoint, the Alaskan also challenged the unspoken rules of the Cold War by advocating a more prominent role for the Senate. He illustrated the point in his attacks on foreign aid, which he termed "a radical departure from the historically established conduct of

[8] Gruening to Felix Frankfurter, n.d. [1954], box 60, Felix Frankfurter Papers, Langdell Library, Harvard Law School; Gruening to Robert Atwood, March 18, 1955, series 36, box 1, Ernest Gruening Papers [hereafter GP], Elmer Rasmuson Library, University of Alaska, Fairbanks; Gruening address, "Let Us End Colonialism," Fairbanks, November 9, 1955, reproduced in Ernest Gruening, *The Battle for Alaskan Statehood* (College: University of Alaska Press, 1967), pp. 72–91.

[9] Jack Germond, interview with author, June 18, 1995; Mike Gravel, interview with author, August 22, 1995; Gruening to Lyndon Johnson, December 16, 1958, box 366, LBJ Senate Papers, Lyndon Baines Johnson Presidential Library, Austin; "Phantom Senator," *New York Times*, July 1, 1958; on the Senate of the 1950s, see Robert Mann, *To the Walls of Jericho: Lyndon Johnson, Hubert Humphrey, Richard Russell and the Struggle for Civil Rights* (New York: Harcourt, Brace, and Company, 1996), pp. 135–146, 236–239; Fred Harris, *Deadlock or Decision: The U.S. Senate and the Rise of National Politics* (New York: Oxford University Press, 1993), pp. 33–158; Michael Foley, *The New Senate: Liberal Influence on a Conservative Institution, 1959–1972* (New Haven: Yale University Press, 1980); Donald Matthews, *U.S. Senators and Their World* (Chapel Hill: University of North Carolina Press, 1960).

our foreign relations." Although Gruening maintained that the Senate's traditionally prominent "role in the conduct of foreign affairs" gave it a special responsibility for oversight, behind his constitutional theories lay fundamental disagreements with mainstream policy. Little more than a fear of losing ground to the Russians, he claimed, motivated most military and economic assastance. The entire policy reminded him of the discredited "Dollar Diplomacy" of the interwar era, to which he also looked for an alternative approach. In a long letter to an old anti-imperialist comrade, Samuel Guy Inman, Gruening noted that in the Senate he was continuing his search for ways to encourage crossnational reformist alliances. His proposal to confine assistance "to countries that were performing in accordance" with reformist principles separated him not only from the executive branch but from most of his Democratic colleagues. For example, J. William Fulbright (D-AR) described the Alaskan's foreign aid opinions as "mistaken" and "extreme." In general, the Foreign Relations Committee chair maintained, the "primary obligation of the Senate" was to facilitate "the establishment of a national consensus" by explaining basic principles to the people, not legislating foreign policy. He tartly informed Gruening to stop trying to "act as Secretary of State."[10]

The full range of Gruening's dissent most clearly appeared on a matter of personal and professional concern: U.S. relations with Latin America. The success of Fidel Castro's revolution in Cuba caused John Kennedy, hoping to dissociate social revolution "from Communism and its power politics," to promise a Latin American policy combining generous economic aid with support for social democrats such as Venezuelan President Romulo Betancourt. The anticommunist rationale behind the Alliance for Progress, however, also led to increased military assistance to the region – over $77 million by fiscal year 1963 – for internal security purposes, this despite the threat of bolstering reactionary forces in Latin American militaries.[11]

---

[10] Gruening draft speech, 1959, box 42, Gruening Senatorial Papers [hereafter GSP], Rasmuson Library, University of Alaska, Fairbanks; Gruening to Samuel Guy Inman, January 16, 1962, box 19, Samuel Guy Inman papers, Library of Congress; Fulbright to Gruening, June 2, 1959, box BCN 140, folder 48, 1943–1960 series, J. William Fulbright papers, Mullins Library, University of Arkansas; U.S. Senate, Committee on Foreign Relations, *Hearings, Mutual Security Act of 1959*, 86th Congress, 1st session, May 21, 1959, pp. 942–945.

[11] Juan De Onís and Jerome Levinson, *The Alliance that Lost Its Way* (Chicago: Quadrangle Books, 1970); Stephen Rabe, "Controlling Revolutions: Latin America, the Alliance for Progress, and Cold War Anti-Communism," in Thomas Paterson, ed., *Kennedy's Quest for Victory: American Foreign Policy, 1961–1963* (New York: Oxford University Press, 1989); William Walker, "Mixing the Sweet with the Sour: Kennedy, Johnson, and Latin

Speaking as "both an idealist and a realist," Gruening challenged the rationale behind the Alliance from its inception. He reasoned that the United States should concern itself not with the recipient regime's anti-communist fervor but with its willingness to enact social, economic, and political reforms. Learning from his own difficulties in Puerto Rico in the 1930s, he doubted that an agenda could be imposed from the outside, and he pressed the administration to allow Latin American reformers – whom, he pointedly noted, expressed far less concern about communism in the region than did Kennedy – more freedom of action. (Gruening's aggressive championing of the Latin American point of view prompted one colleague to dub him "Ernesto.") The Alaskan feared that Kennedy's agenda would result in the United States aligning itself only with vehement anticommunist forces, thus reinforcing "the impression, which already exists, that we are in favor of the oligarchical and feudal setup which exists down there."[12]

Even more boldly, Gruening argued that "a number of countries need a revolution" in Latin America. Again drawing on his own extensive background in Latin American affairs, he pointed to Mexican history. There, a "purely indigenous" revolt responding to the Mexicans' "appraisal of what their country needed" produced a "continuing revolution." "Unfortunately," he admitted, most post–World War II uprisings were "infiltrated by the Communists," thus ensuring that Latin America was exchanging one form of totalitarianism for another. Still, Washington's fears that that reform could spiral out of control did not in his opinion justify U.S. support for dictatorships. The success of popularly elected leaders such as Romulo Betancourt in Venezuela, Luis Muñoz Marín in Puerto Rico, and José Figueres in Costa Rica demonstrated that "a Latin American country can have both social and economic progress under democratic procedures." By the 1960s, Gruening was celebrating democracy more than he had in the past, but not because he had transformed into a Wilsonian. Instead, he believed that in the postwar climate, free elections represented a first step to achieving social and economic reform.[13]

America," in Diane Kunz, ed., *The Diplomacy of the Crucial Decade: American Foreign Relations during the 1960s* (New York: Columbia University Press, 1994), pp. 42–56; Tony Smith, "The Alliance for Progress: The 1960s," in Abraham Lowenthal, ed., *Exporting Democracy: Themes and Issues* (Baltimore: Johns Hopkins University Press, 1991), pp. 71–89.

[12] *CR*, 87th Congress, 1st session, August 11, 1961 p. 15632; Thomas Kuchel to Gruening, November 8, 1963, box 455, Thomas Kuchel papers, Bancroft Library, University of California, Berkeley.

[13] Gruening to Romulo Betancourt, June 15, 1964, box 30, GSP.

Because administration operatives dismissed the "old curmudgeon," Gruening understood that legislative initiatives represented the clearest way to reform foreign aid. He took up the challenge, eager, as always, to be "a liberal yet an effective politician." This pragmatic streak had earlier accounted for his embrace of the Cold War consensus, but by the 1960s Gruening sought to employ his oratorical, bureaucratic, and intellectual skills on behalf of his traditional dissenting agenda. Sometimes, this effort involved high-profile speeches, designed to expand the range of options considered by the Senate, as in his call to terminate all assistance to all Latin American juntas after a military coup toppled the democratically elected government of Peru. On other occasions, Gruening worked behind the scenes to assemble coalitions to push through policy-related amendments to foreign aid legislation. At other times, the senator demonstrated his bureaucratic skills by using his position on the Government Operations Committee, whose charter granted it vague powers over a wide array of international matters, to establish his own foreign policy subcommittee. Though not persuaded by the Alaskan's recommendations, one foe within the Kennedy administration nonetheless could not help but to "admire the old goat still carrying on in his independent fashion."[14]

By the end of Kennedy's presidency, this persistence gave Gruening a disproportionate amount of influence on the two foreign policy issues which had defined his career to date – inter-American relations and foreign aid. After a military coup in the Dominican Republic ousted the reformist, democratic government of Juan Bosch, the Alaskan delivered his highest profile critique of the Alliance for Progress in late September, 1963. Gruening called on the administration, which had cut off aid but also begun to plan how to resume relations with the new regime, to show some "courage" and "take whatever steps are necessary" to restore Bosch to power. As one "very familiar" with the Dominican situation – he was the only man in the Senate who had been "down there before Trujillo" – Gruening believed his plan could succeed. As frequently occurred with the Alaskan's suggestions, most other Senate liberals were unsure about the plan's practicality. Still, Frank Church (D-ID) termed the initiative "characteristic" of Gruening's tendency to offer "refreshingly bold"

---

[14] Gruening Diaries [hereafter GD], September 1, 1964; Jack Germond interview; Maurine Neuberger, interview with author, September 10, 1995; Ralph Dungan, interview with author, May 31, 1995; John Carver oral history, JFK Presidential Library, vol. 8, p. 101; Garison Nelson with Clark Bensen, *Committees in the U.S. Congress, 1947–1992, Volume 1: Committee Jurisdictions and Member Rosters* (Washington, D.C.: Congressional Quarterly Press, 1993), p. 158.

positions. Moreover, although it failed to draw widespread support, Gruening's proposal made the senator a player in the Senate's response to the Dominican crisis, with the effect of encouraging colleagues to adopt more outspoken opposition to the administration's course. In this sense, the affair provided a good example of how, as one commentator noted, the Alaskan "defined the limits of the issues" about which he cared passionately. In the process, Gruening goaded the administration into a public response, which, as he planned, further polarized the situation: pressed by Kennedy to refute the claims of "certain quarters" in the Senate that the coup "reflected a collapse of the Alliance for Progress," Assistant Secretary of State Edwin Martin recommended that the "impatient idealists" understand how "men should and do operate in a complex world." As Martin privately conceded, however, the fierce attacks offered by Gruening and a few like-minded colleagues forced the administration to register a public protest and sever aid to the new regime. Privately, the president admitted that he would be inclined to extend diplomatic recognition to the new Dominican government "if it were not for the Congress."[15]

Gruening also played a key role in what *U.S. News & World Report* labeled the "foreign aid revolt" of 1963, during which he helped to cobble together an alliance of antiforeign aid conservatives and liberals who called for making the ideological character of the recipient regime the key factor in determining whether it would receive assistance. Congressional conservatives of both parties had been skeptical of economic assistance from the start. The likes of Bourke Hickenlooper, a Republican senator from Iowa, and Otto Passman, a Democratic congressman from Louisiana, criticized the program as impractical and a waste of taxpayers's dollars. But although Passman used his position as chair of the Foreign Operations Subcommittee to slash foreign aid appropriations, a bipartisan bloc in the Senate generally restored most of Passman's cuts and provided consistent support for boosting both economic and military aid. The defection of Gruening and like-minded liberals, however, changed the legislative dynamic in the upper chamber, opening up the possibility, for the first time, that the Senate might be as inhospitable to foreign aid as the House. Unlike conservative critics of foreign aid, for whom opposition to the program was reflexive and motivated in large part by political

---

[15] Gruening to Mrs. E. H. Bell, October 3, 1963, box 30, GSP; *Executive Sessions of the Senate Foreign Relations Committee (Historical Series)*, vol. XV, 88th Congress, 1st session, October 3, 1963, pp. 662–665, 668–675; 109 CR, 88th Congress, 1st session, September 30, 1963, pp. 18320–18321, 18326–18328; Jack Germond interview; Edwin Martin oral history, pp. 101, 107–111, JFK Presidential Library; *Washington Post*, September 30, 1963.

concerns, Gruening's chief complaint about foreign aid was ideological. For the Alaskan, "the acid test of U.S. common sense, determination, and backbone is whether we are going to continue to be blackmailed by foreign governments which are allegedly anticommunist." Instead, Gruening hoped to use the leverage obtained by foreign aid to prod recalcitrant governments in the Third World to reform. And, for the first time in his Senate career, he had the political strength to push his ideas into policy. The coalition of ideological extremes not only placed new restrictions on the foreign aid program, but also produced severe cuts in the administration's authorizataon request. Gruening himself introduced two of the most significant policy-related amendments, measures to sever military aid to Latin American regimes which came to power through coups and to governments which threatened aggressive warfare against their neighbors. Again, his activism drew criticism from the executive branch: after the vote on the anti-aggressor amendment, Kennedy rebuked the Alaskan publicly, urging Gruening to recognize that "it's a very dangerous, untidy world, but . . . we're going to have to live within it."[16]

By late 1963, then, Gruening had established a reputation for frenetic activity and, given the radical nature of his program, surprising effectiveness on foreign policy matters. Much of his success, though, rested upon an unusual combination of factors. Gruening worked on issues – foreign aid, U.S. policy toward nations like Peru and the Dominican Republic – which attracted little attention from most colleagues and posed a relatively small political risk to challenging executive authority. His persistence alone thus made him a player. Also, his long personal and intellectual involvement with the two issues earned respect for his opinions even from senators of differing views. As he would discover, neither condition would apply to his next foreign policy crusade.

By the end of Kennedy's presidency, Gruening had outlined an international vision which updated his interwar, anti-imperialist ideals, making them applicable to the Cold War era. To the Alaskan, viewing international relations as solely a no-win contest with the USSR had prevented policymakers from recognizing that the United States lacked the power to freeze the postwar international climate through military means. In any case, he noted, adjustments to the status quo, even those that employed violence, did not necessarily threaten U.S. interests. More important,

---

[16] Gruening to Gordon Skrede, September 4, 1963, box 32, GS 63–65, GP; *U.S. News & World Report*, November 25, 1963; *Congressional Quarterly Almanac*: 19; (1963), pp. 278, 280.

Gruening reasoned, the antirevolutionary mindset inherent in Cold War foreign policy had weakened the standing of the United States as a symbol to the world. In its most elemental form, his dissent represented an alternative conception of power in the international arena and a continuation of the process that he began in the 1920s of structuring an anti-imperialist alternative to Wilsonianism.

During Senate consideration of the 1963 foreign aid bill, Kennedy's congressional liaison, Lawrence O'Brien, complained that the upper chamber was accomplishing "nothing whatever" because of a general "antipathy to AID and frustration over Vietnam, military coups in Latin America, etc." O'Brien was not the only figure to discern the linkage between the two events. In fact, the foreign aid revolt prompted Gruening to consider Southeast Asian affairs for the first time in his career. Amid press reports of mounting U.S. casualties, he wondered whether the involvement was another of Kennedy's misguided policies. Gruening privately concluded that if his son died in Vietnam, he would not feel that he had perished in "the defense of my country." He frankly admitted that withdrawal might allow the communists to assume power throughout Southeast Asia, but he saw no viable alternative. Indeed, the revolutionary, reformist heritage of the United States and its commitment to the principle of national self-determination made any other option irreconcilable with the country's traditional ideals. Certainly, he reasoned, any policy in which U.S. troops defended the regime of Ngo Dinh Diem was unacceptable. Embellishing his continued call for the United States to take the lead in creating cross-national alliances, he argued that it was acceptable to consider military intervention to assist a reformer such as Juan Bosch, but not a dictator like Diem.[17]

Gruening's decision to oppose the military involvement in Vietnam thus flowed logically from his long-held international beliefs. He went public with his concerns on March 10, 1964, when he delivered the first full-length Senate speech demanding withdrawal. Urging President Johnson to repudiate "the dead hand of past mistakes," Gruening suggested as a "basic truth" that foreign troops could not win the war. Unconsciously, perhaps, harking back to the Haitian intervention of the 1920s, he used the critical portrayals from correspondents on the scene to describe the

---

[17] Gruening to Gordon Skrede, September 4, 1963, box 32, GSP; George McGovern oral history, LBJ Presidential Library; Lawrence O'Brien, "Memorandum for the President," October 7, 1963, box 53, President's Official File, John F. Kennedy Presidential Library, Boston.

conflict as a civil war matching a broad-based coalition of reformers, including indigenous communists, against Diem's corrupt coalition of Catholic émigrés and large landowners. Having challenged the basis of the commitment, Gruening then offered his solution. The time had come for "a little hard rethinking" based on the fact that the conflict already had tarnished the nation's image and Americans could not "jump into every fracas all over the world ... and stay in blindly and stubbornly." Accordingly, the United States should pull out "with the knowledge that the game was not worth the candle."[18]

The *New York Times* commented that the "normally mild-spoken" senator "surprised colleagues by his choice of strong words." In fact, Gruening hoped that his charged rhetoric would spark outspoken criticism from other senators, as had occurred after the coup in the Dominican Republic. But, in this case, he misjudged badly. Few in Washington considered his arguments particularly innovative, aware that, unlike colleagues such as Mike Mansfield (D-MO), Gruening lacked a background in Southeast Asian history. (Cognizant of the problem, the Alaskan spent free time throughout the spring and summer of 1964 poring through background reading material on Vietnam.) In the event, Gruening's high profile dissent only seemed to isolate him. With U.S. troops already on the ground in Southeast Asia and the specter of Chinese expansionism looming, Bryce Nelson, then an aide to Frank Church, recalled that his boss and like-minded senators worried about the "strident" nature of Gruening's rhetoric; they "did not want to be lumped in" with such a figure. In addition, the Alaskan's somewhat "doddery" appearance provided a tailor-made excuse for his opponents to dismiss him as a "curiosity" without addressing his often perceptive criticisms.[19]

Gruening's outspokenness also exposed him to personal attack. His opposition to foreign aid and Latin American policies had poisoned his relations with most of Kennedy and Johnson's foreign policy team, but in particular had alienated him from Dean Rusk. On March 19, the secretary of state looked to settle the score in an address which one aide admitted was intended to start "a quiet campaign to answer those who said, 'South Vietnam is not worth the life of one American boy.'" Rusk ended his

---

[18] *CR*, 88th Congress, 2nd session, March 10, 1964, pp. 4831–4835.

[19] Jack Germond interview; William Bundy, interview with author, June 22, 1995; *New York Times*, March 21, 1964; Nelson quoted in Gibbons, *U.S. Government and the Vietnam War*, vol. 2, p. 277; for hard-line reaction to the speech, see 110 CR, 88th Congress, 2nd session, March 11, 1964; pp. 4986–4992; Larry Berman, *Planning a Tragedy: The Americanization of the War in Vietnam* (New York: W.W. Norton, 1982), p. 32.

speech by attacking "those who would quit the struggle by letting down our own defenses, by gutting our foreign aid programs." Such policies, he claimed, would abandon "the field to our adversaries." He then pointedly added that "insofar as anybody here or abroad pays attention to the quitters, they are lending aid and comfort to our enemies."[20]

In the wake of Rusk's thinly disguised accusation of treason, Gruening quickly abandoned hope that the behind-the-scenes persuasion of the type favored by other Democratic senators would modify the administration's course. But the attack did cause him to focus on Vietnam, at the expense of his earlier concentration on Latin America and foreign aid. For Gruening, Vietnam seemed to embody all of the flaws in twentieth century American foreign policy. The Alaskan chastised policymakers for blindly applying the principles of containment, a doctrine he once had embraced but now considered "disastrous" and irrelevant to international relations beyond Europe. The stakes in Southeast Asia were high, Gruening maintained, but for a different reason than Rusk seemed to think. With the United States supporting "puppet governments, dictatorships that elicit little or no enthusiasm from the people they rule" throughout the Third World, intervening to prevent one such regime from falling, as in Vietnam, could establish a dangerous precedent. Vietnam thus perfectly illustrated the faults of U.S. foreign policy: a tendency to address political problems through military means; a pattern of supporting dictatorships in the name of anti-Communism; a policymaking apparatus which too often excluded congressional input; and a lack of concern with maintaining the U.S. commitment to reform on all levels of international politics. Determined to strike back at Rusk and convinced that the administration's approach in Vietnam violated the basic tenets of his creed – indeed, the policy seemed destined to "have the United States reverse its traditional principles" – the senator "reveled" in his dissent. As his son, Hunt, recalled, his father, who always "thrived on controversy" anyway, told him about this time to "show me a man who's controversial, and I'll show you someone who stands for something."[21]

---

[20] Rusk, "The True Blessings of Peace," Salt Lake City, March 19, 1964, reproduced in 110 CR, 88th Congress, 2nd session, March 20, 1964 pp. 5975–5977; *Washington News; Washington Post*, March 23, 1964; Brian VanDeMark, *Into the Quagmire: Lyndon Johnson and the Escalation of the Vietnam War* (New York: Oxford University Press, 1991), pp. 10–11; *Congressional Quarterly Almanac*: 19; (1963), pp. 278, 280.

[21] Hunt Gruening, interview with author, February 22, 1995; for Gruening's public reaction to Rusk's address, see CR, 88th Congress, 2nd session, March 20, 1964, pp. 5827–5828, March 23, 1964, 5977–5978, May 13, 1964, 10820, May 27, 1964, 12142, 12144, June 3, 1964, 12581.

Having established the rationale for his dissent, Gruening then looked, as always, to affect policy by generating a forceful Senate response. The reaction to his March 10 address, however, suggested that high-profile speeches would not do the job. Gruening spent the spring of 1964 trying to replicate the tactic that had yielded victory the year before: searching for a way to take advantage of unusual legislative splits in the makeup of the Senate. But Vietnam was not the Dominican Republic or the foreign aid bill, and appeals to seemingly like-minded colleagues, ranging from Fulbright to Church, fell flat. By the summer, only Wayne Morse (D-OR) had joined the Alaskan in calling for a withdrawal of U.S. troops.

Vietnam differed from inter-American policy and foreign aid matters in another important way. Gruening had shown patience on the latter issues, slowly building support for his proposals. Regarding Vietnam, however, he quickly grew frustrated. Advancing age and anger at the personal attacks on him by members of the administration fueled his impatience, but so too did the senator's conviction that the deteriorating situation in Southeast Asia demanded quick Senate action. With a touch of desperation, Gruening returned to the position that had inaugurated his foreign policy activism four decades before – that of an anti-imperialist muckraker. As with Haiti, the Alaskan hoped that the people would recognize that military escalation violated traditional U.S. ideals. Vietnam, no less than any other foreign policy matter, then would "largely be settled by public opinion," and he did not doubt the final outcome. Gruening claimed that upwards of 99 percent of his constituent mail opposed the war. Such wildly exaggerated claims only exposed the Alaskan to ridicule. One prowar colleague, Gale McGee (D-WY), scoffed that the stakes in Vietnam were too high for the United States "to project its foreign policy with a five-cent postage stamp."[22]

Ironically, Gruening's outspokenness had more impact than he realized, at least in the spring and early summer of 1964. Earlier plans to introduce a resolution authorizing the use of force in Southeast Asia had fizzled due to Johnson's fear, in the words of one administration official, that "Morse and Gruening would have fought it, and stirred up a big

---

[22] 110 CR, 88th Congress, 2nd session, March 24, 1964, pp. 6068, March 25, 1964, 6245–6246. Ironically, the White House shared Gruening's conception of the state of public opinion. In May, Johnson expressed his belief that, even though few others had expressed the sentiment publicly, Senate support for withdrawing U.S. troops from Vietnam ranged well beyond "just Morse and [Richard] Russell and Gruening." National Security Advisor McGeorge Bundy agreed, asserting that "90 percent of the people . . . don't want any part of this" war. Beschloss, ed., *Taking Charge*, p. 372.

debate about the war." Being one of a minority of two on the Tonkin Gulf vote, however, isolated the Alaskan in the upper chamber on Vietnam. As McGovern later recalled, other Senate Democrats considered Gruening's interpretation of the administration's long-term intentions and his calls for a unilateral withdrawal "just wrong." They also noted that, whatever its faults, Johnson's policy on the war was clearly superior to that of Republican presidential nominee Barry Goldwater. Consequently, no one "really sympathized" with the Alaskan on the issue.[23]

That did not mean that most Senate liberals were comfortable with Johnson's policies. In early 1965, McGovern, Church, and Gaylord Nelson (D-WI) all publicly expressed their doubts about the administration's course in Vietnam. But since they refrained from calling for an immediate U.S. withdrawal, Gruening concluded that they had framed their dissents "so moderately that it means little." As an alternative, he turned to public opinion. In the first few months of 1965 alone, Gruening missed roll call votes to appear at teach-ins or lectures at the University of Alabama, Hofstra, UCLA, University of California, the University of Miami, Albion College, and the University of Puerto Rico, in public protests in Washington, Chicago, and several times in New York City, and in debates from Des Moinĕs Iowa to Laurinburg, North Carolina.[24] The activist clearly enjoyed the fight, in contrast to the frustration of trying to build an antiwar Senate coalition. He privately confided to one friend his pleasure at knowing that his dissent "drove Lyndon Johnson crazy."[25]

Even so, Gruening's public relations offensive accomplished little. Seemingly oblivious to the way in which the tactics and agenda of the more radical protesters created a public backlash, he was the sole member of Congress to address an April, 1965, Washington rally sponsored by the

[23] Gruening to William Bauer, July 22, 1964, Vietnam 1964 file, Brown Boxes series, GSP; George McGovern, interview with author, December 8, 1994; Gruening oral history, LBJ Library; Gibbons, *U.S. Government and the Vietnam War,* vol. 2, pp. 280–342.

[24] GD, January 15, 1965; for Gruening's public appearances, see GD, March 25, 1965, March 27, 1965, April 1, 1965, April 3, 1965; *Miami News,* May 12, 1965; *Detroit Free Press,* May 14, 1965; *San Francisco Examiner,* May 18, 1965; all in 1965 Scrapbook, vol. 1, Gruening Papers; *New York Times,* May 23, 1965.

[25] Wayne Crabtree to Gruening, November 7, 1965, Alaska Con 1966–1968 file, Brown boxes series, GSP, Gruening Papers; Gruening to Wayne Crabtree, December 6, 1965, Alaska Con 1966–1967 file, Brown boxes series, GSP, Gruening Papers; GD, February 15, 1965. Gruening was correct on this point; the president feared that his "Congressional support was very uncertain and wobbly" and could disintegrate "rapidly" under the pressure of "speeches by Morse [and] Gruening." LBJ quoted in John McCone, "Memorandum for the Record," April 22, 1965, *Foreign Relations of the United States, 1964–1968,* vol. II, p. 599.

Students for a Democratic Society (SDS), an event which even the liberal *New York Post* dismissed as little more than "a one-sided anti-American sideshow."[26]

Within the Senate, meanwhile, Gruening's outspokenness prompted strong criticism from the likes of Gale McGee[27] but private acclaim from more sympathetic colleagues. McGovern, for example, admired Gruening's "great moral courage on Vietnam and other issues," and confidentially told his colleague that he had "not supported you 100% on all your efforts because of the extremely conservative nature of my state . . . but my heart is always with you even when I have not been able to vote with you." Despite the complement, Gruening characterized McGovern's dissent as "always minor," and expressed frustration with "those who cry 'peace, peace,' and support the escalation of the undeclared war." In the end, meanwhile, McGovern and Church considered the Alaskan more interested in preserving the purity of his dissent than in proposing politically and strategically realistic alternatives. As Church privately noted, "Morse and Gruening may be right, but they have been written off, and so exercise no influence on a future course of events." From the Idaho senator's point of view, the pair occupied "the 'never-never-land' of radically ineffectual dissent."[28]

For most of his Senate tenure, however, such sentiments did not prevent Gruening from maintaining his effectiveness on issues such as Latin American policy. Between 1964 and 1966, he used his position on the Government Operations Committee to launch an inquiry into the state

[26] Gruening to Rhea Miller, April 21, 1964, Vietnam File, Brown boxes series, GSP; *New York Post*, April 19, 1965; Adam Garfinkle, *Telltale Hearts: The Origins and Impact of the Vietnam Antiwar Movement* (New York: St. Martin's Press, 1995), pp. 44–65; DeBenedetti, *American Ordeal*, pp. 111–112; Wells, *The War Within*, pp. 24–25; Garfinkle, *Telltale Hearts*, pp. 44–51.

[27] On one occasion, the contention of the Wyoming senator, a history professor before entering the upper chamber, that history, not specific decisions by individual policymakers, best explained the administration's policies, provided too much of an opening for someone with Gruening's debating skills to resist. The Alaskan mockingly replied that such reasoning constituted the first time he "ever knew that history had that kind of motive power." Furious, McGee retorted that "history creates events that even Republicans and Democrats, or the Senator from Alaska, sometimes cannot control." *CR*, 89th Congress, 1st session, June 9, 1965, pp. 12985–12987.

[28] Frank Church to George McGovern, box 70A2445/11, George McGovern papers, Mudd Library, Princeton University; Church to Eli Oboler, July 28, 1965, series 2.2, box 8, Frank Church papers, Albertson's Library, Boise State University; George McGovern to Gruening, May 18, 1967, box 72A3053/11, McGovern papers; Jack Germond interview; George McGovern interview; GD, June 9, 1965; 111 CR, 89th Congress, 1st session, June 9, 1965, pp. 12985–12987; Small, *Johnson, Nixon, and the Doves*, pp. 94–95.

of the Alliance for Progress, a study which solidified his credentials as the most innovative thinker among the Senate dissenters on the issue and earned praise from Morse, Fulbright, Church, and Albert Gore (D-TN). Gruening's efforts also helped to sidetrack a March, 1967, resolution for advanced congressional approval for increased economic aid to Latin America. Remarking that the "eloquent" nature of Gruening's testimony against the bill had forced him to reconsider his support even for multilateral aid, Fulbright hailed his colleague for having "inspired one of the most interesting hearings we have had this year." Finally, the Alaskan played a prominent role in rallying liberal swing votes to defeat the last legislative attempt to revive the Alliance for Progress, a 1967 amendment offered by Robert Kennedy (D-New York) to increase economic assistance to Latin America by nearly 20 percent.[29]

But Gruening could not develop a politically palatable alternative to Johnson's Southeast Asian policies. Sometimes he dismissed the problem by arguing that "recommendations for extrication ... are not the responsibility of those who for years have dissented from United States policy in Vietnam." More often, though, he offered unrealistic suggestions, such as permitting conscientious objection for individual wars. Privately, he even hinted at supporting draft resistance, and instructed his staff to counsel those who requested assistance in averting conscription, describing such aid as "part of the service that we should render." In the end, however, despite his oratorical abilities, Gruening was not at his most effective in his crusade against the Vietnam War. As McGovern later noted, Gruening "hated" the conflict "with such a passion" that he "couldn't contain himself." The war became his "obsession."[30]

[29] Wayne Morse press release, March 27, 1967, box B-47, Wayne Morse papers, University of Oregon Library, Eugene; U.S. Senate, Committee on Government Operations, *Report, United States Foreign Aid in Action: A Case Study,* 89th Congress, 2nd session, CIS Document #S0918; *CR,* 90th Congress, 1st session, August 17, 1967, pp. 22965–22972; U.S. Senate, Committee on Foreign Relations, *Hearings, Latin American Summit Conference,* 90th Congress, 1st session, March 21, 1967, p. 155; *Hanson's Latin American Newsletter,* July 30, 1966, September 3, 1966; both in 1966 scrapbook, vol. 2, Gruening papers; *Congressional Quarterly Almanac:* 23; (1967), p. 337; *New York Times,* August 19, 1967; *Washington Post,* August 18, 1967; Robert Packenham, *Liberal America and the Third World: Political Development Ideas in Foreign Aid and Political Science* (Princeton: Princeton University Press, 1973), pp. 180–181.

[30] Gruening to Paul Wagner, February 9, 1966, box 3, SFAE papers; Gruening to Phil Kirby, August 25, 1966, Vietnam 1966 file, Brown boxes series, GSP, Gruening papers; Milton (Pennsylvania) *Standard,* May 9, 1966, 1966 Scrapbook, vol. 1, Gruening papers; George McGovern interview; Laura Olson, interview with author, October 15, 1995; *CR,* 89th Congress, February 17, 1966, p. 3391.

In fact, by the end of the 1960s, the senator's "real priority was opposing the war in Vietnam." The conflict obviously made the Alaskan more willing to assume a position of outspoken dissent, even at the cost of influence among his colleagues. But his antiwar views also affected more than his tactical approach. His crusade against the war began with Gruening applying to a new foreign policy issue his traditional dissenting framework, one which had not "modified except by being intensified with the passage of time." And, indeed, some of his anti-war efforts featured remarkable connections to his dissenting past. During a 1965 debate between Gruening and William Bundy, the recently appointed assistant secretary of state for East Asian affairs, Freda Kirchwey, a former associate from *The Nation*, "was suddenly jerked back to those early twenties when Gruening was denouncing in the pages of *The Nation* the same – exactly the same – acts; only then it was Haiti." Likewise, upon hearing of the exchange, Hubert Herring, a colleague among the admirers of the Mexican Revolution, detected the links between the principles of Gruening's Vietnam dissent and their earlier crusades in the Caribbean Basin.[31]

But the blinding passion of which McGovern spoke separated Gruening from other senators skeptical about Johnson's foreign policy. For instance, in an April, 1965, address at Johns Hopkins University, the president announced his willingness to enter into "unconditional discussions" and to fund a $1 billion development of the Mekong River delta if the North Vietnamese ended the war. Then, for five days in early May, Johnson halted the bombing of North Vietnam. Most Senate dissenters warmly welcomed these developments, which to Church vindicated "those of us who have tried to influence policy by tempering our criticism with restraint." Gruening, by contrast, interpreted Johnson's "very phony performance" quite differently. He correctly noted that the president's insistence upon "a free and independent South Vietnam" eliminated any possibility for successful negotiations. The senator also dismissed the Mekong Delta development proposal as nothing less than a "bribe": however much the administration wanted to cloak its aggressive actions with talk of massive economic aid, "the disguise is too thin."[32]

---

[31] Hubert Herring to Gruening, April 22, 1965, series 38, box 8, Gruening papers; Gruening to Rick Goodfellow and Bruce Gazaway, September 9, 1966, Vietnam 1966 file, Brown boxes series, GSP, Gruening papers; Kirchwey quoted in *The Nation*, September 20, 1965.

[32] GD, April 7, 1965, April 14, 1965; CR, 89th Congress, May 6, 1965, 1st session, pp. 9762–9766; Frank Church to Eugene Chase, April 21, 1965, series 2.2, box 28, Church Papers; Melvin Small, *Johnson, Nixon, and the Doves* (New Brunswick: Rutgers University Press, 1988), pp. 36–42; George Herring, *America's Longest War: The United States and Vietnam, 1950–1975* (New York: Knopf, 1979), pp. 134–135.

The only tangible effect of the address on Gruening came in causing him to reevaluate his perspective on foreign aid. Through early 1965, despite his often caustic criticism of the program, he continued, as he had in the 1930s with Puerto Rico, to entertain the possibility of positive U.S. action to assist the cause of reform overseas. During his 1964 visit to South America, for instance, embassy staffers with whom he came into contact regularly expressed surprise about his abstract commitment to the principle of foreign aid. But after the president's transparent attempt to salvage his Vietnam policy through promises of economic assistance, Gruening returned to his 1920s framework, in which the U.S. government itself stood as the chief barrier to international reform. Abolishing the foreign aid program now represented a worthy goal.

In the 1920s, Gruening's articles had featured outspoken criticisms of Marine atrocities in Haiti, but, adjusting to the political realities of both the Alaskan economy and the climate of the Cold War, he generally refrained from sharp attacks on the military after World War II. But, as with his anti-imperialism, his anti-militarism resurfaced after he entered the Senate. He already had emerged as perhaps the upper chamber's most vociferous opponent of military aid, arguing that it tarnished the U.S. image by aiding reactionary forces in Third World societies. Now, he began to question the wisdom of the Cold War defense budget itself. In 1967, after Undersecretary of State Nicholas Katzenbach taunted antiwar senators by noting that those who really wanted to express displeasure with the war could vote against the defense appropriation bill, Gruening needed no more encouragement. The year before, the Alaskan had charged the Pentagon with embarking on a "military binge." After Katzenbach's challenge, Gruening translated his concerns into concrete action, and began voting against all military appropriations measures. Perhaps, he reasoned, a lower military budget would yield a more restrained executive policy. This decision obviously ended his promilitary posture from his period as governor. As he had in the 1920s, the senator again considered it tactically and ideologically acceptable to oppose the defense budget as a whole.[33]

Free of all restraint, Gruening gave full expression to his radical antimilitarism. In August, 1966, the seventy-nine-year-old senator led a protest of 2,000 in Los Angeles criticizing the United States for both its Vietnam policy and having used the atomic bomb against Japan in World War II.

---

[33] Gruening to Robert McNamara, April 26, 1966; Gruening to Paul Ignatius, June 6, 1966; both in box 2, SFAE papers; *Congressional Quarterly Almanac:* 23; (1967), pp. 307, 314; CR, 90th Congress, 1st session, August 22, 1967, p. 23502.

Joined by folk singer Joan Baez, he spoke from a platform bearing the sign "Shame America" with red, white, and blue bombs falling on a cowering nude woman clutching two infants. These views made Gruening a polarizing figure; he was hung in effigy before an appearance at Ohio State. One headless dummy bore the caption "Senator Gruening seems to have lost his head," while the other (which retained its head) equated him with Benedict Arnold. The senator proceeded with his Columbus speech anyway, announcing his "painful" conclusion that the United States was the aggressor in the war.[34]

The Alaskan complemented his antimilitarism with a sharpened anti-imperialist viewpoint. He long had asserted that most Latin American countries "need a revolution." By 1967, however, he was also claiming that peaceful evolutionary change could not meet Latin America's needs. Given this conclusion, violent upheaval constituted the region's best hope – he recalled that "our colonial forefathers practiced a little violence in our revolution." The roots of these ideas existed in his earlier positions on inter-American affairs, but in the 1960s, he much more strongly championed revolutionary change. The senator even reevaluated the core application of the containment doctrine: U.S. policy toward Western Europe. Asserting that "NATO is obsolete" because the conditions which prompted its founding had passed, Gruening maintained that its continued existence prevented Europe from moving beyond the divisions of the immediate postwar years. In addition, he claimed, fulfilling NATO's military requirements provided an excuse to keep U.S. military spending needlessly high. As with his positions on Latin American and national security issues, Gruening's disillusionment with NATO was not inconsistent with beliefs he had articulated throughout his career. At the same time, however, his position in the 1960s was more uncompromising and extreme than that which he had expressed earlier.[35]

Despite his advanced age and increasingly radical views, Gruening did not hesitate to stand for reelection in 1968. But unlike most other dissenting senators, including Morse, he did not tone down his attacks against Johnson's policies. In 1967, he promised that he would oppose the war "whatever may be the political consequences," confident that, in the end, public opinion would rally to his cause. This belief, however, flew in the

---

[34] GD, June 27, 1966; *Columbus Dispatch*, May 27, 1966; *Ohio State Lantern*, May 31, 1966; both in 1966 Scrapbook, Vol. 1, Gruening papers; *New York Times*, August 21, 1966.
[35] Gruening, "Our Obsolete Concepts about NATO," August 23, 1966, copy in series 25, box 3, Gruening papers.

face of a copious amount of contrary evidence. Gruening's votes against the defense budget badly weakened his standing in Alaska, the state with the highest proportion of voters serving in the military. Moreover, on the issue at hand, one poll revealed that 83 percent of Alaskans favored escalating U.S. military activity in Vietnam, a position which also appeared in a substantial amount of negative constituent feedback. Hoping to tap into these sentiments, Mike Gravel, the former speaker of the State House of Representatives and a one-time admirer of the senator's, launched a primary challenge. Gravel portrayed the senator, in the words of the *New York Times*, as a "senile, cantankerous, doddering dabbler with baggy pants," preoccupied by a "concern with world affairs." Gruening, meanwhile, hoped to rally support from the older Alaskans who remembered his effective tenure as governor. In one advertisement, the challenger promised to work for Alaska first, inviting those who preferred to elect a senator for Laos or Thailand to cast ballots for the incumbent. In the end, perhaps the senator had believed his own propaganda that his antiwar position enjoyed vast popular support. On primary night, Gravel prevailed by 2,000 votes. Gruening then refused to concede defeat, and instead undertook an independent write-in campaign in the general election. As his final campaign got underway, he did not tone down his actions. Briefly returning to Washington following the primary, he voted against the fiscal year 1969 defense budget, even though he knew that doing so would not affect the upper chamber's final tally. Fittingly, the vote was the final one that he cast in the Senate. The next day, he left for Alaska, where the underfunded write-in effort drew only 16 percent of the vote, a distant third behind Gravel, who narrowly defeated Republican Elmer Rasmuson.[36]

---

[36] George Sundborg interview; Mike Gravel interview; Hugh Gallagher, interview with author, January 15, 1996; *New York Times*, April 28, 1968; *CR*, 90th Congress, 2nd session, October 3, 1968, p. 29310; *Anchorage Daily Times*, August 24, 1968; Edwin Webking, Jr., "The 1968 Gruening Write-In Campaign," (Ph.D. dissertation, Claremont Graduate School, 1972), pp. 38–63; C. Robert Zelnick, "A Dove's Struggle in Alaska," *The Progressive*, August 1968; George Sundborg, "Senator Gruening's Last Campaign: What an Alaska Political Race Looked Like from the Inside," (unpublished manuscript). For examples of negative reaction by Alaska Democrats to Gruening's opposition to the war, see Al Haylor to *Anchorage Daily Times*, August 1, 1966; William Ullom to Gruening, September 15, 1967; Murleen Isaacs to Gruening, November 10, 1967; all in Alaska Con 1966–1968 file, Brown boxes series, GSP, Gruening papers. For staff concern with the political effects of Gruening's antiwar activism, see Don Greeley, "Note to File," April 5, 1967, Gun control file, Brown boxes series, GSP, Gruening papers; Laura Olson, "Memo to Senator," February 20, 1967, Soviet consular treaty file, Brown boxes series, GSP, Gruening papers; George Sundborg interview; Don Greeley, interview with author, January 23, 1996.

Upon his death in 1974, most remembered Gruening for his early and outspoken opposition to the involvement in Vietnam. Taking a broader view, the *Washington Post* noted that the eulogies for the late senator unsurprisingly focused on his early and consistent opposition to the U.S. involvement in Vietnam. Yet, the newspaper concluded, Gruening's crusade against the war represented "only the continuation of a career always remarkable for its versatility and for the fidelity it revealed to certain ideas."[37] Still, the fact that his decision to oppose the war flowed logically from his previously articulated principles should not obscure the conflict's effect on Gruening. Even before Vietnam, the Alaskan had positioned himself as an anti-imperialist icon on Latin American and foreign aid policies, revealing the intellectual range of his dissent and the tactical strengths and limitations of using the Senate as an institution from which to launch reform-minded international crusades. Once Vietnam emerged as a major issue, Gruening's role in the Senate and elements of his ideology began to change. Tactically, he emphasized using his powers as a senator to mobilize public opinion, at the expense of building legislative coalitions. Ideologically, the senator ended his term far more enthusiastically welcoming the prospects of revolutionary change – even at the expense of short-term U.S. strategic interests – than had been the case earlier in his career. In this sense, Gruening ended the 1960s as he had begun the decade, defining the ideological and tactical range of anti-imperialism in the Senate.

---

[37] *Memorial Addresses*, pp. 41, 71; "Ernest Gruening," *The Nation*, July 20, 1974; Jack Germond and Jules Witcover, "Gruening, Doctor of Diversity," *Washington Star*, October 10, 1977; A. Robert Smith, "Gruening of Alaska," *Argus Magazine*, January 6, 1978; *Washington Post*, June 28, 1974.

"Come Home, America":
The Story of George McGovern

Thomas J. Knock

The Senate chamber was nearly empty on the afternoon of September 24, 1963. George McGovern, the young South Dakotan who had the floor, could have counted his listeners in a single glance if he had thought to do so. But first-year junior senators from states with small populations knew not to expect large audiences. At forty-one, his tall frame was still spare, and suggested physical strength. Receding hair made his lean, rectangular face look a little more seasoned than it otherwise might have, though his overall mien was professorial. As he spoke, his voice was strong and his diction clear, but the tone was generally unvarying. Journalists described him as "mild mannered," "a gentle intellectual," or "a shy and modest professor" who "speaks with a Western twang." Yet his future prestige as a commentator on national affairs would stand less on how he sounded than on what he said, for people were impressed by his unaffected eloquence and earnestness and by the persuasiveness of his arguments.

For a politician, his résumé was somewhat unusual. He was neither a lawyer nor a businessman, nor was he wealthy. His family background was deeply rooted in the church, and he was a highly decorated war hero. He hailed from a province of the Middle Border and held a Ph.D. from a leading university. He possessed the "all-American" asset of an attractive family – a smart and beautiful wife, four daughters, and a son. He also

For their helpful criticisms, the author would like to thank the following individuals: Randall Woods of the University of Arkansas, David F. Schmitz of Whitman College, Robert Johnson of Brooklyn College, John Milton Cooper of the University of Wisconsin; Dennis D. Cordell, James K. Hopkins, Donald L. Niewyk, David Price, David J. Weber, and Kathleen A. Wellman, all of the SMU Department of History; and, especially, Bruce Levy of the SMU Department of English.

had served two terms in the House of Representatives, with the distinction of being the first Democrat that South Dakota had sent to Washington in twenty-two years. In 1961, the Kennedy administration had brought him onboard as Director of Food for Peace and his reputation flourished. In the Senate, he continued to enjoy the status of protégé of the President of the United States.

McGovern's speech that afternoon was not calculated to please the White House. His main subjects were the arms race and the pending military budget which, at $55 billion, amounted to over half the entire federal budget. The senator proposed to reverse course by cutting appropriations by 10 percent. In the European theater alone, he observed, the United States already had 10,000 nuclear weapons deployed, and the two superpowers together had amassed in their lethal stockpiles the equivalent of from forty to sixty billion tons of TNT, or a ten- to twenty-ton bomb for every human being on the face of the earth. The threat of annihilation was not his only concern, however. He felt discouraged, he said, that debate typically grew heated over government spending for mental health facilities or that provisions for youth conservation training programs took months to make it to a vote while, staggering expenditures for armaments flew through the legislature. Weapons systems were one thing, but the size of this appropriation was so immense that, in evaluating it, "we are to a considerable degree determining the priorities of our national life." And so, what, in this instance, could his proposed $5 billion savings mean? It could "build a $1 million school in every one of the nation's 3,000 counties, plus 500 hospitals costing $1 million apiece, plus college scholarships worth $5,000 each to 100,000 students – and still permit a tax reduction of a billion dollars."

He cited additional examples – all of them sources of domestic strength, he reasoned – which languished because of the obsession with military power in the struggle to contain Communism. Regrettably, policymakers disdained any other approach to that challenge. The senator then pointed to the "current dilemma in Vietnam" as "a clear demonstration of the limitations of military power," to which his colleagues seemed oblivious. The $55 billion arms budget had proved useless in coping with "a ragged band of illiterate guerillas fighting with homemade weapons." Moreover, in Saigon, the United States financed a government that tyrannized its own citizens. Alas, President Kennedy's course was scarcely one of victory or even stalemate. It was, rather, "a policy of moral debacle and political defeat" in which American resources were being "used to suppress the very liberties we went in to defend." If the Senate neglected to reexamine the policy – the core of which could be traced to the military spending bill – it would "stand derelict before history." He closed with a warning: "[T]he failure in Vietnam will not remain confined to Vietnam. The trap we have fallen into there will haunt us in every corner of this revolutionary world if we do not properly appraise its lessons . . . [and] rely less on armaments and more on the economic, political, and moral sources of our strength."[1]

The speech was at least a minor historic occasion – the earliest trenchant commentary by any senator on the nation's growing entanglement in Southeast Asia. (Some of his future supporters would commit the last lines to memory; more than thirty years later the feminist Gloria Steinem could recite them verbatim.[2]) But the full significance of his words went beyond the ringing of a fire bell in the night. In essence, McGovern had called into question the basic assumptions that had guided his country since the onset of the Cold War. On one hand, he cautioned that the foreign policy of the United States increasingly risked the designation of imperialism; and, on the other, that its architects grievously ignored serious material and spiritual inadequacies in the lives of millions of Americans. Given the nature of the times, it was an unusual indictment. From this early pass onward to his campaign for the presidency in 1972 and beyond, his message would remain the same: The historic potentiality of the nation was indivisible; it could not fulfill its promise around the globe if it did not fulfill its promise at home.

McGovern's coupling of the pursuit of peace and progressive change was not simply premonitory. The propositions that he asked his fellow citizens to consider had long roots in his own past and in his distinctive synthesis of the American liberal and progressive traditions. Although historians have yet to accord the subject the attention it deserves, few political careers offer an alternative understanding of the American Century as compelling and instructive as McGovern's.[3] Whereas it embodies a highly consequential example of the impact that a single individual sometimes

---

[1] "A Proposal to Reverse the Arms Race," in the papers of George S. McGovern, Seeley Mudd Library, Princeton University, container labeled "Speeches and Statements, Sept.–Oct., 1963," and "Senator George McGovern Reports" (constituent newsletter), August 1963, box 10, 66A841. The speech is reprinted in George McGovern, *A Time of War, A Time of Peace* (New York, 1968), pp. 24–35. The personal descriptions of McGovern are in *New York Times*, August 11–13, 1968.

[2] Author's interview with Gloria Steinem, July 5, 1996.

[3] The exception is an excellent campaign biography by the journalist Robert Sam Anson, *McGovern, A Biography* (New York, 1972); see also *Grassroots, the Autobiography of George McGovern* (New York, 1977). The present author is currently writing a biography of McGovern.

can exert on American politics and foreign policy, his career was extraordinary and historic (much like those of George Frost Kennan and J. William Fulbright) primarily because of his impress as searching and prophetic critic. In this respect, one can draw at least as much insight and wisdom from his efforts as from those of any Cold War president. Indeed, as none other than Lyndon Johnson once allowed, George McGovern's life composes "a dramatic and inspiring story of what America is."[4]

McGovern was born on July 19, 1922, in Avon, a tiny hamlet in south-eastern South Dakota, and grew up in Mitchell (pop., 15,000), forty miles north. His mother, Frances McLean McGovern, was a gentle, statuesque Canadian. His father, Joseph C. McGovern, who at the age of nine had begun his working career as a "breaker boy" in the coal mines of Iowa and Illinois, was a former bush-league baseball player turned Wesleyan Methodist minister. As the son of a conservative churchman, the central influence on George's early personal development undoubtedly was his upbringing in a religious household. Every morning before they packed off to school, Joseph McGovern led his four children in the reading of Scripture. Sundays, of course, were filled with formal worship. The Reverend was a man of stern aspect, one whom the camera rarely caught smiling; yet, seldom did he inveigh about sin and punishment to his family or his parishioners. His sermons leaned instead toward the quiet lecture on the meaning of character and faith and the application of Christian values in one's daily life. George himself would never fully embrace the fundamentalism of Wesleyan Methodism. (By the age of twelve he was breaking the rules by sneaking off to the movies a couple of times a week.) But he esteemed his father's philosophical approach to religion, and much of the spiritual curriculum would stay with him. As a politician, no one could quote germane passages from Scripture during debate with greater facility than McGovern. And he always kept framed in his study the quotation from St. Mark that his father had also kept framed in his: "For whosoever will save his life shall lose it; but whosoever shall lose his life for my sake and the gospel's, the same shall save it."[5]

---

4 Johnson, quoted in *Grassroots*, p. 228.
5 This discussion is based on the author's interviews with George McGovern, August 9, 1991 and October 8, 1994; with his wife, Eleanor Stegeberg McGovern, October 27, 1995; his sister, Mildred McGovern Brady, May 26, 1995; and with his daughters and son, Anne McGovern, December 29, 1995; Susan McGovern Rowan, December 29, 1995; and Steven McGovern, December 29, 1995; and on Lefton Stavrianos to Thomas Knock, June 5, 1995, with enclosure. See also *Grassroots*, pp. 4–6; and Anson, *McGovern*, pp. 20–21.

If his lot as a prairie preacher's son was the most decisive factor of McGovern's boyhood, then the Great Depression ran a close second. Its repercussions were all the more pronounced because of the agricultural economy, the climate, and the landscape of the Dakotas. The historian Walter Prescott Webb once described the predicament of McGovern's late-nineteenth century forebears as a people "far from markets, burned by drought, beaten by hail, withered by hot winds, frozen by blizzards, eaten out by grasshoppers, exploited by capitalists, cozened by politicians." Any evocation of the Plains in the 1920s and 1930s would be only slightly less bleak.[6]

Thereon, one of McGovern's earliest memories, at the age of ten, was of learning that adults, even grown men, could cry. The incident took place when he and his father paid a call on Art Kendall, a hardworking local farmer. As they drove up, Mr. Kendall sat sobbing on the back porch steps. In his hand he held a check for his entire year's production of hogs. The amount did not even cover the cost of shipping them to market, let alone for feed. McGovern knew that countless Americans went to bed hungry each night. Hardly a week went by that his mother and father did not invite a penniless stranger into the house to share supper. And yet there was this paradox of Mr. Kendall: even when harvests were plentiful, farmers still struggled to eke out an existence. Such encounters with the ravages of the depression (along with the fact that his Republican parents respected Franklin Roosevelt) would never leave him.[7]

Young George's awareness and sensitivity to the things that went on around him were also manifest in his strivings as a student. He was captivated by American history. At Mitchell High School, he read about his region's progressive statesmen – Robert LaFollette, George Norris, and Peter Norbeck – and admired their achievements on behalf of farmers and laborers. He also had a gifted American history teacher, who coached debate and occasionally philosophized on the meaning of life and the virtue of service to others. In the tenth grade, he decided that he, too, would become a history teacher.[8]

---

[6] Walter Prescott Webb, *The Great Plains* (Boston, 1931), p. 501. See also Herbert S. Schell, *History of South Dakota*, 3rd ed., (Lincoln, NB, 1975), pp. 277–297 and 342–355, and Alan L. Clem, *Prairie State Politics, Popular Democracy in South Dakota* (Washington, D.C., 1967), pp. 1–11 and 21–38.

[7] Author's interview with McGovern, August 9, 1991, and *Grassroots*, pp. 10–11.

[8] Author's interviews with McGovern, Aug. 9, 1991 and October 1, 1991; Mildred McGovern Brady, May 26, 1995; and with Dean Tanner and William Timmins (boyhood friends), October 23 and 24, 1998. See also *Grassroots*, pp. 16–17, and Anson, *McGovern*, pp. 29–31.

McGovern matriculated at Dakota Wesleyan University in the autumn of 1940. By the end of his sophomore year he had become the archetypal "Big Man On Campus." He was elected class president and wrote a regular column for the school's newspaper. Exceedingly bright, well-liked, and handsome, he was voted "Glamour Boy" of 1942–43 by the student body. More important, as in high school, he established a reputation as a star debater, an activity that gave him his first taste of politics and instilled in him an elemental faith in American political institutions and in the power of knowledge. (Forensics also gave him self-confidence and became the chief means of his social ascent.) In 1942, he placed first in a state-wide orator's competition, with a speech entitled "My Brother's Keeper," which the National Council of Churches designated one of the twelve best in the nation. In his junior year, Dakota Wesleyan won a championship against thirty-two teams from a twelve-state region, and George himself was named most outstanding individual speaker. Topics were generally of the times: "The Battle of the Far East," "What Does the Axis Really Want?" and "How Much War News Are We Entitled to Know?" Few challengers ever got the best of him, but a notable exception occurred in his senior year of high school. The proposition was, "Resolved: That Great Britain and the United States should form a permanent alliance." George argued the affirmative while his opponent from Woonsocket High, Eleanor Stegeberg, argued the negative and won. The encounter changed the lives of both debaters, for it led to their marriage four years later.[9]

National contention over the country's stakes in the war in Europe had already reached high pitch when McGovern entered college. In debate tournaments he tended toward the internationalist position and eschewed the isolationist views of America Firsters, whom he regarded as extremists.[10] Almost from the start, World War II seemed to him an unambiguous struggle against a cruel, fascistic totalitarianism. "We are fighting

[9] *The Phreno Cosmian* (Dakota Wesleyan's student newspaper, copies in University Library), September 23 and December 16, 1941, and February 24 and March 3, 1942. For examples of McGovern's column, "As I See It," see *Ibid.*, December 16, 1941, on the impact of Pearl Harbor ("We stand united behind a capable, efficient government – 130 million strong"); January 13, 1942, on the role of civilians and soldiers ("the mightiest warrior for democracy is the educated man or woman"); and January 27, 1942, on a dictatorship vs. a slow-moving democracy (that "moves with a surety which avoids the tragedy that often accompanies rashness"). See also, author's interview with Eleanor Stegeberg McGovern, October 27, 1995; and Eleanor McGovern (with Mary Finch Hoyt), *Uphill, A Personal Story* (Boston, 1974), pp. 53–55.

[10] Author's interview with McGovern, August 9, 1991.

for a freedom which has been bought with the blood of Americans for two centuries," he intoned in his editorial column after Pearl Harbor. In the spring of 1942, to the dismay of his pacifist mother, he enlisted in the Army Air Force and a year later he was called to begin training as a bomber pilot. Eventually he commanded the crew of a B-24, the lumbering, four-engine craft known as the "Liberator." Over Germany, Italy, and Austria McGovern flew thirty-five combat missions (nearly twice the number that comprised the lifespan of the average crew). For his skill and courage under fire – most conspicuously for an emergency landing on a tiny island in the Adriatic and another harrowing predicament that required him to land his disabled plane on one tire – he won the Distinguished Flying Cross with three oak leaf clusters.[11] Although he rarely traded on it politically, no presidential candidate of the twentieth century could boast of a more exemplary or heroic military record.

McGovern had gone off to war with a sense of conviction and purpose. Although he reacted viscerally to the mass killings in which he had participated, the Allied victory over the Axis and his own exploits imbued him with fresh confidence in America's future. "I was really carried away by the vision of Roosevelt and Churchill and the Four Freedoms and the United Nations," he recalled. Flying his crew home across the Atlantic in 1945, he "had that Wilsonian view that this time it was over," and he felt as if he were "going back to participate in the launching of a new day in world affairs."[12]

His wartime experiences thus tended to nurture his interest in politics and rekindle his desire to study American history and the prospects for international cooperation. When tempting, lucrative job opportunities came his way, he declined them. "I'm afraid I'm 'doomed' to the life of a student and teacher," he confided to an intimate. "[T]hat old driving interest to learn rather than make money is still dominant."[13] With the help of the G.I. Bill, he completed his degree at Dakota Wesleyan and, in the fall of 1947, enrolled at Northwestern University to pursue a Ph.D.

---

[11] *Ibid.*; "As I See It," *The Phreno Cosmian*, December 16, 1941; for details on McGovern's service, see Records of the Army Air Forces, World War II Combat Operations Reports, 1942–46, 455th Bomber Group, boxes 1762–1767, National Archives, College Park, MD; and Stephen E. Ambrose, *The Wild Blue: The Men and Boys who Flew the B-24s Over Germany* (New York, 2001).

[12] Author's interview with McGovern, August 9, 1991.

[13] McGovern to Robert Pennington (Eleanor McGovern's brother-in-law), May 30, 1945, Pennington family papers, privately held (copy provided to author by Mr. Pennington).

Though somewhat small, Northwestern's history graduate program ranked among the country's finest. Several of McGovern's classmates – William H. Harbaugh, Robert W. Towner, and Alfred F. Young – would go on to become eminent scholars. His professors included Ray Allen Billington, the distinguished historian of the American frontier; Richard Leopold, one of the early deans of diplomatic history; and Lefton Stavrianos, a specialist in Eastern European and Russian history. Above all, there was the young Arthur S. Link, who would become one of the great American historians of the twentieth century and McGovern's dissertation supervisor and life-long friend. Link's devotion to the subjects of progressive reform, the life of Woodrow Wilson, and American internationalism influenced his student in both subtle and conclusive ways; in particular, McGovern acquired from him an enduring respect for the father of the League of Nations and an appreciation of the practical virtues of international organization.[14]

Whereas Link grew increasingly disposed to the so-called Consensus School that prevailed in the historical profession in the 1950s, McGovern was equally impressed by the Progressive historians of the previous generation – practitioners such as Vernon Parrington and Charles Beard – who emphasized, not *consensus*, but the role that *conflict* had played in bringing about change in American history. Then, too, there were the writings on the Social Gospel by Walter Rauschenbusch and Harry Emerson Fosdick. Their entreaties – directed at "young and serious minds" of the 1910s and 1920s to set their "religious motive power and zeal" to the task of solving social problems born of industrial capitalism – struck a chord in the aspiring scholar who was a minister's son.[15] Thus had McGovern embarked upon a wide-ranging examination of Progressive America – through the eyes of social activists who had lived it and under the guidance of scholars who undertook to interpret the era for the post – New Deal generation.

In the same regard, McGovern's dissertation, "The Colorado Coal Strike of 1913–14" (1953), is instructive. This 500-page study reconstructed the year-long battle for union recognition on the part of ten thousand miners and their families in southern Colorado – a conflict

---

[14] Author's interviews with William H. Harbaugh, October 23, 1995; Alfred F. Young, January 9, 2000; and McGovern, October 1, 1991; unrecorded conversations between the author and Arthur S. Link (1991–95); Young to Knock, December 15, 1996; and Stavrianos to Knock, June 5, 1995.

[15] Author's interviews with McGovern, August 9 and October 1, 1991; see also, *Grassroots*, pp. 34–36.

that culminated in the infamous "Ludlow Massacre" perpetrated by John
D. Rockefeller, Jr.'s paid army of 800 troops. The subject resonated for
McGovern. It reminded him of stories about his breaker-boy father having
to be carried to the mines at dawn at the age of nine, still asleep in his
father's arms; of the travails of organized labor during the Depression;
and of South Dakota farmers who had struggled against economic forces
beyond their control.[16] Through the process of becoming a historian and
of rendering the great coal mine war, then, McGovern's view of politics
and social conflict had begun to crystallize.

His thoughts on foreign policy were acquiring a definite shape as
well. Graduate readings included Owen Lattimore's *The Situation in Asia*,
E. H. Carr's *The Soviet Impact on the Western World*, Edwin Reischauer's
The United States and China, and John K. Fairbanks' *The United States
and Japan*. Their work – which in part emphasized western imperialist
depredations in understanding the sources of revolutionary nationalism –
made it impossible for him to regard Harry Truman and Dean Acheson
with anything but skepticism. ("There would have been no American intervention in Vietnam," he later wrote, "if the views of Lattimore and
other competent Asia scholars had been heeded.")[17]

The Cold War had already thrown the Northwestern history
department into discord by the time McGovern had arrived. Like many
of his peers and some of his professors, he supported Henry Wallace's
third-party presidential bid in 1948. Wallace, an Iowa-born agricultural
scientist and multimillionaire, had served as FDR's Secretary of Agriculture and second Vice President; in 1946, Truman fired him from his
cabinet post as Secretary of Commerce for publicly criticizing the administration's new hard-line toward the Soviet Union. The President's
decision to expand the nuclear arsenal, as well as his proclivity to regard the Russians as aggressive by nature, formed the basis of Wallace's
criticism. For his part, McGovern believed that Truman had abandoned
diplomacy too soon and exaggerated the Soviet threat, and so he and
Eleanor decided to attend the Progressive party's nominating convention
in Philadelphia. The behavior of fanatical elements within the party's left
wing, however, deeply troubled the young couple. Returning somewhat

---

[16] Author's interviews with McGovern, October 1, 1991, and Harbaugh, October, 23, 1995.
Though it cost the lives of scores of people and still failed to win recognition for the
United Mine Workers, McGovern concludes that the strike played an important role "in
bringing a larger measure of democracy and economic security to the miners of southern
Colorado" (*Dissertation Abstracts International*, vol. 13–6, pp. 1166–1167).
[17] Author's interview with McGovern, October 1, 1991, and *Grassroots*, pp. 40–42.

chastened, if not wholly disillusioned, they ended up not voting at all that year.[18]

Nonetheless, by the summer of 1950, McGovern had reached the conclusion that the Cold War was the result, as he put it in a letter to Arthur Link, "of U.S. blundering and allegiance to reactionary regimes on the one hand and Soviet stubbornness and opportunism on the other hand." He worried that, "unless we can quickly replace [Truman's] 'Get Tough Policy' with the thought and action that characterized Roosevelt's relations with the Russians, we shall find ourselves in an eastern war against 120 crack Chinese and Russian divisions." What was all the fuss supposed to be about, the twenty-eight-year-old asked, "when we have such allies as Franco, Chiang, Rhee and the most reactionary elements of the Republican party?" He could agree with Link's invocation of Reinhold Niebuhr's declaration that "the Christian must often choose between sinful alternatives if he is to survive"; yet he could not help feeling that America's course had been flawed since the death of Franklin Roosevelt. "We seem to be unaware that two-thirds of the world is either in revolution or on the verge of it," he wrote in September 1950. "I somehow feel that Russia has understood and exploited the forces of nationalism and socialism which are convulsing Asia ... whereas we are engaged in a hopeless process of sitting on the lid in the tension centers of the world."[19]

Like any perceptive diplomatic historian, McGovern made connections between domestic politics and foreign policy. The Korean War and McCarthyism had stymied the Fair Deal, he said to his mentor. He considered the McCarran Internal Security Act of 1950 "possibly a greater loss of freedom than any previous measure in our history." And he prayed that Truman would not permit Korea to blow up into a bigger war which, he feared, "would mean the death blow to what ever liberalism remains in the United States." A few months later, addressing two hundred Methodist

---

[18] Author's interviews with McGovern, August 9 and October 1, 1991; Eleanor McGovern, October 27, 1995; Robert Pennington, March 27, 1996; and Alfred F. Young, January 9, 2000. For interesting local coverage of the Wallace convention, see news reports in the *Mitchell Daily Republic*, July 24, 26, and 27, and August 31, 1948, and letter-to-the-editor by McGovern, "The American Way," September 22, 1948; see also, *Grassroots*, pp. 40–45. John C. Culver, *American Dreamer: The Life and Times of Henry A. Wallace* (New York, 2000) and Graham White and John Maze, *Henry A. Wallace: His Search for a New World Order* (Chapel Hill, N.C., 1995) are fine biographies. McGovern's opinion of the thirty-third president has changed little over the years: "I've never been a big Truman admirer; some people have, but I never have." (author's interview, April 4, 1994).

[19] McGovern to Link, September 30, 1950, papers of Arthur S. Link, Seeley Mudd Library, Princeton University.

ministers in Mitchell, he called for a cease-fire in Korea and for diplomatic recognition of the People's Republic of China and its admission to the United Nations.[20] Thus, long before he ran for office, McGovern had found his compass; and, if not quite revealing the final destination, it pointed in an unmistakable direction.

In the meantime, before he was awarded his Ph.D. in 1953, McGovern had accepted a faculty position at his alma mater. He was at once a highly successful and (for his candid opinions on contemporary issues) a controversial teacher. The students were so impressed with his courses and his outstanding record as debate coach that they dedicated the college yearbook to him in 1952.[21] Politics, however, held an irresistible attraction. To various groups around Mitchell, he continued to speak out on national affairs. On behalf of Adlai Stevenson's presidential candidacy he published in the *Daily Republic* a series of seven historical Op-ed pieces about the evolution of the Democratic party. And, in his spare time, he somehow managed to reorganize the moribund Democratic party of South Dakota, an unenviable task at best.

Since statehood in 1889, South Dakotans had sent only five Democrats to Washington. In 1952, they gave Eisenhower a two-to-one margin over Stevenson and elected 108 Republicans to the 110-seat assembly. (The state's Republican governor had said the contest was "between New Dealism and Americanism.") Then, in order to facilitate his objective, McGovern did something that stupefied his academic friends – he resigned a tenure-track job. ("What a loss to history!" Arthur Link exclaimed when he heard the news.) But his friends' skepticism evaporated when, miraculously and almost single-handedly, he revived competitive two-party politics and, in 1956 and 1958, won election to the House of Representatives.[22] As a congressman, he distinguished himself in the fields

---

[20] McGovern to Link, August 19, 1950, Link Papers; *Mitchell Daily Republic*, June 8, 1951 (news report) and June 18, 1951 (McGovern letter-to-the-editor).

[21] See Dakota Wesleyan's year book, *The Tumbleweed*, for 1952, 1953, and 1955; *The Phreno Cosmian*, February 13, 1952 and September 16, 1955 (news story and editorial on his service), in University Library; and author's interviews with Gordon Rollins (DWU's former vice-president of finance) October 23, 1998, and Barbara Rollins Nemer (former student of McGovern), October 27, 1998.

[22] McGovern's essays on the Democratic Party appeared in the *MDR* between August and October 1952. (South Dakota's governor is quoted in *ibid.*, October 10, 1952.) See also Clem, *Prairie State Politics* (pp. 11–15, 38–45, and 118), according to whom, "More than any other figure," McGovern was "responsible for the existence of both a partisan and an ideological choice in contemporary South Dakota politics" (p. 55); and Schell, *History of South Dakota*, pp. 313–315. Link is quoted by Harbaugh (author's

of agriculture and education and gained renown for superb constituency work. By 1960 he was ready to challenge the red-baiting Karl Mundt for his Senate seat. Yet the combination of the latter's incumbency, constant reminders of McGovern's sympathy for Henry Wallace, and the issue of John F. Kennedy's Catholicism precluded an upset.[23]

Almost daily throughout his four years in the House McGovern "took a bite out of" Ezra Taft Benson, the Secretary of Agriculture who had overthrown the Democrats' regime of generous commodity price supports. A few days after ascending Capitol Hill (and notwithstanding his lowly status), he offered an amendment to a farm bill which would have established 90 percent parity payments; he presented the case so well that it came within four votes of adoption. His most consequential first-term feat, however, occurred the next year – a major broadening of the scope of the National Defense Education Act of 1958. An early draft of this legislation, spurred by the Soviet Union's launching of Sputnik, provided federal loans to college students, but solely to those concentrating in the sciences. The former history teacher lobbied the Committee on Education and Labor, arguing that the nation would be best served by extending the benefits to all students regardless of their major. This time his proposal became law, and it helped to lay the foundation for full-scale federal aid to education during the next decade.[24]

With regard to international relations, McGovern was no sooner sworn in than he confronted a resolution related to presidential warmaking powers. The immediate issue was the "Eisenhower Doctrine," a pledge to defend the interests of the United States in the Middle East through military aid or, possibly, military intervention. McGovern voted nay. He did so in the belief that the measure usurped congressional prerogatives under the Constitution, but also because it left untouched the social and political problems that threatened the peace in the region. The Eisenhower Doctrine, he said, "provides no practical plan to use American aid dollars to eradicate the swamplands of poverty and disease that open the way for Communist inroads." He wondered as well how the government hoped to advance its long-term interests, not to mention its own historic ideals, by expending its moral and economic resources to prop up feudal despots "who embody everything that is alien to our tradition of liberty

interview, October 23, 1995); for the congressional campaigns, see *Grassroots*, pp. 63–70 and 79–80.

[23] For these developments, see *Ibid.*, pp. 52–83 and Anson, *McGovern*, pp. 63–98.

[24] Author's interview with McGovern, October 1, 1991; *Grassroots*, pp. 77–78.

and equality." The following year he joined sixteen members who refused to endorse the president's decision to send 14,000 Marines into Lebanon.[25]

Taken together, McGovern's early stand against Cold War interventionism and his domestic initiatives constituted an important first step along a path from which he would rarely stray. Most of his analyses of contemporary events in one way or another proceeded from his experiences during the Great Depression and World War II and in his training as a historian. "[W]e have allowed ourselves to become identified with those who seek to freeze the status quo," he lamented, for example, in a floor speech in 1958, echoing his letters to Arthur Link. "Most of the people of the world are not looking primarily for military hardware. They are hungry, sick, or illiterate." The test for foreign aid ought to be "how effectively it enables the people of the underdeveloped areas to build up the kind of society where better standards of life are possible."[26]

In his second term in the House, he continued to articulate the same anti-imperialist and humane values, drawing a bead on President Eisenhower's and Secretary Benson's narrow construction of the Agricultural Trade Development and Assistance Act. Known as Public Law 480 (or PL 480), this program had been established in 1954 primarily to alleviate the burden of America's huge agricultural surpluses by distributing them abroad. But, because the administration's chief emphasis was on "surplus disposal," recipient countries had come to regard it with suspicion, and critics at home and abroad branded it a Republican "dumping" program.[27] In 1959, McGovern worked with Senator Hubert Humphrey

---

[25] Congressional Record, House, 85th Congress, 1st session, January 31, 1957. "That's the way I should have voted on the Gulf of Tonkin resolution," he later said ruefully about the Lebanon incident (author's interview, October 1, 1991).

[26] Congressional Record, House, 85th Congress, 2nd session, vol. 104, parts 16–17, pp. 1100–1101.

[27] The following discussion is based on Thomas J. Knock, "Feeding the World and Thwarting the Communists: George McGovern and Food for Peace," in J. Christopher Jespersen and David F. Schmitz eds., *Architects of the American Century: Essays on American Foreign Policymakers and the Organizations They Have Shaped* (Chicago, 2000), pp. 98–120. See also Senate Committee on Foreign Relations, *Hearings: Mutual Security Act of 1954*, Senate, 83rd Congress, 2nd session, 1954; McGovern, *War Against Want: America's Food for Peace Program* (New York, 1964); Peter A. Toma, *The Politics of Food for Peace, Executive-Legislative Interaction* (Tucson, 1967); Mitchell B. Wallerstein, *Food for War – Food for Peace, United States Food Aid in the Global Context* (Cambridge, MA, 1980); Vernon W. Ruttan, *United States Development Assistance Policy, the Domestic Politics of Foreign Economic Aid* (Baltimore and London, 1996); and Michael Maren, *The Road to Hell: The Ravaging Effects of Foreign Aid and International Charity* (New York, 1997).

of Minnesota to craft legislation to transform PL 480 into what Humphrey now christened, "Food for Peace." Their aim was to redress the absence of any overtly humanitarian component as well as to fight the Cold War more creatively. A generous expansion of the program, the two farm state progressives submitted, not only would relieve hunger but also could underwrite economic and social development projects. As Humphrey put it, "Russia cannot supply food. The United States can."[28]

McGovern struck a characteristic tone of idealism and pragmatism. Citing the drop in exports shipped under PL 480 in 1958, he pointed out that American storage facilities would soon be bulging with a record carryover of 1.3 billion bushels of wheat (more than double the annual domestic requirement). Instead of spending $1 billion for storage, would it not be better to use that money to feed the world's hungry and help to build more just societies? Could the president not see that, rather than a "burden" to bemoan, agricultural abundance was "one of America's greatest assets for raising living standards and promoting peace and stability in the free world"? McGovern wondered just what it would take to get Eisenhower and Benson to jettison their "myopic view of this extremely important program" in favor of "vigor, boldness, and imagination."[29]

The country would soon be hearing a lot about "vigor, boldness, and imagination" as the Kennedy presidential movement got underway. But the "farm problem" was a question that largely bored the candidate from Massachusetts. "I don't want to hear about agriculture from anyone but Ken Galbraith," he once quipped, "and I don't want to hear about it from him."[30] Even so, he could not avoid the subject during the campaign, and McGovern's and Humphrey's ideas about PL 480 helped him find his voice. Kennedy now linked an ostensibly unexciting domestic issue to foreign policy in a fairly dynamic way. "I don't regard the agricultural surplus as a problem. I regard it as an opportunity," he declared to thousands of South Dakotans in McGovern's hometown. "[F]ood is strength, and food is peace, and food is freedom, and food is a helping hand to people

Although some resources were set aside for humanitarian purposes, the paramount intent behind PL 480, as General Foods board chairman Charles Francis insisted, was to "get rid of surpluses" (see Ruttan, pp. 70–72 and 152–156).

[28] See "International Food for Peace Act of 1959," and speech by Humphrey, Congressional Record, Senate, April 21, 1959, 86th Congress, 1st session.

[29] For McGovern's speech, see Congressional Record, House, 86th Congress, 1st session, January 29, 1959; and press release on "Food for Peace Resolution," box FFP-1, McGovern papers.

[30] Author's interview with John Kenneth Galbraith, May 7, 1996; see also Anson, *McGovern*, 115.

around the world whose good will and friendship we want."[31] He also wove the idea into his inaugural address. Thus, to "those peoples in the huts and villages of half the globe struggling to break the bonds of mass misery," he pledged his administration's "best efforts to help them help themselves" – for however long it might take and "because it is right." Two days later, he created the post of "Director" of Food for Peace and charged him with the responsibility of using America's bounty to narrow the gap between the haves and the have-nots. "Humanity and prudence, alike," he stated, counsel a major effort on our part."[32]

McGovern's appointment came as no surprise. Both John and Robert Kennedy appreciated his credentials and personal qualities and, not incidentally, his loyalty during the recent campaign. South Dakota was one of those states where Kennedy's religion had hurt Democrats, and he lost it to Richard Nixon by 50,000 votes out of 306,000. McGovern had steadfastly stood by the national ticket; yet, in an acrimonious, uphill battle, he came within 15,000 votes of denying Karl Mundt a third term. Robert Kennedy, among others, believed his brother had cost McGovern the election. The consolation prize was Food for Peace and the cocurricular title, "Special Assistant to the President."[33]

For someone of McGovern's background and inclinations, the assignment was well-nigh perfect. As Director, he intended to do nothing less than bury the old "surplus disposal" concept forever and engineer a vast expansion of the program. In the process, he managed (for the while) to turn Food for Peace into a progressive instrument of American foreign policy. As he set about the task, he was not unmindful of the

---

[31] Remarks at the Corn Palace, Mitchell, S. D., September 22, 1960, in *Freedom of Communications, Final Report of the Committee on Commerce, United States Senate. Part I. The Speeches ... of Senator John F. Kennedy, August 1–November 7, 1960* (Washington, D.C.: U. S. Government Printing Office, 1961), pp. 325–328. See also, press release, "Food For Peace: A Program, Not A Slogan," by Kennedy, October 31, 1960, copy in McGovern papers, box FFP-1. Kennedy also commissioned a study of the program, January 19, 1961, copy in President's office files (POF), box 78, papers of John F. Kennedy, John F. Kennedy Library (JFKL), Boston, MA.

[32] John F. Kennedy Inaugural Address, *Public Papers of the Presidents, 1961* (Washington, U. S. Government Printing Office, 1961), pp. 1–3; and Executive Order 10915 and Memorandum for Heads of Executive Departments and Agencies, January 24, 1961, copies in Richard Reuter papers, box 13, JFK Library.

[33] The issue of Catholicism is discussed in a series of letters to and from McGovern, c. November 1960, box 17, 67A1819, McGovern papers. See also, McGovern interview (April 24, 1964) in JFK Library Oral History Project; and author's interviews with McGovern, August 9, 1991; Galbraith, May 3, 1996; and with Arthur M. Schlesinger, Jr., July 10, 1996.

political motives behind food aid, or of the administration's preference for the "tough, pragmatic" approach to foreign aid in keeping with Walt Whitman Rostow's *Stages of Economic Growth* and Kennedy's notion of the 1960s as the "Decade of Development." At the same time, McGovern told the President, Food for Peace should dedicate itself to "the cause of feeding hungry people even if the economic benefit [to the United States] is an indirect one."[34]

All of these considerations were manifest in the "Food for Wages" program, the "long-term investment in progress" that McGovern had advocated as a Congressman. For two years, he traveled constantly – to Latin America, the Middle East, Africa, and Asia – marshalling and overseeing countless allotments of immense quantities of cheap food and fiber to fuel labor-intensive economic development projects. In his first six months in office, the United States shipped 264,000 tons for this purpose, or six times the amount that the Eisenhower administration had shipped in six years. By 1963, twenty-two third world countries were participating, and the volume of commodities had surpassed a million tons. In all, Food for Wages provided partial wage payments for upwards of 700,000 workers engaged in land clearance, reclamation, reforestation, and irrigation, and in the construction of bridges, dams, roads, wells, hospitals, schools, and agricultural cooperatives.[35] For McGovern, launching public works projects was the way to fight the Cold War. To audiences at home, he liked to say, "American food has done more to prevent ... communism than all the military hardware we have shipped around the world." Indeed, the historian declared, in an agreeable rhetorical compound of Thomas Jefferson and Woodrow Wilson, farmers were "the new internationalists." Once the cradle of isolationism, America's rural heartland was now a dynamic force in foreign policy, supplying the sort of "self-help capital" that the Soviet system simply could never amass, let alone parcel out. It was all rather crisply summed up by Walt Rostow: "Marx was a city boy."[36]

---

[34] W. W. Rostow, *The Stages of Economic Growth: A Non-Communist Manifesto* (Cambridge, England, 1960); McGovern to Kennedy, Memorandum and Report on Food For Peace (p. 20), March 10, 1961, POF, box 78, Kennedy Papers, JFK; and Knock, "Feeding the World and Thwarting the Communists: George McGovern and Food for Peace," pp. 106–107.

[35] *Ibid.*, pp. 105–107.

[36] "I was willing to use some of that rhetoric," he has said, "but my own inner sense of the program was that it should not be used in any major way as a Cold War tool" (author's interview with McGovern, August 9, 1991). See also McGovern address to the 59th Convention of the National Farmers Union, Washington, D.C., March 16, 1961, and similar examples in Speeches Files, 1961 and 1962, McGovern Papers; and Memorandum

But this was only the half of it. In his travels, McGovern frequently encountered scenes of appalling misery, particularly in Latin America. To be sure, he advised President Kennedy, the administration should devote resources to help stimulate development projects; but it must "not ignore the vital need for purely humanitarian programs to feed the hungry."[37] Here, then, dearest to the Director's heart was the overseas school lunch program, which he worked extremely hard to revitalize. Among other things, it resulted in dramatic improvements in the health of millions of children, not to mention in increases in school attendance as high as forty percent. By mid-1962, some thirty-five million children worldwide were receiving daily Food for Peace lunches. By 1964, the children at the Food for Peace table numbered one million in Peru, two million in Korea, three and a half million in Egypt, four and a half million in Brazil, nine million in India, and over ten million in Southeast Asia.[38] With the possible exception of the Peace Corps, George McGovern had superintended arguably the greatest humanitarian achievement of the Kennedy-Johnson era.

Despite universal acclaim, McGovern still longed to be a senator. With the President's blessing and a glowing public acknowledgment of his services, he entered the race in South Dakota in 1962 and won.[39] Whereas he would always be grateful for the rare opportunity Kennedy had bestowed, he did not hesitate to establish a little independence upon entering the world's most exclusive deliberative body.

His first speech, "Our Castro Fixation versus the Alliance for Progress," was an incisive discourse grounded in his scholarly background, his earlier stand against military interventionism, and insights he had gained from Food for Peace. He began by defending the President against right-wing attacks for his disinclination to undertake a post–missile-crisis invasion of Cuba. At the same time, he characterized as a "tragic mistake" the administration's own trespasses against that island,

to Kennedy, August 3, 1961, POF, Kennedy Papers, box 78, JFKL. Rostow is quoted in *War Against Want*, p. 115.

[37] See McGovern to Kennedy, Memorandum and Report on Food For Peace, March 10, 1961, POF, Kennedy Papers, Box 78, JFKL, p. 18.

[38] See McGovern to Kennedy ("1961 Report to the President"), January 3, 1961, POF, box 78; McGovern to Kennedy, March 29 and July 18, 1962, POF, box 79, Kennedy Papers; and McGovern's account in *War Against Want*, pp. 32–42.

[39] Drew Pearson, for example, hailed Food for Peace as one of the "most spectacular achievements of the young Kennedy administration" (quoted in Knock, "Feeding the World and Thwarting the Communists," p. 107); for McGovern's resignation, see McGovern to Kennedy and Kennedy to McGovern, both July 18, 1962, POF, box 79, Kennedy Papers. For his senatorial campaign, see *Grassroots*, pp. 88–92 and Anson, pp. 119–128.

adding that the Bay of Pigs invasion "might have damaged our standing in the hemisphere more if it had succeeded ... than it did as a miserable flop." He then submitted an inventory of the region's *real* problems: that the richest two percent of the people of Latin America possessed over half of all its wealth, while eighty percent lived in shacks or huts; that Latin America's rate of illiteracy exceeded one-third, and disease and malnourishment afflicted fifty percent of its people. He also enumerated the burdens of swelling populations, one-crop economies, unjust tax structures, and military establishments designed to keep the system intact.

What Fidel's revolution had done, McGovern proffered, was to have "forced every government of the hemisphere to take a new and more searching look at the crying needs of the great masses of human beings," though he doubted (quite perceptively) whether the ruling classes were as yet "aroused sufficiently ... to make the Alliance [for Progress] succeed on a broad scale." As for his fellow citizens, rather than losing sleep over Cuba, they might do better to refrain from ill-advised military interventions in the name of anti-Communism and "point the way to a better life for the hemisphere and, indeed, for all mankind."[40]

The *New York Times* was taken with the speech enough to publish it as an article in the *New York Times Magazine*. The President, however, was annoyed. McGovern had not submitted an advance copy and, notwithstanding praise for the Alliance for Progress, he had implied that the adminstration – not just its right-wing critics – was hobbled by a "Castro fixation" that failed to plumb the causes of modern revolutions.[41] At any rate, it was an exceptional debut.

The initial stage of McGovern's apprenticeship in the Senate occurred between the aftermath of the Missile Crisis and the escalation of the war in Vietnam. During that promising interlude, he perceived a historic opportunity for the United States to alter the trend born of the Cold War. The prevailing state of international relations, he believed, held possibilities for curbing the arms race and dismantling (at least partially) America's colossal military-industrial complex – this, by way of a gradual, orderly shift in the nation's economy toward more pacific industrial enterprises.

---

[40] "Our Castro Fixation versus the Alliance for Progress," *Congressional Record*, Senate, March 15, 1963, 88th Congress, 1st session, vol. 109, reprinted in McGovern, *A Time of War, A Time of Peace*, pp. 96–102.

[41] See "Is Castro an Obsession With Us?" *New York Times Sunday Magazine*, May 19, 1963, in which McGovern sharpened his criticism of the administration. McGovern learned of JFK's displeasure through Theodore Sorensen (author's interview with McGovern, August, 9, 1991).

As he had said before, if the United States were "to fulfill its promise both at home and around the globe," there was an unfinished domestic agenda to attend to: the work of creating new jobs and greater educational opportunities for young people; of doing something about rising medical costs confronting older people; and of addressing the deeper causes behind both poverty and a sluggish national economy. It was no longer possible, therefore, "to separate America's domestic health from our position in world affairs."[42]

To these ends, the senator introduced singularly striking legislation in August and September 1963. For example, he proposed his $5 billion cut in the defense budget – appropriations that would consume more than half of every dollar of federal revenue.[43] He made a good case for pruning. In virtually all categories – from ICBMs and Polaris submarines to strategic bombers and tactical nuclear weapons – the United States far and away outpaced Soviet capabilities. He noted that, during World War II, his B-24 had carried the equivalent of five tons of TNT, a force rendered trifling by the "the 20,000-ton destroyer of Hiroshima"; but today the U.S. nuclear arsenal was more than "one and a half million times as powerful as the bomb that wiped out Hiroshima." For further evidence that the quest for nuclear superiority was meaningless, he cited Secretary of Defense Robert McNamara's recent estimates that an all-out nuclear exchange would yield fatalities approaching 90 million in Western Europe, 100 million in the United States, and 100 million in the Soviet Union. In light of such "overkill capacity," he asked, "what possible advantage" could accrue from "appropriating additional billions of dollars to build more missiles and bombs"? Of course, "America ought to have a defense force that is second to none"; but the time had come for a fundamental reconsideration of national security needs and their implications for American society.[44]

Not far from his mind was President Eisenhower's heretofore uncelebrated farewell address warning of the dangers that the military-industrial complex posed to democratic government and liberal capitalism.[45] But

---

[42] Ibid., as he put it in "Our Castro Fixation."

[43] This discussion is based on materials in a box labeled "Speeches and Statements, September–October, 1963," McGovern Papers, and on the text of two Senate speeches, "New Perspectives on American Security," August 2, 1963, and "A Proposal to Reverse the Arms Race," September 24, 1963, reprinted in *A Time of War, A Time of Peace*, pp. 5–22 and 24–35.

[44] *Ibid.*, pp. 5, 10, 11, 12–13, and 28–29.

[45] Among politicians, McGovern was an early "Eisenhower revisionist." He has characterized his farewell address as "brilliant" and the "most thoughtful" since George Washington's. As a congressman, McGovern rarely found himself in accord with the

McGovern recognized as well – when one-tenth of the country's gross national product was devoted to military spending year in and year out – that many a corporation and member of Congress would oppose any substantial reductions. These were among the considerations that went into another of his legislative initiatives, the National Economic Conversion Act, introduced just three weeks before Kennedy's fateful trip to Dallas.[46]

Counseling a coordinated effort between industry and government, this bill called upon the president to establish a national commission to study, in consultation with the governors of the states, "any reasonable future opportunities for converting the instruments of war to the tools of peace." It also would require major defense contractors to appoint their own committees to study ways to ease the coming transition to a peacetime economy. Systematic planning of this sort was the key: it would relieve the anxieties of all concerned who had grown dependent upon the "gigantic WPA" that the Pentagon had become; it would "add new force to disarmament discussions by removing fear of the economic consequences"; and it could "cause a boom, rather than a drag on our economy."[47]

Indeed, he argued, alluding to Eisenhower, the present level of military spending actually distorted the nation's economy, for it weakened the competitive position of civilian industries and aggravated the balance of payments problem. For instance, while both Japan and Western Europe were busy modernizing their civilian industrial plants at a far faster rate, the United States still devoted some three-fourths of all its scientific and engineering talent to weapons research and development. Although it once ranked first in machine tool production, the United States, he pointed out, had slipped to fifth place; and, already (as of 1963), thousands of public school teachers were failing to meet reasonable teaching standards. Apart

president, but his estimation has grown over the years, in part because of the books about Eisenhower by his good friend, the historian Stephen Ambrose: "When Steve Ambrose's volumes came out, I realized how tenacious he was in blocking these expenditures for the military that broke the budget. He wouldn't permit it. For eight years, he sat there saying 'No, no.'" (McGovern interviews, October 1, 1991 and April 4, 1994.)

[46] "The National Economic Conversion Act," Octoberober 31, 1963, is reprinted in *A Time of Peace, A Time of War*, pp. 49–60. See supporting materials in acc. no. 67A1881, boxes 1 and 3, 71A3482, box 21, and "Speeches and Statements, September–October, 1963," in McGovern Papers. In drafting the bill, McGovern consulted with Seymour Melman, professor of industrial engineering at Columbia, an activist in the nuclear disarmament movement and critic of the military-industrial formula for the nation's political economy.

[47] "The National Economic Conversion Act," in *A Time of Peace, A Time of War*, pp. 49, 54, and 57.

from everything else, then, a gradual reordering of priorities seemed a matter of common sense.[48]

There were other reasons to commend economic conversion planning, in tandem with the proposal to reverse the arms race. That summer, McGovern had given his first speech on civil rights, once more linking his agenda for social and economic progress at home to ongoing developments in international affairs.[49] The crusade went beyond the struggle for legal equality, he said. "The Negro's demand for civil justice is greatly complicated by his hunger for better jobs and better schools and better housing at a time when all of these are in short supply for both whites and Negroes." Meeting these domestic needs was "fundamental to the strength of our nation" – hence, again, the imperative "to shift some of our massive military budget to constructive purposes here at home." To McGovern, then, American priorities in conducting the Cold War itself had placed obstacles in the path toward simple justice.[50]

"Four out of five human beings of the globe are non-whites," he reminded his fellow senators in subsequent remarks that reflected on the wages of Western imperialism. "Since World War II, they have been largely caught up in an irrepressible demand for national independence. They have sounded the death knell to colonialism and they are demanding the right to be treated as equals. . . . And they will mock the pretensions of those who preach democracy but practice discrimination." Thus, in the case of race relations, too, it was "no longer possible to separate

---

[48] *Ibid.*, pp. 54–56. Thirty-one senators co-sponsored the legislation. Although President Johnson established a high-level "Committee on Defense and Economic Agencies" in December 1964, the administration was nonetheless decidedly cool. Because of Vietnam, McGovern admitted at a UAW Conference two months later, "I don't think defense spending is going to drop drastically next year or the year after" (in San Diego, February 26, 1965 in "Speeches and Statements 1965," McGovern Papers.) See also *New York Times*, December 22, 1963; Congressional *Record*, December 30, 1963 88th Congress, 1st session; and McGovern, "Swords into Plowshares," *The Progressive* (January 1965), pp. 10–12.

[49] "The Continuing American Revolution and the American Negro," address before the New York State Young Democrats Convention, June 15, 1963, in 71A3482, box 21, McGovern Papers. A modified version, is printed in *A Time of Peace, A Time of War*, pp. 149–163.

[50] *Ibid.*, pp. 151 and 152. "I think if we can understand the spirit of 1776, we can better appreciate the rising expectations that are convulsing the American Negro community and the developing continents of the globe," the former historian also said. "We should not forget that once the colonists launched the war for independence from England, they unleashed forces that led also to a social revolution in American life," pp. 150 and 152.

our domestic condition from our international posture." Our communist adversaries, he declared, possessed no weapon more potent than "the stark truth about race relations in the United States."[51] (Martin Luther King would make virtually the same arguments four years later, in his famous declaration of conscience concerning the Vietnam War.)

In part owing to Vietnam, McGovern's perception of a "peace dividend" was fleeting. But he would always insist that the Cold War could not be won through military means. The conflict in Southeast Asia (even before Kennedy's assassination, as we have seen) only strengthened that conviction. That was why, in September, 1963, he had combined his commentary on Vietnam with his proposal to reverse the arms race. A series of coincidental misfortunes that Food for Peace suffered also had a bearing on his alarm. A month before expressing his apprehensions about Kennedy's willingness to have walked at least ankle-deep into the Big Muddy, McGovern had received disturbing information from the American embassy in Saigon. Food for Peace was proving "a valuable and flexible tool in the achievement of U.S. policy goals in Viet Nam," William C. Trueheart, Charge d'Affaires *ad interim*, reported. In fact, it had become "integral" to the feeding of militia trainees in the Strategic Hamlet program as well as to other counterinsurgency efforts.[52]

Trueheart apparently had assumed that the former Director would be gratified. McGovern's priorities, of course, lay elsewhere; in 1961, for instance, he had coordinated a huge emergency shipment of food for thousands of flood victims along the Mekong.[53] Now he discovered that the proceeds from the sale of Food for Peace commodities were being delivered over to Ngo Dinh Diem to enhance the regime's ability "to maintain a high level of military expenditures for the prosecution of the war."[54] But it was only the beginning. By 1965–66, as much as half – and by 1973–74, two-thirds – of the total program was being thus diverted, much like a shell-game, so that more money would be left over to fight

---

[51] "The Point of No Return," *A Time of Peace, A Time of War*, pp. 155–56.

[52] Trueheart to McGovern, August 16, 1963, box 5, 67A1881 and box FFP-4, McGovern papers. (McGovern requested status reports on Food for Peace from a number of embassies; Trueheart's letter was among the responses.)

[53] McGovern, *War Against Want*, pp. 55–59; see also, "Pigs Plus Corn Plus Cement Equals Success in Vietnam," October 10, 1964, box 8, 67A802, McGovern papers.

[54] Trueheart to McGovern, August 16, 1963, cited above. The process had actually begun, covertly, in late 1961, unbeknownst to McGovern. See Top Secret memorandum, U. Alexis Johnson to McGeorge Bundy, November 28, 1961, POF, box 128, Countries, Vietnam, Security Files, JFKL.

the war.[55] What Arthur Schlesinger, Jr., had once described as "one of the visible embodiments of the idealism of the New Frontier" would become one of invisible casualties of the Vietnam war. The mutation of Food for Peace into "Food for War" would have a lasting impact on McGovern's thinking about the ways that powerful nations might figure in the life of weaker nations.[56]

In early August, 1964, McGovern listened to the admonitions of senators Wayne Morse and Ernest Gruening. Although he suspected the two lone naysayers might turn out to be right about the Gulf of Tonkin Resolution, he believed that Lyndon Johnson "was more interested in domestic policy and that he did not quite know how to liquidate the Kennedy policy in Vietnam before the election." Moreover, J. William Fulbright, chair of the Senate Foreign Relations Committee, had assured him (and a small group of other interlocutors) that the resolution "doesn't mean anything," except to take Vietnam out of politics and foil the warhawk Republican presidential candidate, Barry Goldwater.[57] And so he voted in favor – mainly for the sake of a Great Society but nonetheless with great misgivings.

Just five days before Johnson's inauguration, on January 15, 1965, McGovern publicly raised questions about the war, which had already begun to metastasize. "We are not winning in South Vietnam," he declared in the Senate. "We are backing a government that is incapable of winning a military struggle or of governing its people." His contention was that the problem was fundamentally political, and he urged the administration seriously to pursue negotiations to neutralize the conflict. He then laid out a program of his own. It involved the gradual elimination of foreign troops and military advisers and the introduction of United Nations peacekeeping forces; a confederation between North and South

---

[55] "[I]f there was some way to use Food for Peace to reduce the budget here at home and also to assist the South Vietnamese budget," McGovern lamented years afterward, "I think [Johnson] would have been willing to put the whole thing in South Vietnam, and that became the view of Walt Rostow, [McGeorge] Bundy, and the others" (author's interview with McGovern, August 9, 1991); see also Wallerstein, *Food for War*, pp. 45–47, 16–17, 134–135, 193–197.

[56] Schlesinger to Kennedy, April 30, 1962, copy in FFP-1, McGovern papers; and McGovern interview, August 9, 1991.

[57] Interview with McGovern, December 29, 1992, quoting Fulbright who, according to McGovern, would also say to skeptics, "You pass this thing [and] it gives Lyndon a tool in the campaign. I wouldn't support it if I thought it would lead to any escalation of the war." See also, *Grassroots*, pp. 102–104, and Randall Bennett Woods, *Fulbright, A Biography* (New York, 1995), pp. 353–355.

Vietnam; and a cooperative venture to harness the Mekong River Valley. For the present, he did not advise military withdrawal until such a settlement could be effected.[58]

McGovern's speech made headlines throughout the country. Then, in March, once the American bombing campaign was under way, CBS News invited him to debate the issue on a prime-time special, "Vietnam – The Hawks and the Doves." His copanelists were Senator Gale McGee of Wyoming, Hanson Baldwin of the *New York Times*, and Roger Hilsman, former Assistant Secretary of State for Far Eastern Affairs. (Thus McGovern was outnumbered 3–1 in this particular aviary.) Baldwin, the most hawkish, contemplated massive bombing and a naval blockade of North Vietnam; if the Chinese intervened, he said, one could rest assured "the upper limit" of our response would not exceed one million men. McGovern, in making his case for negotiations, offered a spirited and prophetic rebuttal:

[E]ven if we could obliterate North Vietnam, with the kind of massive bombing attacks that you suggest, the war would still continue in the South, the guerrillas would continue to fight, [and] the political situation would continue to deteriorate.... I think there will be a staggering loss of life out of all proportion to the stakes involved [with] no guarantee that... the situation out there will be any better. In fact, I think that there will be such enormous political instability... that indeed we invite a much worse situation than the one that exists.... [I]t's far better for politicians to take some political risks than for us to risk a course that might cost the lives of hundreds of thousands of our citizens.[59]

For all of his impassioned dissent, McGovern avoided personal criticism of Johnson in this and other instances; he appreciated the significance of the latter's historic legislative achievements as well as the need to preserve the lines of communication, although efforts to reason with the President proved barren. On one such occasion in the Oval Office, a few days after the CBS broadcast, McGovern attempted to refute the Johnsonian article of faith that Ho Chi Minh was a stooge of the Chinese who wanted "to take over the world." The Vietnamese and Chinese had hated each other for a thousand years, McGovern rejoined, and Ho might well serve as a barrier against Chinese expansion. "Goddamn it, George,

---

[58] *Congressional Record*, 89th Congress, 1st session, January 15, 1965 vol. III, pp. 784–86. For coverage of the speech, see the *New York Times* and the *Washington Post*, January 16, 1964. McGovern's ideas were informed by personal consultations with the journalist Bernard Fall, by General James Gavin's enclave theory, and by Charles DeGaulle's controversial proposal for reconvening the Geneva conference.

[59] See thirty-four-page transcript of CBS Special Report: "Vietnam: The Hawks and the Doves," March 8, 1965, box Speeches and Statements 1965, McGovern papers.

don't give me another history lesson," Johnson interrupted. "I don't have time to be sitting around this desk reading history books."[60]

Shortly after the administration embarked upon escalation in July, 1965, McGovern outlined another moderate peace plan in a speech in New Hampshire. While praising Johnson's unprecedented domestic record, he also admonished him for "preaching that the fate of the human race and the cause of all mankind center in Saigon" and deplored the waste of energy and talent that might otherwise have been devoted to "the strengthening of the Atlantic Community, the Alliance for Progress... and other steps toward peace that promise a better life for the people of the earth." In November, he took the first of many trips to Vietnam. The former bomber pilot was not unaccustomed to scenes of cruel war, but what he saw in an American military hospital made him heartsick – eighteen-year-old G.I.s without arms or faces; a handsome Marine lieutenant (with a Purple Heart pinned to his gown) who had both feet blown off. Flying over the countryside, McGovern beheld the endless jungle terrain; overwhelmed by a sinking feeling, he thought to himself, "How are we going to fight in this?"[61]

Back in Washington, he expressed his alarm more openly than ever before as the war began to undermine the Great Society, and Johnson would soar to great heights of apoplexy at the mere mention of McGovern's name. "The boss gets wild about him sometimes," Harry McPherson told Joe Califano. As he had done with Fulbright, the President eventually banned the senator from all White House functions. (Not until Gerald Ford's ascension would he be invited back.) Nonetheless, by the spring of 1967, McGovern and his principal kindred spirits, Fulbright and Frank Church of Idaho, had become the foremost critics within the Liberal Establishment which had itself conceived the war.[62]

---

[60] Interview with McGovern, December 29, 1992; and "Statement of Senator George McGovern to President Johnson, Private Conversation at the White House, March 26, 1965," in Office Files of Horace Busby, Lyndon B. Johnson papers, lyndon B. Johnson Library, Austin, Texas (hereinafter, LBJL).

[61] See speech to international affairs workshop sponsored by Unitarian Universalists at Star Island, NH, July 25, 1965, printed in *Register Leader*, October, 1965, pp. 3–4; and another version in *Congressional Record*, Senate, July 27, 1965. McGovern described the trip to Vietnam at a town meeting in Mitchell, *Daily Republic*, December 17, 1965 and in *Grassroots*, pp. 106–107.

[62] McPherson to Califano, February 23, 1966, White House Congressional file (file "M"), box 270, LBJL; author's interview with McGovern, December 30, 1997. See also LeRoy Ashby and Rod Gramer, *Fighting the Odds: The Life of Senator Frank Church* (Washington: Pullman, 1994), pp. 183–186 and 200–202; and David F. Schmitz and Natalie Fousekis, "Senator Frank Church, the Senate, and the Emergence of Dissent on the Vietnam War, 1963–1966," in *Pacific Historical Review* (August 1995), pp. 561–581.

At that point, no country in the history of warfare had been subjected to more intensive air assaults than Vietnam. American B-52s had rained down upon the "little piss-ant country," as LBJ referred to it, 1.5 million tons of bombs, a magnitude exceeding the combined tonnage dropped by all belligerents in World War II. Most of North Vietnam's infrastructure, such as it was, lay in ruins. Napalm and Agent Orange had destroyed literally half of South Vietnam's forests. In addition to hundreds of thousands killed, one in four South Vietnamese peasants was homeless. At year's end, nearly 16,000 American soldiers were dead, while troop levels had climbed beyond 500,000. In Saigon, two American-sponsored quasidictators, Nguyen Cao Ky and Nguyen Van Thieu, controlled the government. To accomplish these feats, the United States was spending $2 billion a month. And still, the capacity and the will of the National Liberation Front and the North Vietnamese seemed undiminished.[63]

In late April, 1967, President Johnson summoned General William C. Westmoreland home to tell the American people there was light at the end of the tunnel and to spurn the cowards, defeatists, and traitors within the antiwar movement and without. The pitch and substance of the public relations campaign – especially attacks on the patriotism of critics – angered McGovern. In response, on April 25, he made a momentous Senate speech that captured perhaps better than any other so far the depth and range of his thoughts. Published simultaneously in *The Progressive* magazine, "The Lessons of Vietnam" was historically well-informed, soundly reasoned, and (once again) remarkably prophetic in virtually all aspects. Indeed, decades later, it reads like the summary chapter of the best scholarly monographs on the subject.

The Vietnam conflict, McGovern began, represented "the most tragic diplomatic and moral failure in our national experience," for it was "degenerating into a defeat for America whether we 'win' or 'lose.'" He reminded his listeners of Douglas MacArthur's remark – that "'Anyone who commits American forces to a land war in Asia ought to have his head

---

[63] The historiography on the war is now enormous. But a good place to start is George C. Herring, *America's Longest War: The United States and Vietnam*, (New York, 1979; 3rd ed., 1996); Larry Berman, *Planning a Tragedy: The Americanization of the War in Vietnam* (New York, 1982); Marilyn Blatt Young, *The Vietnam Wars, 1945–1990* (New York, 1991); and Lloyd C. Gardner, *Pay Any Price: Lyndon Johnson and the Wars for Vietnam* (Chicago, 1995). Among the more recent, outstanding studies, see Fredrik Logevall, *Choosing War: The Lost Chance for Peace and the Escalation of War in Vietnam* (Berkeley, CA, 1999); David Kaiser, *American Tragedy: Kennedy, Johnson, and the Origins of the Vietnam War* (Cambridge, MA, 2000); and Robert Mann, *Grand Delusions, America's Descent into Vietnam* (New York, 2001).

examined'" – and warned that if the fighting continued the consequences would be severe, that "dreams of a Great Society and a peaceful world will turn to ashes."

He also noted that only "by a crude misreading of history and a distortion of our most treasured ideals" was the administration able to rationalize its actions. He then spoke of the warhawks' incessant invocations of Hitler and Munich and the domino theory. "This, I think, is a piece of historical nonsense," McGovern said. "There is no analogy between Munich and Vietnam, and countries are not dominoes." As for tyrants, ironically, Adolf Hitler was Vice President Ky's "only political hero." Ho Chi Minh, though a Marxist, was first, last, and always a nationalist, and the struggle he led "grew out of local conditions." For this was "essentially a civil conflict among various groups of Vietnamese," not one of northern aggression against neighbors to the south, as the administration claimed. In any case, the challenge of communism could not be met "by forcing an American solution on a people still in search of their own national identity." The United States had "no obligation to play policeman...especially in Asia, which is so sensitive to heavy-handed interference by even well-meaning white men." Above all, Americans must learn that "conflicts of this kind have historical dimensions that are essentially political, economic, and psychological; they do not respond readily to military force from the outside." Moreover, "corrupt regimes" like the one in Saigon "do not deserve to be saved by the blood of American boys." Congress, he concluded, "must never again surrender its power under our constitutional system by permitting an ill-advised, undeclared war," thus rendering its function "very largely one of acquiescence." Dissent among his colleagues recently had been sharp; but, alas, "it has come late in the day."[64]

From this pass onward McGovern would grow ever more vehement (some observers said "obsessive") in his views. The baleful events of 1968 – the Tet Offensive, Johnson's retreat from politics, the assassinations of Martin Luther King and Robert Kennedy, and the disastrous Democratic National Convention in Chicago, where McGovern himself, urged on by Kennedy's bereft disciples, launched a last-minute

---

[64] McGovern, "The Lessons of Vietnam, April 25, 1967, *Congressional Record*, Senate, 90th Congress, 1st session, reprinted in McGovern, *A Time of War*, pp. 128–145. McGovern still did not counsel an immediate withdrawal. His proposal actually approximated the Paris Peace Accords of some six years hence: a cease fire and a negotiated settlement (involving all parties, including the Vietcong) to be followed by internationally supervised elections, and then the withdrawal of all outside forces and the conversion of military bases to peacetime uses. Herein lay the "path to sanity and peace in southeast Asia."

campaign for the presidential nomination – would only increase that tendency.[65]

When Richard Nixon and Henry Kissinger took over the conduct of the war in January, 1969, and said to Fulbright, "Just give us a year," most Democrats seemed content to oblige.[66] After only two months, however, with American casualties still running as high as 2,000 a week, an impatient McGovern decided to abbreviate Nixon's honeymoon. "In the name of decency and common sense, there must be no further continuation of the present policy," he said in a hard-hitting floor speech on March 17. "I believe the only acceptable objective now is an immediate end to the killing." Not a single senator joined him that afternoon. For his troubles he was chastised in the press and on Capitol Hill as "precipitate."[67] Then, just before the Fourth of July, the graduation photographs of one week's dead, some 242 U.S. servicemen, appeared in *Life* magazine, their eyes staring out from the pages almost accusingly. The publication caused a sensation, and many members of both parties worried whether there really was an end in sight. Yet another McGovern speech, on July 2, prompted a remarkable colloquy. One by one, Fulbright, Church, McGee, Eagleton, and others stepped forward to rejoin the struggle and to commend the South Dakotan for his "intellectual and political courage" and for having "stood on this floor – alone – when others were maintaining a respectful honeymoon silence."[68]

The White House reacted to attacks like these by attempting to stigmatize McGovern and company as "neoisolationists," a reproach that neither he nor the others (especially Fulbright) was unused to hearing. But Nixon easily topped Lyndon Johnson; he had an unusually astringent Vice President, Spiro T. Agnew, to unleash on his tormentors. To the Midwestern Governors Conference, for example, Agnew denounced

---

[65] Author's interviews with McGovern, December 29, 1992, August 7, 1993, and December 30, 1997; and *Grassroots*, pp. 108–127.

[66] Woods, *Fulbright*, p. 504. The Chair of the SFRC was nonetheless pessimistic; *Ibid.*, pp. 504–506.

[67] *New York Times*, March 18, 1969; author's interview with McGovern, August 7, 1993; and transcripts of "The Evans and Novak Report," March 30, 1969, and "Issues and Answers," April 6, 1969, Speeches and Statements files, box March–May 1969, McGovern Papers. (On the latter program the Senator said: "These young men that are dying in Viet Nam, in my judgment, should not have their lives jeopardized because of any tradition of a hundred days silence.") See also Anson, *McGovern*, pp. 168–169.

[68] See "Vietnam, One Week's Dead, May 28–June 3, 1969," *Life*, June 27, 1969, pp. 20–32; and McGovern speech, "Vietnam and the Declaration of Independence," and Colloquy, July 2, 1969, *Congressional Record*, Senate, 91st Congress, 1st session.

the "self-professed experts" (alternately, the "Fulbright-crats" and the "McGovern-crats") whose "stock in trade [was] to downgrade patriotism" while "prolonging the war." At a convention of the Veterans of Foreign Wars, he wondered if "the isolationists in the Senate really give a damn" and assailed their proposals as "a blueprint for the first defeat in the history of the United States."[69]

Against the likes of McGovern and Fulbright, the charge of neoisolationism – a contrivance of infinite resilience since the 1960s – was as absurd as it was disingenuous. In their unwavering patronage of the United Nations, of intercultural exchange, and of the principle of international cooperation and the peaceful settlement of disputes, they had no peers. But, of course, that was the problem. As McGovern once had written sarcastically when the accusation was leveled by the Johnson White House, "A preference for the peacekeeping actions of the United Nations over freewheeling unilateral interventionism . . . is a sure sign of 'neo-isolationism.' "[70] In a very real sense, none of the antagonists was an isolationist. Since 1945, the larger contention was, in fact, between two competing forms of internationalism – one, "progressive," the other, "conservative" – and Vietnam had become its crucible. As exemplars of progressive internationalism, McGovern and Fulbright's great sin was to have rejected the American obsession with national sovereignty and to have shunned "strategic monstrosities" that failed to apprehend the limits of American power. Increasingly appalled by Vietnam, they began to draw sharper distinctions between, on one hand, the authentic internationalism of balanced justice and cooperation, of which they were the great champions, and, on the other hand, unilateralist Cold War globalism and the impulse to hegemonic power. In responding to *its* practitioners, McGovern used the term, "neo-imperialist."

By the spring of 1970, Nixon had been in office nearly a year and a half. His "secret plan" for closing down the war had proved to be a transparent

[69] Agnew quoted in Woods, *Fulbright*, p. 531, and the *New York Times*, August 18, 1970. (For McGovern, Hatfield, and Fulbright's reply, see *Ibid.*, August 19, 1970.) In other statements, Agnew referred to them as "troglodytic leftists" and opined, "Ultraliberalism today translates into a whimpering isolationism in foreign policy . . . and a pusillanimous pussy-footng on the critical issue of law and order." ("Let Us Elevate the Rhetoric," compiled by Democratic National Committee, September 1970, in Campaign Issues 1972, box 6, McGovern papers.)

[70] "Foreign Policy and the Crisis Mentality," *Atlantic Monthly*, January, 1967, reprinted in *A Time of Peace, A Time of War*, p. 178.

campaign deception and "Vietnamization" had little credibility. Though he had begun the process of piecemeal deescalation, hundreds of thousands of American soldiers remained in Southeast Asia and the intensity of the bombing campaign was approaching (eventually to exceed) the equivalent of yet another World War II. McGovern's faith in the search for "peace with honor" was exhausted. He now believed that, if the policy were ever to change, Congress would have to exercise the power of the purse. And so, he looked about for a legislative remedy. His on-staff foreign-policy specialist, John Holum, pointed out that a bill actually to terminate the war would never get to the floor. But, Holum suggested, if the measure took the form of an amendment to a pending bill, the Senate would have to vote on it.[71]

For such an undertaking, McGovern needed a reliable Republican cosponsor. It was almost inevitable that his choice would be Mark Hatfield of Oregon, the war's staunchest foe within the GOP. A naval officer during World War II, Hatfield had always believed, in part on the basis of his assignment to Hanoi in the autumn of 1945, that the United States had erred from the moment it had lent support to the French colonial war against Ho Chi Minh. For his persistence, he had not only incurred the wrath of Lyndon Johnson, but also eventually wound up on Nixon's infamous "enemies list." Hatfield welcomed McGovern's invitation.[72]

The two senators rested their proposition on a historical as well as a political foundation. They prepared and circulated a pamphlet of evidence from the past, with an emphasis on the Mexican War – another war "unnecessarily and unconstitutionally begun by the President" (as a censorious congressional resolution of 1848 had asserted). From the pens of Hamilton, Adams, Marshall, Madison, Webster, and Lincoln, among others, they made their case – that the "whole powers of war" were "vested in Congress" (as Marshall had opined) and that to "[a]llow the President to invade a neighboring nation whenever he shall deem it necessary" was to "allow him to make war at his pleasure" (as Lincoln once had warned). Thus Vietnam illustrated how badly the war power had deteriorated – "and for only one reason," John Holum explained to

---

[71] Interview with John Holum, Nov. 17, 1994; and with McGovern, August 7, 1993. (Holum later served in the Clinton administration as Director of the U.S. Arms Control and Disarmament Agency, 1993–99, and as Undersecretary of State, 1999–2001).

[72] Interview with Mark Hatfield, October 7, 1994. (Hatfield had placed Nixon's name in nomination at the 1960 Republican convention and had seconded his nomination in 1968.)

potential cosponsors. "Congress has not insisted that its prerogative be respected."[73]

On April 30, 1970 – only hours before American and South Vietnamese forces invaded Cambodia – McGovern and Hatfield introduced their amendment to the Military Procurement Authorization bill. The rider would have prohibited the use of funds to support American military operations in Southeast Asia after December 31, 1970, and would have set a timetable for an orderly withdrawal of combat troops by June 30, 1971 – barring a declaration of war. The so-called Amendment to End the War was the first serious attempt by either house of Congress to reclaim its exclusive grants to raise and support armies and to declare war.[74]

This dramatic initiative was the culmination of years of frustration on the part of *many* members of Congress. At the same time, more specifically, it proceeded from McGovern's perspective that the war, while killing tens of thousands of G.I.s and hundreds of thousands of Vietnamese, also was relentlessly devouring precious resources and degrading the quality of American life and politics. Unemployment and war-induced inflation, now both at six percent, had practically doubled since Johnson left office. The investment in the blood-soaked jungle continued to drain American gold reserves. Great American cities and universities were in turmoil. Nixon had vetoed major health and education bills, and disapproved of McGovern's proposals for an expansion of the Food Stamp program. As part of its southern electoral strategy, the White House had slammed the brakes on school desegregation. And, just as important, McGovern and Hatfield were deeply troubled by the temper of the antiwar movement as well as the president's statements that "under no circumstances" would he be affected by peace demonstrations.[75]

---

[73] See *The Amendment to End the War: The Constitutional Question*, "Material Submitted by the Senate Steering Committee... for a Vote on the War (Not Printed at Government Expense)," copy in series 329-78-229, box 37, McGovern Papers; interview with John Holum, November 17, 1994.

[74] See Amendment 609, attached to H. R. 17123, referred to the Armed Services Committee, May 5, 1970, Congressional *Record*, 91st Congress, 2nd session, copy in series 329-78-229, senator's personal amendments file/Legislative Hist 1970, McGovern papers.

[75] See, for example, McGovern speeches at the Colorado Jefferson-Jackson Day Dinner, March 21, 1970, and the Allegheny County Labor Council, in Pittsburgh, April 12, 1970, Speeches and Statements files, Feb.–March and April, 1970, McGovern Papers; and author's interview with Hatfield, October 7, 1994. Fulbright, too, was deeply distressed. "If the President is going to close his mind," he said, "the likely result will be disillusionment on the part of young people who still have faith in their country's democratic procedures and the swelling of the ranks of that dissident, violent minority whose excesses the President himself has so frequently and so eloquently deplored"

Indeed, a sense of alienation and powerlessness had begun to permeate the antiwar movement by 1970. (It was one thing to have driven Johnson from office, but quite another to get Nixon to close down the war.) This was manifest in a widening breach between radical activists in the minority and disillusioned young liberals in the majority, and all of them frustrated at every turn by the imperviousness of the political system.[76] Ironically, although his views placed him in the mainstream of the antiwar coalition, McGovern's relationship with it had always been uneasy. Invitations to speak at antiwar rallies – as he did, for instance, in November, 1969, before some 350,000 protesters gathered in Washington, D.C. for the "Mobilization" – always threw his staff into uncharacteristically rancorous arguments over whether he should attend. Moreover, despite the fact that by 1972 many voters would identify him with the counterculture as well as with "peaceniks," McGovern was a conventional, middle-aged, middle-class family man whose own children thought he was too conservative, and he was as bewildered as anyone of his generation by the way younger activists sometimes behaved and expressed themselves.[77] Without question, his entire career was a testament to the belief that dissent formed the marrow of American citizenship. "[T]he willingness to question and challenge all that we are and all we do" constituted the "higher patriotism," he averred in a commencement address at Grinnell College in 1967, to cite but one example. But he also deplored "the folly of undisciplined radicalism," as he called it when, in August, 1970, he condemned the late-night bombing of the University of Wisconsin's Math Center, which had only succeeded in killing an innocent graduate student. Violence of this sort was senseless, he said, and it alienated the very people whose support was essential to changing the system that had produced the war. "The blunt fact," he added two months later, "is that the

---

(Statement, Oct. 1, 1969, series 71, box 35, papers of J. William Fulbright, University of Arkansas).

[76] The best studies include Charles DeBenedetti and Charles Chatfield, *An American Ordeal: The Antiwar Movement of the Vietnam Era* (Syracuse, N.Y., 1990); Melvin Small, *Johnson, Nixon, and the Doves*; Melvin Small and William D. Hoover, eds., *Give Peace A Chance, Exploring the Vietnam Antiwar Movement* (Syracuse, NY, 1992); Todd Gitlin, *The Sixties: Days of Hope, Days of Rage* (NY, 1987); Terry Anderson, *The Movement and the Sixties* (NY, 1995); James Miller, *Democracy is in the Streets: From Port Huron to the Siege of Chicago* (NY, 1987); Paul Buhle, ed. *History and the New Left: Madison, Wisconsin, 1950–1970* (Philadelphia, 1990); Peter B. Levy, *American and the Sixties–Right, Left, and Center: A Documentary History* (Westport CT, 1998).

[77] All of his family members and political associates have characterized him so. See, for example, author's interview with Steven McGovern, December 29, 1995; John Holum, November 17, 1994; and George Cunningham, May 21, 1995.

violence-prone extremists on the left and the inflammatory Agnew-type orators on the right are natural allies."[78]

And yet McGovern realized how, after so many years of unabated war, his own more traditional methods and prescriptions for change might lack credibility from the perspective of not only radicals, but also many young antiwar liberals. And that made him all the more fearful for the future health of America's institutions of popular representation and civil debate. Few politicians were in greater demand on the campus speaker's circuit than McGovern and Hatfield. "We had been out there," the latter recalled. "We walked into those places. Students wanted some sort of focused leadership vehicle that they could get organized around, to mobilize and expand this concern."[79] McGovern and Hatfield thus intended to craft a "prudent alternative" to the rising radicalism within the movement – that is, to bring the war issue "fully within the political system."[80]

And so they submitted a measure that had teeth, one that would compel the Senate to take a stand and demonstrate, once and for all, the breadth of opposition within that chamber. Win or lose, they also hoped to give millions of Americans, especially the young, the opportunity to make their voices heard.[81] These considerations became even more acute after

---

[78] "The Folly of Undisciplined Radicalism," August 31, 1970, box 1A, McGovern Papers; Anson, *McGovern*, 173; and author's interview with McGovern, August 7, 1993. McGovern has recounted other incidents that he considered "cruelly self-defeating." For example, in 1971, with Coretta Scott King and Leonard Woodcock, he participated in a "March for Peace and Justice," in Atlanta. The march was an effort on the part of the Southern Christian Leadership Conference, the United Auto Workers, and various religious and antiwar groups to demonstrate their belief that the war must be ended in order "to begin rebuilding and the healing of America." When they entered the downtown area, McGovern recalled, "there was a young guy with his girlfriend, I guess, who had taken a flag and torn it up and turned it into a bikini for the girl and crude jock strap for the guy. They jumped in ahead of the parade, with a big sign saying, 'McGovern for President,' or something. I was furious because everything had been peaceful and constructive." As for the couple wrapped in the flag, "that's what played on television" (interview, August 7, 1993).

[79] Author's interview with Mark Hatfield, October 7, 1994. On this subject, see also, McGovern, "Reconciling the Generations," *Playboy* magazine, January 1970, 128, 132, and 266–67; Senate speech, May, 1970, copy in McGovern papers, series 327-78-229, box 37; and two other commencement addresses at Xavier University (of Chicago), June 4, 1969, and Dartmouth, June 13, 1970, Speeches and Statements files, June–August 1969 and June–July 1970, respectively.

[80] As DeBenedetti and Chatfield observed about McGovern's 1972 candidacy, in *An American Ordeal*, p. 3 (see also p. 242).

[81] On May 4, McGovern sent identical telegrams to the student body presidents of fifty major colleges and universities across the nation. "May I urge you to direct at least a portion of your efforts to supporting Congressional action to cut off further funds," he

April 30. Nixon's unexpected "incursion" into Cambodia set in motion the events at Kent State University, where Ohio National Guardsmen opened fire on student protesters, killing four and wounding eleven, on May 4. This tragedy, in turn, incited even greater demonstrations that shut down hundreds of campuses – "the most massive and shattering protest in the history of higher education," according to one authority.[82]

Suddenly the Amendment became what the authors hoped it would – the pivot for a wide variety of groups arrayed against the war. A few days after Kent State, McGovern and Hatfield (along with senators Frank Church, Harold Hughes, and Charles Goodell) arranged a $60,000 loan in order to produce a thirty-minute, televised discussion, on NBC, about the war and their initiative; a closing entreaty for funds to pay for the program garnered a record $500,000 from around the country. Starting in May, thousands of college students descended on Washington to lobby for the passage of "McGovern-Hatfield." The Amendment won the cosponsorship of twenty-five senators and the endorsement of preeminent legal scholars, and spurred the heaviest volume of letters ever to inundate the Capitol post office. Network news programs discussed it exhaustively. Then, in June, the Senate finally repealed the Gulf of Tonkin Resolution and passed the so-called Cooper-Church Amendment to terminate the Cambodian incursion – good auguries all around.[83] Even so, after a full summer of debate, a majority of senators could not be mustered for

enjoined them, adding, "I pledge to you that there will be an official roll call," series 329-78-229, box 37, McGovern papers.

[82] DeBenedetti and Chatfield, *An American Ordeal*, pp. 279–270. Ten days after the shootings at Kent State, Mississippi National Guardsmen killed two students and injured twelve more at all-black Jackson State University.

[83] See McGovern Senate speech on the Amendment, June 29, 1970, *Congressional Record*, Senate, 91st Congress, 1st session, copy in McGovern papers, series 329-78-229, box 37; *New York Times*, June 25, July 1, and September 2, 1970; and transcripts of "Issues and Answers" June 21 and August 22, 1970, and CBS News Special: "The Senate and the War," part I, June 5, 1970 and part II, August 29, 1970, in McGovern Papers, Speeches and Statements file, boxes, June 1970 and August 1970. See also DeBennetti and Chatfield, *An American Ordeal*, pp. 285–287. By August, in order to attract more supporters, McGovern and Hatfield had revised the Amendment: they pushed back the date for complete withdrawal from June 30 to December 31, 1971 and inserted an emergency provision to permit the president to extend the deadline for sixty days should circumstances so warrant; beyond that, Congress would have to give its explicit approval. The revision was intended to assuage senators who believed that a definite timetable was too extreme. Yet, the idea of shared responsibility between the Executive and Legislative for policy in Indochina remained intact. See McGovern to Senator Len Jordan, with enclosure (Amendment 609 – Proposed New Language), August 14, 1970, and Press Release, August 17, 1970, series 329-78-229, box 37, McGovern Papers.

the more far-reaching Amendment to End the War, and many privately
regarded it a lost cause.[84]

Perhaps by then McGovern did, too. For just before the final roll call,
on September 1, 1970, he allowed the emotional appeal to eclipse the
intellectual. Seven years earlier, the chamber was practically empty when
he had first spoken about Vietnam. On this morning, ninety-four senators
were in their seats, and the gallery above, where his family now sat, was
filled to overflowing. The atmosphere was at once electric and hushed.
McGovern took only three minutes to make his case – that the conflict
was no more the property of Johnson or Nixon than of those who let it
continue: The "cruelest, the most barbaric, and the most stupid war in
our national history" still raged because Congress had permitted its constitutional authority "to slip out of our hands until it now resides behind
closed doors ... [in] the basement of the White House," he declared.

And every senator in this chamber is partly responsible for sending 50,000 young
Americans to an early grave. This chamber reeks of blood. Every Senator here is
partly responsible for the human wreckage at Walter Reed and Bethesda Naval
and all across our land–young boys without legs, or arms, or genitals, or faces,
or hopes.... And if we don't end this foolish, damnable war, those young men
will some day curse us for our pitiful willingness to let the Executive carry the
burden that the Constitution places on us. So before we vote, let us ponder the
admonition of Edmund Burke, the great parliamentarian of an earlier day: "A
conscientious man would be cautious how he dealt in blood."[85]

Thirty-two Democrats and seven Republicans voted for the
Amendment to End the War. Twenty-one Democrats and thirty-four Republicans voted nay. It failed, according to Hatfield, because too many
senators "saw it as too radical." Nonetheless, the size of the tally in favor,
at forty-two percent, was significant. As Stephen Young, an Ohio Democrat, said, "Thirty-nine senators today have spoken out in clear and convincing terms that the United States must disengage and withdraw our

---

[84] For instance, Fulbright See Fulbright Office Memorandum, August 25, 1970, series 42:3,
box 6, Fulbright papers. Also, the public discourse was acrimonious. Senator Robert Dole
of Kansas called it "the Amendment to Lose the Peace," John Tower of Texas said that it
would "hamstring" the President, and John Sherman Cooper of Kentucky worried that
passage would undermine prospects for the on-going negotiations in Paris. For its part,
the White House, via Vice President Agnew, practically accused McGovern and Hatfield
of treason. (See *New York Times*, August 18 and 19 and September 1 and 2, 1970; "Issues
and Answers" transcript, August 22, 1970, cited above.)

[85] *Congressional Record*, Senate, 91st Congress, 1st session, September 1, 1970, and as a press
release, Speeches and Statements files, August–September, 1970, McGovern papers; and
author's interview with McGovern, August 7, 1993.

combat troops from Vietnam next year." Hatfield was wont to celebrate a "moral victory," as Nixon now would have to cope with "a quantitative factor" that told his war council "that they were losing public support." In retrospect, he came to see the Amendment as "the beginning of the end of the Vietnam War."[86]

Likewise, the outcome was both disappointing and gratifying for the Senator from South Dakota. The vote had fallen short of its potential to become the most significant one cast by the upper house since the Gulf of Tonkin resolution; yet, his and Hatfield's exertions had made Congress both the focus and the instrument, as it had never been before, of the broad-gauged antiwar movement. Then, too, he took solace in the fact that, in trying to do what he believed needed to be done, millions of people had gotten behind the endeavor. And so the seed was planted. In the end, the only way to change the policy was to change the White House. Five months later, in January, 1971, he announced his candidacy for president and began to wage what one might call a campaign for progressivism and peace, a campaign that stressed that as between domestic politics and foreign policy there was scarcely any difference. With Vietnam as his point of reference, he argued that the Cold War no longer could be permitted to deplete limited resources that the United States ought more wisely spend on programs for social betterment – whether at home or in Southeast Asia.

Although "Jimmy the Greek," the famous oddsmaker, rated his chances of winning the Democratic nomination at 200 to one, McGovern mounted a "grassroots" primary campaign and went on to capture the prize on the first ballot. His acceptance speech (delivered at 2:48 A.M. to a nonetheless ebullient throng) was entitled "Come Home, America." In this and other addresses, he pledged to end the war within ninety days of his inauguration; to pare down the defense budget and curtail military adventurism that propped up corrupt dictatorships; to begin the slow process of conversion to a peacetime economy; to establish a system of national healthcare; to expand opportunities for higher education; and to ensure that every able-bodied citizen had a job, provided by either the private sector or, if need be, the federal government. The program for the domestic life of the United States and the kind of role it might play in the world, then, were indivisible. "Lend me your strength and your support," he enjoined the

---

[86] Author's interview with Hatfield, October 7, 1994; *New York Times*, September 6, 1970. When another version of the Amendment came to the floor in June 1971, 42 senators voted for it and 55 against.

convention, "and together, we will call America home to the ideals that nourished us in the beginning."[87]

McGovern went down to defeat at the hands of Richard Nixon in one of the most lopsided elections in American political history.[88] But, in 1974, South Dakota sent him back to the senate just three months after Nixon resigned from office in disgrace. Within another year, in tandem with Watergate, the residual impact of "the McGovern movement" and its adherents' persistent prodding of Congress to reclaim its constitutional prerogatives at long last pulled the props out from under America's longest war.

Thereafter, the senator continued to speak out against foreign interventions and the nuclear arms race. In his bid for a fourth term, he was overwhelmed in the Reagan landslide of 1980. Retiring from national politics, he lectured on college campuses, appeared on public affairs television programs, and wrote a host of newspaper and magazine articles. His views did not change substantively over the years. By the 1990s he was still advocating a form of Wilsonian progressive internationalism rather than a post–Cold War incarnation of unilateralist globalism, an outlook that seemed to have gained at least some acceptance by the time Bill Clinton entered the White House.

In 1997, Clinton (who, along with many members of his administration, had worked on the '72 campaign) asked McGovern to represent the United States in Rome as the ambassador to three United Nations agencies dealing with food and agricultural issues (including the World Food Program, which he had helped to establish twenty-five years earlier).[89]

---

[87] "Come Home, America," his acceptance speech at Miami, Florida, July 13, 1972 is printed in *An American Journey, The Presidential Campaign Speeches of George McGovern* (New York, 1973), pp. 16–24. For the campaign, see Gary Warren Hart, *Right from the Start, A Chronicle of the McGovern Campaign* (New York, 1973); Theodore H. White, *The Making of the President 1972* (New York, 1973); and *Grassroots*, pp. 155–249.

[88] Only days after his nomination, McGovern's prospects suffered an irremediable blow when his running mate, Senator Thomas F. Eagleton, was forced off the ticket due to a previously undisclosed history of mental disorders.

[89] The list of "McGoverniks" includes Hillary Rodham Clinton (who, in 1972, assisted her future husband in Texas) and a number of former Clinton administration officials: National Security Adviser Samuel Berger and John Holum, Director of the United States Arms Control and Disarmament Agency (both of whom were McGovern campaign speechwriters); Eli Segal, one-time chief of Americorps; John Podesta, White House Chief-of-Staff; and Jeff Smith, Chairman of the President's Science Advisory Council. Other notables include Senate Majority Leader Tom Daschle, former senator Gary Hart, Judge Richard Stearns of the First Federal District, and Robert Shrum, Democratic party strategist.

During his service the elder statesman set about advancing detailed plans for lifting 500 million people (half of the world's underfed population) out of the grip of hunger by 2015. To that end, he also wrote a book, *The Third Freedom*, in which he recalled the achievements of Food for Peace and the successes that he and Senator Robert Dole had in the 1970s in expanding the domestic School Lunch and Food Stamp programs, thus eradicating hunger in America. The book also lamented President Reagan's cutbacks in Food Stamps and the Clinton administration's reductions in aid to families with dependent children – to the point where, at the turn of the millennium, thirty-one million Americans did not have enough to eat. In a fine alloy of idealism and realism, he went on to explain how it was possible to end hunger in the world by the third decade of the twenty-first century – if only the United States, working with the United Nations and the international community, would make that goal a priority.[90]

McGovern set the mission on course in May, 2000, when he persuaded President Clinton to pledge significant start-up resources for an international school lunch program for the world's 300 million malnourished children. Two months later, with Bob Dole at his side, he testified before the Senate Agriculture Committee, whose members warmly countersigned the enterprise. In a White House ceremony in August, 2000, McGovern was awarded the Presidential Medal of Freedom. The following January, at the request of Secretary of State Colin Powell, he agreed to stay on at his post in Rome – one of a small number of Clinton ambassadorial appointments to be retained by the George W. Bush administration. In 2002, the United Nations itself offered him the position of "Global Ambassador on Hunger," which he accepted.[91]

There is a certain, eloquent symmetry to this latest chapter of McGovern's career. Among other things, it is a felicitous reminder of the cast of his bid for the presidency, a campaign which remains unique in the annals of contemporary American history. For he presented to his fellow citizens what amounted to a critical treatise on the American Century – an analysis that continues to hold implications for interventionism (and its consequences) in the Third World; for the armaments race and the use of

---

[90] George McGovern, *The Third Freedom, Ending Hunger in Our Time* (New York 2001); McGovern to Thomas J. Knock, June 12, 1998. See also, "Interview – George McGovern," by Carl P. Leubsdorf, *Dallas Morning News*, April 5, 1998, front-page Sunday editorial section.

[91] McGovern, *The Third Freedom*, pp. 25–28; Jacqueline Salmon, "The President's Honor Role," *Washington Post*, August 10, 2000; McGovern to Knock (telephone interview), January 30 and December 1, 2001.

force in international relations; for the political economy of the United States relative to other great industrial powers; and, not the least, for the very nature of the nation's political and social institutions. Yet perhaps the most striking thing about this tentative epilogue may be the consistency of the whole of his life's work, not to mention its intrinsic qualities and tangible results: that is, on one hand, his unrelenting sense of duty to explore alternatives to what he regarded as the cumulative perversions of Containment and, on the other, his enduring faith in the possibilities for national redemption through authentic internationalism, education, and humanitarian endeavor. In a sense, George McGovern continues to beckon, "Come Home, America."

Congress Must Draw the Line

Senator Frank Church and Opposition to the Vietnam War and the Imperial Presidency

David F. Schmitz

The career of Senator Frank Church (D-ID) provides a unique perspective for understanding the development of opposition to the Vietnam War and the anti-imperialist position during the 1960s and 1970s. From his first speech in February, 1965, criticizing Operation Rolling Thunder and United States policy in Vietnam to his opposition to the Ford administration's efforts to prevent the final fall of the Saigon government in 1975, no senator had a longer career of opposition to the Vietnam War or a greater impact on American foreign policy than Frank Church. His early opposition to the war in Vietnam helped to provide legitimacy to the then struggling antiwar movement and marked the beginning of a decade-long struggle with the Executive branch concerning the constitutional balance of power and the nature of American foreign policy. Central to Church's critique was his conviction that the American obsession with communism led to an interventionist foreign policy that was damaging to the national interest. In order to change this policy, Church sought to reintroduce to the making of American foreign policy the principles and ideals of the nation, and restore the Senate's constitutional role. Church believed that the United States needed to be willing to accept change in the world and have faith in its own institutions and values as guides to diplomacy.

I want to thank Alan Virta and Mary Carter of the Frank Church Papers, Boise State University, for their generous assistance, and Randall Woods and Amy Portwood for their comments on earlier drafts. My colleagues at Whitman College who make up the "Symposium" reading group, Paul Apostolidis, Julia Davis, Tom Davis, Susan Ferguson, Tim Kaufman-Osborn, Jeannie Morefield, Lynn Sharp, and Bob Tobin, read a final draft and made numerous suggestions to improve this work.

First elected to the Senate from Idaho in 1956, Church quickly rose in prominence in the Democratic Party. He attracted the attention of Senate majority leader Lyndon Johnson who appointed him to the Senate Foreign Relations Committee (SFRC) in 1958. In 1960, John F. Kennedy tapped Church to deliver the keynote address at the Democratic National Convention. By the time of his reelection in 1962, Church had established himself as a person whose views on foreign policy were well respected. His persistent opposition to the war brought him to national prominence and an increasingly influential position within the Senate as more of the nation came to agree with his interpretation of the war and critique of American foreign policy. In the wake of the war, Church would chair the Senate Select Committee on Intelligence in 1975 (Church Committee), that investigated abuses of power by the FBI, multinational corporations, and in particular the CIA, and developed new restrictions on executive action.

The bases of Church's antiwar position, which included broader opposition to American Cold War policies and the "Imperial Presidency," were shaped prior to his election to the Senate. Church came from a tradition of western political independence and progressivism best exemplified by his boyhood idol, Republican Senator William Borah of Idaho. His views were also shaped by Franklin D. Roosevelt and American involvement in World War II. While this at first appears contradictory, especially given Borah's isolationism and opposition to U.S. involvement overseas during the growing international crisis of the 1930s, Church drew inspiration from both men in their opposition to organized wealth and monopolistic power over the economy. World War II led Church to reject his youthful support of Borah's isolationist position, but he still admired his independence of thought, resistance to entangling alliances, and willingness to combat the leaders of his own party. Moreover, he shared Borah's anti-imperialist position and opposition to American intervention abroad that was central to western progressivism. Church represented the intersection of New Deal and Progressive thought, and the seeds of his opposition to the war were present in both. Building on this tradition, Church was able to challenge the prevailing postwar consensus on containment.

Church's opposition to the Vietnam War developed in three stages. Initially, he limited his dissent to questioning the war's necessity and initiating public debate concerning American escalation. Church saw the war as bad policy and a mistaken application of the containment doctrine. By the late 1960s, however, he had concluded that the war was a symptom of a larger problem facing the nation and turned to congressional action to bring the war to an end. By the end of the war, Church was engaged in a sustained effort to change the assumptions and conduct of American foreign policy.

Church readily acknowledged that Borah was "the idol of my boyhood days," and that he continually looked to his career for guidance. Church saw Borah as "splendidly independent," and willing to make "things uncomfortable for men in high station, both in and out of his own party." The "Lion of Idaho" more often than not opposed his party's position on foreign policy, particularly its support of intervention in Latin America. Borah, whom Church termed the "country's foremost spokesman in matters of foreign policy," was in office during a period when there was a proper balance between the executive branch and the Senate in the making of the nation's foreign policy.[1]

In a 1964 speech, Church outlined the importance of Borah's ideas on his own thinking. He saw Borah as the champion of a democratic foreign policy, which meant to Church openness in the conduct of policy, respect for the Constitution, and a commitment to anti-imperialism. Borah, he noted, had a great deal of respect for the press and was "ardent in his belief in the commonsense of the American people, and so he held that diplomacy should be conducted in full view of the public." He believed that Idahoans and the American public respected and often supported Borah's dissent because he always paid "homage to the Constitution," placed his faith "in the wisdom of the Founding Fathers," and demonstrated "respect for fundamental American morality." Borah, Church noted, "was the friend and champion of the smaller countries," could sympathize with revolutionaries in their efforts to promote social progress, and understood that American intervention in Latin America and elsewhere bred a "deep-seated hostility . . . toward the United States." Church declared that "to those who still cannot see that we are . . . harvesting the bitter fruits of our earlier 'gunboat diplomacy' in the Caribbean, and who seem to think that American bayonets will stifle, rather than spread, the seed of communism, I offer the words of Borah in refutation, and I defy anyone to gainsay the prophetic quality of the warnings he sounded many years ago" in his condemnation of American intervention in Cuba, Nicaragua, the Dominican Republic, and Haiti.

[1] Church, "The Role of Borah in American Foreign Policy," March 26, 1964, Frank Church papers, series 8.1, box 4, folder 96, Boise State University, Boise, Idaho (hereafter Church papers followed by series/box/folder).

Most important for Church, so much of what Borah stood for "still remain[s] applicable to our life and times. I think of his reluctance to use force, his anti-imperialism, and his toleration of diversity in the world at large." Who in the 1960s would, Church asked, defend American colonies or the notion of the white man's burden in the Philippines? Yet, "in today's world, where we have permitted ourselves to become so massively involved that we regard every little country's frontier, no matter how remote, as our responsibility, do we not wonder whether we haven't extended our commitments beyond our capacity to fulfill? Was there not some wisdom to Borah's attempt to limit the American sphere of influence?"[2]

This sensitivity to imperialism was central to the Western progressive tradition that influenced Church. It stemmed from the West's own colonial economic relationship to the east. Borah and other western progressives inveighed against the exploitation of large eastern corporations that drained wealth from the west without providing for the development of local markets or manufacturing. Thus they were able to understand the complaints of others concerning outside domination and economic exploitation. Paradoxically, they called upon the same federal government that sponsored imperialism abroad to regulate business and provide the West with its share of the nation's wealth. The coming of the New Deal, and then the massive development of the West prompted by federal policies during World War II, transformed many of these progressives, including a young Frank Church, into liberal Democrats. Investments and programs by the federal government promoted local development and in the process freed local people from outside domination. World War II also led Church to break with Borah on the issue of supporting international organizations such as the United Nations. Yet the differences here are not as great as they first appear. While Borah was a leading opponent of the League of Nations and other international organizations, his opposition stemmed mainly from his fear that membership would entangle the United States in the defense of European imperial holdings and promote American intervention abroad while damaging democratic institutions at home. Church endorsed membership in the United Nations because he believed it would help promote international cooperation and a world without imperialism. It would, therefore, act as a brake against unilateral American action and intervention overseas that

[2] Ibid.

he feared would harm the nation's democratic character and republican institutions.

Church drew upon this Western progressive tradition to question policy in Vietnam and to open up a public debate on the war. In the initial phase of his dissent, Church saw American policy as a mistaken application of the containment policy to a nonvital area of the world. The U.S., Church maintained, had no fundamental interests in Vietnam. Instead, it was being blinded by a rigid anticommunism that was leading it to intervene globally against its best interests. The problem Church faced throughout 1964–65 was how to criticize American policy while still backing the new president, Lyndon Johnson, whose domestic programs he fully supported. Church moved with caution, focusing his comments on the need for new ideas and options beyond the employment of American force.

Central to Church's misgivings about the war was his belief that the struggle was primarily nationalistic and anticolonial. Ho Chi Minh, he noted, was regarded by most Vietnamese "as the authentic architect of independence from the French, as the George Washington of Vietnam, so to speak." A greater military effort by the United States, Church argued, promised little improvement and threatened to involve China directly as it had in the Korean War. The "war in South Vietnam is their war, not ours," and while aid was necessary, he did not "believe that the people of Vietnam in the jungles and in the countryside draw the distinction we draw between American and French uniforms."[3] That is, they saw America as just another colonial power. In place of force, Church urged that the United States seek a negotiated settlement. "If experience proves anything at all," Church declared in a June, 1964, Senate speech, "it is that upheaval among the black, brown, and yellow peoples, now emerging in their own right throughout Africa and Asia, is not likely to be assuaged for long through the unilateral intervention of any white nation." The UN, he believed, could oversee negotiations because it "has proved to be theirs, as well as ours," and could play the role of "honest broker."[4] As Church would later recall, he used the term "negotiated settlement" when it was a "dirty word in Washington."[5]

In private, Church's criticisms of American policy were much sharper. Upon returning from a fact-finding mission in Vietnam, Church noted

[3] *Washington Evening Star*, March 15, 1964.
[4] *Congressional Record*, 88 Congress, 2 session, 1964, pp. 14790–14796.
[5] Church papers, 10.6/8/1.

that "the war was being lost because of the lack of Vietnamese public support for the government."[6] He wrote Undersecretary of State George Ball that he "saw nothing in South Vietnam . . . to mitigate my fears that we may be only digging the grave deeper there."[7] In questioning Secretary of State Dean Rusk during an executive session of the SFRC, Church argued that "the very character of the fight necessarily means that it will either be won or lost by these people themselves. It cannot be won, we cannot win it for them." He contested Rusk's analysis of the war as a "free world" contest with Communism whose successful outcome would block China's quest for world revolution. It was, he argued, "a continuation of the revolution that commenced much earlier, and did not end with the defeat of the French." When Rusk insisted that China was trying to "engulf Southeast Asia," Church responded that the "great bulk of the revolutionaries are South Vietnamese" who viewed Ho Chi Minh "as the authentic architect of independence." The United States was "going to find that we can provide no solution there ultimately and we will be faced with an impossible situation."[8]

Still, Church continued to support the Johnson administration publicly, in no small part because of his fear of Richard Nixon's and Barry Goldwater's militancy and calls for direct attacks on North Vietnam. By contrast, Church believed Johnson's actions were moderate and still offered the hope for a peaceful resolution.[9] Focused on the upcoming election between Johnson and Goldwater, Church voted in favor of the Gulf of Tonkin Resolution in August, 1964. This was a vote, he later confessed, that he "regretted . . . to the end of his life."[10] At the time he, like other leading Democrats, including J. William Fulbright, the Chairman of the SFRC who steered the resolution through the Congress, believed the administration's claim that two attacks had occurred, that both were

---

[6] William Conrad Gibbons, *The U.S. Government and the Vietnam War: Executive and Legislative Roles and Relationships. Part II: 1961–1964*, (Princeton University Press: Princeton, 1986), p. 143; on Church's trip to Vietnam see "Study Mission to Southeast Asia: November–December 1962," Senate Documents 88–12, 88 Congress, 1 session, March 15, 1963; Church's notes from his trip, Church papers, 8.2/2.2/18.

[7] Church to Ball, May 8, 1963, Church papers, 2.2/26/18.

[8] Senate Committee on Foreign Relations, Declassified Records, "Briefing by Secretary of State Dean Rusk on the Situation in Southeast Asia," June 15, 1964, Record Group 46, National Archives.

[9] Church, "The Private World of Barry Goldwater," *Frontier*, November, 1963, pp. 5–7; and Church, "Stemming the Goldwater Flood," speech September 19, 1963, Church papers, 8.1/4/54.

[10] F. Forrester Church, *Father and Son: A Personal Biography of Senator Frank Church of Idaho by His Son* (New York: Harper and Row, 1985), 59.

unjustified, and that Johnson was a "man of peace" committed to keeping the war from escalating.[11]

As the situation in South Vietnam continued to deteriorate throughout the fall of 1964, Church spent more and more time studying the conflict and searching for a means to prevent an American escalation of the war. In particular, Church was impressed with the reporting of David Halberstam and the writing of political scientist Hans Morganthau. Church met Halberstam in November, 1964, to discuss his recently published *Esquire* article that contended that the U.S. was supporting a corrupt, ineffective, and unpopular government in Saigon.[12] Morganthau's "Realities of Containment" questioned the administration's claim that the war in Vietnam was a fight to contain China. Instead, he argued, it was a civil war and he warned against further U.S. involvement. While Church did not accept the basic assumptions of realists such as Morganthau who focused primarily on the use of power, he did find support for his own understanding of the conflict in Morganthau's claim that the United States was overextending itself in an area of little importance. Church arranged a dinner meeting in early 1965 where the University of Chicago professor discussed his ideas with a group of senators and reporters.[13]

Increasingly frustrated by the continued turmoil in Vietnam and indications that the Johnson administration was planning to increase American participation in the war, Church sought to make U.S. policy the focus of national debate. To this end, he believed the SFRC should hold public hearings on the war. The Morganthau dinner was part of his strategy to persuade Fulbright to agree. So was his subsequent decision to be more public about his doubts concerning the war. In December, 1964, Church agreed to be interviewed by *Ramparts* magazine. His comments immediately became front-page news in the *New York Times*. Church voiced his fears about the growing American role and concomitant expansion of the

---

[11] Press Release, August 8, 1964, Church papers, 2.2/27/3; Randall Woods, *Fulbright: A Biography* (New York: Cambridge University Press, 1995), pp. 354–357; Edwin Moise, *Tonkin Gulf and the Escalation of the Vietnam War*, Chapel Hill, NC: University of North Carolina Press 1996).

[12] Church papers, 2.2/27/4; David Halberstam, "The Ugliest American in Vietnam," *Esquire*, LXII, November 1964, pp. 37–40, pp. 114–117.

[13] Hans Morganthau, "Realities of Containment," *New Leader*, June 8, 1964, pp. 3–6; Church to Morganthau, December 28, 1964, Morganthau to Church, December 31, 1964, Church to Morganthau, January 15, 1965, Church papers, 2.2/27/5. Those who attended the dinner-discussion included Senators Fulbright and Jacob Javits, Harry McPherson, and reporters David Broder, Chalmers Roberts, Max Frankel, and Richard Strout.

war, called for the U.S. to undertake "a major shift on Asia," and recommended a UN supervised plan for the neutralization of Southeast Asia. "The thing we must remember," he emphasized, "is that there is no way for us to win their war for them. It is a guerilla war, at root an indigenous revolution against the existing government."

The trenchant nature of Church's critique helps explain his emergence as the leader of the Senate's "doves." "Unless we come to accept the fact that it is neither within the power nor the interest of the United States to preserve the status quo everywhere, our policy is doomed to failure."[14] This was a direct challenge to the policy of containment and the premise that all areas of the globe had to be protected from monolithic communism. In rejecting the verities of Cold War logic, Church drew on the Western progressive tradition of opposition to intervention in smaller countries, anti-imperialism, and commitment to national self-determination. He called for both an abandonment of the bipolar world view that underlay containment and an acknowledgment of the limits of American power. In 1964–65, this was, in the eyes of many, tantamount to accepting defeat.

The escalation of the war that Church had feared and anticipated came in February with the initiation of the bombing campaign against North Vietnam, Operation Rolling Thunder. He responded on February 17, with a major address to the Senate. American actions were part of what he termed an "excess of interventionism" that had come to characterize American relations with the excolonial areas of the world. This intervention, Church contended, had two primary defects. "First, it exceeds our national capability; second, among the newly emerging nations, where the specter of Western imperialism is dreaded more than communism, such a policy can be self-defeating." Church again called for a political settlement in Vietnam, arguing that the United States had to recognize that only a local solution could end the conflict, not great power intervention. The idea that "everything which happens abroad is our business" had to be abandoned. That notion had led to an "intensely ideological view of the cold war." "We have come to treat 'communism,' regardless of what form it may take in any given country, as the enemy.... [W]e fancy ourselves as guardian of the 'free' world ... [and] seek to immunize this world against further Communist infection through massive injections of American aid, and, wherever necessary, through direct American intervention." This produced a misunderstanding of the roots of the Vietnam War

[14] *Ramparts*, January–February 1965, pp. 17–22; *New York Times*, December 27, 1964, p. 1.

and an exaggerated belief in the ability of the United States to determine the outcome of the fighting.[15]

Church, however, avoided directly attacking President Johnson. He hoped to maintain LBJ's confidence while steering him away from escalation and toward negotiations. "I'm reluctant to repudiate the President on Vietnam," Church acknowledged, "because, by doing so, I lose any chance that may be left to me to exert some moderating influence upon the future course of events."[16] Church's hope was short-lived. The day following Church's speech, Johnson invited him and twenty-five other senators to a series of briefings at the White House. That evening, Johnson told Church that "there was once a Senator who thought he knew more about war and peace than the President" and had "predicted there would be no war in Europe a brief two or three months before war broke out." The president mentioned no names, but he was referring to William Borah, who he knew was Church's hero. The current senator from Idaho responded that the "Presidential eagle ... held a bundle of arrows in one claw, and an olive branch in the other." While he approved of his use of the arrows, he thought "that this should be accompanied by an equally aggressive use of the olive branch." Johnson retorted that he had to use force because "Hanoi thinks I'm not in a negotiating position."[17]

Johnson's indication that negotiations were his goal, and his April 7 speech at Johns Hopkins University, gave Church hope that he was having some influence on the president. While Johnson warned that the U.S. would not withdraw, and was "prepared for a long continued conflict," he also indicated his willingness to open "unconditional discussions" with the North and offered $1 billion toward the development of the Mekong River.[18] Invited by Johnson to read the text of the speech the day

---

[15] Church, "Our Overinvolvement in Africa and Asia," Church papers, 8.1/4/136.

[16] Church, undated memorandum, April 1965, Church papers, 10.6/8/7; Church to Oboler, July 28, 1965, Church papers, 2.2/28/10; see also Gibbons, *U.S. Government and the Vietnam War: Part II*, pp. 275–277, 394–397.

[17] Church, undated memorandum, April 1965, Church papers, 10.6/8/7. It was from this meeting that the apocryphal Walter Lippmann story emerged. Johnson told members of the press that during his discussion of Vietnam with Church he asked him who he had talked to before giving his speech on Vietnam. When Church supposedly stated Lippmann, Johnson said he shot back, "Well Frank, next time you need a dam in Idaho, why don't you talk to Walter Lippmann." See David Schmitz and Natalie Fousekis, "Frank Church, the Senate, and the Emergence of Dissent on the Vietnam War," *Pacific Historical Review*, vol. LXIII, no. 4, November 1994, pp. 572–574.

[18] *Public Papers of the Presidents: Lyndon B. Johnson, 1965*, Washington, D.C., 1966, part I, pp. 394–399.

before he delivered it, Church recalled thinking that this was the "first break, the first indication, of a Presidential willingness to negotiate a settlement."[19]

Continued escalation of the war, however, led Church to question Johnson's sincerity and eventually to renew his criticisms. "Our continued bombings," he wrote in late April, "make me wonder whether the President's address was intended more as a ploy than as an expression of serious purpose."[20] By June, Church decided he again had to address the issue in the Senate. He spoke on what he termed "The Vietnam Imbroglio" and called upon his colleagues to discuss ways to facilitate a negotiated settlement. He suggested three steps: working through the United Nations, a U.S. commitment "to deal with representatives of the Vietcong" as part of any talks, and making self-determination for the people of South Vietnam the basis of any agreement. Ho Chi Minh, Church argued, saw his hopes for victory resting on the weakness of Saigon, not the will of Washington, and with good reason. "An endemic instability engulfs the city. One coup follows another with such frequency that correspondence with the Government might well be addressed: 'To Whom It May Concern.'" Negotiations represented the only means to salvage American prestige and avoid the danger of acting as a "global policeman with the duty of imposing a Pax American." Continued escalation and emphasis on military action, Church warned, were "actually working against our larger interests in Asia" of containing Chinese influence. The administration had to realize that the "war in Vietnam is as much a political struggle as it is a military one."[21]

What Church desired was a broader forum for discussion of the war. In late July, 1965, he again urged the SFRC to hold public hearings. In an executive session hearing, Church explained that the "impact of our inquiry is extremely limited on the Executive Department" due to the secret nature of the committee's hearings with administration officials. This left the president in control of the information that reached the American public. "Public hearings," he stated, would allow the committee to invite "a lot of very knowledgeable and gifted people to give us some balanced judgment as to the correctness of the course we are pursuing." There should be an examination of the "whole philosophical argument

---

[19] Frank Church, Oral History, Lyndon B. Johnson Library, Austin, Texas (hereafter Johnson Library).
[20] Church to Chase, April 21, 1965, Church papers, 2.2/28/8.
[21] "The Vietnam Imbroglio," June 24, 1965, Church papers, 2.2/28/8.

as it affects American foreign policy generally, which has led us into Vietnam."[22]

Church's appeal again fell on deaf ears as most members of the committee either accepted the same basic assumptions and policy of the administration or were unwilling to oppose the president publicly on an issue of national security. As summer gave way to fall and Johnson increased the number of American troops in Vietnam, Church gave up on the idea that he could influence the President and instead turned to the American people through the pages of the *New York Times Magazine*. In the article "How Many Dominican Republics and Vietnams Can We Take On?" he bluntly answered his own inquiry. In the twenty years since World War II, he explained, nationalist revolutions had exploded all over the world. Faced with that reality, "no nation – not even our own – possesses an arsenal so large, or a treasury so rich, as to damp down the fires of smoldering revolution throughout the whole awakening world." The United States had to "escape the trap of becoming so preoccupied with Communism ... that we dissipate our strength in a vain attempt to enforce a global guarantee against it." Church rejected the idea that there was any danger in Vietnam from China or the Soviet Union. Indeed, he believed that "as an international force under one directorate ... Communism is a bust. China and Russia are bitter enemies." The communist world, he concluded, "bears no resemblance to a monolithic mass." The United States should "exercise a prudent restraint and develop a foreign policy more closely tied to a sober assessment of our own national interests."[23]

In December, when Johnson ordered a pause in the bombing of North Vietnam, Church saw the action as mainly a gesture to pacify administration critics.[24] Church feared that the president had lost touch with reality, had "personalized the war," and was "losing his capacity to render objective judgment."[25] Johnson, Church concluded, had come "to regard Vietnam as some kind of Asian Alamo."[26] When the bombing halt failed

---

[22] Senate Committee on Foreign Relations, *Executive Sessions of the Senate Foreign Relations Committee*, Historical Series, vol. XVII, 89 Congress, 1 session 1965, (Washington, D.C., 1990), pp. 939–53.

[23] Church, "How Many Dominican Republics and Vietnams Can We Take On?" *New York Times Magazine*, November 28, 1965, 44–45, 177–178.

[24] Church to Chase, January 20, 1966, Church papers, 2.2/29/8.

[25] Gibbons, *U.S. Government and the Vietnam War: Executive and Legislative Roles and Relationships, Part III: January–July, 1965,* (Princeton University Press: Princeton, NJ, 1989) p. 310.

[26] Frank Church, Oral History, Johnson Library.

to produce serious negotiations, and with the prospect of a lengthy and ever escalating war looming large, Church finally succeeded in convincing Fulbright to hold public hearings in February, 1966. To Church, the significance of the hearings was profound. As he recalled, "once it became apparent to the American people that there were members of this committee, who obviously were good, loyal Americans, knowledgeable in public affairs and informed on foreign policy, who disagreed with the war" and its continued escalation, "then the general resistance to the war and the debate itself over the war began to spread in the country. But if we had not gone out from behind closed doors, this never would have happened."

During the hearings, Church went immediately to the heart of what he considered the fundamental flaw in American policy: a failure to recognize the difference between the type of aggression the United States faced in Europe and the revolution that was taking place in Vietnam. On the first day of the hearings he expressed his concern to Secretary of State Dean Rusk. "I gather that wherever a revolution occurs against an established government, and that revolution ... is infiltrated by Communists, that the United States regards it in its interests to prevent the success of the Communist uprising." Church saw such a policy as "self-defeating" and urged the Secretary to focus on the question, "How can we best cope with the phenomena of revolt in the underdeveloped world in the years ahead?"[27]

Containment worked well in Europe, Church believed, because of shared values and institutions. The fundamental mistake of American policy was believing that a "design that was suitable for Europe would also be suitable for those regions of the world that have just thrust off European rule," and failing to recognize "how very different the underlying situation was in Asia and Africa."[28] Church believed the United States had to play an active role in world affairs, yet he was in agreement with the sentiment expressed in 1821 by John Quincy Adams that the United States should not go abroad "in search of monsters to destroy"; the country was better served by the "countenance of her voice, and by the benignant sympathy of her example." If it continued to intervene around the world, it might "become the dictatress of the world." But it "would no longer be the ruler of her own spirit."[29]

---

[27] J. William Fulbright, ed., *The Vietnam Hearings*, (Vintage: New York, 1966), pp. 52–56.
[28] Ibid., p. 136.
[29] Ibid., p. 115.

The Senate hearings marked Church's effort to apply American principles to the policy of Cold War intervention. He believed that only a full, painful open debate could turn American policy around. Aware of the limits of his power as a United States senator, and especially conscious that as a Democratic senator he was supposed to support the party's president, Church sought out a wider forum for his views. Following Borah's example of independence and dissent, Church helped establish the parameters of dissent that were vital to the emergence of opposition in the Senate and the nation. He brought a distinct philosophy and regional tradition to the debate, attributes that in turn allowed him to view the conflict in Vietnam from an anti-imperialist perspective rather than through the prism of the Cold War. While his role as the leading voice of dissent in the Senate would be eclipsed by Fulbright due to the latter's position as chair of the SFRC, Church played a crucial role in shaping public opinion toward the war and eroding the postwar consensus on containment.

In the end, the Church-Fulbright public relations campaign proved inadequate as a means for bringing the war to an end. The continued escalation convinced Church by 1969 that the war was not merely a policy mistake but a symptom of a larger problem: executive dominance of the foreign policy-making process that allowed the president to continue policies even if they were unpopular with the nation. This led him to the second phase of his opposition to the Vietnam War, efforts to control the president's freedom in conducting policy and bring an end to the war through congressional action. Church now insisted that unless Congress gained a greater control over policy, the war would expand to all of Southeast Asia, continue indefinitely, and, moreover, threaten constitutional government in the United States. Out of this concern would emerge the landmark Cooper-Church and Case-Church amendments. Again, Church was drawing on a Western progressive perspective that saw excessive American intervention abroad as not only misguided, but dangerous to the democratic institutions of the nation.

In June, 1969, Church compared the growth of executive power, and the creation of the "Imperial Presidency," to the Caesars' grab for power in ancient Rome, and predicted similar negative consequences for the Senate and the Republic unless action was taken to restore the constitutional balance of power. In his speech "Of Presidents and Caesars," Church spoke on the decline of constitutional government in the making of American foreign policy. The president reminded him of those Roman rulers who "subtly and insidiously ... stole their powers away from an unsuspecting Senate." The "Senate has acquiesced, while Presidents have steadily drawn to themselves much of the power delegated to Congress by the Constitution." He noted that "as crisis has followed upon crisis in these last thirty years, the concentration of power in the hands of the President has grown ever more rapidly, while the Congress has been reduced to virtual impotence in the making of foreign policy." Church argued that the Vietnam War demanded that constitutional issues be addressed "because nothing less than the survival of Constitutional government is at stake. Our democratic processes ... are being undermined by the very methods we have chosen to defend these processes against real or fancied foreign dangers."[30]

Matching deeds with words, Church moved in 1969–70 to limit the executive's power and bring the war to an end. The first step, as he saw it, was for Congress to limit the area of the war in order to contain its scope. Such a move would simultaneously begin to force a change in American policy and lead to the reassertion of the role of the Senate in the making of foreign policy.[31] It was crucial, Church surmised, that the senators who opposed the war win in their first major confrontation with the Nixon White House and effectively demonstrate the Senate's ability to limit the power of the president. A defeat caused by overreaching might divide the opposition and actually enhance Nixon's ability to continue the war. That many Senators feared being blamed for a failure to win the war made a piecemeal strategy all the more attractive to Church.[32]

In the fall of 1969, Church began to work with John Sherman Cooper (R-KY) on bi-partisan measures to restrict the power of the president. Cooper was one of the first Republicans to publicly oppose the war, and he and Church complemented each other in their battles to limit the power of the presidency and bring an end to the war. Known as a maverick among Republicans, Cooper was more than willing to cross the aisle to work with Democrats. Moreover, both strongly believed that Congress had a constitutional right to play a role in foreign affairs, checking presidential power, and agreed that the opposition had to work in stages to counter the Executive's actions effectively.[33]

---

[30] Church, "Of Presidents and Caesars: The Decline of Constitutional Government In the Conduct of American Foreign Policy," June 19, 1969, Church papers 8.1/6/12.

[31] LeRoy Ashby and Rod Gramer, *Fighting the Odds: The Life of Senator Frank Church*, (Pullman, WA, Washington State University Press: 1994), p. 293.

[32] Author's Interview with Bethine Church, May 27, 1992.

[33] On Cooper see Robert Schulman, *John Sherman Cooper: The Global Kentuckian*, (Lexington: The University Press of Kentucky, 1976).

Church was under no illusions about the Nixon administration's commitment to total victory in Vietnam. On May 15, 1969, the day after Nixon's first major address on the Vietnam War, Church told a national audience on NBC's the *Today Show* that he was disappointed. "We've waited for months for Mr. Nixon to reveal his plans for ending the war in Vietnam; he said he had one during the campaign. His statement last night was merely a restatement of the position that President Johnson had taken many times." He rejected the idea that the United States had to stay to fulfill its commitment to the South Vietnamese. "We've done everything that can be done to fulfill our commitment," Church stated. "If, by now, the Saigon Government cannot field an army in its own country against an enemy, that, after all, is no larger than they ... then they never are going to be."[34]

Church attacked "the favored euphemism ... 'honorable settlement,' " as a mask for continued war. "It is time to stop the prideful nonsense about winning an 'honorable settlement' and avoiding a 'disguised defeat'; it is time to acknowledge the failure of our involvement in Vietnam." The only obligation the United States government has is "to the American people." Church concluded that "national interest shows compelling reasons why we must extricate ourselves from Vietnam. A process of deterioration spreads through our society which cannot be arrested, much less reversed, until we disengage."[35]

In addition, Church began to criticize Nixon's policy of "Vietnamization." Church argued that "our strategy in Vietnam has failed," but the Nixon administration has refused "to acknowledge that failure." Instead, "in recent weeks there has been increasing talk of changing the military mix in Vietnam by replacing American troops with Vietnamese.... This is not a formula for extricating the United States from Vietnam; it is, rather, a formula for keeping up to 300,000 American troops engaged in Vietnam indefinitely. Its purpose is not to get out, but to stay in."[36]

It was Nixon's November 3, "Silent Majority" speech that provided the context for the introduction of the Cooper-Church amendments. That soliloquy was a response to the growing antiwar movement. He used it to explain his policy, buy time for his efforts to force a military solution on the North Vietnamese, and attack his domestic opponents. Nixon asserted

---

[34] Transcript of NBC's the *Today Show*, May 15, 1969, Church papers 8.1/6/11.

[35] Church, August 19, 1969, Church papers 8.3/2/24.

[36] Church, "Vietnam: Disengagement Now," *Vital Speeches*, vol. XXXVI, no. 2, November 1, 1969, pp. 34–39.

that the "great question is: How can we win America's peace?" He rehearsed the, by then, familiar argument of credibility and juxtaposed his policy of Vietnamization against the calls for "an immediate, precipitate withdrawal ... without regard to the effects of that action." Warming to his task, Nixon concluded:

Let historians not record that when America was the most powerful nation in the world we passed on the other side of the road and allowed the last hopes for peace and freedom of millions of people to be suffocated by the forces of totalitarianism.... I pledged in campaign ... to end the war in a way that we could win the peace.... The more support I can have from the American people, the sooner that pledge can be redeemed; for the more divided we are at home, the less likely the enemy is to negotiate at Paris. Let us be united for peace. Let us also be united against defeat.... North Viet-Nam cannot defeat or humiliate the United States. Only Americans can do that.[37]

This attempt to discredit the opposition incensed Frank Church. He challenged the president's position in a series of talks and essays in November and December and took his first active steps to limit the president's ability to conduct the war. Church noted that the president's speech was designed to ask the country for "more time." Adding, "To [Nixon's] credit, he stressed that 'we are finally bringing American men home,' but ... he could not find the resolution to cut the knot that binds us to the Saigon generals." Church argued that there "is no 'victory' we can win in Vietnam worthy of the name." Vietnamization, he reiterated, was not a scheme for American disengagement from Vietnam but rather a plan to ensure that U.S. troops would remain there indifinitely. As long as Vietnamization was tied to maintaining the Thieu regime, all avenues to a final withdrawal were blocked.

"Nearly everyone now recognizes," Church stated, "that our intervention in Vietnam was in error. Two years ago, our political skies were still filled with hawks; today scarcely a hawk can be seen." Accordingly, Church took issue with the notion that the nation's credibility would be harmed by a withdrawal. By ending the war "we shall suffer no lasting injury to our power or presting." Rather, "the termination of our war in Vietnam would represent a ... liberation for America, and even a victory of sorts – a victory of principle over pride and of intelligent self-interest over messianic delusion."[38]

---

[37] *Public Papers of the Presidents: Nixon, 1969*, (Washington, D.C.: Government Printing Office, 1971), p. 909.

[38] Church, "The Only Alternative: A Reply to the President on Vietnam," *The Washington Monthly* December, 1969. This was based on a speech he delivered in the Senate on

While he favored a quick and complete withdrawal that was not tied to the preservation of the regime in Saigon, and was certain that the administration intended on continuing the war, Church did not believe it was yet politically possible to mandate a removal of American troops. Indeed, Nixon's speech was well received by the public. He had succeeded in portraying himself as a moderate pursuing a prudent course of gradual withdrawal and negotiation while protecting American security and credibility. With the president making it clear that he preferred conflict rather than compromise, Senate doves found themselves on the defensive. In search of a victory, they turned their attention to Laos.

In a three hour executive session on December 15, the Senate debated an amendment to the Department of Defense Procurement and Development Act that would prohibit the use of American forces in Laos and Thailand. There was disagreement over the extent of the original amendment, with some doves opposing the restriction on American bombing in Laos. Church broke the deadlock by submitting a compromise proposal that only blocked the use of ground troops without Congressional approval. With no opposition from the administration, the first Cooper-Church amendment easily passed by a vote of 73–17.[39] While Church realized that this measure did not significantly restrict the action of the president, the first Cooper-Church amendment provided an important precedent that Church would build on when he concluded the time was right for a more all-encompassing restriction of the president's ability to wage an undeclared war.

The overthrow of the government of Prince Norodom Sihanouk by the Cambodian military in mid-March, and the U.S. rush to support the new Lon Nol regime, led Church to believe that Nixon would use Lon Nol's seizure of power to extend the war into Cambodia. He, therefore, turned again to Cooper, and the two began drafting a bipartisan measure to ban United States combat troops from Cambodia. On April 12, Church and Cooper announced that they were planning to introduce legislation to "extend to Cambodia the present prohibition against introduction of

December 19, 1969, Church Papers 8.1/6/51. Another version of this speech was syndicated under the title "Vietnam: The Other Alternative," Church Papers 8.3/4/10.

39 Church, "War Without End," May 1, 1970, Church papers 2.2/32/9; *New York Times*, December 16, 1969. The full amendment stated" "In line with the expressed intention of the President of the United States, none of the funds appropriated by this Act shall be used to finance the introduction of American ground combat troops into Laos or Thailand." Church Papers, "Significant Events Relating to the Cooper-Church Amendment," 2.2/39/9.

American combat troops into Laos and Thailand." Church stated that the "recent events in Southeast Asia – including the ouster of Prince Sihanouk by a military junta in Cambodia, the intensification of the conflict in Laos and the extension of the ground battle into Cambodia – create dangerous pressures for deepening America's involvement." He noted that "it has been reported ... that armed American military personnel have already crossed into Cambodian territory several times in recent days. In light of our tragic experience in Viet Nam, the United States must avoid being pulled into a wider war." Furthermore, he noted that the amendment "continues Congress' efforts to reassert its constitutional role in the formulation of foreign policy."[40]

Church feared a "new front" in the war was opening up that would place the policy of "de-escalation in the gravest jeopardy."[41] He saw the introduction of the Cooper-Church amendment as "an effort to hasten a close to the war in a safe and orderly manner, and to bring back to Congress those powers which, over the years since Franklin Roosevelt, have subtly drifted into the hand of one man, the President."[42] What Church did not know was that Nixon had already decided to invade Cambodia, a move that would set off a new round of protests and making the second Cooper-Church amendment the central issue of the battle between opponents and supporters of the war.

When Nixon announced to the nation on April 30, 1970, his decision to send troops into Cambodia, Church had already prepared a speech on the issue. On May 1, 1970, an angry Church addressed the Senate concerning American policy in Vietnam and the invasion of Cambodia. He blamed the failure to end the war and the new expansion of the fighting into a neighboring nation on the Nixon administration's refusal to "acknowledge the futility of our continued military intervention in Vietnam." The nation, Church declared, had to admit "the impossibility of sustaining at any acceptable cost an anticommunist regime in Saigon, allied with, dependent on, and supported by the United States." Church found that the "policy itself was deeply unsound, extraneous to American interests and offensive to American values."[43]

While deeply troubled by the president's action, Church believed it provided an opportunity for Congress and the people to take the initiative in

[40] Joint Press Release by Senators Frank Church and John Sherman Cooper, April 12, 1970, Church papers 2.2/39/9.
[41] Church, News Release, April 29, 1970, Church papers 2.2/39/9.
[42] Church to Pfc. Robin Crawford, June 19, 1970, Church papers 2.2/32/10.
[43] Church, "War Without End," May 1, 1970, Church papers 2.2/32/9.

Vietnam away from the executive branch, to limit the expansion of the war, and bring the war itself to an end. As Church stated, it was time "for the Congress to draw the line against an expanded American involvement" in the war and begin to put an end to it. "If the Executive Branch will not take the initiative, the Congress and the people must." The best method was for Congress to immediately pass the Cooper-Church amendment to force the withdrawal of American forces from Cambodia. "Too much blood has been lost, too much patience gone unrewarded, while the war continues to poison our society."[44] He was now convinced that enough pressure could be exerted on the Nixon administration to force it to abandon its policy of victory in Vietnam and settle for a negotiated agreement that would end the war.

In the ultimately successful battles to ward off the administration's efforts to block the Cooper-Church amendment and decree that no United States troops could be engaged in Cambodia without specific Congressional approval after June 30, Church was the leader of the opposition's fight over the direction of the war. Church outlined the importance he attached to the amendment in a series of speeches in May, 1970. Criticizing Congress for permitting the "president to exercise blank check authority," he argued that it was now faced with "another front ... in this endless war." "This new crisis," Church argued, "presents the Congress with an historic opportunity to draw the limits on American intervention...." It was time for Congress to reassert its power "so as to avoid a deepening American involvement" in Cambodia.[45] When the Cooper-Church amendment was formally introduced on May 11, Church noted that the Congress's failure to use its powers in relation to funding and declaring wars "is one for which historians may judge us harshly." Yet he quickly noted that "there is a precedent for what we are asking the Senate to do," referring to the first Cooper-Church amendment. What was new was the attempt to restrict the use of troops in a country where they were already committed. "Unquestionably," Church declared, "Congress had the power to accomplish" this objective.

In addition to the need to reassert Congressional power and bring an end to the war, Church noted that the adoption of the measure was necessary to assure young Americans that the political system worked and that they should not give up on the government. That May, the alienation of American youth had come to a head with the shootings

---

44 Ibid.
45 Church, News Release, May 7, 1970, Church papers 3.2/32/8.

at Kent State and Jackson State, and the closing of over 500 colleges and universities across the nation. "This war," Church stated, "has already stretched the generation gap so wide that it threatens to pull the country apart." Many rejected the idea that the war in Vietnam was necessary to national security, and had little to do with the safety of Americans or American society. "We now reap the bitter harvest," Church warned, "manifested in the angry uprising on campuses from coast to coast. . . . Once the moral authority of the government is rejected on an issue so fundamental as an unacceptable war, every lesser institution of society is placed in jeopardy." It was futile, Church asserted, to "tell these young people that our 'will and character are being tested,' that we shall not be humiliated or accept our first defeat." They never believed that Vietnam was about the nation's security, and "they do not believe that a mistaken war should be won. They believe it should be stopped. That, for them, is the path of honor." It was thus all the more imperative that Congress "draw the line against an expanded American involvement in the widening war."[46]

The administration adamantly opposed the second Cooper-Church amendment. Central to its position was the claim that the restriction would interfere with the president's role as Commander-in-Chief, and that Congress only had the authority to limit the civilian acts of the president. Church argued that there was nothing in the amendment that prevented the president from fulfilling his duties as Commander-in-Chief, and noted that Nixon had supported the first Cooper-Church amendment without invoking this argument. The issue at hand was the warmaking power. The purpose of the amendment, Church insisted, was to return that power to Congress where it rightfully belonged.

In the face of a mounting challenge in the Senate and the massive protests against his policy, Nixon began to remove American forces from Cambodia. The president set the end of June as his deadline, and declared the Cooper-Church amendment moot.[47] On June 3, Nixon proclaimed the Cambodian invasion "the most successful operation of this long and very difficult war," and that all of the "major military objectives have been achieved."[48]

---

[46] Statement by Senator Frank Church Before the Senate Foreign Relations Committee, 11 May 1970; see also Church's statement to the full Senate, May 13, 1970, both Church papers 2.2/32/8.

[47] Statement by Senator Frank Church Before the Senate Foreign Relations Committee, May 11, 1970, Church papers 2.2/32/8.

[48] Ashby and Gramer, p. 315.

Church responded that whether or not Nixon was withdrawing American troops from Cambodia, the amendment was still necessary. Cooper-Church was not designed to "undo what's been done. Instead, it is addressed to the immediate need of preventing the United States from bogging down in Cambodia," and committing itself to the defense of another nation in Southeast Asia.[49] "The Cooper-Church amendment is the opening move" in extricating the United States from the Vietnam War by "setting the outer limits ... to American involvement in Cambodia." More importantly for Church, "its adoption would also signal that the Congress recognizes and stands willing to reassert its share of the responsibility for bringing the war to a close." Opponents of this measure "would concede all power to the Presidency. They would reduce the Congress of the United States to impotence, while making the President an autocrat supreme." Finally, the Cooper-Church amendment was vital as a rebuttal to those who believed the government cannot work.[50]

On June 30, after seven weeks of debate and the defeat of all of the administration's qualifying amendments, the Senate passed Cooper-Church 58–37. While the House of Representatives did not finally approve a modified version of the amendment until December, passage of the amendment marked a milestone in the Vietnam War. It was the first time that Congress restricted the deployment of troops during the war and voted against the wishes of a president. Moreover, it provided a means for both the Congress and the public to demonstrate the full extent of their opposition to the war. Cooper-Church was, therefore, a landmark in the history of opposition to the war, congressional initiatives to bring the fighting to an end, and efforts to control Executive power in foreign policy.

That fall, Church announced on television and in speeches across the country that "the doves have won."[51] He based his argument on the fact that the two key propositions of the dove position, "a negotiated peace and the withdrawal of American troops" were now official policy. The debate would now be over when to withdraw, not whether to do so.

---

[49] Statement of Senator Frank Church Before the Senate Foreign Relations Committee, May 11, 1970, Church papers 2.2/32/8.

[50] Remarks of Senator Frank Church in the U.S. Senate, June 3, 1970, Church papers, 2.2/39/10.

[51] See for example Church, "The Doves Have Won and Don't Know It," September 6, 1970 on CBS television, Church papers 2.2/32/15; "The Doves Have Won," September 11, 1970 speech at Mills College of Education; "The Doves Are Winning – Don't Despair," September 26, 1970 speech at Colorado State University; and "The Unsung Victory of the Doves," December, 1970, all Church papers 10.6/8/8.

"So the last service the doves can perform for their country," Church concluded, "is to insist that President Nixon's withdrawal program truly leads to a 'Vietnamization' of the war. It must not become a device for lowering – and then perpetuating – an American military presence in South Vietnam for the indefinite future. Our long ordeal in this mistaken war must end," Church continued. "The gathering crisis in our own land, the deepening divisions among our people, the festering, unattended problems here at home, bear far more importantly on the future of our Republic than anything we ever had at stake in Indochina." The opponents of the war needed to prevent the corruption of the nation and its institutions. Their opposition was, for Church, the "highest concept of patriotism – which is not the patriotism of conformity – but the patriotism of Senator Carl Shurz, a dissenter from an earlier period, who proclaimed: 'Our country, right or wrong. When right, to be kept right; when wrong, to be put right.' "[52]

The emerging antiwar majority in the Senate would challenge the executive on a number of foreign policy issues. Passage of Cooper-Church paved the way for Congress to repeal the Gulf of Tonkin Resolution, and to the passage of the War Powers Act. In 1973, Church cosponsored the Case-Church amendment that prohibited any reintroduction of American forces into Southeast Asia without congressional authorization. Beginning that same year, the Idaho senator chaired the Senate Select Committee hearings on the abuses of power by American multinational corporations. These investigation would eventually expand to include examinations of abuses of power by the president, the FBI, and the CIA, including covert actions to overthrow governments and assassinate foreign leaders. By 1975, Church was using his position as chair of the Special Committee to fundamentally reshape and redirect American foreign policy.

The Watergate crisis confirmed all of Church's fears about the growth of presidential power, and made clear to him the need for a greater congressional role in the making of the nation's foreign policy and the renewal of democratic ideals as a component of American policymaking. Church doubted that Watergate could have occurred without the "moral and political perversion generated by Vietnam." American policy had come "full circle." "If 'dirty tricks' were acceptable in foreign policy, why, in the view of the White House ... were they any less so in domestic affairs?" Connecting the battles over the direction of American policy in Vietnam with

---

[52] Church, "The Doves Have Won and Don't Know It," September 6, 1970, Church papers 2.2/32/15.

the political crisis at home, Church asked: "If it showed commendable realism for the President to circumvent Congress's war and treaty powers in the interest of a war policy he believed to be right, why ... was it any less respectable to sabotage the electoral process, in order to reelect a President whose policies they believed to be right?"

For Church, the only solution was a broader definition of "national security in all of its varied dimensions." The problem was that "over the last thirty years, the United States has expended its major energies on the foreign military and political aspects of national security, but gradually necessity gave way to habit, pride, and even arrogance." This led "people at the apex of power ... to manipulate and circumvent the processes of American democracy." The tragedies of Vietnam and Watergate demanded a return to democratic values as a guide to American policymaking and a "renewed idealism – not the soaring idealism which bred in us the illusion of divine mandate to set the world right, but rather a chastened, realistic, nonperfectionist idealism which will enable us to strike a balance between our highest aspirations and our human limitations."[53]

This point of view, however, clashed directly with efforts by the new president, Gerald Ford, and Henry Kissinger, whom he kept on as secretary of state, to maintain containment and preserve executive control over the making of foreign policy. Ford had supported U.S. policy in Vietnam since entering Congress during the Truman administration. He and Kissinger were very much a part of that generation of post–World War II leaders who embraced containment and supported a global role for the United States that included covert action and the use of military force abroad. Vietnam did not shake either the president's or his secretary of state's convictions that anticommunism, containment, intervention, and executive freedom of action must be the basis of American foreign policy.

For Church, the opposite was true. The final end of the Vietnam War on April 30, 1975, appeared to him to provide "an opportune time for some reflections on America's role in the world," and for a reevaluation of the policies that led the United States to intervene. Frustrated by what he saw as the persistent exaggeration of the Soviet threat in the Third World and American intervention abroad, he believed that Vietnam should have convinced the nation that many of its old policies were flawed; indeed counterproductive.[54] These convictions were reinforced by the revelations

[53] Church, "Beyond Vietnam," June 6, 1973, Church papers 10.6/8/13.
[54] Church, "A Post-Vietnam Foreign Policy," Church papers, 10.6/8/13.

concerning the CIA covert operations to overthrow foreign governments and assassinate foreign leaders.

Church decided that Chile would be the case study that the committee would use in its examination of covert activities. The American effort to block Salvadore Allende's election, and subsequent role in his overthrow, convinced Church that the U.S. had completely lost its moral compass. Chile, Church stated, "contained all of the elements ... that are normally associated with covert operations" and "contained the most dramatic examples of abuse conflicting with our professed principles as a Nation and interfering with the right of the Chilean people to choose their own government by peaceful means in accordance with their own constitutional processes."[55]

As the investigation proceeded, Church managed to control leaks and maintain a spirit of bipartisanship. The spring and summer were, however, full of rumors and reports of assassination attempts and coups against such foreign leaders as Fidel Castro of Cuba, Rafael Trujillo of the Dominican Republic, and Allende. Matters came to a head that fall when the Church Committee launched public hearings and made plans to publish its findings.[56] Claiming "executive privilege," the Ford White House sought to block the publication of any documents and to discredit the committee's work. In a memorandum approved by the president, White House aide Jack Marsh contended that the documents in question "were highly classified and unsanitized." The president had "provided the documents on the express assumption that they would be used by the Committee in a responsible manner."[57] Kissinger and other senior staff agreed that the publication of the reports "will be extremely damaging to the United States" and have "an appalling and shattering impact in the international community. Without question, it would do the gravest damage to our ability to play a positive role of leadership in world affairs ... [and] would deal a serious blow to our foreign policy from which we could recover only with difficulty."[58]

---

[55] U.S. Congress, Senate Select Committee to Study Governmental Operations with Respect to Intelligence Activities (hereafter cited as Church Committee) *Hearings on Covert Action*, vol. 5, 94th Congress, 2d session, December 18, 1975, pp. 63–64.

[56] Memorandum, September 18, 1975, Rockefeller, Kissinger, and others to the president, box 5, ND6, White House Central File, Gerald R. Ford Library, Ann Arbor, Michigan (hereafter Ford Library).

[57] Memorandum October 29, 1975, Marsh to Cheney, box 7, Cheney Files, Ford Library; see also Memorandum 14 November 1975, Connor to Marsh, box 31, presidential handwriting files, Ford Library.

[58] Ibid.

The administration's efforts to control the documents were not surprising, but the effort masked the larger issue at stake: the direction of American foreign policy. The investigations confirmed that the United States was involved in the overthrow of the Chilean and other governments, and had attempted to assassinate foreign rulers. For Church, American opposition to Allende was groundless, and he dismissed the claim that Chile was a danger to U.S. national security. As the report on Chile made clear, U.S. policy was still based upon the same assumptions that had led the nation into the Vietnam War. Kissinger explained American covert action against Allende in terms of blocking the expansion of communism; for his part Ford claimed that the domino theory had "a great deal of credibility."[59] Kissinger stated that he had "yet to meet somebody who firmly believes that if Allende wins, there is likely to be another free election in Chile.... Now it is fairly easy for one to predict ... he will establish over a period of years some sort of communist government. In that case, we would have one not on an island ... but in a major Latin American country.... So I don't think we should delude ourselves on an Allende takeover and [the fact that] Chile would not present massive problems for us."[60]

The Church Committee's final conclusions centered on the need for better statutory guidelines for the intelligence community and control over the "excessive, and at times self-defeating use of covert action" through better congressional oversight and "lawful disclosure of unneeded or unlawful secrets." Specifically, the committee sought a ban on assassination plans and the subversion of democratically elected governments, combined with routine reviews of covert operations by Congress. There was no blanket prohibition against covert operations. The committee recognized a need to use such methods, but only "when no other means will suffice to meet extraordinary circumstances involving grave threats to national security."[61]

By the time the Committee's *Final Report* was submitted in April, 1976, the climate of opinion had begun to swing away from sweeping reforms. The assassination of Richard Welch, CIA station chief for Greece, on December 23, 1975, brought charges from Agency supporters that the

---

[59] *Department of State Bulletin*, April 28, 1975, p. 544.

[60] U.S. Congress, Church Committee, *Covert Action in Chile: 1963–1973*, 94th Congress, 2d session, December 18, 1975, p. 9.

[61] The Church Committee's recommendations are summarized in the *Congressional Quarterly Almanac 32*, Washington D.C., 1976, pp. 304–307; see also Church Committee, *Final Report* 94th Congress, 2d session.

congressional investigation was releasing too much information and undermining U.S. security.[62] Ford sought to prevent drastic reforms by submitting his own list of restrictions to Congress. Executive Order 11905
prohibited the undertaking of assassination efforts and other already
illegal actions and recognized the principle of congressional oversight.
The Senate and House, in turn, established new intelligence committees.

Church summarized his findings and views in a bicentennial speech
entitled, "The Erosion of Principle in American Foreign Policy: A Call for
a New Morality." He found the proper guide to balance security interests
with morality in the thoughts of the nation's founders. The senator noted
that "an objective close to the hearts of our founders was to place the
United States at the helm of moral leadership in the world." Yet since
the end of World War II the notion of leading by example had been replaced by intervention and the support of some of the most brutal dictatorships in the world. As evidence he listed CIA-orchestrated coups in
Iran, Guatemala, and Chile, various assassination plots by three administrations against foreign leaders, and support for dictators in Africa, Asia,
and Latin America. For all of its efforts, the country found itself involved
in a divisive, immoral war in Vietnam and allied with nations that mock
"the professed ideals of the United States." Church asked, "If we have
gained little" from these policies, "what then have we lost? I suggest we
have lost – or grievously impaired – the good name of the United States
from which we once drew a unique capacity to exercise matchless moral
leadership." The damage stemmed from an "arrogance of power" that
led the United States into Vietnam and allowed Nixon to declare "like
Caesar peering into the colonies from distant Rome" that the government of Chile was "unacceptable to the President of the United States."
Church concluded, "[T]he remedy is clear. American foreign policy must
be made to conform once more to our historic ideals, the . . . fundamental
belief in freedom and popular government."[63] As the Church Committee
concluded: "The United States must not adopt the tactics of the enemy. . . .
Crisis makes it tempting to ignore the wise restraints that make men free.
But each time we do so, each time the means we use are wrong, our inner
strength, the strength which makes us free, is lessened."[64]

---

[62] Rhodri Jeffreys-Jones, *The CIA and American Democracy*, (Yale University Press: New
   Haven, 1989), pp. 211–212.
[63] Church, "The Erosion of Principle in American Foreign Policy: A Call for a New
   Morality," Church papers, 10.6/1/17.
[64] Church Committee, *Alleged Assassination Plots Involving Foreign Leaders*, Interim Report,
   94th Congress, 1st session, November 20, 1975.

Given the passions aroused by the Vietnam War and the distrust engendered by the Church Committee investigations, it should not be surprising that no new consensus emerged concerning the direction of American foreign policy. Subsequently, Church was attacked from all sides in 1975–1976. Critics of U.S. foreign policy did not believe that the investigations went far enough or that the restrictions produced sufficient checks on executive power. Conversely, supporters of the CIA denounced Church for impairing the Agency's ability to act. Such disagreements, Church believed, were to be expected, and he found the whole debate healthy for the nation and the future of its foreign policy.

Building on a decade of mounting criticism of American imperialism and the imperial presidency, the Church Committee conducted one of the most far-reaching examinations and discussions of American foreign policy the nation had ever witnessed. Moreover, Church's challenge to the policy of containment, the national security state, and the imperial presidency helped legitimize alternative views about what should be the basis of America's policy and role in the world. It certainly helped open the door for Jimmy Carter's emphasis on human rights. In his inaugural address, Carter echoed Church when he called upon the nation to "take on those moral duties which, when assumed, seem inevitably to be in our own best interests," and to let the "recent mistakes bring a resurgent commitment to the basic principles of our Nation." The best means to enhance freedom and advance the national interest, Carter asserted, "is to demonstrate here that our democratic system is worth emulation. . . . We will not behave in foreign places so as to violate our rules and standards here at home, for we know that the trust which our Nation earns is essential to our strength."[65] Four months later, Carter announced that the nation had to overcome its "inordinate fear of communism" that had led it to so many mistakes.[66] Such views led to breakthroughs such as the Camp David Accords, and the Panama Canal Treaties, which Church steered through the Senate, and provided the basis for the checks during the 1980s on Ronald Reagan's efforts to intervene in Central America.

Church, of course, did not act alone. But his was a unique voice offering an alternative perspective to the conventional cold war wisdom at a time when real change was possible in American foreign policy. In Frank Church, the nation found a penetrating and often eloquent voice examining fundamental assumptions that wove together his western political

---

[65] *Public Papers of the Presidents: Jimmy Carter, 1977*, Washington, D.C., 1977, pp. 1–4.
[66] Ibid., pp. 955–957.

independence and anti-imperialism and the moral outrage of the Vietnam generation. He knew that for substantive changes in the direction of American foreign policy to occur it was necessary to discredit the old verities of the Cold War and restore power to the Senate. That Church was not completely successful does not diminish his accomplishment of forcing vital questions into the mainstream of political debate and mobilizing the institutional power of the Senate to challenge the imperial policies of the nation and power of the president. The Cooper-Church amendment marked a shift in national attitudes and the end of the Cold War consensus; it constituted a starting point for efforts to restore the proper balance in American government and for the prevention of despotism at home as well as abroad. Church had revived the Western progressives' opposition to imperialism and in so doing had helped to draw the line against American intervention abroad and abuses of power at home.

Dixie's Dove

J. William Fulbright, the Vietnam War, and the American South

Randall B. Woods

During the two years following his shepherding of the Gulf of Tonkin resolution through the United States Senate in 1964, J. William Fulbright of Arkansas, chairman of the Senate Foreign Relations Committee (SFRC), came to the conclusion that the war in Vietnam was essentially a civil war and that the United States was simply supporting one side against the other. By the time President Lyndon B. Johnson left the White House in 1969, Fulbright was insisting that the insurgency in South Vietnam was chiefly a response to the repressive policies of the government in Saigon and its American ally, that the war had no bearing on the vital interests of the United States, and that the nation's involvement there was corroding its institutions and corrupting its public life. Though he was a true internationalist, Fulbright, anguished by what he perceived to be America's uncontrollable impulse to dominate, eventually sought refuge in a realism that bordered on neoisolationism. In "The Price of Empire" (1967) and *The Arrogance of Power* (1966) he advocated an Asian policy similar to that espoused in 1950 by former President Herbert Hoover and Senator Robert A. Taft.[1]

---

[1] "The Price of Empire," in Haynes Johnson and Bernard M. Gwertzman, eds, *Fulbright: The Dissenter* (Garden City, NY, 1968) and J. William Fulbright, *The Arrogance of Power* (New York, 1966). For Hoover's and Taft's views see John W. Spanier, *The Truman-MacArthur Controversy and the Korean War* (Harvard University Press: Cambridge, MA, 1959), 156–157. The Johnson administration, Fulbright wrote, should abandon its efforts to "extend unilaterally its power in such a way as to promote its conception of 'world peace' generally, or the defense of 'free people' and seek to maintain such base facilities there as will protect the sea and air routes of the area from domination by hostile forces." "Summary Proposal for Disengagement in Vietnam," Folder April–June 1967, box 7, papers of Carl M. Marcy, Records of the U.S. Senate, Record Group 46 (National Archives,

In public hearings, on television, and in Congress, the junior senator from Arkansas worked assiduously to erode national support for
the Johnson administration's policies in Vietnam. The motives and circumstances surrounding Fulbright's decision to confront Lyndon Johnson
were hotly debated by his contemporaries and are of increasing interest to
historians.[2] The Arkansan's dissent was a product of his fear of the burgeoning radical right, his growing pexception of the strength of the military industrial complex, his love-hate relationship with Lyndon Johnson,
and his commitment to détente with the Soviet Union. But, somewhat
ironically, Fulbright's perspective on Vietnam and the sharpness of his
critique of American policy grew out of his Southern background and his
commitment to Wilsonian internationalism as he defined it. His ties to
both the upland South and the Delta, his Anglophilia, his classic liberal
education, and his opposition to the Civil Rights Movement contributed
to the form and substance of his opposition to the war. Perhaps most important, his Southern background and perspective enabled him to communicate with those on the political right, to act as a bridge between
conservative supporters and liberal opponents of the war.

In trying to understand Fulbright and his antiwar position it is helpful to compare his social agenda with that of prowar Southerners. In
his 1968 essay on the Cold War and the burden of Southern history
C. Vann Woodward lamented that such cosmopolitan Southemers as
Lyndon Johnson and Secretary of State Dean Rusk had helped expand

Washington, D.C.; hereinafter cited as RG 46). Like Hiram Johnson and Charles Beard
before him, he called upon America to retreat within itself and work to perfect its own
institutions and social system and thus to become an example to the rest of the world. "If
America has a service to perform in the world – and I believe it has – it is in large part the
service of its own example," he declared to a Johns Hopkins University audience. "In our
excessive involvement in the affairs of other countries, we are not only living off our assets
and denying our own people the proper enjoyment of their resources; we are also denying
the world the example of a free society enjoying its freedom to the fullest." *Congressional
Record*, 89 Congress, 2 session, 10808 (May 17, 1966).

[2] Several books have been written on Fulbright's life and his opposition to the war. The two
best are Johnson and Gwertzman, *Fulbright*, and William C. Berman, *William Fulbright
and the Vietnam War: The Dissent of a Political Realist* (Kent, Ohio, and London, 1988). It
should be noted that two of the most comprehensive and careful histories of the antiwar
movement, Melvin Small's *Johnson, Nixon, and the Doves* and Charles DeBenedetti and
Charles Chatfield's *An American Ordeal*, discuss Fulbright only in terms of his actions
in opposition to the war. They make no attempt to portray him as representative of a
particular culture or philosophy. Small, *Johnson, Nixon, and the Doves* (New Brunswick,
NJ, 1988), pp. 49, 72, 788 1, and 1078, and DeBenedetti and Chatfield, *An American
Ordeal: The Antiwar Movement of the Vietnam Era* (Syracuse, NY: Syracuse Univ. Press,
1990), pp. 110, 113, 124, 152–154, and 358–359.

America's presence in Southeast Asia, invoking themes of invincibility and cultural superiority, which had long constituted the core of America's missionary mentality.[3] Woodward believed that Johnson and Rusk had not heeded his call for a new generation of Southern politicians to shape a foreign policy based on empathy and restraint. According to Woodward, these bellicose sons of Dixie had betrayed their regional heritage by rejecting the South's history of "defeat and failure ... frustration and poverty ... slavery and its long aftermath of racial injustice," a tradition that should have led them to an understanding of other nations and engendered a sense of cultural relativity.[4] Woodward failed to acknowledge, however, that their very appreciation of the burden of Southern history – the historical suffering of the South and its endemic problems – had in part impelled Lyndon Johnson and other idealistic Southerners to intervene in Vietnam.

In the spring of 1966, Henry Cabot Lodge, then in the midst of his second tour of duty as United States Ambassador to South Vietnam, wrote a concise, impressionistic description of the South Vietnamese people for Lyndon Johnson. The similarity between Vietnam and the American South, with its heritage of defeat in civil war, northern economic domination, and voluble patriotism, was striking. He observed that "they have had one-hundred years of colonial domination followed by ten years of Diem's dictatorship and in their subconscious is the feeling that they don't have to take responsibility for their actions ... At the same time, because of their colonial past, they are touchy about sovereignty and independence – about 'face.'"[5] Like American Southerners, the Vietnamese possessed a strong sense of family as well as long experience of farm tenancy and sharecropping. Neither people had enjoyed a strong tradition of economic or political democracy. Moreover, both Vietnam and the South had proved remarkably resistant to reform – and for roughly the same reasons.[6]

These similarities were not lost on certain key members of the Johnson administration. Indeed, the perceived presence in South Vietnam of conditions and traits traditionally associated with the American South played a role in Washington's decision in 1965 to commit combat troops to the conflict in Indochina. In many ways Dean Rusk and Lyndon Johnson

[3] C. Vann Woodward, *The Burden of Southern History*, rev. ed., (Baton Rouge, LA: Louisiana State Univ. Press, 1968). 219, 220, and 230. Many of the phrases that Woodward employs, "welfare imperialism," p. 220, for example, are taken directly from Fulbright's speeches.

[4] Ibid., 229.

[5] See Henry Cabot Lodge to Johnson, April 29. 1966. National Security files – Memos to president, Wait W. Rostow, box 7, papers of Lyndon B. Johnson (Johnson Library, Austin, Texas; hereinafter cited as LBJ papers).

[6] Ibid.

represented Southern liberalism at its best and at its worst. They were the
Southerners of C. Vann Woodward's hopes, men who had encountered
in their history "guilt" rather than "innocence ... the reality of evil,"
rather than "the dream of perfection," which were almost universal in
the human experience.[7] Contrary to Woodward's expectations, however,
this experience did not produce in them a realism that would constrain
America's imperial impulse. In the Hill Country of Texas and the hills
of Georgia, Lyndon Johnson and Dean Rusk had encountered poverty,
racial exploitation, ignorance, and human degradation. The Southern
experience generated in them a reformist zeal that would culminate in
the Civil Rights Acts of 1964 and 1965, Medicare, the War on Poverty,
and other Great Society programs.[8] It also engendered in them, if not a
desire to carry the blessings of liberty and democracy to Southeast Asia,
at least a wish to create a viable society in South Vietnam when forced
by the exigencies of the Cold War to do so. Following John F. Kennedy's
assassination, the historian Eric Goldman touched a responsive chord in
Johnson by invoking a presidency based on unity and ministration to the
needs of all the people; and following Johnson's victory in the 1964 presidential election, W. Averell Harriman, veteran diplomat and adviser to
presidents, appealed to Johnson to extend that vision to the international
arena. Harriman argued that because of Johnson's overwhelming mandate, he had the opportunity to unify the peoples of the free world through
the proclamation of an updated version of Franklin D. Roosevelt's Four
Freedoms. Harriman called upon Johnson to do nothing less than extend
the War on Poverty to foreign lands; the Texan responded enthusiastically.[9] Thus Johnson and his secretary of state came to see the war in
Southeast Asia as a corollary and not as a contravention of the Great

[7] Woodward, *Burden of Southern History*, p. 21.
[8] Dean Rusk interview with author, Athens, Georgia, October 14, 1988; and Harry
McPherson interview with author, Washington, D. C., July 13, 1990 (transcripts in possession of author).
[9] Harriman to Johnson, November 19, 1964, box 439, papers of W. Averell Harriman
(Library of Congress, Washington, D.C.). In truth Johnson was caught in a bind. Shortly
after he became president he observed to his advisers that there had been too much emphasis on social reconstruction in the aid program in Vietnam. All too often when the
U. S. became involved in the affairs of another country, he admonished, it tried to make
the other country over in its own image. Meeting of the president with Rusk, Robert
McNamara, George Ball, McGeorge Bundy, John McCone, and Lodge, November 24,
1963, meeting note file, box 1, LBJ Papers. *But* as he became aware of the political vacuum in South Vietnam and as he became caught up in the effort to build a society able
to stand on its own, Johnson's fears concerning American imperialism receded into the
background.

Society. They thrust America into Vietnam not only out of a desire to contain Sino-Soviet imperialism but also out of a determination to uplift the downtrodden. It was very much in character for Lyndon Johnson to identify the peasantry of Southeast Asia with the rural laborers of the South.

J. William Fulbright acknowledged the noble motives behind the Johnson–Rusk dream while also recognizing in it the seeds of America's destruction. Indeed, Rusk and Fulbright believed that there was an intimate relationship between domestic and foreign affairs. Yet while Rusk was sure that the war in Southeast Asia was necessary to preserve democracy, free enterprise, and individual liberty at home and abroad, Fulbright was convinced that the war was undermining those very principles in the United States and overseas. Rusk never seemed to perceive the contradiction between Woodrow Wilson's desire to see other nations enjoy the right of self-determination and his efforts early in his administration to export democracy forcibly. Fulbright did.

As the Arkansan's dissent bit ever deeper into the Vietnam consensus that Lyndon Johnson desperately tried to maintain, a number of administration supporters and members of the Johnson foreign policy establishment came to attribute Fulbright's opposition to the war to his Southerness, or rather to what they regarded as the worst of the Southern tradition. A member of Fulbright's staff who was interviewed by *Life* magazine noted the Senator's Arkansas roots and explained Fulbright's antiwar stance by asserting: "He appreciates the pride a little country has in telling off a big country." Members of the White House staff carried the argument somewhat further. "In other words," Fred Panzer wrote Hayes Redmon, "it appears that Fulbright, identifying with the antibellum [sic] Southern gentry is still wrangling from the seething hatreds of the Civil War; Vietnam is his ancestral plantation, the Vietnamese, especially the Vietcong, are an amalgam of his tattered gallant Rebels and his devoted and dedicated darkies, and the American presence is those hated carpet baggers and damn Yankees.[10] In fact, Dean Rusk and Walt W. Rostow, former State Department official and National Security Adviser under Kennedy and Johnson, have argued that Fulbright's opposition to the war was a direct outgrowth of his racism. According to them, he simply thought it abhorrent that white men should have to spill their blood to

[10] Brock Brower, "The Roots of the Arkansas Questioner," *Life*, LX, May 13, 1966, p. 108; and Fred Panzer to Hayes Redmon, May 10, 1966, office files of Fred Panzer, box 361, LBJ papers.

safeguard the freedom and independence of yellow men.[11] His position on civil rights and traits that he shared with both the planting aristocracy and yeomen farmers affected Fulbright's stance on foreign affairs but not in the ways that his enemies have argued.

In many ways Fulbright was the very antithesis of W. J. Cash's "glandular, God obsessed, hedonistic" Southerners, people "doomed by their savage ideal," in whom a propensity for violence was combined with religious fundamentalism and deep distrust of intellectual inquiry and discipline. Nor did he resemble the upland planters a few notches above Cash's rednecks whom Ben Robertson writes about in *Red Hills and Cotton:* "We are farmers, all Democrats and Baptists, a strange people, complicated and simple and proud and religious and family-loving, a divorceless, Bible-reading murdersome lot of folks, all of us rich in ancestry and steeped in tradition and emotionally quick on the trigger."[12] Fulbright was as different from these visceral and tempestuous Southerners as his views on the Vietnam War were atypical of the South.[13]

Nonetheless, J. William Fulbright was very much a Southerner. As a United States Senator from Arkansas for thirty years, Fulbright represented both the Ozarks and the Delta. Stubborn, independent, and refined, he exhibited strains of both highlander and planter in his personality. Although there were populist echoes in his philosophy and legislative agenda, Fulbright was in many ways a paternalistic patrician. Above all, these influences bred in him a determination to preserve the traditional features of Anglo-American civilization – a republican form of government, rule by an educated elite, reverence for the law and tradition, political stability, and a humane free-enterprise system.

Certainly Anglophilia and especially a devotion to classic English liberalism is typically, if not exclusively, Southern. During his tenure as

---

[11] Walt W. Rostow interview with author, November 15, 1988, Austin, Texas (transcript in possession of author); and Rusk interview with author.

[12] Quoted in Jack Temple Kirby, *Rural Worlds Lost: The American South, 1920–1960* (Baton Rouge and London: Louisiana State University Press, 1987), p. 226.

[13] In 1968 and 1972 the great majority of white southerners supported Richard Nixon. The South was the most patient region in the nation with the president's deliberate withdrawal from Vietnam. Indeed, one of George C. Wallace's main appeals as a presidential candidate was his call for an "honorable" peace in Vietnam. Compared with the universities of the north and far west the Southern schools were models of decorum and stability in the 1960s. Often the core of dissidents on the southern campuses was composed of students and instructors whose origins were outside the region. Such radical organizations as the Students for a Democratic Society (SDS) made little gain against the deeprooted conservatism and respect for authority among Southern youth. Charles P. Roland, *The Improbable Era: The South since World War II* (Lexington, KY, 1975), pp. 94–96 and 112.

a Rhodes scholar, Fulbright immersed himself in the writings of Adam Smith, John Stuart Mill, and their Whiggish descendants. The chairman of the Senate Foreign Relations Committee was singled out by C. Vann Woodward as one of a new generation of intellectuals called upon to articulate a foreign policy grounded in empathy and restraint. Fulbright's opposition to the war in Vietnam, however, along with his antimilitarism and anti-imperialism, stemmed not from a liberalism born of contact with suffering but rather from a deep-seated conservatism. "Despite a persistent malaise from their heritage of slavery, secession, defeat, and poverty," writes Charles P. Roland, "Southerners looked upon themselves as defenders of the ancient American virtues."[14] "He is not a liberal at all," I. F. Stone once remarked of Fulbright. " 'This is the landed civilized gentleman type . . . foreign to the American egalitarian tradition."[15]

It is indisputable that J. William Fulbright was a racist. To his mind, the blacks he knew were not equal to whites nor could they be made so by legislative decree. His answer to the problem of prejudice and poverty was federal aid to education. Throughout his career he regarded involuntary integration as anathema. In 1956, Fulbright signed the Southern Manifesto, an attack on the Supreme Court's Brown decision, and remained conspicuously aloof from the Little Rock school crisis of 1957. When Fulbright's sister, Anne Teasdale, wrote and urged him to speak out against the lawlessness and violence spawned by Governor Orval Faubus's defiance lest the world think that he shared the provincial prejudices of his native region, he refused.[16] In the spring of 1960, he participated in the Southern filibuster in the Senate against pending civil rights legislation. No new law was needed in Arkansas to protect the voting rights of African Americans, he declared during his three-and-a-half-hour tour of duty: "In Arkansas the Negroes take advantage of their right to vote by the thousands. It is only individual unconcern or apathy that keeps the number from being greater; it is not caused by any discrimination or interference on the part of the officials or citizens in Arkansas."[17] In the spring of 1962, he argued against a Constitutional amendment to eliminate the poll tax, and he testified before a subcommittee of the Senate Judiciary

---

[14] Ibid., p. 2.

[15] Newsclippings, folder 98, box control number 155, first accession, papers of J. William Fulbright (Mullins Library, University of Arkansas, Fayetteville; hereinafter cited as JWF Papers with references to F and *BCN*).

[16] Teasdale to Fulbright, May 20, 1958, and Fulbright to Teasdale, May 27, 1958, F 67, BCN 105, ibid.

[17] *Congressional Record*, 86 Congress, 2nd session, 3981, March 1, 1960.

Committee against bills outlawing literacy tests by states.[18] In March, 1964, he participated prominently in a Senate filibuster designed to defeat Title VII of the Civil Rights Bill. The northern approach in Congress, Fulbright proclaimed, had been to enact bills merely declaring equality, while the Southern approach had been to enact legislation that would help Negroes upgrade themselves through vocational training and other educational programs. "The people of the South are burdened with a historical legacy that the rest of the Nation does not share," he told the Senate. "They are marked in some strange ways by a strange disproportion inherited from the age of Negro slavery" and no one – neither he, nor Congress, nor the Supreme Court – could change that.[19] J. William Fulbright – his name sonorous as a lord's title – patrician, educated, "senatorial," upper class, and Anglo, was thus vividly and concretely yoked with that which was disreputable and reprehensible.

But Fulbright was no racist in the Vardaman–Talmadge–Russell tradition, with its race-baiting and vicious discrimination. To argue that Fulbright was filled with a visceral hatred toward blacks is patently absurd. He founded the Fulbright Exchange Program and advocated the notion of cultural relativity. He was no more hostile or resentful toward African Americans than he was toward Indonesians. But he did not feel compelled by Christian duty or social conscience to use the power of the state to remedy historical wrongs, correct maldistribution of wealth, or legislate equal opportunity. "In theory no one approves of discrimination just as no one approves of bad manners or meanness or sin of any kind," he wrote a constituent in 1946. However, flaws in human nature could not and should not be corrected through legislative statute or judicial edict. In a democratic, secular state the government had no business acting in this realm.[20] Fulbright did work behind the scenes to desegregate the University of Arkansas School of Law in 1948.[21] A year later, he tacitly supported the "Arkansas Plan," a scheme put forward by Congressman Brooks Hays and *Arkansas Gazette* editorial writer Harry

---

[18] "Keep Poll Tax, Says Fulbright." *Little Rock Arkansas Gazetie*, March 15, 1962, P. 1A and "Literacy Test Bills Violate States' Rights, Fulbright Says," ibid., April 12, 1962, p. 18A.

[19] *Congressional Record*, 88 Congress, 2nd session, 5639 (March 18, 1964).

[20] Fulbright to Theron Raines, February 1, 1946, F19, BCN 48, JWF Papers. See also Fulbright to J. Lewis Henderson, June 15, 1945, F 18, BCN 50, and Fulbright to Rose Stenzler, August 29, 1946, F 9, BCN 48, ibid.

[21] Fulbright to Herbert Thomas, February 25, 1946, F 16, BCN 25, ibid., and Jack Yingling interview with author, October 12, 1988, Savannah, Georgia (transcript in possession of author).

Ashmore whereby the white South would grant African Americans the right to vote and equal protection under the law in return for the freedom to continue to segregate public facilities and discriminate in hiring.[22] Though the Arkansas legislator signed the Southern Manifesto in 1956, it was with great reluctance and only after he worked vigorously and successfully to moderate the extremist original version penned by Senator Strom Thurmond of South Carolina and Senator Sam J. Ervin, Jr. of North Carolina.[23] Indeed, Fulbright was featured on the cover of the first issue of the *Citizen*, the national publication of the white supremacist Citizens' Councils of America, and branded as one of the nation's most dangerous liberals.[24] Nevertheless, not until 1970 did he cast his first vote for a civil rights bill, a measure extending the Voting Rights Act of 1965.

Fulbright continually justified his civil rights voting record on the grounds of political expediency, though he never denied believing that education and time rather than legally mandated integration and nondiscrimination were the true avenues to improved race relations. "In an issue of this kind which affects a person's children, you have to go along or you can't be in the Senate," he remarked frankly. "They always imagined the black would rape their daughter. This was the worst possible thing ... I was justly criticized as an opportunist," he later recalled, but he added, "I don't think anything has happened to shake my belief that I wouldn't have survived politically if I hadn't taken the course I did."[25] Whatever the politics of the situation, Fulbright believed that race relations fell into the area of folkways and mores and that in these fields all peoples are entitled to control their own destiny.

In truth Fulbright's racism was born of the blindness of the Southern highlander who had not experienced black life and culture. Lee Williams, his longtime administrative assistant, recalled, "He shares the class and caste consciousness of his planter friends from eastern Arkansas but he

---

[22] "The Area of Compromise," *Little Rock Arkansas Gazette*, December 29, 1948; "Excerpts From 'The Arkansas Plan,'" ibid., February 3, 1949; and Fulbright to Harry Ashmore, January 3, 1949, F 2, BCN 48, JWF papers.

[23] Ervin Draft and Holland, Fulbright, et al., draft, 1956, Southern Manifesto, papers of Richard B. Russell (University of Georgia Library, Athens); and Yingling interview with author.

[24] "Racist Magazine Scores Fulbright," *New York Times*, November 12, 1961, sect. 1, p. 78.

[25] J. W. Fulbright interview with author, Washington, D.C., October 11–20, 1988 (transcript in possession of author). Fulbright's fears were hardly groundless. In his first campaign for the Senate in 1944, his opponent, Homer Adkins, declared him to be both a communist sympathizer and a "nigger lover." Undated advertisement, F 39, BCN 6, JWF papers.

does not share their fear of 'racemixing.'[26] Indeed, Fulbright had almost no personal contact with the poverty and racism characteristic of much of the South. His father was a wealthy farmer and banker who settled in Fayetteville, a small university town tucked away in the northwest comer of the state, just after the turn of the century. The future senator led a sheltered, privileged life in a region in which African Americans were less than 2 percent of the population and sharecropping was virtually unknown.[27] In Fulbright's youth northwest Arkansas was made up of independent mountain folk, proud, reclusive, stubborn, and poor. The population of the state became blacker, the land flatter, and the planter class more numerous as one moved from northwest to southeast, toward a land of cotton and rice plantations, tenant farmers and sharecroppers. Of course Fulbright was aware of the South's miserable living standards and meager personal incomes, but he had personally witnessed little of the human suffering that was the wrenching by-product of those statistics. His maternal great-grandparents had owned slaves in Virginia.[28] Some of his strongest political supporters were planters, men like Robert E. Lee Wilson and Hugh Brinkley, who owned tens of thousands of acres in eastern Arkansas. Nonetheless, the African Americans whom his ancestors had owned and whom his friends exploited were for him primarily abstractions. Fulbright's status as a white Southerner affected his views on Vietnam; but it was the South's concern with class and with preserving the status quo, rather than its obsession with race, that was important in the formation of his views.

As previously noted, Fulbright's upperclass background, his Rhodes scholarship, and his contacts with the masters of the Delta combined to produce in him a deepseated Anglophilia. Indeed, the characterization of him as "British Billy" by his political enemies had substantial truth to it.[29] In March, 1945, the newly elected senator from Arkansas

---

[26] Lee Williams interview with author, Washington, D.C., June 20, 1989 (transcript in possession of author).

[27] The Appalachian and Ozark highlands "was a different South, without plantations. many black people, or a palpable Confederate mystique," writes Jack Temple Kirby. Northwestern Arkansas in 1930 resembled the southern rim of Appalachia. Benton and Washington Counties in the extreme northwest enjoyed relative commercial prosperity with their diversified grain-dairy-livestock and fruitbased economies. By 1959 eleven of the fourteen counties in the quadrant had adopted grain-dairy-livestock economies. Kirby, *Rural Worlds Lost*, pp. 80, 96, and 1067.

[28] Allan Gilbert, A *Fulbright Chronicle* ... (Fayetteville: Privately published by the Fulbright Family, 1980), p. 710.

[29] Johnson and Gwertzman, *Fulbright*, p. 79.

appeared before the Joint Committee on the Organization of Congress to suggest the creation of an executive-legislative cabinet that would have the power to dissolve the government and call general elections when the two branches deadlocked over an important issue.[30] A year later when the Republicans gained control of Congress in the midterm elections, Fulbright suggested that President Harry S. Truman follow parliamentary procedure and resign in favor of a prominent Republican senator such as Arthur H. Vandenberg of Michigan.[31] Fulbright was an ardent supporter of postwar aid to Britain and a committed Atlanticist. Like many other members of the southern and English aristocracy, Fulbright's education was grounded in the classics and in the literature of the Enlightenment. His degrees at the University of Arkansas and at Oxford were in history; his reading focused on Republican Rome, Greece, and modern Europe.

As a classicist and an Anglophile, Fulbright was devoted to the republican form of government. Indeed he considered pure democracy in many ways a dangerous experiment, declaring during the debate over the 1957 Civil Rights bill: "The Constitution does not provide in any place that every citizen shall have the right to vote. The truth of the matter is that during the early days of this Republic few if any responsible leaders of the country believed in universal suffrage.... The idea that in some mysterious way vast masses of voters possess a wisdom and sanctity superior to that of a more restricted electorate gained its greatest momentum under Hitler and Mussolini ..."[32] He held to the Lockean notion that humans were born a blank slate. Over time, events, circumstance, experience, and education etched out a distinct person and personality. Implicit in this philosophy was the notion that humankind could be improved through education and a rationally ordered society.[33] "Our form of government is the product of great human effort," Fulbright asserted. "It was created by our forefathers with the realization that man is potentially good, but also potentially a beast. Wise actions by our people will always be needed to keep the beast from seizing control. Through education we strive to bring out the good in our young people and to cultivate in them a desire to preserve and protect the values of our society."[34] Care for the commonweal

---

[30] *Congressional Record*, 79 Congress, 1st session, A 15 86, March 29, 1945.

[31] Johnson and Gwertzman, *Fulbright*, p. 103.

[32] *Congressional Record*, 85 Congress, 1st session, p. 11080, July 9, 1957.

[33] See Forrest McDonald, *Novus Ordo Seclorum: The Intellectual Origins of the Constitution* (Lawrence, KS: University Press of Kansas, 1985), p. 53.

[34] Unpublished speech draft, April 18, 1946 (Fulbright family papers in possession of author).

must reside, he believed, with an elite that practiced public virtue – that vital characteristic of all republics. According to Forrest McDonald, public virtue has meant traditionally "firmness, courage, endurance, industry, frugal living, strength, and, above all, unremitting devotion to the weal of the public's corporate self, the community of virtuous men." To Anglo-Americans of two centuries ago, "the public" included only independent adult males.[35] For Fulbright it comprised the educated and publicminded, those who brought discernment and commitment to public affairs.[36]

From convictions shaped by reading Plato, Thucydides, and Montesquieu during his formative years, Fulbright became persuaded that the Vietnam War was eroding the political liberties of the American people. As a student of empires, Fulbright was acutely conscious both of America's military and economic dominance at the close of World War II and of the inevitability of decline from that lofty status. He was fearful that in its efforts to retain its power America was destroying its political institutions. In 1967, he told a meeting of the American Bar Association that America was "fighting a two-front war and doing badly in both." In the same speech he declared that "one is ... the war of power politics which our soldiers are fighting in the jungles of Southeast Asia. The other is a war for America's soul which is being fought in the streets of Newark and Detroit and in the halls of Congress, in churches and protest meetings and on college campuses, and in the hearts and minds of silent Americans from Maine to Hawaii.[37] The great question before America was whether it could simultaneously pursue imperialism abroad and republicanism at home, which were to him "morally incompatible roles."[38] The "arrogance of power," the "tragedy of American foreign policy," "myth and reality in Soviet-American relations," those and other phrases in Fulbright's rhetoric pointed to the era in Athenian history when democracy was devolving into empire. A recurrent theme in Fulbright's speeches was that in seeking to impose its will on Vietnam, the United States, like Athens, was perverting its idealism and abandoning its search for excellence. Decrying the federal government's massive military budget and the Johnson administration's Asian Doctrine, Fulbright told a joint congressional committee: "Contrary to the traditions which have guided our nation since the days of the Founding

---

[35] McDonald, *Novus Ordo Seclorum*, p. 70.
[36] Congressional *Record*, 80 Congress, 2nd session, pp. 39–49, April 1, 1948.
[37] J. William Fulbright, "The Price of Empire," in Johnson and Gwertzman, eds, *Fulbright*, p. 308 (first quotation) and 304 (second quotation).
[38] Ibid., p. 304.

Fathers, we are in grave danger of becoming a Sparta bent on policing the world.[39]

The war in Vietnam threatened republicanism in Fulbright's view because the corridors of power were walked by persons who were incapable of restraint or sound judgment, unwilling or unable to practice "public virtue." During his days at Oxford, Fulbright studied under Ronald Buchanan McCallum, a historian of contemporary Europe and a disciple of Woodrow Wilson. Among the many authors McCallum had his student read was David Hume. According to Forrest McDonald, Hume believed that "parties arising 'from *principle*, especially abstract speculative principle' . . . were 'known only to modern times' and were destructive to the point of 'madness.' "[40] It was Fulbright's fear of an ideologically driven foreign policy that was in part responsible for his opposition to the war. "The fears and passions of ideological conflict have diverted the minds and energies of our people from the constructive tasks of a free society to a morbid preoccupation with the dangers of Communist aggression abroad and subversion and disloyalty at home," he told an audience at the University of North Carolina in 1964.[41] From approximately 1965 through 1972 Fulbright operated on the assumption that an unholy alliance of Russophobe interventionists and liberal zealots driven by speculative principle had seized control of the executive and were attempting to build an American empire in Asia. In turn, the war in Asia was polarizing American society and stimulating the growth of extremist groups from the John Birch Society to black nationalists.[42]

The war in Southeast Asia was especially offensive to Fulbright because it contravened the principles of Wilsonian internationalism as he perceived them.[43] Throughout twenty-five years of correspondence

---

[39] Statement before Joint Congressional Committee, July 5, 1970, series 78:5, folder 9:11, second accession, JWF papers.

[40] Quoted in McDonald, *Novus Ordo Seclorum*, p. 163.

[41] Fulbright, "The Cold War in American Life," in Johnson and Gwertzman, *Fulbright*, p. 287.

[42] Fulbright, "Price of Empire," ibid., p. 3058.

[43] Recently the notion of Southern internationalism has come under attack. What is clearly absent in the traditional Southern exegesis of foreign policy, argues Paul Seabury and Charles O. Lerche Jr., is a sense of "multilateralism." There is nowhere in the Southern ethos any appreciation of the interdependence of peoples and states and the necessity facing the United States of adapting itself and its desires to the demands of a sometimes hostile environment. Those participating in the formulation of policy and those commenting on that policy between 1919 and 1953 have spoken in xenophobic and unilateralist terms even when calling for support of America's allies. The *Walking Tall* image of the rugged individualist going it alone even within such bodies as the League of Nations

with his former pupil, Fulbright's Oxford tutor and friend, Ronald McCallum, defended the Wilsonian vision of an interdependent, peaceful world.[44] Like Wilson's biographer, Arthur S. Link, Fulbright believed that Wilson's pledge to "make the world safe for democracy" indicated (at least by 1917) not a determination to export American culture and institutions but rather a commitment to the principle of national self-determination. And he focused throughout his public life on Wilson's dream of an international collective security organization in which the community of nations acted for the common good. Contemporary internationalists, he told the Cubberly Conference in the summer of 1962, were trying to create "a system of permanent processes for the gradual improvement of the human condition on earth, in trying to make – in Woodrow Wilson's words' – a society instead of a set of barbarians out of the governments of the world.' "[45]

Fulbright authored the Fulbright-Connally Resolution, which committed the United States to participation in an international collective security organization following World War II. He was an ardent supporter of the concept of a federation of Europe and, like his friend Assistant Secretary of State William L. Clayton, a multilateralist in international economic matters.[46] As early as the debate over ratification of the United Nations Charter in 1945, Fulbright had blasted his Senate colleagues for clinging to the principle of national sovereignty, and as the Cold War progressed he lamented Washington's tendency to ignore the world organization.[47] The Vietnam War did not have the support of the United Nations, he

and United Nations was always implicit and frequently explicit in Southern discourse. Charles O. Lerche Jr., "Southern Internationalism Myth and Reality," in Patrick Gerster and Nicholas Cords, eds., *Myth and Southern History*), (Chicago: University of Chicago Press, 1974), pp. 262–263; and Paul Seabury, *The Waning of Southern Internationalism* (Princeton: Princeton University Press, 1957), 139–143. Despite his being a Southerner. Fulbright's internationalism, under the criteria established by these critics, is authentic.

[44] In 1944 McCallum published *Public Opinion and the Lost Peace* in which he challenged the longstanding view of John Maynard Keynes that the peace structure hammered out at the Versailles Conference was predestined to fail. The concept of the League of Nations was sound. McCallum argued the organization had not worked because political figures on both sides of the Atlantic had never been willing to make a true commitment to the principles that underlay it and had attempted to use it for their own selfish. political purposes. Herb Gunn, "The Continuing Friendship of James William Fulbright and Ronald Buchanan McCallum," South *Atlantic Quarterly* vol., LXXXIII (Autumn 1984), pp. 417–419.

[45] "National Goals and National Consensus," July 28. 1962, series 4:19, box 29:7. JWF papers.

[46] *Congressional Record*, 80 Congress, 1st session, pp. 31–38 April 7. 1947.

[47] Ibid., 79 Congress, 1st session, p. 7962–7964 July 23, 1945.

frequently observed, and by 1967 America's Southeast Asian adventure was deeply dividing the North Atlantic Treaty Organization (NATO). In acting outside the framework of the United Nations, in refusing its offers of mediation, in violating the provisions of the 1954 Geneva Accords, the United States was not only destroying Vietnam and itself but also undermining the principles of collective security and international cooperation.

It should be noted that in arguing that nation states would have to relinquish a portion of their sovereignty if a system of world government were to work, Fulbright was not typically southern or typical of Southern internationalists. Tennant S. McWilliams and others have shown that most Dixie advocates of international cooperation were nationalists under the skin. Indeed, Woodrow Wilson, although born a Southerner, had acquired his views on multilateralism and world government as part of his immersion in the politics and culture of the urban Northeast. Many southerners touted Wilsonian internationalism because they perceived it to be a vehicle that would restore to the region a degree of dignity and respect, that would act as an antidote to slavery, civil war, and reconstruction. What in truth they favored was an association of nations in which each member retained complete freedom of action. Indeed, influenced by the Cold War and McCarthyism, many Southern politicians came to define internationalism as an American-led crusade to defeat communism.[48] Fulbright certainly shared the region's pride in Woodrow Wilson and in Wilson's vision of international cooperation, but unlike many of his fellow Southerners (and perhaps unlike Wilson), Fulbright took Wilson's principles at face value.[49] In part the exchange of persons program that he founded was designed to eradicate the nationalism and xenophobia that made internationalism unworkable.[50]

Fulbright's perception that U. S. foreign policy had been captured by unilateralists and imperialists was responsible for his well-known reversal on the relative powers of the executive and legislative branches in the field of foreign policy. Fulbright began his career as a champion of the executive's prerogatives in foreign affairs. He defended the Yalta Accords, the

[48] Tennant S. McWilliams, *The New South Faces the World: Foreign Affairs and the Southern Sense of Self 1877–1950* (Baton Rouge and London, 1988), p. 142–145.

[49] "I have always suspected that if Wilson had not suffered a stroke on his train in Colorado and had been able in full vigor to carry out his campaign to educate the American people," Fulbright once observed, "he might have succeeded and the history of twentieth century might have been incalculably different." Fulbright, "National Goals," series, 4:19, box 29:7, JWF papers.

[50] Fulbright to George A. Home, February 6, 1946, F 50, BCN 24, ibid.

Bretton Woods Accords, the Dumbarton Oaks Conference, the Truman Doctrine, the Marshall Plan, and NATO; he identified executive domination of foreign policy with internationalism and congressional control with isolationism. Those perceptions did not really change, but Fulbright's perception of internationalism and isolationism altered dramatically. The executive, he believed, had perverted internationalism, converting it exclusively into Cold War interventionism. While Fulbright's critique of American foreign policy and its perversion may not have been typically Southern, it had its roots in his southern heritage and education.

If Fulbright's philosophy was rooted in the Anglophilia and class-consciousness of Arkansas's planting aristocracy, it grew also out of the mindset of the southern highlanders who populated the Ozark mountains. Their salient features – a stubborn independence and an ingrained tendency to resist established authority – contributed significantly to Fulbright's stance toward the war in Vietnam. Throughout his public career he seemed determined to swim upstream – against Harry Truman and the cronyism of the early 1950s, against Senator Joseph R. McCarthy and his Russophobe supporters, against the complacency and materialism that marked Dwight D. Eisenhower's years as president, and against Lyndon Johnson, the larger-than-life Texan and the military industrial complex that supported him. Like many southern highlanders, Fulbright embraced dissent for dissent's sake. In "A Higher Patriotism," an antiwar speech he delivered at Storrs, Connecticut, in 1966, the Arkansan observed with distaste that intolerance of dissent was a typically American characteristic. He echoed Alexis de Tocqueville's thoughts on the United States 150 years earlier: "I know of no country in which there is so little independence of mind and real freedom of discussion." Fulbright insisted that unanimity was tantamount to complacency: in the absence of debate and dissension, errors – the war in Vietnam being the most glaring – were sure to be made.[51] And, in fact, it was his penchant for dissent that helped the junior senator survive in office until 1974. A large majority of Arkansans believed that North Vietnam was the aggressor and that the American cause was just, but they distrusted Johnson because he was a Texan, because he seemed to epitomize big government, and because he was seen as a bully. Fulbright, cast in the role of the courageous underdog struggling against insuperable odds, appealed to the average Arkansan whose immense inferiority complex lay always just beneath the surface. "If the present Administration is half as vindictive against its

---

[51] *Congressional Record*, 89 Congress, 2nd session, pp. 886–972, April 25, 1966.

foreign policy critics as was the Roosevelt regime," a prowar constituent from northwest Arkansas wrote, "you may well find yourself being undercut, patronage-wise and in other ways, here in Arkansas in order to render you ineffective and sour the voters on you. In any event, you must have courage – a quality I greatly admire in any man."[52]

Fulbright's opposition to the war in Vietnam, then, stemmed from his attachment to republicanism, his traditional English liberalism, and his Southern highlander independence. It also flowed from his views on the South and its place in American history. Senator Fulbright, whose paternal great-grandparents' home in Missouri had been burned by Union raiders, bought into the myth of Reconstruction that held sway in the South well into the 1960s, namely, that from 1867 through 1877 Dixie had been forcibly occupied by federal troops and compelled to accept governments run by ignorant field hands, exploitative carpetbaggers, and unscrupulous scalawags. During that supposedly terrible period, radical Republicans in Congress turned the South's cavalier social system upside down; the poor, the ignorant, and the corrupt ruled the virtuous, educated, and civilized. "Even today," he observed to the Senate, "although the South has long since recovered its political rights and has begun at last to share in the nation's economic prosperity, the very word 'Yankee' still awakens in Southern minds historical memories of defeat and humiliation, of the burning of Atlanta and Sherman's march to the sea, or of an ancestral farmhouse burned by Cantrell's raiders...."[53]

To him the civil rights movement was in large part just another attempt by the North to impose its will and culture on the South. "The South lost the war in 1865," he observed to the Senate with some bitterness during the debate over the Civil Rights Act of 1960. "Why are there so many

---

[52] David M. Baxter to Fulbright, March 20, 1966, series 48: 11, box 35:3, JWF papers. A Little Rock television survey taken in the fall of 1967 indicates that 54 percent of the viewers questioned responded that they opposed Fulbright's stand on the war while 46 percent approved. For socioeconomic and educational reasons opposition to the war was greater in this, the state's only urban area, than in other regions of Arkansas. "Fulbright's Stand Tested by TV Poll," *Little Rock Arkansas Democrat*, November 2, 1967. Fortner governor and marine veteran Sid McMath, one of Arkansas's most popular figures, repeatedly and Publicly denounced the junior senator's opposition to the war. The state's equally popular sitting governor, Winthrop Rockefeller, a Republican, refused to criticize Fulbright. "The folks here in Arkansas are proud of our boy who stands up and takes a position," he told Peter Jennings of ABC News. "Fulbright Facing '68 Fight," *Washington Evening* Star, May 15, 1967. Most important, during the 1968 senatorial campaign Fulbright repeatedly defended his stance on the war before Arkansas crowds and he won handily.

[53] Statement by Senator J. W. Fulbright, March 7, 1966, box 462, Harriman papers.

in the North who wish to prolong it?"[54] Fulbright's historical memory led him to identify both with his own nation, embroiled in a hopeless war half a world away, and with Vietnam, struggling desperately to fend off a larger imperial power. Like Edmund Burke, an Irishman who became one of eighteenth-century England's most powerful politicians and a man whom Fulbright was fond of quoting, the Arkansan represented the experience of defeat in the halls of the national legislature. "Perhaps we Southerners have a sensitivity to this sort of thing [the stalemate in Vietnam] that other Americans cannot fully share," he remarked in 1966. "We – or our forebears – experienced both the hotheaded romanticism that led to Fort Sumter and the bitter humiliation of defeat and a vindictive Reconstruction." The South's burden, he observed, had become the nation's burden.[55]

As an individual with a strong sense of class, kinship, and place, he believed it no less abhorrent that the United States should force its culture, political institutions, and economic theories on another society than that the North should impose its mores on the South. Fulbright acknowledged that most Americans supported the war in Vietnam for admirable reasons – to extend the blessings of democracy and individual liberty and to guarantee stability and prosperity to a people threatened by communist imperialism. But he also believed that popular and official ignorance of Indochinese history and culture prevented Americans from perceiving that nationalism was a stronger component in the ideology of Vietnamese communists than was Marxism-Leninism, that respect for authority and continuity were more important political values in Vietnamese society than democracy and freedom, and that China and Vietnam were age-old enemies rather than coconspirators out to communize the world. America's efforts to remake Vietnam in its image were as absurd as the North's efforts to legislate racial equality in the South.[56] If the Vietnamese wanted to live under communist rule, so be it. His was a live-and-let-live mentality, a mentality that had led to the Compromise of 1877, and that had been used for a hundred years to block federal action to help African Americans. Nonetheless, that same perspective

---

[54] *Congressional Record*, 86 Congress, 2nd session, pp. 7312 and 7324 (quotation), April 5, 1960.

[55] *Ibid.*, 89 Congress, 2nd session. p. 5145, March 7, 1966.

[56] "U S. efforts to preserve the independence of States in Asia and to promote their economic growth will fail unless greater indigenous Asian . . . support is forthcoming," he advised President Kennedy in 1961. Fulbright to Kennedy, May 19, 1961, box 1, Fulbright papers, Records of the Senate Foreign Relations Committee, RG 46.

produced a much-needed critique of the notion of American diplomatic omnipotence.

Further contributing to Fulbright's determination to protect the sanctity of indigenous cultures was his dislike of colonialism, a Southern and Wilsonian preoccupation. Like so many other leaders of the New South, Fulbright never forgot that Arkansas and the entire region were economic colonies of the North. In 1964, during an exchange with Senator Jacob Javits, he declared: "Where did New York get its many dollars? It did not take the money out of the ground, out of a gold mine.... For many years Mr. Joseph Eastman [a New York industrialist] dominated the Interstate Commerce Commission. The Interstate Commerce Commission set up freight rates so that we in the South could not start an industry..."[57] From 1943 through 1955, which covered his term in the House and his first decade in the Senate, Fulbright devoted much of his energy to freeing his constituents from their economic bondage. His views on the South as an exploited economic colony of the North, his adherence to the Wilsonian principle of national self-determination, as well as his resentment at what he believed to be the North's efforts to impose its racial views on the South instilled in him an intense anticolonialism.

From late 1956 through 1960 the Arkansan repeatedly castigated John Foster Dulles and Dwight Eisenhower for adopting a rigidly counterrevolutionary position in regard to the anticolonial, nationalist revolutions that were beginning to sweep the developing world. In propping up military dictators and aging colonial regimes, Washington was merely adding fuel to the flames of regional disputes and blocking healthy change. The second Indochinese war was the bitter fruit of that neocolonial stance. As visualized by its architects, containment was designed to prevent the spread of Soviet aggression, Fulbright told journalists Martin Agronsky and Eric Sevareid in 1966. As it had evolved under Johnson, it was an attempt to contain a worldwide movement toward self-government and self-expression by peoples formerly yoked to European empires.[58] From being one of foreign aid's staunchest supporters Fulbright moved during the Vietnam era to being one of its most adamant opponents.[59] The Vietnamese were suffering from the " 'fatal impact' of the rich and strong on the poor and weak," he told a Johns Hopkins audience in the spring

---

[57] *Congressional Record*, 88 Congress, 2nd session, pp. 95–96, April 29, 1964.

[58] Berman, *Fulbright and the Vietnam War*, p. 55. See also Congressional Record, 89 Congress, 2nd session, 6749–6753, March 25, 1966.

[59] "From Fulbright: A Sweeping Attack on LBJ's 'Asian Doctrine,' " *U.S. News and World Report*, August 1, 1966, p. 12.

of 1966. "Dependent on it though the Vietnamese are, our very strength is a reproach to their weakness, our wealth a mockery of their poverty, our success a reminder of their failures."[60]

In part it was his sensitivity to imperialism, particularly cultural imperialism, that set Fulbright apart from conservative nonsouthern critics of the war. George F. Kennan, who although still enamored of the domino theory and concerned about a possible loss of credibility should the United States pull out of Vietnam, had during the 1966 SFRC televised hearings on Vietnam called for "a resolute and courageous liquidation of unsound positions" in that war-torn country.[61] Like Fulbright, Kennan distrusted democracy, recommending the establishment of rule by an "elite ... of mind and character."[62] He believed that the key to winning the Cold War was maintaining a healthy society at home. He was a conservative who bemoaned the erosion of traditional American virtues; however, unlike Fulbright, who denounced perceived efforts by the United States to foist its values, virtuous or otherwise, on other nations, Kennan worried that mistakes made in Vietnam and the impact of the war on America would undermine the nation's ability to lead the free world.

Fulbright's position on civil rights, if not his Southernness, posed a problem for antiwar dissidents, many of whom looked to him for leadership and for most of whom opposition to the war in Vietnam and support for the second reconstruction were part of the same moral and philosophical cloth. Most accepted the political argument that he put forward in justification of his racist voting record. Nevertheless, they could never quite forget or forgive Fulbright for signing the Southern Manifesto and voting against every civil rights bill until 1970.[63]

---

[60] *Congressional Record*, 89 Congress, 2nd session, p. 10807, May 17, 1966. Fulbright believed that in its effort to save Vietnam, the United States was destructively projecting its values and goals on a foreign culture. As Lyndon Johnson prepared to pour thousands of additional troops into Vietnam in the summer of 1965, Carl Marcy, Fulbright's chief of staff on the SFRC, lamented the change that had come over America since John Kennedy's inauguration. "We have tried to force upon the rest of the world a righteous American point of view which we maintain is the consensus that others must accept," he told Fulbright. "Most of the tragedies of the world have come from such righteousness." Marcy to Fulbright, August 17, 1965, series 48:1, box 16:2, JWF papers.

[61] Walter L. Hixson, "Containment on the Perimeter: George F. Kennan and Vietnam" *Diplomatic History*, X11; Spring, 1988, p. 161.

[62] Ibid., p. 162.

[63] In later years Fulbright responded to those who questioned at the time how he could take such apparently incongruous positions on the war and civil rights. Philosophical questions aside. Arkansans were willing to listen to arguments in behalf of an enlightened foreign policy; this was patently not the case in the area of civil rights. "They [the people

The great irony was that Fulbright's participation in the struggle against civil rights enabled him to communicate with Southern hawks who were beginning to have doubts concerning the war. And the alienation of the hawks was the key to the destruction of the prowar consensus in Congress. Throughout 1967, Fulbright worked to convince Richard B. Russell of Georgia, Sam Ervin of North Carolina, and other strict constructionists in the Senate to apply the same constitutional standards to the Johnson administration's foreign policy as they did to its civil rights program. Russell and Ervin had initially opposed the introduction of troops into Vietnam but had subsequently taken the position that, once there, they should be supported to the fullest. By 1967, they were frustrated with the stalemate on the battlefield and angry at Johnson's deception and arrogance.[64] In the issues of executive usurpation of congressional prerogatives and the "unconstitutional" extension of American power abroad, Fulbright offered the disillusioned hawks of Dixie a face-saving way to oppose the war. When in July, 1967, the chairman of the SFRC offered his national commitments resolution, a proposal requiring explicit congressional approval of executive agreements with foreign countries, Russell and Ervin leaped to their feet to support it. "I know of nothing that is more in need of clarification than the present state of the alleged commitment of the United States all over the world," Russell told his colleagues.[65] That attitude, in turn, led to the passage of the Cooper-Church amendment, setting a deadline for withdrawal of American troops from Cambodia, and eventually to enactment of various end-the-war resolutions during the administration of Richard M. Nixon.[66]

of Arkansas] know what their daughter is and they know what the conditions are in their local school. It's not over in Vietnam or the Middle East. There they are subject to persuasion.... They didn't agree with my view on Vietnam. But I could make them shake their view of it by saying, 'After all, I know more about it.' " On the other hand, "You had a hell of a chance of persuading them that it's a good thing for their daughter to go to school with a black man." Fulbright Interview with author.

[64] Russell to General L. O. Grice, March 21, 1967, dictation series, box IT 34e., Vietnam folder, Russell papers.

[65] *Congressional Record*, 90 Congress. 1st session, pp. 207–227, July 31, 1967. Congress eventually passed the national commitments resolution during the Nixon administration.

[66] Into 1970 and early 1971 Fulbright continued to try to convince Senator Sam Ervin, to apply the same constitutional standards to Nixon's foreign policy as he did to civil rights, impoundment. and other issues. Ervin put him off and cast one hawkish vote after another. Like Richard Russell, Ervin believed that U.S. involvement in the Second Indochinese War had been a mistake, but that once the "boys" were committed to battle, the nation could not look back. But Fulbright's persistence, coupled with the brouhaha over publication of the Pentagon papers (the secret history of the war commissioned by Secretary of Defense Robert McNamara), and the declared intention of Senator John C. Stennis of

Fulbright's opposition to the Vietnam War thus stemmed from southern and conservative roots that most of his followers would neither have
understood nor appreciated. Deeply conservative and even racist, he was
treated as a hero by war protesters and widely heralded for a time by the
New Left. Committed to aristocratic values and to an elitist perception of
society, he was viewed as a crusader against the establishment.[67] It may be,
as Sheldon Hackney argues, that the South is a counterculture; however,
only in that special sense may Fulbright be considered a rebel.[68] Nevertheless, Fulbright put forward a searching critique of American policy at
a crucial point in the nation's history. That indictment, particularly as it
pertained to cultural imperialism, was in part an expression of Fulbright's
Southern and aristocratic background, compounded alike of his classical
education, Ozark roots, Delta associations, and historical memory.

Mississippi to seek a congressional limit on the warmaking powers of the president finally
turned Ervin. In August the selfstyled country lawyer, his jowels shimmying and eyes
flashing, opened hearings before his Judiciary subcommittee on various pending measures
designed to keep the executive branch from withholding information from Congress. The
first item on the agenda was the Fulbright bill, which would compel the president either
to furnish full information to Congress upon request or to invoke executive privilege. and
it was clear from the beginning that the North Carolinian was now ready to support his
Arkansas colleague. "Senate G.O.P. Chief Backs Restrictions on President's Warmaking
Powers," *New York Times*, July 28, 1971, sec. 1, p. 7. From the summer of 1971 on,
Ervin consistently supported endthewar resolutions. Karl Campbell, "The Triumph of
Conservatism: Senator Sam Ervin and the Road to Watergate," paper presented to the
1993 American Historical Association meeting in Washington, D.C.

[67] Fulbright always shunned the mantle of leadership that radical America sought to thrust
upon him, however. One of Fulbright's aides asserted: "Fulbright is not a zealot. He gave
respectability to the antiwar movement, but he based his opposition on rational judgment
rather than emotion, and he was always worried by the longhaired demonstrators who
saluted him as their *leader*," quoted in Stanley Karnow, "Henry and Bill: The Kissinger
Fulbright Courtship," *New Republic*, December 29, 1973, p. 16.

[68] Sheldon Hackney, "The South as a Counterculture," *American Scholar*, XLII; Spring,
1973, pp. 283–293.

Advice and Dissent: Mike Mansfield and the Vietnam War

Donald A. Ritchie

Mike Mansfield came to Congress in 1943 as the United States put aside isolationism to forge military commitments around the globe. Part of a generation shaped by Munich and Pearl Harbor, Mansfield accepted as imperatives international resistance to aggression, strong presidential leadership, and a bipartisan foreign policy. The United States, he believed, emerged from World War II with a moral vision and a sense of national purpose. "Our goal was the defense of liberty, and the triumph of political and economic freedom." Immediately after the war, when the nation had been the most powerful, "we were in our most cooperative and international mode, showing a decent respect for the opinions of others, and seeking their cooperation and support." He considered it a great irony that as other nations grew economically and militarily stronger relative to the United States in the 1960s and 70s, "we started to try to change the world on our own."[1]

Those who observed him most closely found Mansfield difficult to define. Taciturn, retiring, and contemplative in nature, this "deceptively mild" man could turn forceful in asserting his convictions. A politician

[1] "Senator Mike Mansfield Recipient of the 1990 Sylvanus Thayer Award," *Assembly*, (January 1991), p. 8.

Donald A. Ritchie is associate historian of the U.S. Senate Historical Office, where he has conducted an oral history program with retired members of the Senate staff and edited the *Executive Sessions of the Senate Foreign Relations Committee, "Historical Series,"* and the *Minutes of the U.S. Senate Democratic Conference, 1903–1964.* His other publications include *Press Gallery: Congress and the Washington Correspondents* (Harvard Press, 1991), *Doing Oral History* (Twayne, 1995), and *The Oxford Guide to the United States Government* (Oxford, 2001).

who was "not a compulsive seeker of power"and "not all-consumed with politics," he held onto the reigns of political power longer than any other Senate majority leader. A party leader who shunned excessive partisanship, he exerted a unique moral authority over colleagues from both parties. A key member of the congressional leadership, he followed a publicly deferential course toward presidents in matters of foreign policy, even while opposing many of those policies in private. A veteran of three branches of the military, he disliked militarism. A scholar of foreign affairs, he never fit comfortably into any prevailing school of thought, from realist to neo-isolationist. Although Mansfield generally voted as a liberal internationalist, he "was neither purely liberal nor conservative, isolationist nor internationalist," marveled his long-time aide Francis R. (Frank) Valeo. "He did not correspond to any of the particular touchstones by which politicians of the period were pigeonholed by the press."[2]

Holding global views while representing a state with isolationist tendencies, Mansfield developed a centrist approach to foreign policy during the Cold War. He supported western containment of communism as well as an end to European colonization of the Third World, particularly in Asia. He preferred that the United States encourage the independence and self-determination of nations through economic and technical assistance rather than armed force, and he warned that assuming too large a military role could cast Americans as neocolonialists. Although he initially supported American military participation in NATO and a combat role in Korea, Mansfield gradually reexamined American overseas obligations, and took the lead in attempting to reduce U.S. troop commitments in Europe and Asia. He also demanded greater congressional scrutiny of U.S. intelligence agencies and reductions in foreign aid. "In a government such as ours," he once explained, "a senator lives with a Constitution, a constituency, and a conscience." Mansfield believed that the president could best speak for the nation, but he never lost sight of the legislative branch's constitutional rights responsibilities. As a senator, he urged his Montana constituency to put aside "that nineteenth century dream of a safe and contented America, removed from the troubles of the world,"

[2] Richard Langham Riedel, *Halls of the Mighty: My 47 Years at the Senate* (Washington: Robert B. Luce, 1969), p. 153; Bobby Baker, *Wheeling and Dealing: Confessions of a Capitol Hill Operator* (New York: W. W. Norton, 1978), pp. 65, 140; Samuel Shaffer, *On and Off the Senate Floor: Thirty Years as a Correspondent on Capitol Hill* (New York: Newsweek Books, 1980), p. 116; Francis R. Valeo, *Mike Mansfield, Majority Leader: A Different Kind of Senate, 1961–1976* (Armonk, NY: M.E. Sharpe, 1999), pp. 31–32.

and reminded them that the United States was part of the world, "whether we like it or not." Nor did he hesitate to express his conscience directly to presidents, reserving his right to dissent from their policies, most notably on the war in Vietnam.[3]

As a specialist in Asian affairs, Mansfield himself bore some of the responsibility for the American commitment in Vietnam. He participated in the creation of the Southeast Asian Treaty Organization and endorsed the South Vietnamese government of Ngo Dinh Diem as a democratic alternative to colonialism and communism. Yet he also promoted Asian nationalism and neutrality, and he objected to the escalating American military intervention in Southeast Asia. The veteran Washington correspondent William S. White likened Mansfield's disagreement with Democratic presidents John Kennedy and Lyndon Johnson over Vietnam to former Vice President Henry Wallace's opposition to President Harry Truman's policies toward the Soviet Union in the 1940s. Unlike Wallace or Foreign Relations Committee chairman J. William Fulbright, however, Mansfield never openly broke with the Democratic presidents with whom he served. As the Democratic majority leader of the Senate, he loyally supported most of Kennedy's and Johnson's initiatives. Mansfield's private dissent on Vietnam rankled both presidents, but they could not afford to ignore him given his standing on Capitol Hill. With Republicans Richard Nixon and Gerald Ford in the White House, Mansfield felt freer to take an open lead in bringing a legislative end to the conflict.[4]

Born to Irish-Catholic immigrants in New York City on March 16, 1903, Michael Joseph Mansfield was only six years old when his mother died. He and two younger sisters went to live with relatives in Great Falls, Montana, where they grew up in rooms behind the family's grocery store. As a boy he liked to mingle with the miners, farmers, and cowpunchers who shopped there, and he adopted their casual, unpretentious style. "They were free souls who drifted or were driven to seek a new life on the Western frontier," he reminisced; and in politics they were "Democrats or nothing – almost all of them." An inattentive student who dreamed of seeing the world, Mike Mansfield dropped out of grade school at fourteen

---

[3] Louis Baldwin, *Hon. Politician: Mike Mansfield of Montana*, (Missoula: Mountain Publishing, 1979), p. 173; *Congressional Record*, 84th Congress, 2nd session, p. 2635.
[4] William S. White, *The Making of a Journalist* (Lexington: University Press of Kentucky, 1986), p. 196.

to join the Navy during World War I. He made seven convoy voyages across the Atlantic before his age was discovered and he was discharged. He subsequently enlisted briefly in the Army but found stateside duty boring. Still in his teens, he joined the Marine Corps, which sent him to the Philippines and to China, experiences that engendered his lifelong fascination with Asia.[5]

Mansfield returned to Butte, Montana, as a copper miner. There he met high school teacher Maureen Hayes, who "inspired and literally forced" him to get a college education, selling her life insurance to pay his tuition. They married while he was a student at the University of Montana. Graduating during the Depression in 1933, Mansfield felt that he was passed over for several high school teaching jobs because he was a Catholic. He returned to graduate school to earn a master's degree in history and political science, writing a thesis on U.S. relations with Korea. He joined the faculty of the University of Montana in Missoula to teach Latin American and Far Eastern history and also worked on a doctorate at UCLA until political ambitions intruded upon his academic career.[6]

Butte and Missoula lay in Montana's First Congressional District, which covered the mountainous western region of the state. The First District's high concentration of Irish Catholics and union miners generally carried elections for the Democrats. The state's Second District encompassed its vast eastern plains populated by sheep and cattle ranchers, with a predominantly Protestant population that voted Republican. During the 1930s both districts exhibited strong isolationist sentiments. Montana's Democratic Senator Burton K. Wheeler broke with the Democratic administration in Washington to oppose American intervention in European affairs, and won reelection. In 1938, an isolationist Republican, Jacob Thorkelson, upset the incumbent Democratic representative in the First District. Thorkelson's eccentric behavior (he was an avid nudist) and his blatantly pro-Nazi pronouncements in Congress stimulated intense efforts to defeat him for reelection. Two years later, Jeannette Rankin, a more respectable isolationist, beat Thorkelson in the Republican primary. In the same primary elections, Mike Mansfield suffered his only defeat at

[5] "Remarks of Senator Mike Mansfield at the 1976 Democratic Congressional Dinner, May 11, 1976, Senate Historical Office files.
[6] Address by Senator Mike Mansfield, in Trent Lott, *The Leader's Lecture Series: Leading the United States Senate* (Washington: Government Printing Office, 1998), p. 7; Gregory Allen Olson, *Mansfield and Vietnam: A Study in Rhetorical Adaptation* (East Lansing: Michigan State University Press, 1995), pp. 7–9.

the polls when he failed in his bid to be the Democratic nominee for the House seat.[7]

Reflecting prevailing public opinion, all candidates in both party primaries in 1940 had opposed American entry into World War II. In November, the Republicans once again carried the First District and elected Jeannette Rankin, who two decades earlier had achieved notoriety as the first woman member of Congress. A pacifist, she had voted against American entry into World War I in 1917, one of fifty representatives who opposed the war resolution. Now elected to a second term, Rankin would cast the sole vote against war with Japan in December, 1941, giving her the historical distinction of being the only member of Congress to vote against both world wars. But Pearl Harbor had discredited the isolationists' arguments and turned public opinion against them. Rankin's unpopular stand destroyed any hope of her reelection, and she chose not to run again. By contrast, Mansfield's status as a veteran of three branches of the armed services resonated with wartime voters. With his students running his campaign he recaptured the First District for the Democrats.[8]

In the House, Mansfield was appointed to the Foreign Affairs Committee, where he focused on Asian policy. His delivery of a series of radio addresses on the war in the Pacific bolstered his standing as one of the few Asian authorities in Congress, and prompted President Franklin D. Roosevelt to send him on a confidential mission to China. After his five-week trip, Mansfield reported back to Roosevelt and the House of Representatives in January, 1945. He presented a sober assessment of the chaotic conditions in China, although his references to the Chinese communists as "more reformers than revolutionaries" (which reflected the prevalent thinking among American diplomats in China) would come back to haunt his future campaigns. President Harry Truman later sent Mansfield as a delegate to the United Nations Assembly in Paris and offered to appoint him Assistant Secretary of State for public affairs. Instead, Mansfield chose to run for the Senate in 1952.[9]

---

7 Burton K. Wheeler with Paul F. Healy, *Yankee from the West* (Garden City: Double-day, 1962), pp. 378–409; see also Thomas Payne, "Montana; Politics Under the Copper Dome," in Frank H. Jonas, ed., *Politics in the American West* (Salt Lake City: University of Utah Press, 1969), pp. 203–30; and Neal R. Peirce, *The Mountain States of America: People, Politics, and power in the Eight Rocky Mountain States* (New York: W. W. Norton, 1972), pp. 90–119.

8 See Kevin S. Giles, *Flight of the Dove: The Story of Jeannette Rankin* (Beaverton, OR: Touchstone Press, 1980).

9 Olson, *Mansfield and Vietnam*, pp. 9–13; *Congressional Record*, 79th Congress, 1st session, pp. 279–280.

The campaign between Mansfield and the incumbent Republican Senator Zales Ecton was a scorcher. Ecton invited the fiery Wisconsin Senator Joseph R. McCarthy to campaign personally against the man they called "China Mike." McCarthy dubbed Mansfield "either stupid or a dupe" for his portrayal of the Chinese communists as reformers, and Ecton depicted Mansfield as soft on communism. Angrily, Mansfield denounced the "slick and ugly way" that the McCarthyites smeared anyone who opposed them. Although Republican presidential candidate Dwight Eisenhower carried Montana that year, Mansfield narrowly defeated Ecton with 50.7 percent of the vote (in his three subsequent races for the Senate, Mansfield never received less than 60 percent of the vote). "How are things in Montana these days?" Joe McCarthy jovially asked the new senator back in Washington. "Much better since you left, sir," Mansfield replied.[10]

Senator Mansfield became the only freshman on the prestigious Foreign Relations Committee. Although some senators considered the committee a "debating society" without much influence over legislation, its handling of diplomatic nominations, treaties, and foreign aid gave Mansfield the opportunity to focus on the issues that most interested him. Leadership posts in later years left him less time for the Foreign Relations Committee. He often missed its meetings and rarely chaired a subcommittee. The committee served as a better forum for its chairman, the erudite J. William Fulbright of Arkansas, and for more voluble members like Wayne Morse, Hubert Humphrey, and Frank Church. In foreign affairs, Mansfield operated essentially as a committee of one.[11]

To supplement its small professional staff, the Foreign Relations Committee borrowed specialists from the Library of Congress' Legislative Reference Service (later renamed the Congressional Research Service). Among them was Frank Valeo, an expert on the Far East. Like Mansfield, Valeo boasted military service in China. He also held a master's degree in international relations from New York University. Valeo recalled his first meeting with the rawboned, "sort of gangling fellow" from Montana who wanted background material for a speech on Japan and China. Valeo prepared drafts that were comprehensive but complex, causing Mansfield to tell him that in the future he preferred "much more conversational" statements. Throughout Mansfield's congressional

---

[10] William "Fishbait" Miller, *Fishbait: The Memoirs of the Congressional Doorkeeper* (New York: Warner, 1977), pp. 440–441; Olson, *Mansfield and Vietnam*, pp. 13–16.
[11] George A. Smathers oral history interviews, Senate Historical Office, pp. 100–101.

career, Valeo would draft most of his foreign policy speeches and memoranda. He drew on Mansfield's own attitudes and experiences and on the newspaper clippings and other reading materials that so intrigued the senator. Their partnership of thought and style enabled Mansfield, a naturally laconic man, to become an eloquent critic of American foreign policy.[12]

Interested in China, Japan, and Korea, Mansfield paid little notice to Southeast Asia until May, 1953, when Supreme Court Justice William O. Douglas invited him and Senator John F. Kennedy to a luncheon for the Vietnamese nationalist Ngo Dinh Diem. Anti-French as well as anticommunist, Diem was seeking American support for an independent Vietnamese government. Then living in exile at Maryknoll seminaries in the United States, Diem lobbied American political and religious leaders, and won the admiration of liberal and conservative Catholics alike. French missionaries had implanted Catholicism more firmly in Vietnam than in most other Asian nations, although Catholics remained a tiny minority in the midst of an overwhelming Buddhist majority. American Catholics naturally sympathized with their religious kinsmen. The Church's ardent anticommunism and the appeal of McCarthyism among many Catholic voters further prompted Catholic politicians like Mansfield and Kennedy to embrace Diem as an anticommunist leader. Increasingly curious about Southeast Asia, Mansfield planned his first fact-finding trip there with Frank Valeo in late 1953. They knew so little about the region that Valeo had trouble determining which of the two starred cities on his French map was the capital of Laos. "Well, let's put both places on the itinerary," Mansfield suggested pragmatically.[13]

Although American policymakers were initially ambivalent toward the communist-led Vietminh, the nationalist force that had fought against

---

[12] Francis R. Valeo, oral history interviews, Senate Historical Office, pp. 15–16; Francis R. Valeo, *Mike Mansfield, Majority Leader: A Different Kind of Senate* (Armong, NY: M.E. Sharpe, 1999); many of Mansfield's memos are included in David M. Barrett, ed., *Lyndon B. Johnson's Vietnam Papers: A Documentary Collection* (College Station: Texas A&M University Press, 1997).

[13] Valeo, oral history, pp. 85–95; Robert Mann, *A Grand Delusion: America's Descent into Vietnam* (New York: Basic Books, 2001), pp. 101–106; Stanley Karnow, *Vietnam: A History* (New York: Viking Press, 1983), pp. 58–59; Frances FitzGerald, *Fire In the Lake: The Vietnamese and the Americans in Vietnam* (Boston: Little, Brown, 1972), pp. 82–84; see also Donald F. Crosby, S.J., *God, Church and Flag: Senator Joseph R. McCarthy and the Catholic Church, 1950–1957* (Chapel Hill: University of North Carolina Press, 1978); and Thomas E. Quigley, ed., *American Catholics and Vietnam* (Grand Rapids: William E. Erdmans Publishing, 1968).

Japanese occupation during World War II, Cold War tensions eventually swung the United States behind a reassertion of French colonial authority in Indochina. Echoing the State Department, Senator Mansfield insisted that American security was "no less involved in Indochina than in Korea." He accepted the domino theory and asserted that if Indochina fell "that means all of Southeast Asia, and perhaps all of Asia will follow suit." But his first visit to the region also instilled in him an appreciation of nationalism as a means of defeating communism. Mansfield called on the French to grant more political freedom to the people of Indochina, and on the United States to recognize Vietnam, Laos and Cambodia as independent governments. To survive, these governments needed to appeal to popular sentiment by confronting social and economic inequalities. He supported increased economic aid, but warned against going "to the extreme of sending in American combat forces." The only ones who could defeat communism in Indochina, he declared, were the people of the region themselves.[14]

The "strange and elusive struggle" in Indochina, Mansfield reported, was "a shadowy war without battle lines." The French defeat at Dien Bien Phu in May, 1954, ended any confidence he had in a military solution. "I always thought that if the French could not win there," he later reflected, "what should make us think we could?" While debating Republican majority leader William F. Knowland during the Dien Bien Phu crisis, Mansfield asserted that Montanans were opposed to the United States taking military action in Vietnam, convinced that "with the communist's superiority of manpower and material, that there isn't much we could do." He strongly doubted that modern mechanized armed forces could cope with the terrain of Indochina conflict, with its thick jungles, flooded deltas, and thousands of scattered villages.[15]

---

[14] Lloyd C. Gardner, *Approaching Vietnam: From World War II Through Dienbienphu, 1941–1954* (New York: W. W. Norton, 1988), pp. 54–87; George C. Herring, *America's Longest War: The United States and Vietnam, 1950–1975* (New York: Alfred A. Knopf, 1996), pp. 3–45; Senate Committee on Foreign Relations, *Indochina: Report of Senator Mike Mansfield on a Study Mission to the Associated States of Indochina: Vietnam, Cambodia, Laos,* October 27, 1953, 83rd Congress, 1st session, (Washington: Government Printing Office, 1953), pp. iii, 1–9; U.S. Congress, Senate Foreign Relations Committee [William Conrad Gibbons], *The U.S. Congress and the Vietnam War: Executive and Legislative Roles and Relationships, 1945–1961,* S. print 98–185, pt. 1, (Washington: Government Printing Office, 1984), pp. 144–45, 160–62, 209.

[15] *Indochina: Report of Senator Mice Mansfield,* 4; Julius Duscha, "Mike Mansfield: Straight Shooter in the Senate," *Washingtonian,* 5 (September 1970) 43; *Congressional Record,* 83rd Congress, 2nd session, p. A3606.

In search of bipartisan support, Secretary of State John Foster Dulles enlisted the Democratic senator from Montana in his effort to see the United States fill the vacuum caused by the French defeat. Dulles invited Mansfield to serve as a U.S. delegate to the Manila conference in September, 1954, that established the Southeast Asian Treaty Organization (SEATO). From Manila, Mansfield and Valeo returned to Indochina. They flew to Hanoi during the last days of French control. Going on to Phnom Penh, they met Prince Norodom Sihanouk, who impressed Mansfield with the intensity of his nationalism and passion for Cambodian independence. In Laos they talked with Souvanna Phouma, and Mansfield formed mutually respectful relationships with each of these leaders, for whom he would serve as a conduit in Washington. On his return to the Senate, Mansfield reiterated that the United States should not act in Asia except through authentic nationalist governments.[16]

It was the Montanan's position that the United States could neither retreat back into an isolationist "Fortress America" nor charge out in every direction "with bombast, billions or bombs." American policy makers needed to weigh each international venture against two general standards: "Does the activity contribute to the preservation of peace and the security of freedom? Does it contribute to these ends in reasonable degree commensurate with the costs?" Mansfield counted on universal desires for independence, material progress, and humane government to spur change in Southeast Asia, and he urged that the United States "take these forces fully into consideration." This approach echoed George F. Kennan's prescription for containing communism through the economic rehabilitation of Europe and Japan rather than through military might. Known as "asymmetrical response," the concept involved applying Western economic strength against the communist bloc's weakness to promote regional stability. Mansfield applied much the same reasoning to Southeast Asia.[17]

The Geneva Accords of 1954 divided Vietnam, and some 860,000 refugees, mostly Vietnamese Catholics, fled to the South. Their plight was widely publicized by the American Catholic missionary doctor, Thomas Dooley, whose correspondence kept Mansfield personally apprised of the situation. Dooley's enthusiasm for Ngo Dinh Diem reinforced the

[16] Mann, *A Grand Delusion*, pp. 180–186; Baldwin, *Hon. Politician*, p. 56. Valeo, oral history, pp. 95–98; Gibbons, *The U.S. Congress and the Vietnam War*, pp. 291–295.

[17] *Congressional Record*, 84th Congress, 2nd session, pp. 2635–2639; John Lewis Gaddis, *Strategies of Containment: A Critical Appraisal of Postwar American National Security Policy* (New York: Oxford University Press, 1982), pp. 61–65.

senator's own sentiments after Diem was appointed president of the South Vietnamese council of ministers. Senator Mansfield pressed the State Department to support Diem, whom he argued had "a reputation throughout Vietnam for intense nationalism and equally intense incorruptibility." He considered Diem the only democratic nationalist who might rival the authority of North Vietnamese leader Ho Chi Minh. When the senator returned to Southeast Asia for his third visit in 1955, he met with Diem at the presidential palace in Saigon. Mansfield noted that the South Vietnamese leader and his cabinet were still wearing the colonial uniform of white linen suits, and urged him to get out as much as possible into the countryside "in his shirtsleeves" to maintain rapport with his people. Reinforcing his shirtsleeves metaphor, Mansfield removed his own jacket and hung it over the back of his chair, and one by one Diem and his cabinet officers did the same.[18]

Impressed by Diem's courage and determination, Mansfield called him "the right man, in the right place, in the right country." As Diem encountered mounting opposition from South Vietnam's Buddhist majority, Mansfield warned that the alternative to Diem's government would likely be a military regime, in which case the U.S. should terminate its aid to Vietnam. Mansfield approved of Diem's decision not to hold a reunification election in 1956 as provided under the Geneva Accords – a decision he later came to regret. Mansfield's zeal for the regime reached its peak in 1957, when he called Diem the savior of Vietnam and of all Southeast Asia, "a man of the people; a man whom the Vietnamese admire and trust; and a man in whom the United States has unbounded confidence and great faith." Soon after, however, the Vietminh resumed armed struggle in South Vietnam and Diem's government grew more repressive.[19]

In 1957, Mansfield was forced to turn his attentions from foreign affairs to domestic politics when he reluctantly agreed to serve as the Senate Democrats' assistant leader (or whip). He quickly discovered that Senate leadership rested firmly in Lyndon Johnson's back pocket, leaving little

---

[18] Olson, *Mansfield and Vietnam*, pp. 42–44, 74; Valeo, oral history, pp. 99–107; Senate Committee on Foreign Relations, *Report on Indochina: Report of Senator Mike Mansfield on a Study Mission to Vietnam, Cambodia, Laos*, October 15, 1954, 83rd Congress, 2nd session (Washington: Government Printing Office, 1954), pp. 2, 10.

[19] *Congressional Record*, 84th Congress, 2nd session, p. 11808; Gibbons, *The U.S. Government and the Vietnam War*, pt. 1: pp. 283–284, 331–333; Olson, *Mansfield and Vietnam*, pp. 53–62, 73; David L. Anderson, *Trapped by Success: The Eisenhower Administration and Vietnam, 1953–1961* (New York: Columbia University Press, 1991), pp. 82–84.

independent room for the whip. In his role as Democratic floor leader, conference chairman, and chairman of the policy and steering committees, Johnson insisted that everyone clear everything with him before doing anything. During Johnson's absences from the Senate, Mansfield substituted as floor leader. Yet whenever he attempted to move legislation, Johnson's chief aide, Senate Democratic party secretary Bobby Baker, would circulate through the chamber delaying action until Johnson's return.[20]

Montana reelected Mike Mansfield with a whopping 76 percent of the vote in 1958. Sweeping Democratic victories in the congressional elections across the nation swelled the party's majorities in the Senate and the House, and raised expectations that it could elect a Democratic president in 1960. Majority leader Johnson considered himself his party's natural standard bearer but did not actively campaign for the nomination. To Johnson's surprise, Senator John F. Kennedy won most of the primaries, took the Democratic nomination, and selected Johnson as his running mate. Kennedy's narrow victory in November thrust Johnson into the vice presidency. The powerful majority leadership that he vacated went by default to Mike Mansfield. Although the Montanan worried over the appearance of a Catholic majority leader serving simultaneously with the first Catholic president, Kennedy insisted that he take the post. Most senators welcomed Mansfield as an antidote to Johnson. As Senator George Smathers observed, "there was a big sign of relief when Johnson departed the Senate. Not that they didn't like Johnson ... but he was so strong, and so difficult, and so tough, that it was a relief to get him over to the vice president's office."[21]

As majority leader, Mansfield adopted a modest style. He liked to quote the Chinese philosopher Lao Tsu, that "a leader is best when the people hardly know he exists." The Senate staff described Mansfield as a "selfless" man with "little vanity and great stoicism," who sought to avoid antagonism and "let things run their course." He worked by persuasion rather than intimidation and expected all senators to act responsibly. Frank Valeo, who replaced Bobby Baker as Democratic party secretary, thought it significant that Mansfield had trained as a historian rather than a lawyer. "He could ignore minor things in bills and it would not trouble him at all, whereas lawyers have great difficulty doing that," Valeo

[20] Mann, *A Grand Delusion*, p. 206; Darrell St. Claire, oral history interviews, Senate Historical Office, pp. 133–135.
[21] *New York Times*, March 5, 1976; Smathers, oral history, p. 121.

observed. "Very few of them can take a broad view." Mansfield could bide his time because he saw things in a longer perspective and "thought like a historian."[22]

More activist senators grew frustrated at the Senate's glacial pace in handling Kennedy's legislative agenda, but Mansfield recognized that the Southern chairmen of the key committees were more conservative than the administration. By accommodating the chairmen rather than pressuring them, he hoped to win more cooperation, while at the same time he worked to reduce their influence by spreading legislative responsibilities among junior senators. To his critics, Mansfield professed that he was "neither a circus ringmaster, the master of ceremonies of a Senate night club, a tamer of Senate lions, or a wheeler and dealer." He thought that every senator "ought to be equal in fact, no less than in theory." The Senate would then advance "by accommodation, by respect for one another, by mutual restraint and, as necessary, adjustments in the procedures of this body."[23]

Mansfield adopted the same deferential approach in his public dealings with the White House. A president bore a greater burden of responsibility than did individual senators, Mansfield maintained, "for he alone can speak for the nation abroad." In private, however, Mansfield felt entitled to speak his own mind. Tapping his personal friendship with John Kennedy from their years together in Congress, he communicated regularly on matters concerning Southeast Asia. In departing from office, President Eisenhower had cited Laos as the first foreign policy crisis Kennedy would face. The day after Kennedy's inauguration in January, 1961, Mansfield advised that the new president would find it difficult to limit any U.S. military commitment in Laos, and recommended neutrality as the only practical course. In May, Mansfield urged Kennedy to move Laos "out of the center" of policy concern "and into a position more commensurate with our limited interests, our practical capabilities, and

---

[22] Riedel, *Halls of the Mighty*, pp. 152–155; Francis J. Attig oral history interviews, Senate Historical Office, p. 60; Valeo, oral history, pp. 334–335; Ross K. Baker, "Mike Mansfield and the Birth of the Modern Senate," in Richard A. Baker and Roger H Davidson, eds., *First Among Equals: Outstanding Senate Leaders of the Twentieth Century* (Washington: Congressional Quarterly Press, 1991), pp. 264–296.

[23] *Congressional Record*, 83rd Congress, 1st session, pp. 22857–22862; Valeo, *Mike Mansfield, Majority Leader*, pp. 6–47; see also "Mike Mansfield's Senate: The Great Society Years," and "The Vietnam Years," in Robert C. Byrd, *The Senate, 1789–1989: Addresses on the History of the United States Senate*, S. doc, pp. 100–120 (Washington, Government Printing Office, 1989), pp. 673–697; see also Donald A. Ritchie, "The Senate of Mike Mansfield," *Montana: The Magazine of Western History*, 48 (Winter 1998), pp. 50–62.

our political realities at home." The public would support Kennedy at first if he sent troops to Laos, but as casualty figures rose people would surely ask: "What are we doing in Laos?"[24]

The senator urged Kennedy to seek a negotiated settlement in Laos and instead concentrate U.S. assistance on South Vietnam, which had the "greatest potential of leadership, human capacities and resources" in Indochina: he had economic aid in mind. When Kennedy decided to send military advisers, an alarmed Mansfield warned that Vietnam "could be quicksand for us." The U.S. would have no significant allies in a military conflict in Vietnam, and the presence of American troops might draw the Chinese communists into the conflict as had happened in Korea. "While Viet Nam is very important," Mansfield cautioned, "we cannot hope to substitute armed power for the kind of political and economic social changes that offer the best resistance to communism."[25]

The administration's military response suggested to Mansfield that the president was getting poor advice from the Departments of State and Defense. The bureaucracy had been badly shaken by the public outcry over the "loss of China" along with the shock of McCarthyism, and officials seemed afraid of repeating those experiences over Vietnam. Believing that Kennedy needed other opinions, Mansfield bombarded him with a steady stream of memoranda. He would pick out items in the newspapers and from other sources and tell Valeo: "Let's get a memorandum out on this. I'll make a statement on the floor, and let's get a memorandum to the President."[26]

In June, 1962, Mansfield delivered a commencement address at Michigan State University and used the occasion to call for a new U.S. policy that placed more emphasis on economic rather than military aid to Southeast Asia. That November, at Kennedy's invitation, Mansfield returned to Vietnam for the first time in seven years. Having grown concerned about reports of government corruption and the failure to implement economic and political reforms in South Vietnam, Mansfield could not help but notice Diem's deterioration. "He seemed to be faltering in speech," Frank Valeo recalled, "and not at all certain about what he was

---

[24] *Congressional Record*, 83rd Cong., 1st sess., 22862; U.S. Congress, Senate Foreign Relations Committee [William Conrad Gibbons], *The U.S. Government and the Vietnam War: Executive and Legislative Roles and Relationships, 1961–1964*, S. prt, 98–185, pt. 2 (Washington: Government Printing Office, 1984), pp. 10, 31.

[25] Gibbons, *The U.S. Government and the Vietnam War*, pt. 2, pp. 32, 84–85; Richard Reeves, *President Kennedy: A Profile in Power* (New York: Simon & Schuster, 1993), pp. 255–256.

[26] Valeo, oral history, 252–255.

saying, and very noncommital, which contrasted sharply with the way he had been earlier with us." News stories out of South Vietnam painted an increasingly bleak portrait of Diem's government and the war effort. While in Saigon, Mansfield skipped some of the official briefings that Ambassador Frederick Nolting had arranged and instead held a four-hour lunch with David Halberstam, Neil Sheehan, Peter Arnett, and other reporters who offered discouraging personal assessments. The Saigon press corps impressed Mansfield, who later defended them from Pentagon attacks. He described them as having "the same objectivity, alertness, and appropriate skepticism of official handouts which are characteristic of American reporters everywhere." When Mansfield departed from Saigon, the U.S. embassy handed him an optimistic statement to release to the press. To Ambassador Nolting's chagrin, Mansfield gave his own less cheerful estimation.[27]

On his return, Mansfield delivered a blunt report to President Kennedy that warned against U.S. involvement in a futile conflict. Diem remained "a dedicated, sincere, hardworking, incorruptible and patriotic leader," Mansfield wrote, but he was older and faced problems more intractable than ever. Diem's brother, Ngo Dinh Nhu, had assumed the "energizing" role in Diem's government, but lacked a popular mandate to govern. Mansfield insisted that any solution to Vietnam's problems must come from within Vietnam. A massive military commitment by the United States would make it the "neocolonial" ruler of Vietnam. "It is their country," Mansfield reminded the president, "their future which is most at stake, not ours."[28]

Kennedy was vacationing in Palm Beach, Florida. "He read my report on a boat on Lake Worth," Mansfield later recalled. "He didn't like it." Mansfield's bleak assessment was not what Kennedy had expected, given their long-held mutual support for Diem and for the anticommunist effort in South Vietnam. When Kennedy objected, Mansfield pointed out that the president had asked him to go to Vietnam and those were his

[27] Ibid., pp. 249, 355–358; Mann, *A Grand Delusion,* pp. 216–219, 262–266, 270–276; Gibbons, *The U.S. Government and the Vietnam War,* pt. 2, pp. 32, 131–132; *Congressional Record,* 88th Congress, 1st session, pp. 2786, A2552–54; Herring, *America's Longest War,* pp. 101–102; David Halberstam, *The Best and the Brightest* (New York: Random House, 1972), p. 208; Olson, *Mansfield and Vietnam,* 109–11; see also William M. Hammond, *Public Affairs: The Military and the Media, 1962–1968* (Washington: Center for Military History, 1988).

[28] *Two Reports on Vietnam and Southeast Asia to the President of the United States by Senator Mike Mansfield,* S. doc., 93–111, 93rd Congress, 1st session. (Washington; Government Printing Office, 1973), pp. 5–14.

conclusions. "This isn't what my people are telling me," Kennedy snapped. Afterwards, Kennedy told his aide Kenneth O'Donnell: "I got angry with Mike for disagreeing with our policy so completely, and I got angry with myself because I found myself agreeing with him." Some months later, in the spring of 1963, Kennedy called Mansfield to the White House and admitted having second thoughts about his report. "I think you're right," Kennedy told him – as Mansfield later reconstructed the conversation. "We've just got to get out. We're in too deep."[29]

At Kennedy's request, Mansfield prepared another lengthy reassessment of the Vietnamese situation in August, 1963. Equally as gloomy as his previous reports, the memo warned that the bureaucracy's tendency to rationalize its "erroneous initial over-extension" could transition South Vietnam into a central problem of American foreign policymaking. Mansfield reminded Kennedy that both General Eisenhower and General Douglas MacArthur had warned the United States against becoming involved in a land war in Asia, and he recommended making a symbolic gesture by cutting the number of U.S. military advisers in Vietnam to demonstrate the limited nature of the American commitment. In a televised interview on September 3, Kennedy seemed to paraphrase Mansfield when he referred to Vietnam as "their war. They are the ones who have to win it or lose it.... the people of Vietnam." Similarly, Secretary of Defense Robert McNamara announced that the U.S. would withdraw a thousand troops from Vietnam by the end of the year.[30]

Mansfield knew nothing about the intrigue in Washington and Saigon that led to the South Vietnamese coup early in November, 1963, and he felt deeply dismayed over the assassinations of Diem and Nhu. Although patriotic enthusiasm for an American defense of South Vietnam remained strong among American Catholics even after Diem's death, a minority within the Church began to campaign for peace. Some took to the streets, but Mansfield, who disapproved of civil disobedience, continued to work through the political process. Three weeks after Diem's death, John F. Kennedy was assassinated, and Mansfield delivered a moving eulogy at his funeral. The senator promptly provided the new president, Lyndon Johnson, with copies of all the memos he had sent to Kennedy, coupled

[29] *Baltimore Sun* November 15, 1976; Karnow, *Vietnam: A History*, p. 268; Olson, *Mansfield and Vietnam*, 111-12; Mann, *A Grand Delusion*, 282-84; John Newman, *JFK and Vietnam: Deception, Intrigue and the Struggle for Power* (New York: Warner Books, 1992), pp. 319-325.

[30] Reeves, *President Kennedy*, pp. 556-557; Arthur M. Schlesinger, Jr., *A Thousand Days: John F. Kennedy in the White House* (Boston: Houghton Mifflin, 1965), pp. 992-996.

with a warning that it might not be possible to win a war in Vietnam. "What national interests in Asia would steel the American people for the massive costs of ever-deepening involvement of that kind?" he asked. As an alternative, Mansfield proposed a truce that would leave Southeast Asia less dependent on U.S. aid, "less under our control, not cut off from China, but, still, not overwhelmed by China." As Mansfield tried to convince Johnson, the new president was trying to sway him. "I need to tell you what's happening in Vietnam that I don't think you know," Johnson told him over the phone. "I don't think you know how serious it is." Recalling the political reaction to the fall of China to the communists in 1949, Johnson asked whether he wanted another China in Vietnam. No, said Mansfield, but neither did he want another Korea. A key factor in both situations, he added, "was a tendency to bite off more than we were prepared in the end to chew."[31]

In 1964, Mansfield publicly endorsed French President Charles de Gaulle's call for neutralization of North and South Vietnam, and the reconvening of the Geneva Conference, which he suggested might well be "the last train out for peace in Southeast Asia." An angry Johnson grumbled to Georgia Senator Richard Russell that Mansfield favored neutralization "but there ain't nobody [in Vietnam] wants to agree to neutralization." Seeing Mansfield's preference for negotiation over military force as a sign of weakness, Johnson dismissed the senator's latest memo as "just milquetoast as it can be. He's got no spine at all." Johnson felt the need to stand tall and appear strong. In conversations with Mansfield, Johnson insisted that he was "anxious to follow any conference route that we can. . . . But we've got to keep our strength there and show them that we will take action in order to have them where they'll talk to us at all."[32]

Johnson's national security staff vehemently opposed Mansfield's call for neutralization, predicting that it would lead to a rapid collapse of anticommunist forces in South Vietnam, unification of the country under communist leadership, neutrality in neighboring countries, and the

[31] Quigley, ed., *American Catholics and Vietnam*, pp. 61–91; Baldwin, *Hon. Politician*, 1979), 110–113; Gibbons, *The U.S. Government and the Vietnam War*, pt. 2, pp. 206–207, 215; David M. Barrett, *Lyndon B. Johnson's Vietnam Papers*, p. 13; Michael R. Beschloss, ed., *Taking Charge: The Johnson White House Tapes. 1963–1964* (New York: Simon & Schuster, 1997), pp. 115, 123–124.

[32] Gibbons, *The U.S. Government and the Vietnam War*, pt. 2, pp. 219, 252; Beschloss, ed., *Taking Charge*, pp. 367, 370, 394; Gerald Gold, et al., eds., *The Pentagon Papers as Published by the New York Times* (New York: Bantam, 1971), p. 285; Olson, *Mansfield and Vietnam*, pp. 129–131.

erosion of American prestige throughout Asia. Rereading his advice to Johnson years later, Defense Secretary McNamara conceded how "limited and shallow" his analysis of Mansfield's proposals had been, and that his arguments had led Johnson gradually toward the direct use of U.S. military force. Johnson's staff never calculated the political, financial, and human cost that might be needed to win. After a second military coup in Saigon in January, 1964, Mansfield argued that Diem's assassination had "severed the slim cord of political legitimacy" of the South Vietnamese government. But National Security Advisor McGeorge Bundy responded that the new government "may be our last best chance, and we simply cannot afford to be the ones who seem to pull the plug." Bundy suggested that Johnson persuade Mansfield not to express his doubts in public, "at least for a while."[33]

When two U.S. reconnaissance planes were downed over Laos in June, 1964, Johnson announced that U.S. fighter planes would escort all future intelligence gathering. This triggered another cautionary memo from Mansfield, which Johnson summarized for Defense Secretary McNamara: "So what he comes out and says is he thinks we ought to get out of there. Which we can't and we're not going to." While testing sentiments on Capitol Hill in a phone conversation with Armed Services Committee Chairman Richard Russell, Johnson explained that U.S. planes would shoot back if shot upon. "Now Mansfield's got a four-page memo saying that I'm getting ourselves involved and I'm gonna get in another war if I do it anymore," Johnson grumbled. "I in a way share some of his fears," Russell injected. "I do too," Johnson replied, "but the fear the other way is more."[34]

Reports that North Vietnamese torpedo boats had attacked American destroyers in the Tonkin Gulf enabled Johnson to ask for a congressional resolution of support for military retaliation. On August 4, a bipartisan delegation of Senate and House leaders met at the White House. After everyone else around the table had spoken in support of a resolution, Mansfield said: "I suppose you want us to be frank. I don't know how much good it will do." He then pointed out the vast differences between earlier resolutions on Cuba and Berlin and the current situation. The United States "may be getting all involved with a minor third rate state,"

[33] Mann, *A Grand Delusion*, pp. 306–314; Barrett *Lyndon B. Johnson's Vietnam Papers*, pp. 21, 25–26; Robert S. McNamara, *In Retrospect: The Tragedy and Lessons of Vietnam* (New York: Random House, 1995), pp. 106–107.
[34] Beschloss, ed., *Taking Charge*, pp. 398, 403.

Mansfield said, and he speculated on the responses from North Vietnam and China. "Do you give me a formula?" Johnson demanded. Mansfield suggested treating the attacks as "isolated acts of terror" and taking the matter to the United Nations. While other congressional leaders fretted about an open-ended resolution, none would oppose the commander-in-chief in a time of crisis. Despite Mansfield's private reservations, he agreed to support the resolution as majority leader. Pat Holt, the acting staff director of the Foreign Relations Committee, observed that most Democratic senators accepted the resolution as "a measured, moderate response to the alleged provocations in the Gulf," particularly when compared to the bellicose statements of Republican presidential candidate Barry Goldwater. Congress overwhelmingly adopted the resolution, trusting the president to use it with restraint.[35]

Mansfield won reelection in 1964 with 64 percent of the vote; and Johnson's landslide victory included Montana (becoming the only Democratic presidential candidate to carry the state during Mansfield's twenty-four years in the Senate). During the campaign, Johnson repeatedly pledged that he sought no wider war, but as the political and military situation in South Vietnam deteriorated, his administration drafted plans for air strikes against North Vietnamese infiltration routes. After the election, Mansfield sent another memo warning that "We remain on a course in Viet Nam which takes us further and further out on the sagging limb." The more military pressure applied to the Vietcong, the less likely that the communists would accept a peaceful settlement. The inability of the military regimes that replaced Diem to govern or to prosecute the war adequately would place the same burden on United States that had once rested on the French. Mansfield urged that military actions within South Vietnam not be allowed to spread across its borders into Laos and Cambodia. National Security Adviser Bundy drafted a vague reply for Johnson's signature. "We could get into a stronger debate," Bundy advised the president, "but I doubt if it is worth it."[36]

Congressional dissent, even from such influential senior senators as Mansfield, Fulbright, and Russell, simply could not compete with the weight of advice the president received from his National Security

[35] Barrett, *Lyndon B. Johnson's Vietnam Papers*, pp. 71–72; Mark A. Stoler, "Aiken, Mansfield and The Tonkin Gulf Crisis: Notes from the Congressional Leadership Meeting at the White House, August 4, 1964," *Vermont History*; 50 (Spring 1982), pp. 80–94; Holt, oral history, p. 179.

[36] Mann, *A Grand Delusion*, pp. 383–385; Barrett, *Lyndon B. Johnson's Vietnam Papers*, p. 96; Gibbons, *The U.S. Government and the Vietnam War*, Pt. 2, 377–379.

Council. In their support for military escalation, officials in the State and Defense Departments provided detailed reports, statistical analyses, classified data, and elaborate contingency plans. Members of Congress worried about wading into a quagmire, but lacked ready accesses to military and intelligence data and could not refute it. In January, 1965, the Senate Democratic Policy Committee sent its chairman, Mansfield, on a private mission to urge President Johnson to find a way of withdrawing from Vietnam. He advised Johnson that committee members "felt strongly that we were wrong in being in Vietnam and that we should find an expeditious and honorable way to get out." Mansfield noted that the president thanked him and "that was about it."[37]

The following month, after the Vietcong raided a U.S. base at Pleiku, Johnson decided on retaliatory bombing of North Vietnam. Before ordering the aerial assault, he invited Mansfield to an emergency meeting of the National Security Council. Once again, everyone else endorsed retaliation. "We are not now in a penny ante game," Mansfield dissented. "It appears that the local populace in South Vietnam is not behind us, else the Viet Cong could not have carried out their surprise attack." Assistant Secretary of State William Bundy noted that Mansfield expressed himself "dryly, but very feelingly," and he was surprised by Johnson's brusque dismissal of the majority leader's views. It suggested how firmly the president had already made up his mind. "We have kept our gun over the mantel and our shells in the cupboard for a long time now," Johnson observed. "And what was the result? They are killing our men while they sleep in the night. I can't ask American soldiers out there to continue to fight with one hand tied behind their backs."[38]

Consistently, Mansfield advocated multilateral diplomatic efforts rather than unilateral military intervention. He pointed to the instability of the South Vietnamese government and reminded Johnson that North Vietnamese General Giap had an Army of 350,000 well-trained soldiers and was "one of the best military tacticians in Asia." In March, 1965,

---

[37] Doris Kearns, *Lyndon Johnson and the American Dream* (New York: Harper & Row, 1976), p. 262; John A. Goldsmith, *Colleagues: Richard B. Russell and His Apprentice, Lyndon B. Johnson* (Washington: Seven Locks Press, 1993), p. 119.

[38] Lyndon Baines Johnson, *The Vantage Point: Perspectives on the Presidency, 1963–1969* (New York: Holt, Rinehart and Winston, 1971), pp. 124–125; U.S. Congress, Senate Foreign Relations Committee [William Conrad Gibbons], *The U.S. Government and the Vietnam War: Executive and Legislative Roles and Relationships, 1961–1964*, S. prt., pp. 100–163, pt. 3 (Washington: Government Printing Office, 1988), pp. 60–64; Halberstam, *The Best and the Brightest*, p. 522; Barrett, *Lyndon B. Johnson's Vietnam Papers*, p. 106; Barrett, *Uncertain Warriors*, pp. 17–18.

Mansfield questioned whether U.S. interests in Southeast Asia were strong enough to justify the cost of a war "in American lives and resources," and called for limiting military involvement to "at most, a very judicious use of air and sea power." He urged the president to take the issue to the UN Security Council. Denying that his approach meant "a return to isolationism," he insisted that it would be preferable to "the kind of isolated internationalism in which we presently find ourselves in Viet Nam." Johnson delayed replying until after delivering an address at Johns Hopkins University in April, in which he offered massive economic aid to Vietnam in return for a cessation of fighting. But when the North Vietnamese failed to respond positively to either the Johns Hopkins offer or the bombing pause that followed it, Johnson reverted to military pressure. Secretary McNamara commented that "Mansfield ought to know Hanoi spit in our face." Following the advice of congressional doves had produced no results, Johnson concluded. "My judgment is the public has never wanted us to stop the bombing," he said. "We have stopped in deference to Mansfield and Fulbright, but we don't want to do it too long else we lose our base of support."[39]

By July, 1965, Secretary of Defense McNamara was recommending that the president send 100,000 troops to South Vietnam, have Congress declare a national emergency, call up the reserves, increase the draft, and commit U.S. forces to all-out combat. Johnson agreed to the additional troops but rejected the declaration of national emergency and reserve call-up as too dramatic. Before making a public announcement, Johnson met with congressional leaders, and again Mansfield advised against sending troops. The next day, the first thing Johnson saw was a nineteen-point memorandum from Mansfield warning that Vietnam was already being called an American war and would soon become Johnson's war. The president directed McNamara to prepare a rebuttal to each of Mansfield's points; then he proceeded with the announcement as planned.[40]

In the midst of the American military buildup in Vietnam, Mansfield decided once again to view things firsthand. He had Valeo draft a letter

[39] Barrett, *Lyndon B. Johnson's Vietnam Papers*, pp. 110–112, 136–137, 159–160; Senate Committee on Foreign Relations [William Conrad Gibbons], *The U.S. Government and the Vietnam War: Executive and Legislative Roles and Relationships, January-June, 1965*, S. Prt. 100-163, pt. 3, (Washington: Government Printing Office, 1988), pp. 205–208, 306–307.

[40] Ibid., pp. 245–246, 257–262; Gibbons, *The U.S. Government and the Vietnam War*, pt. 3, pp. 390, 430–436; Mann, *A Grand Delusion*, 455–461; Joseph A. Califano, Jr., *The Triumph and Tragedy of Lyndon Johnson: The White House Years* (New York: Simon & Schuster, 1991), pp. 35–47.

for Johnson's signature, in which the president asked Mansfield to lead a congressional fact-finding mission to Vietnam. "I'm sure this was the farthest thing from Johnson's desires," Valeo mused, "but Mansfield asked him about it and he couldn't say no to him. He was still trying to win and keep his support for what he was doing, not only in Vietnam but elsewhere." The request gave the trip greater stature and gave Mansfield a reason for reporting back to the president on his return. Indirectly, Mansfield's mission also fostered Senator Fulbright's continuing education on Vietnam. President Johnson had promised Fulbright the use of a military jet to attend a meeting of the British Commonwealth Parliamentarians' Association in New Zealand. When Fulbright publicly criticized Johnson's intervention in the Dominican Republic (where Johnson sent 22,000 troops without congressional authorization), the Defense Department abruptly informed him that Mansfield's delegation would use the jet plane instead. Staff member Pat Holt recalled that the Foreign Relations Committee members traveled across the Pacific "in a propeller plane and Fulbright took along a bunch of books on Southeast Asia and the Far East generally; he had a lot of time to read!" A Europeanist by training, Fulbright returned more steeped in Asian history and determined to hold "educational" hearings on Vietnam in early 1966.[41]

Although they traveled more comfortably than Fulbright, the Mansfield delegation got a sobering look at the Vietnam war. On previous visits Saigon had seemed "a little Paris in the tropics," Frank Valeo recalled, but now it had become a military bastion filled with soldiers "There's no way you can turn this around," a depressed Valeo concluded. Although Mansfield held out some hope for General Nguyen Cao Ky, who had taken charge in Saigon after several other military regimes had collapsed, he did not believe that sending more American troops to South Vietnam would solve its political problems. More troops might only cause the war to spill over into Laos, Cambodia, and Thailand and destabilize the entire region. In his report to Johnson he urged the president "to bring the matter to the Conference table as soon as possible." He pressed for a diplomatic solution because he could see no chance of military victory. "This is a conflict in which all the choices open to us are bad choices," Mansfield concluded. The United States stood only to lose at

[41] Valeo, oral history, 384–85; Holt, oral history interviews, 1980, Senate Historical Office, pp. 201–202; Randall Bennett Woods, *Fulbright: A Biography* (New York: Cambridge University Press, 1995), pp. 385–392.

home and abroad "by the pursuit of an elusive and ephemeral object in Viet Nam."[42]

On his return, Mansfield presented a grave assessment of the war to his Senate colleagues at a closed-door hearing of the Senate Foreign Relations Committee. If the war escalated any further, he predicted, "the amount of men who will be needed will be a lot more than we have been reading about in the papers." The United States could not count on Hanoi and the Vietcong simply giving up their war effort. At the same time, he insisted that he remained "100 percent in favor" of Johnson's efforts "to achieve a peaceful settlement on honorable terms, if it is at all possible." Nor would the majority leader advocate American military withdrawal until a diplomatic solution had assured South Vietnam's independence. In February, he moved to table Oregon Senator Wayne Morse's motion to repeal the Tonkin Gulf Resolution. The vote of 95–5 demonstrated the Senate's continued support for the president and the war. For Senator Eugene McCarthy the vote dashed any hope of the Senate's taking a stand against the war. "I never thought that Mike did as much as he should have in challenging the involvement in Vietnam," a disgruntled McCarthy later complained.[43]

Although opposed to the steady escalation of American combat in Vietnam, Mansfield never broke publicly with the president, as did Fulbright, Morse, and McCarthy. The majority leader met regularly with Johnson to plan legislative strategy, and their teamwork helped break open the legislative logjam of the Kennedy years. Under Mansfield, the Senate voted cloture to end a protracted filibuster and pass the landmark Civil Rights Act of 1964. In the next Congress, the enlarged Democratic majorities that swept in with Johnson's reelection enacted a flood of Great Society programs. "We galloped into the War on Poverty and the Great Society," recalled Stewart McClure, chief clerk of the Senate Labor and Education Committee. "I had never seen so much activity in my life around here! We were passing major bills every week. It was unbelievable. Just a great dam broke." Unlike Fulbright, who found himself isolated from the White House, Mansfield as a legislative lieutenant maintained his contacts and continued to express his opinions on Vietnam directly to the president. Dealing with Lyndon Johnson was never easy. In their many

---

[42] Valeo, oral history, pp. 390–391; *Two Reports on Vietnam and Southeast Asia*, pp. 17–33, 36.

[43] *Executive Sessions of the Senate Foreign Relations Committee (Historical Series)*, vol . XVIII, 89th Congress, 2nd session, 1966 (Washington: Government Printing Office, 1993), pp. 17–32.

meetings, Mansfield recalled, "everything was MY in his vocabulary, he talked about the Army – MY Army, MY Air Force or MY Navy." But Mansfield refused to let Johnson call him MY leader. "I wasn't his leader, I was the Senate's leader. And on too many occasions I was the only one who would raise any objections ... I don't think that set well with the president. And it was awfully hard for me to do it because everybody else said yes sir!"[44]

Unable to brush aside the Senate majority leader, Johnson responded to Mansfield's appeals by extending a cease-fire for twelve days between Christmas in 1966 and the Vietnamese new year, Tet, in 1967. Before the bombing of North Vietnam resumed, the president summoned congressional leaders to the Cabinet Room. All endorsed the resumption except for Fulbright and Mansfield. When his turn came to speak, Mansfield unfolded a three-page memo that argued for an indefinite halt to the air raids. The United States should declare a cease-fire, call for elections, contemplate withdrawing its military forces, and reactivate the Geneva Accords. Unfortunately, Johnson had already made up his mind to resume bombing. Later, when Mansfield watched Johnson's televised announcement of the bombing resumption, he told colleagues: "I feel so sorry for him. I can imagine what he's going through." Reporters took this remarks as illumination of "the compassionate side of Mansfield's complex character." Journalists marveled that the Senate's foremost advocate of an Asian detente could bring himself to defend the Johnson Administration "without quite agreeing with it." The *Washington Post* commented that despite Mansfield's reserve and self-effacing manner, he was capable of generating "great hand-wringing within the State Department" because of his independent views on ending the Vietnam war and reducing American troop strength in Europe. Mansfield felt increasingly irritated over the curt way that administration officials dismissed each of his plans for deescalation. "They shouldn't say 'no' to every suggestion we make up here," he complained. "We should miss no opportunity to light a candle to the negotiating table."[45]

44 Stuart E. McClure, oral history interview, Senate Historical Office, p. 97; *Baltimore Sun*, November 15, 1976; Eugene McCarthy, *Up 'Til Now: A Memoir* (New York: Harcourt Brace Jovanovich, 1987), p. 184; Baker, "Mike Mansfield and the Birth of the Modern Senate," pp. 287–288.

45 Senate Committee on Foreign Relations [William Conrad Gibbons], *The U.S. Government and the Vietnam War, July 1965–January 1968*, S. prt., 103–183, pt. 4, (Washington: Government Printing Office, 1994), pp. 145–147; Andrew J. Glass, "Mike Mansfield, Majority Leader," in Norman J. Ornstein, ed., *Congress in Change: Evolution and Reform*

Expansion of the war broadened the ranks of antiwar senators, which dampened the president's willingness to consult with Congress. *Washington Post* columnist Mary McGrory noted that Johnson so disdained the antiwar senators "that he did not even bother to tell his long-suffering majority leader about the new bombing targets in the north." The growing division of Senate Democrats into hawks and doves made it harder for them to unify behind any plan to end the war. Seeking common ground, Mansfield suggested taking the war to the United Nations. He encouraged senators who had served on UN delegations to speak out on the need to involve the world body, and "to raise their voices so that the clamor would be heard on Pennsylvania Avenue." His mail from home began running heavily in support of finding some way out of Vietnam.[46]

While he muted his public criticism, the majority leader also refrained from endorsing the war. Presidential aide Harry McPherson recorded that Mansfield's "silence was almost as irritating to the White House as exposed confrontation." Mansfield's stream of memoranda had long urged a cease-fire, negotiations, and a unilateral withdrawal of U.S. forces, and now other senators, such as the Idaho Democrat Frank Church, began making similar suggestions in public. In February, Pennsylvania Democrat Joseph Clark introduced an amendment to a defense authorization to restrict military action in Vietnam unless Congress passed a declaration of war. Mansfield offered a substitute amendment that declared Congress' support for American armed forces in Vietnam but also endorsed the Geneva Accords and the president's efforts "to prevent an expansion of the war in Vietnam." Despite its ambiguity, the Mansfield-Clark amendment marked the first congressional declaration in behalf of limiting the war.[47]

Personally appealing to Johnson to take the war to the United Nations, Mansfield reminded him how when they had sat next to each other in the Senate chamber, Mansfield would lean over "and tug the back of your coat to signal that it was either time to close the debate or to sit down. Most of the time, but not all the time, you would do what I was trying to suggest.

(New York: Praeger, 1975), p. 142; Barrett, *Lyndon B. Johnson's Vietnam Papers*, pp. 314, 318; *Washington Post*, September 25, 1966.

[46] *Washington Evening Star*, August 29, 1967; Valeo, oral history, pp. 433–435.

[47] David M. Barrett, *Uncertain Warriors: Lyndon Johnson and His Vietnam Advisers* (Lawrence: University Press of Kansas, 1993), pp. 4–5; Harry McPherson, *A Political Education: A Washington Memoir* (Austin: University of Texas Press, 1995 [1972]), pp. 74–75; Olson, *Mansfield and Vietnam*, 189–91; Gibbons, *The U.S. Government and the Vietnam War*, pt. 4, pp. 447, 587–592.

Since you have been President I have been figuratively tugging your coat, now and again." He warned Johnson that "the hour is growing late, very late." Secretary of State Dean Rusk told the president that he was ready to take Mansfield's proposal to the Security Council, but Johnson, in a breakfast meeting with Mansfield, asked: "Would it make us look weaker and more foolish than we are?" Nothing that Mansfield could say would allay his fears.[48]

By the fall of 1967, McNamara was having second thoughts about the war and told the president that it would be a mistake to let the public "think we can win the war overnight with bombing. We cannot." The only congressional leader to side with McNamara was Mike Mansfield. "We could bomb North Vietnam, into the stone age if we wanted to," Mansfield said. "I do not believe we have reached the objective which was stopping the flow of men and materials into the South." Perhaps the answer lay not with the United States, he suggested, but with direct negotiations between Saigon and the Vietcong. "We should not delude ourselves by such phrases as a 'phase-down' of the level of American troops," Mansfield said in an unusually open assault on Johnson's rhetoric. "Rather we should face up to the very strong possibility that the war in Vietnam may well take years." On November 30, 1967, the Senate voted 82–0 in favor of Mansfield's resolution to enlist the UN Security Council in the search for peace in Vietnam.[49]

Despite his disapproval of the war, Mansfield distanced himself from antiwar demonstrations. "I am not for personal insults, rowdyism, harassment, violence, intolerance and disregard of the law," he insisted. "I am sure that everyone knows how I stand on Vietnam. But regardless of how I stand, the office of the Presidency must and should be respected by all American citizens." Yet Mansfield – unlike most government officials of the 1960s – always encountered receptive audiences at universities. Speaking at the University of Indiana in February, 1968, just after the surprise Tet offensive, Mansfield called the war "grim, pitiless, and devastating." The lives of too many Americans were at stake. The war had divided the nation, diverted its energies and resources, knocked the economy out of equilibrium, and damaged American relations abroad. Nor was there any indication that the North Vietnamese or the Vietcong were "nearing

---

[48] Barrett, *Lyndon B. Johnson's Vietnam Papers*, pp. 416–417; Olson, *Mansfield and Vietnam*, pp. 181–186.

[49] Gibbons, *The U.S. Government and the Vietnam War*, pt. 4, pp. 795–797, 825–826; Olson, *Mansfield and Vietnam*, pp. 186–189; *Congressional Record*, 90th Congress, 1st session, pp. 33131, 35543.

the end of their rope." His remarks exasperated Lyndon Johnson, who complained at a congressional leadership meeting: "I wish Mike would make a speech on Ho Chi Minh. Nothing is as dirty as to violate a truce during the holidays. But nobody says anything bad about Ho. They call me a murderer. But Ho has a great image."[50]

Following Tet, public opinion polls showed a majority of Americans opposed to the war. On the evening of March 27, 1968, Johnson called Mansfield to the White House. During three hours of talks, Johnson described the need for sending more troops to Vietnam. Such a move would be suicidal, Mansfield declared, and told Johnson that he would oppose the increase in the Senate. "You're just getting in so deep you'll never get out," he protested. Johnson then read him the draft of a speech he intended to make to the nation. "I don't like it," Mansfield responded flatly. "You are offering the people no hope." At the meeting's end, Johnson stopped at the door. "Mike, I'm sorry we can't agree on more things, but . . . I want you to know that I appreciate your honesty and your candor," he said. "You've been frank with me all along." Four nights later, Mansfield listened as Johnson announced his decisions to limit the bombing of North Vietnam and not to seek another term as president. It "was not the speech he read to me," Mansfield subsequently noted.[51]

The war that crushed Johnson's presidency brought Republican Richard Nixon to the White House. Nixon and Mansfield had known each other since their days in the House of Representatives and had managed to get along at arms' length. "He felt insecure with me," Mansfield admitted, "and I felt insecure with him." As Senate majority leader throughout Nixon's presidency, Mansfield met with the president for breakfast at least once a month. At their first breakfast, Nixon confided that he believed the United States should establish ties with the Peoples Republic of China. Mansfield, who had long called for improved relations with China, was pleased, observing that "you can't ignore eight, nine hundred million people." After Nixon visited China in 1972, Mansfield and Senate Republican leader Hugh Scott led the first congressional delegation to Beijing.[52]

---

[50] *Congressional Record*, 90th Congress, 1st session, p. 32799; Baldwin, *Hon. Politician*, pp. 186–190; Mason Drukman, *Wayne Morse: A Political Biography* (Portland: Oregon Historical Society Press, 1997), p. 234; Barrett, *Lyndon B. Johnson's Vietnam Papers*, p. 584.

[51] Barrett, *Lyndon B. Johnson's Vietnam Papers*, p. 668; *Baltimore Sun* November 15, 1976; Johnson, *The Vantage Point*, pp. 419–420.

[52] Baldwin, *Hon. Politician*, pp. 154–159; *Baltimore Sun* November 15, 1976; William F. Hildenbrand, oral history, 160–177; Valeo, oral history, 532–556.

In hopes that Nixon was not wedded to a military victory in Vietnam, Mansfield gave him time to disengage. After visiting Southeast Asia again in 1969, Mansfield stopped at San Clemente, California, to brief Nixon, telling him that none of the countries he visited had expressed any fear of a Chinese invasion, one of the rationales for the U.S. military presence in the region. Later that fall, on Guam, Nixon spoke of "Asia for the Asians," and of reducing Asian dependence on U.S. military and economic aid. The press referred to this initially as the "Guam Doctrine," but Mansfield never missed an opportunity to call it the "Nixon Doctrine" as a means of raising its importance. Nixon subsequently argued that Mansfield was misinterpreting the Nixon Doctrine, and that he had never meant it as "a formula for getting America *out* of Asia, but one that provided the only sound basis for America's staying *in*." Although Nixon pledged to "Vietnamize" the war by reducing the U.S. combat role as South Vietnamese forces took over more of the fighting, he also worried about the United States losing face.[53]

Privately, Mansfield made an extraordinary offer to the president. In a personal meeting, followed by a detailed memorandum, he lamented the deep divisions that the war had wrought and pledged his full public support for any effort on Nixon's part to end the war rapidly. If the United States announced a cease-fire and withdrawal of its troops, Mansfield promised to declare that the Republican president had made the "best possible end of a bad war" that his Democratic predecessors had begun. Nixon declined this remarkable concession from a leader of the opposition party. He wanted to end the war, but not to lose it. The United States would keep its commitments to Vietnam and fight for a "fair and honorable peace." Nixon realized that Mansfield had given him his last chance to end "Johnson's and Kennedy's war" and to avoid making it his own war.[54]

In the Senate, Mansfield expressed his profound disappointment over the decision to continue the war: Nixon's announcement ended the "wait-and-see" attitude among congressional doves and sparked their drive for a legislative end to the war. The Senate approved Kentucky Republican John Sherman Cooper's amendment prohibiting the use of U.S. troops in Laos and Thailand. More hawkish House conferees dropped the amendment,

[53] Olson, *Mansfield and Vietnam*, pp. 205–211; Richard Nixon, *RN: The Memoirs of Richard Nixon* (New York: Grosset & Dunlap, 1978), p. 395; LeRoy Ashby & Rod Gramer, *Fighting the Odds: The Life of Senator Frank Church* (Pullman: Washington State University Press, 1994), 292–293, 300–301; Valeo oral history, pp. 531–532; Baldwin, *Hon. Politician*, pp. 272–276.
[54] Nixon, *RN*, pp. 408–409; Olson, *Mansfield and Vietnam*, pp. 211–223.

but Senator Cooper announced that he planned to attach it next to the defense appropriations bill. When a family illness caused Cooper to miss the debate, Majority Leader Mansfield introduced the amendment for him. After a closed-door debate involving highly classified material, Senator Frank Church offered substitute language to widen the amendment's appeal, and won passage by a vote of 80–9.[55]

What brought Mansfield finally into open opposition was the 1970 military incursion into Cambodia. This act violated Cambodian neutrality and unleashed renewed student demonstrations across the United States, leading to the notorious Kent State killings. Knowing that Mansfield would object, Nixon did not inform the majority leader in advance. Mansfield felt heartsick over the expansion of the war. "I have reached the point in my thinking where, for the first time, I am giving the most serious consideration to a termination date after which no more funds will be appropriated for military operations in Indochina," he recorded privately at the time. "The American people feel let down, disappointed, concerned. They have appealed to the White House. They have appealed to the Congress. Their only hope, I think, is the Senate." Mansfield set out to build a coalition in the Senate, as *New York Times* correspondent Warren Weaver observed, based on "the proposition that Congress should legitimately share in the momentous decisions of war and peace, that it *must* share if reckless ventures like Vietnam are not to tear apart the fabric of the nation again."[56]

The senator's public opposition to the war did not hinder his reelection to a fourth term in 1970, although his margin of 60.5 percent was lower than his two previous victories. Being a large state with a small population, Montana tended to elect fiscally conservative Republicans as governor while sending liberal Democrats to Washington to bring home federal funding for public works. In 1970, voter concerns over inflation and unemployment generally benefitted Democratic candidates, and Mansfield's Republican opponent concentrated his fire on the senator's support of gun control rather than on his opposition to the Vietnam war. Ultimately, Mansfield's retention of his grassroots popularity throughout

---

[55] Mann, *A Grand Delusion*, pp. 646–648. The legislative maneuvering to end the war is summarized in Congressional Quarterly, *Congress and the Nation, Volume III: 1969–1972* (Washington: Congressional Quarterly, Inc., 1973), 899–931.

[56] Robert W. Merry, *Taking on the World: Joseph and Stewart Alsop–Guardians of the American Century,* (New York: Viking, 1996), p. 487; Olson, *Mansfield and Vietnam*, pp. 213–218; Warren Weaver, Jr. *Both Your Houses: The Truth About Congress* (New York: Praeger, 1972), p. 280.

that turbulent era most likely reflected his meticulous attention to constituent services rather than his principled dissent from the war.[57]

Mansfield wanted Congress – the branch of government "closest to the people" – to reassert its constitutional responsibilities over foreign and military policy and prevent the executive branch from making "expedient decisions." To that end, he now endorsed repeal of the Tonkin Gulf Resolution and passage of the Cooper-Church amendment, which set a date for removal of all U.S. troops from Cambodia, and the McGovern-Hatfield "end-the-war" amendment, which fixed dates for withdrawing U.S. troops from all of Southeast Asia. When the Senate rejected the McGovern-Hatfield amendment, Mansfield offered his own legislation calling for the total withdrawal of U.S. troops after American prisoners of war had been freed. Despite intense lobbying by the Nixon administration, the Senate passed Mansfield's amendment by a vote of 57–42. The House duly rejected it, but after a month-long deadlock the conference committee adopted a softened version that called for an end to U.S. military operations "at the earliest practicable date." The Mansfield amendment marked the first time that a twentieth-century Congress had urged an end to a war that the country was still fighting. Before signing the defense procurement authorization to which it was attached, President Nixon declared that "the so-called Mansfield amendment" would not change the policies of his administration. Nixon taunted the majority leader; if the peace negotiations in Paris collapsed, he told reporters, Mansfield would have to take the blame. Bolstering Nixon's resolve was National Security Advisor Henry Kissinger's argument that Mansfield's effort to cut off funds for the war while they were still negotiating had been "*immoral.*" In truth, North Vietnam had secretly offered a settlement based on the terms similar to those in Mansfield's amendment.[58]

[57] By contrast, Mansfield's colleague from Montana, Senator Lee Metcalf, had won with margins of 53.2 percent in 1966 and 52 percent in 1972; Montana also elected a Democratic governor in 1968 by a 54.1 percent margin and reelected him in 1972 by 54.1 percent. Peirce, *The Mountain States of America*, pp. 118–119; Payne, "Politics Under the Copper Dome," pp. 218–219; *New York Times*, June 10, November 4, 1970.

[58] Passage of the Mansfield amendment received a boost from the publication in the *New York Times* and *Washington Post* of the Pentagon Papers, the still-classified history of America's role in Vietnam from 1945 to 1968, which further shook congressional confidence in the war. David Rudenstein, *The Day the Presses Stopped: A History of the Pentagon Papers Case* (Berkeley: University of California Press, 1996), pp. 122–123, 329–330. Baldwin, *Hon. Politician*, pp. 203–204; Ashby & Gramer, *Fighting the Odds*, 337–339; H.R. Haldeman, *The Haldeman Diaries* (New York: G.P. Putnam's Sons, 1994), 305; Stanley I. Kutler, ed., *Abuse of Power: The New Nixon Tapes* (New York: Free Press, 1997), p. 636.

Determined to end to the war on his own terms, President Nixon ordered the mining of Haiphong Harbor in May, 1972. On the night that he returned to Washington from China, Mansfield went to the White House with other congressional leaders to hear these plans. Presidential aide William Safire noted that Mansfield "looked unusually pale." When Admiral Thomas Moorer briefed the legislators, Mansfield protested that mining the harbor meant enlarging the war. "We are courting danger here that could extend the war, increase the number of prisoners and make peace more difficult to achieve." As he drove home, Mansfield listened to Nixon's announcement on the car radio. The next week, he offered an amendment to end the war in Vietnam by ordering the withdrawal of all U.S. military forces by August 31, 1972. A second provision would terminate U.S. air and naval actions in Vietnam, provided that all prisoners of war were released.[59]

Expectation that peace was at hand helped Nixon win a landslide re-election victory in 1972. Then he authorized a massive bombing campaign over North Vietnam the week before Christmas. Mansfield angrily denounced the Christmas bombing as "a Stone Age tactic," and promised that when Congress reconvened he would introduce new legislation setting a terminal date for the war. At the opening of the 93rd Congress in 1973, the Senate Democratic Conference unanimously endorsed Mansfield's "little state-of-the-union message," in which he declared: "There is no greater national need than the termination, forthwith, of our involvement in Vietnam." It remained for Congress, he insisted, to bring about "complete disinvolvement" by cutting off all funds for American military action in Southeast Asia.[60]

Days later, North Vietnam accepted the U.S. proposals for peace. Although the agreement formally ended the American combat role in the war, the Nixon administration continued to press for military aid to friendly governments in Southeast Asia, for which it sought Mansfield's support. He remained adamantly opposed. At the same time, Mansfield played a key role in launching an investigation of Nixon's role in the Watergate scandal. Not wanting the inquiry to appear partisan, Mansfield decreed that no potential Democratic presidential candidates serve on the

---

[59] George D. Aiken, *Aiken: Senate Diary, January 1972–January 1975* (Brattleboro, VT: Stephen Greene Press, 1976), pp. 55–56; William Safire, *Before the Fall: An Inside View of the Pre-Watergate White House* (Garden City: Doubleday, 1975), pp. 422–427; Mann, *A Grand Delusion*, pp. 699–704.

[60] Jonathan Aitken, *Nixon, A Life* (Washington: Regnery, 1993), pp. 454–457; *Washington Post*, January 4, 1973.

committee. The fairness with which he operated and the restraints he placed on partisan rhetoric helped focus national attention on the evidence that the Watergate committee uncovered and helped prepare public opinion for the resignation of the president less than two years after his landslide reelection. On Nixon's last night in the White House he met with congressional leaders, whom chief of staff Alexander Haig thought all looked ill at ease. "Only Mike Mansfield seemed to be immune to mixed feelings," Haig observed. "Always taciturn, the Senate majority leader was cold in manner, snubbing Nixon's rather halting attempt to lighten the moment with a personal remark."[61]

With Gerald Ford in the White House, Mansfield urged congressional Democrats to refrain from political posturing over Southeast Asia. "If there is any blame to be attached, and there is a great deal, we must all share in it," he said. "None of us is guiltless." Still, Mansfield refused to support Ford's request for additional U.S. aid to the region. More aid meant more fighting and more killing, "and that's got to stop sometime." For the first time in his long career he voted against a defense appropriations bill. The war finally ended, Mansfield asserted, because Congress refused to give the president "a blank check in providing close-out funds."[62]

When Mike Mansfield retired from the Senate in 1976, he listed the war in Southeast Asia as his greatest regret. "Over 55,000 dead, over 300,000 wounded, the cost will stretch to the middle of the next century," he reflected, "and for what?" He trusted that this tragedy would leave the United States with "a better understanding of what it takes to live in peace in a diverse world." In 1977, Mansfield returned to Hanoi on a mission for President Jimmy Carter, to discuss an accounting for Americans missing in action, in anticipation of a rapprochement between the two nations. From 1977–1989, Mansfield served as ambassador to Japan under Presidents Carter and Ronald Reagan, holding that post longer than any previous ambassador. He returned to Washington as a consultant on Asian affairs for an investment firm, and in his nineties advised President Bill Clinton on normalizing relations with Vietnam.[63]

[61] Alexander Haig, *Inner Circles: How America Changed the World: A Memoir* (New York; Time Warner, 1992), p. 502.
[62] *The Hill*, March 18, 1998; Baldwin, *Hon. Politician*, pp. 331–336; Thomas M. Franck and Edward Weisband, *Foreign Policy by Congress* (New York: Oxford University Press, 1979), pp. 13–33.
[63] *Christian Science Monitor*, June 10, 1976; *The Hill*, March 18, 1998; Mike Mansfield, *Charting a New Course: Mike Mansfield and U.S. Asian Policy* (Rutland, VT: Charles E. Tuttle Company, 1978), p. 86; *Washington Post*, March 16, 1993.

A man of quiet dignity, Mike Mansfield lacked the flamboyance of other critics of the Vietnam war. He disappointed his antiwar colleagues by not condemning the conflict more openly. Some wondered why he never resigned from the leadership in protest. One study of senatorial character concluded that Mansfield exhibited the sort of affliction that "immobilizes intellectuals who know what is right but are incapable of acting." Yet no matter how dramatic, resignation would have been a gesture much out of character for someone as patient as Mansfield. Representing a separate branch of government, he saw no contradiction between leading his party in the Senate and taking a different stance from his party's president – although he chose not to make a public display of his dissent. By retaining his majority leadership for sixteen years, through Democratic and Republican administrations, Mansfield managed to keep open his channels of communication to the White House while at the same time mustering congressional opposition to the war.[64]

Mansfield's long life spanned the twentieth century and absorbed elements of a political culture that extended from Wilsonian liberalism through Roosevelt's New Deal to Johnson's Great Society. Although he identified with each of these successive strands of liberalism, four decades of electoral politics in a state divided between Catholics and Protestants, and between Democrats and Republicans, shaped his more cautious, centrist approach to governmental policy. His world view was further influenced by the century's recurring warfare. A sailor in World War I, a congressman during World War II, a senator during the Vietnam War, and a federal officeholder from the beginning to the end of the Cold War, Mansfield constantly reassessed his attitudes according to his personal experiences and studies, adjusting old ideas to meet new realities. He called for scaling back the American military presence abroad but was no isolationist. Instead he advocated diplomacy over military solutions and multilateralism rather than unilateral action. He expected the United States to act responsibly toward other nations and not risk the lives of its citizen soldiers in conflicts not vital to the national defense. He saw danger in overcommitment and demanded clearer goals in foreign policy. This evolution in thinking led one of the earliest supporters of the

[64] *Congressional Record*, 88th Congress, 1st session, p. 22682; Joseph Martin Hernon, *Profiles in Character: Hubris and Heroism in the U.S. Senate, 1789–1990* (Armong, NY: M.E. Sharpe, 1997), pp. 206–207.

government of South Vietnam to oppose American military participation in the Vietnam War. Mansfield's generally refrained from overt confrontation on the Senate floor, but expressed his attitudes privately in the stream of pragmatic and remarkably prescient memoranda he sent to Kennedy, Johnson, and Nixon. It was a national tragedy that their recipients failed to heed his warnings.

The Reluctant "Volunteer"

The Origins of Senator Albert A. Gore's Opposition to the Vietnam War

Kyle Longley

"In our differences over Vietnam, we have let ourselves become hyp-
notized into self delusion," Senator Albert A. Gore of Tennessee wrote
in 1970, "We have gradually accepted the unholy, autistic reality that
war creates. We have let Vietnam become a matter of partisan politics;
and frequently we have devalued our moral currency to compound political nostrums and cater to prejudices, resorting to crude face-saving
devices which counterfeit our highest traditional values and violate our
pride in being the world's greatest democracy." "We must de-mesmerize
ourselves," he concluded, "break through the shell of public relation for-
mulae and jingoist slogans, and dispassionately analyze the kernel of our
national interest. What we must be really concerned about is saving the
soul of our country and our individual honor and conscience."[1]

The issue of Vietnam had become important almost immediately on
Gore's arrival in the Senate in 1953, and he had observed the situation
throughout the decade. Immediately after earning a spot on the Senate
Foreign Relations Committee in 1959, he visited South Vietnam and reported that President Ngo Dinh Diem lacked popular support. From his
position on the Senate Foreign Relations Committee (SFRC), he began
urging the Kennedy administration to exercise restraint. With the inauguration of Lyndon Johnson, he changed his tactics. He voted for the
Tonkin Gulf Resolution in 1964, but by 1965, he had become an outspoken critic of Johnson's policy of escalation and firmly entrenched in the
camp of the Senate "doves." Until his defeat in 1970, Gore questioned

[1] Albert A. Gore, *The Eye of the Storm: A People's Politics for the Seventies* (New York: Herder and Herder, 1970), p. 10.

U.S. policy regarding Vietnam and pushed for solutions that included a negotiated settlement, neutralization of the region, and the withdrawal of U.S. troops. Even after leaving office, he continued criticizing U.S. policy in Southeast Asia through books, articles, and speeches.[2]

Why Gore opposed U.S. involvement in Vietnam remains a perplexing question. A native of the "volunteer" state known for its martial spirit, Gore chose a contrary view. Three factors appear especially important in shaping his choice. Gore's political philosophy, strongly inspired by his region's brand of populism and progressivism, played a significant role. Other components of Upper Cumberland and Middle Tennessee's political culture also shaped his position, primarily the maverick tradition. Finally, his personal distaste for the presidents running U.S. policy affected his stance. All these influences converged to establish the foundations for Gore's opposition to the Vietnam War.

The Boy from Possum Hollow

Gore's background significantly affected his politics. Unlike most of his Senate contemporaries, he came from humble origins. Born in December, 1907, in the Upper Cumberland region of Tennessee, he was the son of a small farmer. Throughout most of his life, the family resided in Smith County near the hamlet of Possum Hollow, not far from the county seat of Carthage. He attended a one-room schoolhouse where he distinguished himself academically. Self motivated, he read everything that he could find, including biographies of Thomas Jefferson, Andrew Jackson, William Jennings Bryan, and Woodrow Wilson. The farm required much hard work, and leisure time consisted of attending church, swimming in the local creeks, and hunting. While the family owned its farm and was comparatively self sufficient, the Gores were not well-to-do by any standard.[3]

---

[2] Robert C. Hodges, "The Cooing of a Dove: Senator Albert Gore Sr.'s Opposition to the War in Vietnam," *Peace and Change* 22; (April 1997): pp. 133–153.

[3] For more information on Gore's life, see his books, *The Eye of the Storm* and *Let the Glory Out: My South and Its Politics* (New York: Viking, 1972). Other good sources include Tape Directory for the Tribute to Al Gore, tape 1, AG-12, Gore Center; Albert A. Gore, interview by Dewey Grantham and James B. Gardner, November 13, 1976, Southern Oral History Collection, Columbia Oral History Project, New York, New York; Albert A. Gore, interview by Bob Bullen, February 4, 1984, Middle Tennessee State University, videotape, Gore Center, Middle Tennessee State University, Murfreesboro, Tennessee [hereafter Gore Center].

The family's comparative poverty limited the career opportunities available to their youngest son. In 1925, Albert graduated from nearby Gordonsville High School. Unable financially to fulfill his dream of attending college full time, he took an intensive teacher training session at Middle Tennessee State College (MTSC) in Murfreesboro and taught the following year in the isolated hamlet of "Booze." For the next six years, he studied at the University of Tennessee and MTSC periodically, typically teaching during the fall semester and attending college in the spring.

Somehow between work and college, Gore found time to participate in local and state politics. He joined the Tennessee Young Democrats' Club, becoming a leader in the group. His political role model became Congressman and later Secretary of State Cordell Hull who also hailed from Carthage. Gore labored on local campaigns and established long time political alliances with people in the Upper Cumberland. In 1932, he ran for school superintendent, but lost to the incumbent. Unemployed at the height of the Great Depression, he became a used furniture peddler and tobacco trader. Fate intervened and the superintendent died. Before doing so, he helped name Gore as his successor.

To enhance his political aspirations, Gore traveled three nights a week fifty miles over country roads to Nashville to study law at the YMCA, earning his degree in 1935. Remaining active in the Young Democrats' organization, he won the attention of an important Tennessee politician, Gordon Browning, who became a political mentor and ally. In 1934, he ran Browning's unsuccessful Senate campaign, but two years later, he helped him win the governor's mansion. For his efforts, the new governor appointed him Commissioner of Labor, and from that position, Gore vaulted into the House of Representatives in 1939.

During his fourteen years in the House, Gore developed a reputation as an independent-minded, progressive Southern Democrat. The young congressman dedicated himself to economic questions such as inequities in the tax system, higher agricultural supports, expansion of the Tennessee Valley Authority (TVA), and job and educational opportunities. He served on committees on banking and finance and worked with the Roosevelt administration on many issues, including atomic power. When Harry S. Truman took over in April, 1945, Gore actively supported many Fair Deal programs. In 1952, he successfully challenged long time Tennessee Senator Kenneth McKellar in a spirited primary contest and moved into the Senate.

The Evolution of the Reluctant Volunteer

Only a few less obvious things in Gore's record on U.S. foreign relations before the late 1950s foretold that he would oppose U.S. intervention in Vietnam. A Wilsonian internationalist, strongly influenced by Hull, he had forcefully supported the U.S. role in World War II. In the House of Representatives, he backed Lend-Lease, the Selective Service Act, and preparations for war. During the conflict, he advocated preparing the country for its role as leader of the United Nations. Furthermore, he resigned his seat in 1945 to serve in the U.S. Army as a private.

After the war, he remained an internationalist. He condemned Soviet aggression and supported Truman's containment policy. He voted for the Truman Doctrine, the Marshall Plan, and the North Atlantic Treaty Organization (NATO). During the Korean War, he went so far as to suggest in October, 1951, that President Truman consider using atomic weapons if the "cease-fire negotiations break down." He also proposed that United States remove civilians and "dehumanize a belt across the Korean Peninsula by surface radiological contamination" and recontaminate the area as needed until a settlement could be reached.[4] While he moderated his views on nuclear weapons soon after, he typically backed Truman's foreign policies.

When he moved to the Senate, Gore parted only in degree from the Eisenhower administration on foreign policy matters. In the 1954 Dien Bien Phu crisis, he indicated he would support Eisenhower's choice of policies, although he expressed reservations about another bloody and costly war in Asia.[5] He also voted for the creation of the Southeast Asian Treaty Organization (SEATO). There were disagreements on several issues

---

[4] Gore to Truman, April 14, 1951, Official File, box 1528, folder 692-A, Harry S. Truman Library, Independence, Missouri.

[5] In mid-April, Gore wrote a constituent that he had just returned from a two-hour conference on the matter. "There is uncertainty as to the extent to which the French want us to become involved. In the second place, great risk would be involved in our actual physical involvement in the conflict in Indo-China. On the other hand, the threat of communist domination of Southeast Asia is starkly real...I am studying the matter as closely as I can...Satisfactory answers to all the perplexing questions are hard to come by." Gore to Howard Parsons, April 14, 1954, SPEC, Indochina Policy, 1954, folder 1, Gore Senate Collection, Gore Center. During debates in which Senator Mike Mansfield (D-MT) took the lead, Gore worried aloud on the Senate floor about the possibility that the Indochina crisis indicated a need to refocus energies on conventional forces, not the thirty percent cut proposed by the Eisenhower administration. *Congressional Record*, Senate, 83rd Congress, 1st session, vol. 100, pt. 13, April 14, 1954: p. 5116.

including nuclear testing and American assistance to dictatorial regimes, but he supported the president's position on the Formosa Straits and the Lebanon crises in 1958. Like most of his colleagues, he feared Communist expansion and wanted to show national unity in the face of the enemy.

Yet, Gore had already begun this questioning of the U.S. intervention in Vietnam as early as 1954, and it became more acute after he received an appointment to the Senate Foreign Relations Committee (SFRC) in 1959. As one of his first duties, he took an extended fact-finding trip to several American posts worldwide. One stop was Vietnam. He traveled the countryside and spent a day with President Diem. Upon his return, he reported that "a taint of corruption and waste hung over Saigon," adding that efforts against the guerrillas were "impractical, wasteful, and doomed to failure."[6] He expressed fears that Diem's "authoritarian policies seem to be growing instead of diminishing" and that "some costly mistakes should be corrected in our aid program" which he described as "loose, confused, and disorganized."[7]

Senator Gore's fears of an increased U.S. commitment to an undemocratic and ineffective South Vietnamese government intensified in 1961. He particularly questioned the wisdom of seeking military victory. He noted that "after the inauguration of my friend, John F. Kennedy, I personally conveyed to him – several times – my deepening concern about our involvement in Vietnam. The more our aid increased, the more urgent was my recommendation that we avoid further entanglement."[8] Restrained by his friendship with Kennedy, Gore chose to express his opinions personally or in executive sessions of the SFRC.[9]

A series of events, especially the Bay of Pigs and Cuban Missile crisis, magnified Gore's feelings about the inability of the United States to shape events in the Third World. As a result, he began issuing more warnings

---

[6] Gore, *The Eye of the Storm*, p. 6.

[7] Gore to Editor of the *Washington Post*, January 10, 1960, Foreign Relations, Correspondence-Members, RG 46, box 169, National Archives, Washington, D.C.; Gore, *Let the Glory Out*, pp. 121–22.

[8] Gore, *The Eye of the Storm*, pp. 6–7.

[9] Gore had worked on Kennedy's campaign as a chief political adviser along with Fulbright and others including Clark Clifford. He was mentioned as a candidate for Secretary of Treasury and Secretary of State. While he and Kennedy clashed over issues of taxes, COMSTAT, and interest rate policies, he remained someone that Kennedy trusted in major battles including one with the steel industry in 1962. His friendship continued with his brother Edward Kennedy who became a close associate when he entered the Senate. Edward Kennedy, letter to the author, November 1, 2001; interview by the author with John Seigenthaler (chief assistant to Attorney General Robert Kennedy), September 22, 2001, Nashville, Tennessee.

about the foolishness of administration policy. In October, 1963, he told Secretary of Defense Robert McNamara:

I certainly can lay no claim to being an expert on the situation in Vietnam. I spent no more time there than you. I am certainly not a military man. I have no more training in that regard than you have, but I must say that as a layman, I have questioned the enormous importance which the military attaches to South Vietnam.... I know of no strategic material that it has. I know of nothing in surplus supply there except poor people and rice. It seems to me we have no need for either. Why must we suffer such great losses in money and lives for an area which seems to me unessential to our welfare, and to freedom, there being none there?[10]

Events in early 1964 moved Gore from muted criticism to open hostility toward official U.S. policy in Vietnam. The change occurred because of the Gulf of Tonkin incident. Several years later, he emphasized that with the Tonkin Gulf Resolution, "the whole Congress was grievously remiss." "I erroneously voted for the Tonkin Gulf Resolution in 1964," Gore added. "I did so, let it be said, upon the representation that our ships had suffered an 'unprovoked attack' in international waters." He complained that "it never occurred to me that such flimsy facts as were later revealed, if indeed they were facts, would be used as either a reason or a pretext for a major military onslaught."[11]

The perceived abuse of power and the Johnson administration's subsequent loose interpretation of the resolution pushed Gore publicly to challenge the president. In late 1964, in Miami, he called for a "negotiated settlement" of the war.[12] In April, 1965, in an executive session of the SFRC, he complained that "we are told that Congress had already endorsed by that resolution that which has been done since then, and whatever other actions may be taken in the future." Adding "Now had I had any notion that such interpretation would be placed on it I would have joined the Senator from Oregon and Senator from Alaska in voting against it."[13] For the next five years, Gore would condemn the

[10] Gore, *The Eye of the Storm*, p. 7.
[11] Ibid., p. 8; Phone interview by the author with George McGovern, August 25, 2001.
[12] *Nashville Tennessean*, January 1, 1965. The *Nashville Banner* ran an editorial by syndicated writer Holmes Alexander denouncing the "peace party" in the Senate in which he included Gore. "Most of the senators who fall in line for hauling down the Stars and Stripes belong to a 'peace party' whose campaigns are financially supported by peace-mongering groups and who consistently agitate for disarmament and for retreat.... I don't suppose there's a weaker chink anywhere in the Free World armor than this pacifist clique within our own Congress." *Nashville Banner*, January 14, 1965.
[13] Gore, *The Eye of the Storm*, pp. 9–10.

Johnson and Nixon administrations' implementation of the resolution, and in 1970, he voted for its repeal.

By February, 1965, he had turned completely against Johnson's policy. He told one constituent that "on the basis of my review of our current policy, I simply do not believe that there is a military victory to be won in Vietnam." He noted that the French had put hundreds of thousands of troops in place but that "religion, race and other factors combine to make for an unstable political situation which complicates the problem immeasurably." Referring to South Vietnam, "I do not accept the so-called domino theory as being valid in every respect.... The people of Vietnam do not fully support our intervention, and as long as this is so, political stability in the area will not be forthcoming."[14]

He became increasingly vocal in late July, 1965. On the Senate floor, he called Johnson's recent statements a "continuation of essentially the same policy that has not thus far worked well in any respect. The policy pursued in Vietnam since 1954 has been a succession of mistakes, each of which compounded the adverse consequences of its predecessors.... The situation in Vietnam is worse than it was 10 years ago; it is worse than it was 1 year ago, or 1 month ago. And it is worse today than it was 1 week ago." He emphasized that the French had "learned that massive military operations conducted thousands of miles from their logistic base in the jungles and rice paddies of southeast Asia are not the answer to a problem that is to a large degree political, ideological, cultural, economic, religious, and racial in nature." He characterized it as "a war that we have scant hope of winning except at a cost which far outweighs the fruits of victory."[15]

As the new year opened, he joined Fulbright and others to publicly challenge the administration's policy in nationally televised hearings in the SFRC. On the first day of the hearings on January 28, Gore grilled Secretary of State Rusk. Regarding Vietnam, he hammered home the point that "many people do not believe, many members of Congress do not believe, that the costs, the risk of nuclear war, the dangers of war with China or perhaps both China and Russia, are worth the endeavor."[16] He also argued against the liberal administration policy of the Gulf of Tonkin Resolution. "I certainly want to disassociate myself [from] any

---

[14] Gore to Mary Toomey, February 18, 1965, Department, State, Vietnam, Gore Senate Collection, Folder, Gore Center.
[15] *Congressional Record*, Senate, July 28, 1965, p. 18571.
[16] *The Vietnam Hearings* (New York: Vintage Books, 1966), p. 15.

interpretation that this was a declaration of war.... Or that it authorized the Administration to take any and all steps toward an all-out war. I specifically interpreted that as an attack which we had experienced as a specific and limited response thereto."[17]

As an increasing number of U.S. troops went to Vietnam in 1966, Gore developed more practical fears of the possible negative effects of the war on the United States. He worried that the war would spread to China, possibly sparking a nuclear confrontation with Peking and Moscow. In April, 1966, at American University, he criticized the administration's "no-sanctuary" policy which granted U.S. planes permission to attack Vietnamese planes fleeing into Chinese airspace. He raised the issue that this policy "might be a torch to the tinder box of World War III," and added that Johnson appeared to have an "Alamo complex in a nuclear age."[18]

In the Fall 1967, Gore continued to speak out in very insightful ways. "The truth, as I see it, is that the war in Vietnam into which we have stumbled, and from which we must extricate ourselves as honorably and cleanly, and as gracefully as possible," he told his colleagues on the Senate floor in late October. He questioned the validity of the argument that the Vietnamese were puppets of the Chinese, pointing out the historical animosity between the two states.[19] Furthermore, the Soviets did not want an emasculated America in Asia. Moscow had been bickering and fighting with the Chinese since the late 1950s, and such a vacuum would only serve their enemy according to Gore. He also believed that Hanoi wanted peace. The war was costly to both countries in material and lives. It was something which could bring the two sides to the bargaining table.[20]

As his fears of the effects on the country intensified, the Tennessean openly called for a negotiated settlement and ultimate U.S. withdrawal. He openly backed Charles DeGaulle's January, 1964, proposal for the neutralization of Southeast Asia. To Gore, the solution lay in bringing everyone to the bargaining table, including the NLF, and seeking the neutralization of Vietnam. He supported others solutions including Mike Mansfield's call that the UN act as a mediator.[21]

---

[17] Ibid., pp. 43–46.
[18] Hodges, "The Cooing of a Dove," pp. 141–42.
[19] *Congressional Record*, Senate, October 24, 1967, p. 29801.
[20] *Congressional Record*, Senate, November 2, 1967, p. 31078.
[21] *Congressional Record*, Senate, November 30, 1967, p. 34355.

As the war heated up during the Tet Offensive in late January, 1968, Gore increased his denunciations of Johnson's policy. He had become a very popular antiwar speaker on university campuses, and he traveled to the University of Idaho to talk about Vietnam. With the assistance of Jim Lowenstein of the SFRC staff, he delivered a blistering critique of Johnson's policy. "However desirable our interests in a pro-Western government in South Vietnam, this interest falls far short of involving our national security." "We are destroying the country we profess to be saving. We are damaging our relations with most other nations of the world. We are destroying any basis of cooperation with the two other major powers upon which the future of world peace depends – the Soviet Union and China. We contaminate ourselves by embracing a corrupt regime in Saigon. And the further tragedy is that we are also seriously damaging – if we are not in danger of destroying, ourselves," he added. "We have stumbled into a morass in Vietnam. We must decide to negotiate ourselves out of it. This will truly serve our national security. We must decide – decide definitely and irrevocably – to negotiate disengagement from Vietnam, not from Asia but from Vietnam, honorably and honestly, which means in my opinion, on condition that Vietnam be neutralized."[22]

In the summer 1968 in Chicago, Gore gave a passionate speech supporting a strong antiwar provision for the Democratic platform. "What harvest do we reap from their gallant sacrifice?" he asked the audience. "An erosion of the moral leadership, a demeaning entanglement with a corrupt political clique in Saigon, disillusionment, despair here at home, and a disastrous postponement of imperative programs to improve our social ills."[23] Gore roared loudly in a short, albeit powerful speech that: "Mr. Chairman, fellow delegates, four years ago our party and the nominee of our party promised the people that American boys would not be sent to fight in a land war in Asia. The people made an overwhelming commitment to peace. They voted for our distinguished leader, President Lyndon B. Johnson, but they got the policies of Senator Goldwater." The Tennessean continued that the United States had lost over 25,000 brave troops and for what? He complained that

---

[22] Albert Gore, "Vietnam," Speech to the Borah Foundation, University of Idaho, February 17, 1968, Senate Foreign Relations Committee, RG 46, 90th Congress, "Gore," box 2, National Archives.
[23] *Nashville Tennessean*, August 29, 1968.

the proposed platform not only validated the policy but applauded it. "I wonder how many American people are applauding it. They don't want to applaud it."[24]

His efforts mattered little as Republican Richard Nixon won the White House. Gore remained an outspoken critic of the war and worried about Nixon's plans. In late March, 1969, he challenged a quote from Admiral John S. McCain, commander of the Pacific theater, that questioned the enemy's capability to ever launch another offensive. Gore warned on the Senate floor that "there is a very sad lesson in this story of self-deception. A revolutionary, political war in Asia cannot be won by white westerners with acceptable risks and losses."[25]

Six weeks later, the *Baltimore Sun* quoted him telling people that the American people should not be "buying another pig in a poke labeled 'secret negotiation.'"[26] Soon after, he made a statement to the SFRC committee that he would support any ideas that extricated the United States from Vietnam. "I tried my very best to keep us out of the Vietnam War. Many times and in various ways, I tried to prevent the war from being widened and deepened, thus bloodier and harder to end. I am now doing everything I can to get us out of this horrible war as quickly, as honorably, and completely as possible. I firmly believe this to be right."[27] Soon after, he rose on the floor of the Senate and pleaded: "Mr. President, this war must end. It must end because it is immoral and because it is wrong. It must end too, because it threatens to destroy us."[28]

After the invasion of Cambodia in May, 1970, Gore joined with Frank Church (D-ID) and others to denounce the action. The Tennessean complained that the president had only eleven days before told the American people that peace was in sight. "Can it possibly be that this major military operation was not in preparation 10 days ago?" Gore asked. He stressed that in an executive session of SFRC, Secretary of State William Rogers had not even mentioned Cambodia. He continued that "if, by reason and logic, the security of the United States impels an invasion of

[24] David Maraniss and Ellen Nakashima, *The Prince of Tennessee: The Rise of Al Gore* (New York: Simon and Schuster, 2000), pp. 87–88; Gore to Philip Livingston, August 21, 1968, Politics, DNC, Chicago, Gore Senate Collection, Folder, Gore Center.

[25] *Congressional Record*, Senate, March 20, 1969, p. 6966.

[26] *Baltimore Sun*, May 9, 1969.

[27] Albert Gore, "The Vietnam War," June 17, 1969, Senate Foreign Relations Committee, 91st Congress, files of "Gore," box 1, National Archives.

[28] As cited in Hodges, "The Cooing of a Dove," p. 147.

another nation, why should we pick upon neutral, little Cambodia?"[29] He complained that the action merely widened the war and that using the administration's logic that the enemy's sanctuaries would extend from the Cambodian border to "all of Asia behind it."[30]

Later, Gore participated in a meeting between the president and the SFRC and House Foreign Affairs Committee on May 6. In the antagonistic meeting, Gore asked whether "you base your action on the principle that the end justifies the means." He then complained that the invasion was "a violation of the border of a sovereign nation" and that the president had done so "without authority or even consultation with Congress." Nixon responded: "The sanctuaries are enemy occupied territory; they are controlled by an enemy that is attacking American forces."[31]

Over the next two months, the Congress and the president would clash over the Cambodian invasion. Republican Senator John Sherman Cooper and Frank Church proposed an amendment to a military sales bill that called for cutting the appropriations for troops in Cambodia on July 1. Another group called for the repeal of the Gulf of Tonkin Resolution. Gore supported both efforts. The Senate repealed the resolution by a vote of 81–10 on June 24. A few days later, it passed the Cooper-Church amendment, 58–37.[32]

As his 1970 campaign for reelection loomed, Gore found his opposition to the war very unpopular among many constituents. Partly in response, he published a book about his political choices, *The Eye of the Storm*. The first chapter focused on Vietnam. "In February, 1970, a young man from Tennessee was killed in Vietnam, another casualty in a war which some have come to accept almost casually," he wrote. "There was nothing about his death to distinguish it from thousands of others except that just a few days before it occurred this nineteen-year-old soldier had sent his family a letter with a request that it be opened and read at his funeral if he were killed." "In that letter," Gore continued writing, "he denounced the futility of the war and the 'uselessness' of his own death. And, indeed, it did seem useless: at nineteen to have one's life arbitrarily snatched away for a cause which its leaders could not carry out, which its defenders could

[29] *Congressional Record*, Senate, May 1, 1970, pp. 13833, 13835.

[30] LeRoy Ashby and Rod Gramer, *Fighting the Odds: The Life of Senator Frank Church* (Pullman: Washington State University Press, 1994), p. 309.

[31] Gore, *The Eye of the Storm*, p. 25; William Safire, *Before the Fall: An Inside View of the Pre-Watergate White House* (New York: Grosset and Dunlap, 1978), p. 193.

[32] Randall Woods, *Fulbright: A Biography* (New York: Cambridge University Press, 1995), pp. 568–575.

not justify, and which the world could not approve."[33] His efforts failed to sway enough opinions in his state regarding Vietnam and other issues, and he lost to the Nixon-backed candidate, Bill Brock.[34]

Despite the recognition of the political costs, throughout the 1960s he had moved from cautious disapproval to open hostility toward U.S. policy in Vietnam. An important question remains why would a senator expose himself to the political consequences of such actions. The obvious reason, the one that he shared with most opponents of the war, was a practical realization that the United States had chosen to fight a costly war in an area of questionable strategic value. On another level, he also believed that the war undermined the democratic system and shredded the social fabric of the country. He and others fought to extricate the United States from the quagmire before it completely destroyed the country. Ultimately, they succeeded.

Yet, what predisposed the senator to view the war as costly and unwinnable? What were the foundations that underlay his antiwar position? The answer lies largely in the political culture of the Upper Cumberland and Middle Tennessee and in his personal and professional relationships with Johnson and Nixon. These influences converged to mold his pragmatic rationales and solutions for ending U.S. involvement in Vietnam.

The Tennessee Progressive

An important foundation of Gore's opposition to the Vietnam war was his political philosophy, one assimilated from family, friends, teachers, and political mentors and role models of Tennessee's Upper Cumberland region and the South. It combined the history and political culture of an area strongly influenced by the ideas of Thomas Jefferson and Andrew Jackson

---

[33] Gore, *The Eye of the Storm*, p. 1.

[34] Gore's opposition to the war clearly contributed to his defeat in 1970. Beside the racial issue, the Vietnam War continued to hurt Gore among ultrapatriotic Tennesseans. One African American insurance adjuster stated that he supported Brock because of his business support, but "not only that, but I have a son in Vietnam, who is proud of his country and glad to fight for it. I can't see how Gore can consider pulling everybody out after everything that's already happened over there." A telephone operator blamed "Gore's stupidity and liberal attitude" for causing "so many college riots in Tennessee. He just keeps egging it on."Kelly Leiter, "Tennesse: Gore vs. the White House," *The Nation*, vol. 211, October 26 1970, p. 398. Future GOP chairman Tom Beasley retold how he was in Vietnam and found statements on a dead NVA that questioned the U.S. role. The former Democrat returned home in 1970 and became a partisan Republican as a result of Gore's position on Vietnam. Bill Frist and Lee Annis, *Tennessee Senators, 1911–2001: Portraits of Leadership in a Century of Change* (New York: Madison Books, 1999), p. 111.

and the major reform movements of populism and progressivism.[35] In this environment, Gore developed strong convictions about the role of government which would significantly influence his response to Vietnam.

The geography and demography of Gore's region were significant. The Upper Cumberland was a comparatively poor region, inhabited by small farmers and businessmen who focused more on self-sufficiency than large agriculture-for-profit enterprises found in western Tennessee. Most people had lived in the area for several generations, having migrated from the frontiers of Virginia, North Carolina, and Kentucky in the eighteenth century. Family and community ties were strengthened by the precarious reliance on farming where people battled the elements, bankers, and others for survival. Strongly independent, they embodied in many ways Jefferson's model of the small yeoman farmer.[36]

A lasting influence on the political culture of the Upper Cumberland came from Jefferson and Jackson. These two men raised the ideal of "equal rights for all, special privilege for none." Both feared the arbitrary rule of a socioeconomic elite and always maintained a healthy skepticism of the power of government in the wrong hands. "There are no necessary evils in government," Jackson had stated, "its evils exist only in its abuses. If it would confine itself to equal protection, and, as Heaven does its rains, shower its favors alike on the high and the low, the rich and the poor, it would be an unqualified blessing."[37] The ideas of Jefferson and Jackson remained strongly imbedded in the political culture of the Upper Cumberland well into the twentieth century and shaped several generations of politicians.

By the time of Gore's birth in 1907, the Upper Cumberland had assimilated ideals from the mainstream reform movements of the late nineteenth and early twentieth centuries. One of the most prominent movements was populism whose ideas found popularity with the hardworking farmers.

---

[35] A working definition of political culture is: "the beliefs about patterns of political interaction and political institutions." Sidney Verba, "Comparative Political Culture," in *Political Culture and Political Development*, ed. Sidney Verba and Lucien Pye (Princeton: Princeton University Press, 1965), pp. 526–527. While Gore and others worked within a large political culture of the country, they each were shaped by their own unique political environments in which demographics and geography played a significant role. They are also many varieties of political culture existing at a local, state, and national level and common themes of political mythology and organization hold the various strains together.

[36] The best work is Jeanette Keith's *Country People in the New South: Tennessee's Upper Cumberland* (Chapel Hill: University of North Carolina Press, 1995).

[37] Robert Remini, *Andrew Jackson* (New York: Twayne Publishers, 1966), p. 152.

The Populists had promised regulation of big business (especially banks), a graduated income tax, government assistance to farmers, and reduction of political corruption. They believed that unadulterated democracy could address the growing socioeconomic inequality in the United States.[38] While the Populists never gained real political strength in the Upper Cumberland due to the peoples' allegiance to the major parties, these concepts grafted nicely onto the region's political culture and found favor among many people who influenced Gore.[39]

From the earliest stages of his political career, Gore liked the Populists and his economic and political principles often resembled the movement in significant ways. "I believe that Populism was an outstanding liberal movement," Gore wrote in 1972.[40] "As one who believes there is much merit in this Populist heritage," he added, "it has always seemed to me perfectly logical that government should play an active role in the nation's business affairs, and I have never lost faith in the government's ability to guarantee economic justice to all people."[41] Throughout his career, many observers avoided the term "liberal" to describe the senator, and typically identified him as a Populist. His interpretation of populism molded his self image which translated into action.

Another important political reform movement that influenced Gore's political philosophy was progressivism. Significant Populist ideas transferred to the progressive movement that swept the country in the early twentieth century in the form of people like William Jennings Bryan. "My earliest recollection of the events which directly shaped my political, social, and economic philosophy," he noted, "are the conversations I had

---

[38] Some of the most important works on populism include: John D. Hicks, *The Populist Revolt* (Minneapolis: University of Minnesota Press, 1931); Norman Pollack,*The Populist Response to Industrial America: Midwestern Populist Thought* (Cambridge: Harvard University Press, 1962); Walter T. K. Nugent, *The Tolerant Populists: Kansas Populism and Nativism* (Chicago: University of Chicago Press, 1963); Lawrence Goodwyn, *The Populist Moment: A Short History of Agrarian Revolt in America* (New York: Oxford University Press, 1978); Robert McMath, *Populist Vanguard: A History of the Southern Farmers' Alliance* (Chapel Hill: University of North Carolina Press, 1975); Steven Hahn, *The Roots of Southern Populism: Yeoman Farmers and the Transformation of the Georgia Upcountry, 1850–1890* (New York: Oxford University Press, 1983); Michael Schwartz, *Radical Protest and Social Structure: The Southern Farmers' Alliance and Cotton Tenancy, 1880–1890* (New York: Academic Press, 1976); Scott G. McNall, *The Road to Rebellion: Class Formation and Kansas Populism, 1965–1900* (Chicago: University of Chicago Press, 1988).

[39] For the impact of the party in Tennessee, see Roger L. Hart, *Redeemers, Bourbons, and Populists: Tennessee, 1870–1896* (Baton Rouge: Louisiana State University Press, 1975).

[40] Gore, *Let the Glory Out*, p. 31.

[41] Gore, *The Eye of the Storm*, p. 107.

with my father sitting around the fire or on the front porch after supper. . . . Often he would refer to William Jennings Bryan, whose achievements as 'the Great Commoner' are still cherished in the memory of the people of my state."[42] Bryan helped bridge the gap between the Populists and progressives, carrying many of the former's ideas into the Democratic Party which Woodrow Wilson later helped shape into law.

Bryan also inoculated Gore with various ideas regarding U.S. behavior in world affairs that later helped shape the senator's response to Vietnam. While an internationalist, Bryan recognized limits of American power. As a particular example, he strongly condemned U.S. intervention in the Philippines. In 1900, in Indianapolis's Military Park, he emphasized that "against us are arrayed a comparatively small but politically and financially powerful number who really profit by Republican policies."[43]

"Imperialism would be profitable to the army contractors; it would be profitable to the ship owners, who carry live soldiers to the Philippines and bring dead soldiers back; it would be profitable to those who seize upon the franchises . . . but to the farmer, to the laboring man and to the vast majority of those engaged in other occupations it would bring expenditure without return and risk without reward." He concluded by calling for Filipino's independence which would allow the United States to progress forward toward his vision of the republic "in which every citizen is a sovereign, but in which no one cares or dares to wear a crown. Behold a republic standing erect while empires all around are bowed beneath the weight of their own armaments – a republic whose flag is loved while other flags are only feared."[44]

In the South, the progressive movement was more an urban and intellectual movement than populism. Still, Carthage's location near the center of Tennessee's progressive center, Nashville, and the interactions of its citizens with others along the Cumberland River, opened areas like Smith County to progressive ideas. Southern progressive reformers pushed for improved infrastructure, better education, and worker safety laws. They also focused on limiting corporate power, especially the railroads, banks,

---

[42] Like many people, Gore identified Bryan with the Populists even though the Nebraskan never joined the party and remained a loyal Democrat. Nor did Bryan ever identify himself as a progressive although many of his positions mirrored progressive policies.

[43] Donald K. Springen, *William Jennings Bryan: Orator of Small-Town America* (New York: Greenwood Press, 1991), pp. 25–26.

[44] Springen, *William Jennings Bryan*, p. 27.

[45] Dewey W. Grantham, *Southern Progressivism: The Reconciliation of Progress and Tradition* (Knoxville: University of Tennessee Press, 1983), pp. xv–xii.

and insurance companies. In many areas, people fought for social justice including anti-lynching laws. They sought to rationalize the economy and society, hoping to move the South forward from its semi-feudal past.[46]

Several progressives especially influenced Gore. The best known was Woodrow Wilson, whom Gore characterized as an important role model.[47] As president, he helped support major changes in the role of government in society. Economic successes included the significant reduction of tariffs on raw materials and some manufactured goods. In other areas, progressives helped create the Federal Reserve Act, the Federal Trade Commission, and passed the Sixteenth Amendment (federal income tax).[48] In the political area, the Congress and state legislatures approved the Seventeenth Amendment (direct election of senators) and Nineteenth Amendment (women's suffrage). To a new generation of politicians such as Gore, the progressives led by Wilson proved that government could alter the lives of people for positive gain.

Perhaps, the most important aspect of Wilson's influence relating to shaping people such as Gore was his idealistic view of the world of where the United States should promote democracy and a rational world system. The best-known manifestation of Wilson's beliefs was his famous 1918 speech on the "Fourteen Points." It called for the freedom of seas, the removal of trade barriers, disarmament, the impartial adjustment of colonial claims, and self determination in the newly freed colonial areas.[49] During his presidency, he also practiced idealistic application of the ideas. In Mexico and elsewhere, he refused to recognize governments that seized power by force. At the same time, Wilson hypocritically used military interventions that suspended civil liberties to protect American interests. However, for Gore and others, Wilson's idealism left an indelible imprint.

---

[46] For the best studies, reference Grantham's, *Southern Progressivism: The Reconciliation of Progress and Tradition* and Arthur Link, *The Paradox of Southern Progressivism, 1880–1930* (Chapel Hill: University of North Carolina Press, 1992). Another interesting work is Michael Dennis, *Lessons in Progress: State Universities and Progressivism in the New South, 1880–1920* (Urbana: University of Illinois Press, 2001).

[47] Albert A. Gore, Interview by Dewey Grantham and James B. Gardner, November 13, 1976, Southern Oral History Collection, Columbia Oral History Project, New York, New York, p. 18.

[48] Initially, it placed only requirements for payment on a progressive scale on people and corporations making more than $4,000 and only reached a top percentage of six percent. Still, it was a move away from reliance on regressive tax structures of tariffs, excise, and sales taxes.

[49] David D. Anderson, *Woodrow Wilson* (New York: Twayne, 1978), p. 135.

The progressive traditions were firmly rooted in Gore's political principles by the time he sought political office and throughout his career Gore consistently referred to himself as a progressive.[50] An especially important influence was Cordell Hull who promoted progressive ideals. A congressman from Carthage, Hull was a primary sponsor of the constitutional amendment creating the income tax. Throughout his congressional career, the Tennessean focused on taxation based on ability to pay and ideas of reciprocal trade and low tariffs. He helped transfer such ideas to a new generation of politicians like Gore. Men such as Speaker of the House Sam Rayburn (D-TX), who became another of Gore's role models when he entered Congress, also represented nicely the ideas of progressive (and populist) traditions that had evolved in the southern political culture in the first half of twentieth century. Others such as Gore's professors and teachers helped transfer to him the populist/progressive ideas that helped shape his political philosophy.

Finally, Gore's experiences as an unemployed worker and marginal farmer during the Depression reinforced Gore's political principles. He later remembered that while at the marketplace, he saw "the face of poverty: grown men who were so desperate, the tears streamed down their cheeks as they stood with me at the window to receive their meager checks for a full year's work."[51] He campaigned for Roosevelt in 1932, emphasizing that FDR's "matchless voice and the confidence and determination in his words seemed to reach every part of our community and to awaken hope where none had been."[52] According to Gore, Roosevelt capitalized on the "roots of social justice. He nourished them on pure water and cheap electricity – and they quickly sprouted."[53] The New Deal would further reinforce Gore's view that the government could responsibly regulate the economy and political system to better serve all Americans.

Roosevelt also shaped Gore's world view. He followed many of the principles of Wilson, yet, added new levels to them. First, Roosevelt dramatically rejected Wilson's interventionism in Latin America through the "Good Neighbor" policy. He recognized the limits of America's ability to affect change by direct military interventions and the costly nature of such exercises. Furthermore, Roosevelt became an anti-imperialist who

---

[50] Interview by the author with Al Gore, September 24, 2001, Nashville, Tennessee.
[51] Gore, *The Eye of the Storm*, pp. 198–199.
[52] Gore, *Let the Glory Out*, p. 42.
[53] Ibid.

pushed in the Atlantic Charter for a pledge that the Allies wanted "to see the sovereign rights and self-government restored to those who have been forcibly deprived of them." He spoke out on the issue of Indochina early. In 1943, he promised that he would try "with all my might and main" to prevent the expansion of "France's imperialistic ambitions." He talked at the end of the war about an international trusteeship for Indochina and complained that the French had "milked it for one hundred years" and that the people were "worse off than they were at the beginning."[54]

As a result of all the aforementioned influences, Gore entered the House of Representatives in 1939 with a comparatively well developed political philosophy that changed little over his thirty-two years in office. As he saw it, the major problems in U.S. society such as poverty and unemployment resulted from the unequal distribution of wealth arising from dominance by a socioeconomic elite. He believed the wealthy benefitted unfairly from government policies, especially the tax structure, and the lack of government supervision of the economy and social system. For him, a democracy should protect the needs of the majority. On another level, it had a responsibility for providing for the basic needs of its citizens. Finally, in foreign policy he believed in an America that supported democracy and corresponding ideas such as respect for civil liberties. This philosophy would shape his positions on the political issues throughout his tenure in Congress.

Gore's political philosophy had a significant influence on his stance on Vietnam for several reasons. His Populist persuasion predisposed him to view skeptically the ideas pushed by the policy making group in the Kennedy and Johnson administrations, one composed primarily of Eastern business and academic elites. Among these were Walt Rostow, Robert McNamara, Arthur M. Schlesinger, Jr., and McGeorge Bundy. To advisers like Bundy, congressmen were a "collection of uninformed yahoos" who needed to "be cajoled and coerced into supporting the policies that the executive in its wisdom had devised."[55] Such attitudes exacerbated tensions with men such as Gore. As journalist David Halberstam noted in 1971: "He has never connected with the Eastern intellectuals, he is not their kind of man, he does not speak their language, not the same style or wit, because, of course, he is a Populist and the sworn enemy of any good Populist is an Eastern intellectual."[56]

---

[54] As cited in Stanley Karnow, *Vietnam: A History* (New York: Viking, 1983), p. 136.
[55] Woods, *Fulbright*, p. 371.
[56] David Halberstam, "The End of a Populist," *Harper's*, vol. 242, January 1971, p. 37.

Gore never tried to curry the favor of the Eastern elites and often distanced himself from them, not unlike Hull, who had clashed with men
such as Sumner Welles.[57] Gore would not forget his roots as a hardworking, self-made man. He spoke with a Tennessee twang and lacked
a prestigious education. While Eastern intellectuals may have liked some
of his political stances (primarily on civil rights and Medicare), few tried
reaching out to him because of his unwillingness to ingratiate himself with
them. Gore's dislike for such men predisposed him to view many of their
ideas with a great deal of skepticism. His position on the SFRC committee
allowed him a forum to challenge the oftentimes arrogant elites and put
them in their place.

Another element of Gore's political philosophy that manifested itself
in his attitudes toward Vietnam was his belief that big business unfairly
profited from the war. This translated into an opposition to what he and
others characterized as the military-industrial complex. While often sim-
plistic in his definition of this union, his stance fit nicely with his political
principles that questioned the power of large corporations. "Eisenhower's
final act, perhaps his most lasting contribution," Gore wrote, "was his
warning to his countrymen of the dangers inherent in the burgeoning
'military-industrial complex'... One will never know, but historians can
meditate upon the knowledge and possibly the anxieties which prompted
this good and simple man of military renown to conclude his service
with that prophetic valedictory warning."[58] Early on, Gore complained
that the "'military-industrial complex'... opposed holding the election"
in 1956 to reunify Vietnam, seeking instead a military solution and expanded conflict and sustained high defense spending.[59]

Throughout his career, he had sought to prevent big business from
profiting from war. When he entered the House in 1939, he began criticizing war manufacturers for exploiting government contracts for personal
gain. In October, 1941, he told an audience that "industry is reaping enormous profits from the expenditures for defense... Profits of 360 leading
corporations increased $132,000,000, or 20 percent, in the first half of
1941, despite a sharp rise in wage payments and taxes."[60] Once the war
started, he continued his attacks. In March, 1942, he supported a bill

---

[57] A good study into the relationship between Hull and Welles is provided in Irwin F.
Gellman's, *Secret Affairs: Franklin Roosevelt, Cordell Hull, and Sumner Welles* (Baltimore:
Johns Hopkins University Press, 1995).

[58] Gore, *Let the Glory Out*, p. 115.

[59] Gore, *The Eye of the Storm*, p. 11.

[60] Gore House Collection, WSM transcripts, October 5, 1941, box 1, Gore Center.

limiting profits for defense contractors. He condemned inordinately high salaries and bonuses for corporation executives and argued that they had learned to evade higher tax brackets.[61] He called for rigid price controls, statutory limits on profits from war contracts and ceilings on salaries and wages, stressing that "exorbitant profits create labor unrest, hinder the sale of war bonds to the general public, add to inflation pressures, and undermine the morale of our soldiers who feel that the cause for which they are called upon to make so great a sacrifice should not be used by so many fellow citizens for selfish gain."[62]

As a member of the Senate Finance and Senate Foreign Relations Committees in the 1950s and 1960s, he continued along the same lines. At that time, he had seen the massive military growth resulting from the Cold War. He maintained a healthy skepticism of those profiting from the buildup including Ford, Northrop, Boeing, and Dow. He believed business leaders had created alliances within the military and government that sustained each other. Military leaders needed Vietnam to advance their careers while politicians such as Lyndon Johnson (D-TX), Richard Russell (D-GA), and Mendel Rivers (D-SC) had massive military industries and bases in their districts. As a result, they supported the ambitions of the business elite for political gains. In this way, Gore denounced the "military industrial" complex with the ease that the Populists and progressives had done the railroad magnates and Eastern manufacturers and bankers years before.

On another level, Vietnam undermined Gore's political priorities. One of his primary concerns was government public works and education programs. The massive military spending on Vietnam, which reached $2 billion a month at its height, damaged his priorities. The primary sponsor of the Interstate Highway System and a strong proponent of programs such as job training, assistance to small farmers, public housing, and Medicare, he saw vast amounts of funds diverted from public assistance to Southeast Asia. Clearly, he preferred money for roads and education rather than guns and tanks.

Equally important, he saw taxes rise. Throughout his career, he sought to increase the tax paid by the wealthy by closing loopholes and to lower taxes on the poor and middle class by raising the standard deduction. During the 1960s, he stepped up his assaults on the wealthy and tax lobbies. He attacked the Kennedy and Johnson administrations' plans for

---

[61] Gore House Collection, WSM transcripts, March 24, 1942, box 1, Gore Center.
[62] Gore House Collection, Speeches, "Can We Head Off Serious Inflation," in "Wake Up, America" radio transcript, May 3, 1942, box 7, Gore Center.

providing tax breaks to the wealthy.[63] In an article for the *New York Times Magazine* in April, 1965, titled, "How to Be Rich Without Paying Taxes," he stressed that the system was not progressive. After revealing that seventeen millionaires had paid no taxes in recent years, he attacked stock options, the deductions for Americans living abroad, and one of Johnson's pet projects, the oil depletion allowance. He underscored that the oil lobby was "the most diabolical influence at work in the nation's capital."[64] He concluded by calling on an "informed and indignant public opinion" to lobby for change and stressed that "the inequity and favoritism of our present laws are a crying injustice."[65]

Already believing in the inequities of the tax code, he concluded that the middle and working classes paid an unfair burden for the war. Taxes rose during the late 1960s to finance the war and the Great Society. In March, 1966, he rose on the Senate floor and warned that inflation appeared on the horizon and that if the administration continued upon its current path to "prosecute an expensive and perhaps long conflict in Vietnam" then cuts in programs would follow.[66]

This perplexed Gore who counterattacked in 1969 with a set of proposals to lower taxes for all Americans, but in particular the poor and middle class. When the Nixon administration proposed a corporate tax rate reduction, Gore pushed for an increase in the personal exemption from $600 to $1,250. Condemned by the Republicans for unbalancing the budget and "tilting the bill's economic bias toward the consumer and away from investment," Gore's proposal won support among his party.

---

[63] During hearings before the Senate Finance Committee in 1964, Gore had grilled Henry Ford II, Chairman of the Board of the Ford Motor Company who had cochaired Johnson's panel of businessmen supporting the tax bill. When Gore stressed that a family of four whose income was $8,000 would received only a five percent cut in taxes while a taxpayer in the $100,000 bracket would receive a 100 percent increase in after tax income, Ford responded "There are always inequities in things and it's too bad, but that's the way things are." Gore noted that: "As I studied him, the thought occurred to me that except for the ingenuity and the fortune of one of his grandfathers this man might be a check-out clerk at a supermarket, or perhaps the manager of a small store after he had 'worked his way up.' Yet because of his gargantuan inheritance from one of America's richest fortunes, permissible by our faulty tax laws, there he sat as chairman of one of the world's largest industrial combines, a frequent guest of the White House, prating on as if his financial position somehow endowed him with a wisdom he must impart to Congress. Many politicians, too, equated money with brains and esteem." Gore, *Let the Glory Out*, p. 171.

[64] Albert A. Gore, "How to Be Rich Without Paying Taxes," *New York Times Magazine*, April 11, 1965, p. 28.

[65] Ibid., p. 86.

[66] *Congressional Record*, Senate, March 7, 1966, p. 5171.

Republicans countered with compromises and the final bill resulted in only a $150 increase. Nevertheless, it demonstrated Gore's concern for the poor and working class when the Democratic and Republican administrations had promoted tax cuts that primarily benefitted the wealthy and relied on trickle down economics while allowing taxes to rise on the majority of Americans to finance the war.[67]

An accompanying problem was the rise in interest rates as the economy recklessly plunged forward as a result of the war and other problems. He complained that by 1965 "Johnson's unwillingness to face the economic facts of an undeclared war soon began to take its toll. High interest rates, for example, cut deeply into a budget strained by the insatiable demands of the Vietnam front."[68] To Gore, the rising interest rates hurt the small businessmen, farmers, and consumers while bankers and financiers became wealthier. He stated that "it is the mass of people – those who must build and buy on credit – who must pay the high interest rates. And repeated cycles of boom and recession only intensify their insecurity." Gore concluded that in practical terms, "in the face of what must appear as systematic injustice, who could be surprised that it is the poor and underprivileged who more and more are tempted to violence?"[69] In this case, Vietnam hurt the people that Gore wanted to represent and in his mind contributed directly to the unrest of the American cities in the 1960s.

Gore's political philosophy was in part a reflection of his political role models. Particularly important were the anti-imperialism of Bryan and FDR, and the democratic imperialism of Wilson. Gore and others such as Wayne Morse (I-OR), Joseph Clark (D-CA), and Ernest Gruening (D-AK) increasingly worked in Congress to question whether a democratic nation could uphold its values while supporting authoritarian regimes and the damage being done to American prestige by the actions. These congressmen and others began issuing warnings about the impact of the assistance to dictatorships.[70]

A representative example occurred in March, 1960, when Gore spoke out on the issue of Castro and Cuba. He focused on the failures of U.S.

---

[67] Rowland Evans, Jr. and Robert D. Novack, *Nixon in the White House* (New York: Random House, pp. 198–200; Allen J. Matusow, *Nixon's Economy: Booms, Busts, Dollars, and Votes* (Lawrence: University of Kansas Press, 1998), pp. 49–50.

[68] Gore, *Let the Glory Out*, p. 186.

[69] Ibid., p. 143.

[70] Robert D. Johnson, "The Origins of Dissent: Senate Liberals and Vietnam, 1959–1964," *Pacific Historical Review*, 1996, pp. 249–275.

policy. "Perhaps of the most glaring illustration of the error of supporting dictators is furnished by our support of Batista in Cuba. Our representatives in Cuba, in my opinion, grossly mismanaged our affairs. We
identified ourselves so closely with the Batista regime that Castro now has
little trouble in turning large segments of the Cuban populace against the
United States."[71] During the same speech, he also talked about Castro.
"Some suggest that we should merely turn back the clock several decades
and send in the marines. Whatever may have been the justification for that
kind of a policy in years gone by, such actions would really solve nothing
in the.... Armed intervention, unilateral or otherwise, however, is not
an appropriate solution for our present difficulties with Cuba. There are
other means by which we can appropriately protect American rights in
Cuba."[72]

There would be other manifestations of this viewpoint as Vietnam remained a secondary issue in the early 1960s. As subcommittee chair on
Africa of the SFRC, Gore spoke out on military assistance and economic
aid to Africa in 1961. He asked why U.S. policy offered the people of
the nonindustrialized world a choice between U.S. supported and Soviet
backed dictatorships. "Our constant identification with the growing number of military dictatorships" concerned him and led him to "seriously
question our chance of winning" the Cold War.[73] He had added that
he could not identify any reason for military assistance other that to
"assuage" the "pride or ego or desire for prestige" among the African
dictators.[74]

Gore had already made the point about the support of Diem in 1959
and would continue to question military and economic assistance to other
authoritarian regimes throughout the early 1960s. Clearly, there existed a
propensity to question aligning with such people and the ultimate result,
prior to his all out opposition regarding Vietnam. The voices of his role
models echoed in his objections, and while they had often ignored their
own rhetoric, the ideas of Bryan, Wilson, and FDR had clearly left an

[71] Albert Gore, Speech for delivery on Senate floor, March 7, 1960, Research, Foreign Policy,
Dictators, 1960, Senate Collection, box 23, Gore Center.
[72] Senate Albert Gore, undated speech for delivery on Senate floor, Research, Foreign Policy,
1960, Senate Collection, box 23, Gore Center; U.S. Congress, Senate, *Executive Session of
the Senate Foreign Relations Committee*, "Developments in U.S. Relations with the OEEC,"
25 February 1960, 86th Congress 2nd session, Washington, Government Printing Office,
1983, p. 176.
[73] Senate Committee on Foreign Relations, *Hearings, International Development and Security*,
87nd Congress, 1st session, June 14, 1961, p. 618.
[74] As cited in Johnson, "The Origins of Dissent," p. 257.

indelible mark on the political philosophy of Gore and affected his views on Vietnam.

Gore's political philosophy strongly affected his views on the war in Vietnam. In large part, it brought him into conflict with sworn enemies of any self-described populist/progressive, primarily Eastern elites and business interests. The conflict undermined his economic priorities that sought more public spending for the working and middle classes. It drove interests rates and taxes higher, placing more of a burden on these groups. Finally, he questioned the wisdom of U.S. policy in the nonindustrialized world, echoing fundamental questions raised by many of the people who helped shape his political identity. In each area, the Vietnam War subverted his political priorities and prompted his opposition.

The Maverick

Beyond shaping his political principles, the political culture of the Upper Cumberland area and Middle Tennessee influenced Gore's opposition to the war in other ways. The region had a political tradition of producing leaders known for their nonconformity and willingness to challenge the entrenched interests. Gore sought to emulate his political heroes who challenged the political tides for the sake of principle. In emulating this trait, he developed a perception of himself as a maverick and sought to perpetuate it.

"Several tags . . . have been attached to me during my political career," Gore wrote in 1970. "One of these is 'maverick,' and if one likes labels, this in some ways is an apt description. It is apt in the sense that most Tennesseans are mavericks, since they are opposed to running thought-lessly with the herd, feel no need to follow the leader, and value their personal and social independence." He concluded "For this reason, only someone who is a maverick, not out of desire to build a political image, but out of the principle, can truly represent such a state."[75] While he exaggerated the extent of most Tennesseans' contrary nature, this perception of himself as a maverick often shaped his political positions.

Gore's pride in being a maverick originated in his region of Tennessee. There are three distinct regions in the state. The more mountainous area of the East was the most independent as witnessed by its opposition to the South during the American Civil War and its tendency to vote Republican. The western part of the state bears the most resemblance to other parts

[75] Gore, *Let the Glory Out*, p. 191.

of the South. It has the largest African American population and a ruling elite that has used boss politics to control the Memphis district. On
the other hand, Gore came from the central region whose proud political
heritage included Andrew Jackson, James K. Polk, and Davy Crockett.
The people that dominated this area were small farmers, fiercely independent by necessity and geography.[76] The region lacked the racial politics
and class divisions of western Tennessee which created conformity among
whites. People in the middle region typically have encouraged their representatives to resist external pressures, especially from Washington or the
Northeast.

Gore had a long history of independence. He noted that when he arrived in Washington in 1939, he kept his mouth closed and learned the system as instructed by Hull. Nevertheless, when he made his maiden speech
in the House after seven months, it was memorable. He spoke against
an $800,000,000 appropriation for the United States Housing Authority,
a plan backed by the Roosevelt administration. *Newsweek* highlighted
that: "Administration stalwarts tried to keep Gore off the floor . . . but his
Southern colleagues, wishing to lick this slum-clearance bill, made a deal
with Joe Martin and the Republicans. The big guns on the conservative
side allowed Gore to deliver the blast, a rip-snorting ten-minute speech.
On that same day the House killed the bill, 191 to 170."[77] This was the
first, but certainly not the last time, Gore would challenge party leaders
over important issues.[78]

Others recognized Gore's maverick nature and his pride in maintaining the image. His chief of staff during his time in the Senate, William
Allen, emphasized that the senator liked to brag that if he found himself
voting with the majority he needed to reconsider his position.[79] A friend
once noted, "Show Albert the grain, so that he can go against it."[80] Jack
Robinson, Sr., an aide in the 1950s, emphasized, "I'd look up on the
board and see a vote that 93 to 3, and I'd think, One of those [3] was

---

[76] Gore's religious roots in the Southern Baptist denomination most likely reinforced the
   maverick perception. Church leaders have glorified those who have taken unpopular
   stands on principle and moved against the crowd.
[77] O'Donnell to Nation and Business, October 30, 1941, "Interview with Congressman
   Gore," *Newsweek* Archives, Washington D.C., p. 4.
[78] During the mid-1950s, Gore expressed a desire for higher office including the vice-
   presidency in 1956 and 1960. At that point, he proved more of a conformist to win
   party favor. Once he moved away for those aspirations by the early 1960s, he returned
   to a more maverick position on many issues.
[79] Interview by the author with William Allen, July 26, 1996, Lexington, Kentucky.
[80] Halberstam, "The End of a Populist," p. 42.

going to be him."[81] Even his wife Pauline recognized the trait. "I tried to persuade Albert [senior] not to butt at a stone wall just for the sheer joy of butting," she recalled.[82] Gore proudly wore the title and actually nurtured the image to the point that it became an important part of his personality, especially after he gave up aspirations of higher office after 1960.[83]

This maverick image was important for several reasons regarding Vietnam. First, it obviously put him onto the side of the other mavericks and dissenting voices. He liked this position. Second, his perception of himself as maverick allowed him to rationalize away opposition. He believed that a well-financed and organized minority often drowned out the majority. He emphasized that "no politician can afford to be, and none wants to be, indifferent to the wishes of the people he represents." Yet, he admitted, "Certainly, I do plead guilty to sometimes ignoring a vociferous minority, and at other times to turning a deaf ear to directives from self-proclaimed spokesmen of nonexistent groups or lobbies of 'thousands of voters.'"[84] While often inundated with mass mailings on Vietnam, Gore resisted their hawkish calls. He regarded his maverick stands on certain issues as best representing the majority of his constituents, a stand bolstered by the fact that he did not lose an election in thirty-two years.

As Vietnam became more divisive, some observers highlighted the importance of his maverick nature. The most apparent came in 1969 when his son, Albert, Jr., had to decide whether to join the military or avoid service. While antiwar, but with a sense of patriotism and concerned with his father's reelection, the younger Gore decided to enlist and received orders to serve in Vietnam. Nevertheless, the family had fretted about their son and encouraged him to make his own decision and not worry about the election. Covering the election, David Halberstam reported, "Those who know the Senator suspect that he would not have minded at all running a campaign with a son who refused to go to Vietnam, that he would in fact have relished it – the drawing of the line, the ethic of it."[85]

Gore proudly considered himself a maverick. Created in part by the political environment in Tennessee and in part his own humble origins, he

---

[81] Interview by the author with Jack Robinson, Sr., November 3, 1998, Nashville, Tennessee.

[82] Halberstam, "The End of a Populist," p. 167.

[83] It is also very possible that arrogance fed this maverick image. His electoral successes saw Gore lose contact with many of the members of his state's party as well as many constituents.

[84] Gore, *The Eye of the Storm*, p. 210.

[85] Halberstam, "The End of a Populist," p. 42.

relished the position of underdog and often refused to follow the crowd. In part, this became such an important component of his personality and public persona that he went to great lengths to perpetuate it. Ultimately this played a role in his demise. In 1970, he recognized the strength of the conservative calls to white working and middle class individuals in his state and throughout the nation on issues such as civil rights, civil disorder, and Vietnam. Yet, he refused to compromise on the controversies and made principled stands.

The Clash of Titans

There were other foundations for his opposition to the Vietnam War in addition to political principles and perceptions. Personal animosities interjected themselves into the equation. At a basic level, his opposition to the war digressed to a rivalry between him and Johnson and a strong dislike for Richard Nixon. While sometimes overlooked, this personal factor made it easier for Gore to question the administrations' policies regarding Vietnam.

The relationship between Gore and Johnson had spanned three decades. They had entered congressional service at approximately the same time and came from comparable backgrounds. Gore noted their similarities, writing, "We had several things in common: a Populist heritage, descent from landed gentry in scrabbly hill country – he in east Texas, I in the Appalachian foothills. Both had scrambled for education and both had taught as youngsters. Both came under the spell of FDR and entered politics early...And, of course, both of us loved our service in Congress, in politics, and in power." "There were some big differences, too," he noted, "One was that I had grown stronger in Populist leanings and had become an inveterate enemy of special privilege, while Johnson had become a bedfellow of big money, oil, and military brass."[86] Gore remembered working with LBJ on the TVA and southwestern power, but acknowledged that "we invariably disagreed on tax policy. I wanted to eliminate special tax privileges, close the big tax loopholes that permit people to escape their fair share of the tax burden; but the creation and preservation of tax favoritisms had long been a strong arch of Johnson's Texas support and one of the keys to his rise to Senate leadership."[87]

[86] Gore, *Let the Glory Out*, p. 168.
[87] Ibid., p. 124.

Observers noted the strained relationship between the two men. Russell Baker of the *New York Times* wrote in 1960 that despite the outwardly friendly personal relations the "two have a mysterious capacity for getting under each other's skin." He added that one Washington insider had commented: "When Gore and Johnson come together, it is like the meeting of a dog and cat." In response, Gore stated, "Lyndon doesn't particularly irritate me, but I seem to irritate him when I disagree with him."[88] Senator George Smathers (D-FL) also noted the tension. He stated that "Johnson picked his people just exactly why I don't know, but I know I was considered one of his favorites," but that "Johnson did not particularly care for Albert Gore. Why, I don't know."[89] Halberstam contended that Gore "remained out-of-step in the Johnson years; Johnson had a Populist streak in him, that and a capacity to get along well with big money, but the difference between the two was personal as much as anything else, a lingering animosity. Johnson, above all else, liked to control and dominate other men, and Albert Gore is a loner, a man not to be controlled."[90]

Even before Johnson obtained the presidency, the two men clashed on numerous occasions. On one particular occasion in January, 1961, Johnson tried holding some of his former congressional power while in the vice-presidency. When Senate Majority leader Mike Mansfield (D-MT) asked the Democratic senators to allow Johnson to preside over party caucuses, Gore and others vigorously protested. "This caucus is not open to former senators," Gore emphasized. While Johnson won the vote handily, he and others noted that even those who voted for him resented the intrusion. Johnson left and later remarked, "I know the difference between a caucus and a cactus. In a cactus all the pricks are on the outside."[91]

While some speculated that Gore was jealous of President Johnson, most likely Gore's independent nature, combined with his disdain for Johnson's slickness and lack of a consistent political philosophy, caused conflict over Vietnam. While they continued to work together on issues of Medicare, job programs, and education, Gore admitted that he believed that "Johnson was going too far." He feared the granting of power to

---

[88] Russell Baker, "Gore also Runs-But for V.P.," *New York Times Magazine*, April 10, 1960, p. 114.

[89] Oral History Interview of Senator George A. Smathers by Donald A. Ritchie, August 1, – October 24, 1989, p. 60, Senate Historical Office, National Archives, Washington, D.C.

[90] David Halberstam, "The End of a Populist," *Harper's*, vol. 242, January 1971, p. 37.

[91] Robert Dallek, *Flawed Giant: Lyndon Johnson and His Times, 1961–1973* (New York: Oxford University Press, 1998), p. 8.

faceless, unelected bureaucrats to administer programs, especially those that had power to withhold federal funding to states. This skepticism, combined with Gore's disillusionment caused by the Gulf of Tonkin issue, predisposed him to challenge Johnson. The personal animosity that had always simmered below the surface spilled over many times on the issue of Vietnam and made Gore defy the president.

In the aftermath of the civil rights battle, Gore concentrated on the election. He recognized the difficulties and spent a lot of time in Tennessee. While always exuding confidence, he knew he had a fight on his hand. He reported to one friend in early July that "Pauline and I got into the farm late last night after four days of campaigning in West Tennessee. My situation is in excellent shape over there but I found more Goldwater supporters than I expected to find."[92] Furthermore, in West Tennessee, he had some other problems. His position on the Civil Rights Bill had left African Americans disenchanted with him. A slogan floated around Memphis promoting, "Ignore Gore in' 64."[93]

Another problem for Gore was that he lacked strong support from the White House. While publicly supportive, Johnson still held a grudge against Gore for his opposition to him heading the caucus and his un-willingness to support his program. Johnson liked pliable people. "I want people around me who kiss my ass on a hot summer's day and say it smells like roses," he liked to say.[94] Yet he noted that during caucus meetings, Gore would always "jack up" against him and that he "didn't want me in," as he complained to George Smathers in early August of 1964. The president also did not like his opposition to the tax plan, civil rights, and other positions. When Smathers reported that Gore had told him that the president disliked him even though he supported him against Goldwater, Johnson instructed Smathers to tell him "I never saw the president show any indication but every time he had a caucus you used to get up and at-tack him and I wouldn't be surprised if he didn't appreciate it." Smathers wanted to offer: "You haven't been for a damn thing we've been for." Finally, Smathers complained, "Why they couldn't get someone to run against him and beat him, I'll never know." Johnson simply responded, "I don't know either."[95]

---

[92] Gore to Joe Jared, July 9, 1964, Politics, General, Gore Senate Collection, Folder, Gore Center.

[93] Interview by the author with Jim Sasser, June 12, 2001, Washington, D.C.

[94] As cited in Dallek, *Flawed Giant*, p. 160.

[95] Telephone conversation of Smathers and Johnson, August 1, 1964, Tapes, WH 6408.01, LBJ Papers, LBJ Library.

The Tennessee senator maintained total disdain for Johnson's successor, Richard Nixon. As early as 1952, he condemned then Senator Nixon for taking money from wealthy constituents to create a special fund to supplement his income and pay for travel, printing bills, and radio broadcasts. The Californian contended that he saved the taxpayers money and used some funds to combat communism. Gore publicly challenged Nixon's integrity, leading some of his constituents to accuse him of slandering the Republican ticket. "Senator Nixon, it seems to me that he slandered himself," Gore responded, "a careful analysis in defense of the subsidization of a United States Senator by a few . . . will reveal the act as an unfortunate example and precedent of conduct in high office."[96] He also wrote a California woman who had defended Nixon that he lived well on his $15,000 salary, and even found opportunities to save and invest in legitimate business opportunities. "I would not consider it right for me to be subsidized by a continuing fund contributed and subscribed to by a few of the people when my fundamental obligation is to all of the people."[97] This would be the first of his many condemnations of Nixon.

He continued to criticize Nixon during the 1960 presidential race. Regarding the election, he stressed that "I never understood how millions of sensible citizens could bring themselves to vote for him for public office. Deficient in grace or charm, unprepossessing in appearance, plebeian in intellect, and painfully humorless, his appeal was to me incomprehensible." "True, he had a certain chauvinistic energy, a cunning shrewdness, an instinct for the narrow prejudice," he added, "and this may have attracted the rough-and-ready element, the social conservatives, and the economic royalists."[98]

Part of the dislike was partisan. Gore had always disagreed with Republican principles, especially economic policies. In 1958, he remarked, "If the Republican Party were ever re-incarnated into a homing pigeon, no matter from where it was released in the universe, whether from a jet plane or in outer space, it would go directly home to Wall Street without a flutter of the wing."[99] In international relations, Gore differed with the Republicans on issues of protectionism, defense spending, and Vietnam. This partisanship made Nixon an easier target for ridicule and resistance.

---

[96] Gore to Nat Williams, October 13, 1952, General Files, Nixon (Senator), box 24, Gore House Files, Gore Center.

[97] Gore to Helen Boyd, September 29, 1952, General Files, Nixon (Senator), box 24, Gore House Files, Gore Center.

[98] Gore, *Let the Glory Out*, p. 141.

[99] Ibid., p. 124.

From the start, Gore attacked Nixon's Vietnam policy. After the election, he asserted that Nixon had claimed a clear mandate from the American people to end the war. Still, Nixon had heavily funded the Vietnamization program, much to the consternation of Gore. Nixon also talked about a "silent majority" of Americans supporting his efforts and warned that "North Vietnam cannot humiliate the United States. Only Americans can do that."[100] Gore responded, "there has been no 'silent majority' quietly egging the warriors on to greater heights up the escalation ladder and urging that carnage be prolonged."[101] "The traditional Southern attraction to violence is assuaged by this," Gore wrote, "just as Nixon's cruel prolongation of the Vietnam war, and his incredible pretension of winning the war, while withdrawing from it, is a prayer to the ghost of Robert E. Lee."[102]

Gore's disagreement with the Nixon administration's policy in Vietnam combined with his opposition to its Anti-Ballistic Missile system, tax policy, and the Supreme Court appointments of G. Harrold Carswell and Clement Haynsworth, caused the Republican administration to strongly oppose Gore's reelection in 1970. This further antagonized Gore who responded by intensifying his attacks on the administration. An example was when U.S. troops invaded Cambodia. Gore pressed Nixon to meet with the SFRC where he asked about the legality of moving into a sovereign nation. Nixon countered "Because this is not a sovereign territory. It had become dominated by the enemy."[103] Such confrontations led Gore to note in August, 1970, that he had been made "Target number one by the Nixon Administration."[104]

Senator Gore correctly appraised the situation. In early 1969, Nixon dispatched Harry Treleaven, head of a New York campaign management firm who had conducted Nixon's 1968 television campaign, to work with Gore's Republican opponent, William Brock. Treleaven's associate, Kenneth Rietz, stayed on with Brock and continued to coordinate attacks on Gore, portraying the senator as too liberal and out of touch with Tennessee voters.[105]

---

[100] George Herring, *America's Longest War: The United States and Vietnam, 1950–1975*, Third Edition (New York: McGraw-Hill, Inc., 1996), p. 251.

[101] Gore, *The Eye of the Storm*, p. 11.

[102] Gore, *Let the Glory Out*, p. 7.

[103] As cited in Glen Moore, "Richard M. Nixon and the 1970 Midterm Elections in the South," *Southern Historian*, p. 62.

[104] Ibid.

[105] Richard Harris, "Annals of Politics: How the People Feel," *The New Yorker*, July 10, 1971, p. 38.

The administration also began illegal activities to help Brock's campaign. John Ehrlichman encouraged a Nixon White House aide, Jackie Gleason, to secure contributions from wealthy Republicans including Richard Scaife ($100,000) and H. Ross Perot ($250,000). He took the money and created a fund to help Republican Senate candidates in 1970 including George Bush and Brock. Designed to circumvent campaign finance laws that limited individual contributions to candidates to $5,000, Gleason funneled contributions, typically $2,500, to groups such as "Friends of Brock Committee," "Brock Boosters," "Women for Brock," and "Brock News Committee." The groups then used the money to purchase attack ads and other campaign materials. Gleason also provided publications such as "Significant Votes of Senator Gore on the Tax Reform Act of 1969" which highlighted the senator's opposition to oil depletion allowance to wealthy donors in oil rich areas. By the end of the campaign, Gleason had delivered over $200,000 into Tennessee races, most of it to Brock. It was the most of any state, except Maryland.[106]

Nixon and Vice-President Spiro Agnew followed these actions with direct attacks on Gore. In May, 1970, Nixon traveled to Knoxville to attend a Billy Graham revival meeting with Brock. As the election approached, Agnew blasted Gore in Memphis. Angry over Gore calling him "our greatest disaster next to Vietnam," Agnew praised Brock for supporting the president. "I do not question the patriotism or the sincerity of the senior Senator from Tennessee," he added, "indeed he is most sincere in his mistaken belief that Tennessee is located somewhere between New York City and Hartford, Connecticut."[107] A month later, Nixon made a speech at East Tennessee State University in Johnson City to a crowd of nearly 30,000. "The President that Tennessee voted for," Nixon told the crowd, "should have a man in the United States Senate who voted with him on the big issues."[108]

The actions of the Nixon administration further antagonized Gore. Already holding the administration in low regard, the attacks made the rift even wider. Ultimately, the endeavors of the Republicans, when combined with the rising conservative movement in the country, led to his defeat in the general election in 1970. The actions of the Republicans, primarily

---

[106] Townhouse File, #807, RG 460, Records of the Watergate Special Prosecution Force, Campaign Contributions Task Force, box 6, Nixon Presidential Materials Project, National Archives II, College Park, Maryland.

[107] Moore, "Richard M. Nixon and the 1970 Midterm Elections in the South," pp. 62, 64.

[108] As cited in Moore, "Richard M. Nixon and the 1970 Midterm Elections in the South," p. 65.

236 *Kyle Longley*

the Nixon White House, had further contributed to Gore's opposition to the war.

The personal rivalry with Johnson and the pure disdain for Nixon and his associates helped shape Gore's position on Vietnam. His friendship with Kennedy had limited his criticisms of the president's policy, but the personal differences between Gore and Johnson and Nixon made it easier to speak out more on the issue and directly challenge the administrations' policies in Vietnam. While other considerations always were important, the personal level often has interjected itself into politics. It did in this case.

Conclusion

Several factors served as foundations for Senator Albert Gore's opposition to U.S. involvement in Vietnam. They include Gore's political philosophy shaped by the political culture of the Upper Cumberland, his maverick nature also created in large part by his political environment, and personal differences with the presidents running U.S. policy in Vietnam. Each played a role in leading Gore to evolve from questioning policy in private and executive sessions of the SFRC to openly breaking with the Johnson and Nixon administrations on the war in Southeast Asia. Understanding these influences should help provide some insight into the role of regional politics and personal issues on U.S. foreign policy and allow comparative analysis of why various individuals chose to challenge U.S. policy in Vietnam.

A Delicate Balance

John Sherman Cooper and the Republican Opposition to the Vietnam War

Fredrik Logevall

In 1969, after Richard Nixon became president of the United States, he and other Republicans liked to complain of the mess they had inherited in Vietnam. "The Democrats' War," they referred to it, or "The Liberals' War." It was a curious charge. That the Nixon team faced an extraordinarily difficult situation in Southeast Asia at the start of 1969 cannot be doubted; the choices were few and awful. But they and their party had much to do with this sordid state of affairs. The initial decision to try to create and sustain a non-communist bastion in southern Vietnam in the mid-1950s had been made under a Republican administration, not a Democratic one. More important, when Lyndon Johnson Americanized the war in 1965 his strongest support on Capitol Hill came from the GOP. As LBJ complained to Senate Minority Leader Everett Dirksen on the phone in late February of that year, "I'm getting kicked around by my own party in the Senate, and getting my support from your side of the aisle."[1] He would make that lament many times in the years that followed. Democrats much more than Republicans were reluctant to make Vietnam an American war, while in the press community pillars of the "liberal" establishment such as the *New York Times* and the *New Republic* were from an early point arguing that Vietnam was not worth the price of a large-scale war. If Vietnam was a liberal and Democratic war it was no less so a conservative and Republican one.

The "liberals' war" charge becomes even more specious when one considers that those few Republican lawmakers who questioned the need for

---

[1] *Newsweek*, 1 March 1965. I would like to thank Andrew L. Johns for his assistance in the preparation of this essay.

a full-scale commitment to South Vietnam came almost exclusively from the moderate-to-liberal wing of the party. (The term "Liberal Republican" was not the oxymoron in the mid 1960s that it would be as the century drew to a close.) In the Senate the group included Clifford Case of New Jersey, George Aiken of Vermont, Margaret Chase Smith of Maine, Mark O. Hatfield of Oregon, Jacob Javits of New York, and John Sherman Cooper of Kentucky. Never the dominant force on Vietnam within the GOP, these senators nevertheless played an important part in the growing congressional dissatisfaction with the war in the last half of the 1960s, and a few of them – notably Aiken, Hatfield, and Cooper – were key players in the winding down of American intervention in Vietnam after 1968.[2]

John Sherman Cooper, in particular, ranks among the most important congressional dissenters on the war – from either party. A chain-smoker who hailed from Kentucky's foothill country, Cooper was tall and courtly and the very model of the Southern gentleman. Despite his good ol' boy mannerisms on the campaign stump, he was thoughtful and learned – his preferred bedside reading ran to Burke, Spinoza, and Santayana. Cooper's judicious handling of legislation, his lack of pretense, his deep experience in both foreign and domestic affairs, made him one of the most respected individuals on Capitol Hill. In a 1960 *Newsweek* poll that asked fifty Washington correspondents to name the ablest persons in Congress, Cooper ranked first among Republicans.[3]

To the uninitiated the ranking no doubt came as a surprise, for Cooper had a comparatively obscure national image. He never mastered or showed much interest in the game played by most other senators, that of promoting their accomplishments through press releases and news conferences. Notoriously absentminded, he paid little attention to such deeds. In addition, Cooper was a poor public orator who tended to mumble his way through speeches. According to one story, a Washington Post reporter had once almost fallen from the press gallery while leaning over the edge with cupped ear to hear the Kentuckian.[4]

---

[2] An insightful study of the liberal Republicans and what became of them is Nicol C. Rae, *The Decline and Fall of the Liberal Republicans: From 1952 to the Present* (New York: Oxford University Press, 1989).

[3] Robert Schulman, *John Sherman Cooper: The Global Kentuckian* (Lexington, KY: The University Press of Kentucky, 1976), p. 6. Any investigation into Cooper's career should begin with this slim but information-packed biography.

[4] LeRoy Ashby and Rod Gramer, *Fighting the Odds: The Life of Senator Frank Church* (Pullman, Wash.: Washington State University Press, 1994), p. 300.

What the Washington reporters knew, however, was that Cooper's low-key, soft-voiced style, combined with his keen intelligence and wide experience, made him very effective behind the scenes. White House officials knew it as well. In the mid-1960s, as the Vietnam War escalated and as Cooper's opposition to American involvement grew apace, U.S. policymakers paid the senator's pronouncements close attention. A White House memo of early 1965 referred to him as a "bellwether" in the emerging Congressional debate on the war, a lawmaker who could have an important influence on undecided colleagues. Two years later, the *New York Times* called the "gentle, white-haired" Cooper a potential leader among Lyndon Johnson's foreign policy critics in the Senate, in view of the seriousness with which the administration viewed his pronouncements.[5]

Cooper's perceived authority on the Vietnam War owed much to his extensive background in foreign policy issues. In World War II he had served as a military police courier with Patton's Third Army and played a key role in the reestablishment after the war of the judicial system in Bavaria. Then, after a short stint in the U.S. Senate, Cooper was appointed by Harry Truman in the fall of 1949 to represent the United States as delegate to the United Nations General Assembly replacing John Foster Dulles. The next year, Secretary of State Dean Acheson named Cooper to be his special assistant in the formation of the North Atlantic Treaty Organization. In 1955–56, following a second brief tenure in the Senate, Cooper served as U.S. ambassador to India, and in December 1960 president-elect John F. Kennedy tapped him for an important fact-finding trip to New Delhi and Moscow. In these positions he won the respect and admiration of important world officials such as Ludwig Erhard, Jawaharlal Nehru, and Anastas Mikoyan.

It must have been heady stuff for this son of Somerset, Kentucky, (population: 11,000) to mingle on the world stage with these statesmen. But then, there was always something of the cosmopolitan in Cooper. At Somerset High School he was president of his class and class poet; his 1918 commencement oration was on "The German Spy System." At Yale he was elected to the elite Skull and Bones senior society and captained the basketball team, and throughout his years in New Haven he displayed a keen interest in international affairs. Cooper's class of 1923 voted him "best liked" and "most likely to succeed," and classmate Stuart Symington,

---

[5] Jonathan Moore to William Bundy, Jan. 1965, box 3, Papers of James C. Thomson, Jr., John F. Kennedy Library, Boston, MA.; *New York Times*, January 15, 1967.

later a Democratic senator from Missouri, called him "far and away the most distinguished member of that Yale class."

In the late 1920s and the 1930s, observing the national political scene and the rising tensions in Europe and East Asia as a state legislator and Pulaski County judge, Cooper never adopted the isolationist unconcern of many in Appalachia and beyond. "In a strongly Republican family in a Republican county, I did not at first feel kindly toward Woodrow Wilson or internationalism," he would later say. "Then I began to read what he'd said." In 1939, in preparation for a speech to the Kentucky Federation of Women's Clubs on isolationism and interventionism, Cooper spent three days at the University of Kentucky library reading up on the Wilsonian approach to foreign affairs. He then gave an address that emphasized America's world-leadership responsibility. "I was deeply impressed with many of FDR's fireside chats to the nation on the subject," he later recalled. "I followed the news of all of Hitler's moves and saw in motion pictures the crowd responses to his inflammatory speeches in places like Nuremberg – commanding, arousing, intense. I did not see how we could avoid reading this as an inevitable, fundamental threat to freedom and a sense of decency everywhere."[6]

Well before American entry into World War II, then, Cooper was a committed internationalist. His experience in the war strengthened his conviction that America must maintain a great-power role on the world stage when hostilities ended, and in the postwar years he voiced frequent and firm support for a policy of containing communist expansion. But he also backed an energetic American effort at negotiating with adversaries on the international stage, criticizing those inside and outside his party who declared negotiations with communists an exercise in futility. At several points of major East-West tension Cooper demonstrated a capacity for independent thinking as he called for superpower negotiations and made clear his belief that American power, no matter how great in relative terms, was ultimately limited.

In May, 1954, for example, when French forces in Indochina faced imminent defeat at the hands of the Vietminh at the outpost of Dien Bien Phu, Cooper voiced strong support for the Eisenhower administration's policy of seeking allied help in bolstering the French cause. He declared that the Paris government, together with the help of the Vietnamese and Laotians, had been engaged in a "fight for freedom." The stakes were high: "Today we are confronted with the same problem which we faced

[6] Schulman, *Cooper*, pp. 26–27.

in Korea and China: whether it is possible to devise measures in concert
with other nations which can prevent the loss of Indochina and other
Asian states vital to the security of the United States and the freedom
of the world." At the same time Cooper took a strong stand in favor
of negotiations. "It is suggested now that it may be possible through
negotiation to find a basis of settlement in Indochina," he said on the day
the French surrender at Dien Bien Phu was announced. "Considering that
our alternatives are losing Indochina entirely, or war with the entry of our
troops, I believe the choice of negotiation may be the only possible choice
available to us."[7]

Strong advocates of negotiations on Indochina were hard to come by
in Congress that year – on either side of the aisle. Nor was it just in foreign
policy that Cooper took an independent road. During his initial stint in the
Senate in 1947–48, he voted with the GOP only 51 percent of the time –
lowest among any of the party's senators. As a member of the Senate
Labor Committee, he offered amendments and backing for changes in
the Taft-Hartley Act that appealed as much to labor as to management
and that won support among key Democrats on Capitol Hill. After winning a return to the Senate in 1952 (to complete the term of Democrat
Virgil Chapman, who had died in office) Cooper was among the first
to oppose the Eisenhower administration's appointment of Albert Cole,
an open opponent of public housing, as Federal Housing Administrator.
Alone among Republicans, he fought the administration's Mexican Farm
Labor bill which, in the absence of agreement between the two countries,
authorized U.S. recruitment of Mexicans for work on American farms at
substandard rates of pay. On civil rights, Cooper called for Republicans,
as the party of Lincoln, to do more to reach out to blacks. All of which
led the left-leaning Americans for Democratic Action (ADA) in late 1953
to name Cooper the Senate's "most liberal" Republican.[8]

A slight exaggeration, maybe, but not much of one. Cooper believed
that the Republican tradition was best represented by Abraham Lincoln
and Theodore Roosevelt, as well as by Henry Clay's Whiggery and
Alexander Hamilton's Federalism. Republicans, he maintained, should
seek to weave the disparate social and economic interests of Americans
into a consensus that sought to maximize individual freedom while maintaining the unity and national security of the nation. In foreign policy,
the party should be determinedly internationalist but not unilateralist; it

---

[7] *Congressional Record*, vol. 100, p. 12434.
[8] Schulman, *Cooper*, p. 59.

should work in concert with allied governments and place faith in the value of international organizations. At home, in Cooper's judgment, the GOP should stand for individual rights and the free-enterprise system, but should not seek to dismantle the Roosevelt New Deal. Government had a responsibility to provide relief for the less fortunate members of society and for defending the right of workers to improve their lot through labor unions and collective bargaining, and it should work to better the civil rights of black Americans. In time, these tenets would come under attack from conservatives who saw liberal Republicanism as being barely distinguishable from the "big government" policies of the Democrats – it was an ideology of "me-tooism," critics charged – but Cooper stood his ground.[9]

Still, a high ranking from the ADA was not something Cooper particularly cared to trumpet in his home state, least of all with a tough 1954 reelection campaign looming. Cooper would go on to lose the election, to former Vice-President Alben Barkley, and the question to be asked is whether Cooper's liberal voting record materially affected the outcome. Probably it did not. Barkley was a grizzled and colorful icon in Kentucky, a man known as "Mr. Democrat" in an overwhelmingly Democratic state. Like Cooper he was an internationalist, and like Cooper he was able and experienced. "We had trouble finding issues," Cooper would later say of his campaign's difficulty in differentiating itself from Barkley's.

All of which suggests that Republican Senator Robert Taft was on to something when he asked Cooper in frustration, some years earlier, "Are you a Democrat or a Republican? When are you going to start voting with us?"[10] Judging by his policy positions, certainly, Cooper could have been mistaken for a Democrat. Had he been born in most any other county in Kentucky, he might well have been one. It may be that being a Republican in a heavily Democratic state made it easier for Cooper to toe an independent line – he did not have a strong party establishment to which he had to answer – and he himself liked to say that his refusal to play the partisan stalwart was in the best tradition of Kentucky politics. In the late 1950s and early 1960s, as key elements in the GOP began moving rightward, Cooper avoided going with them. He would remain a Republican – he returned to the Senate in 1957, and this time would stay for sixteen years – but an independent one.

---

[9] For an impassioned defense of liberal Republicanism, see Jacob K. Javits, *Order of Battle: A Republican's Call to Reason* (New York: Pocket Books, 1966).
[10] Ibid, p. 37.

In foreign policy, Cooper would continue to call for a more forthcoming American position on superpower negotiations. In 1961, when Nikita Khrushchev issued ultimatums about the question of Western access to Berlin, Cooper emphasized the need for diplomacy. He voiced support for a "stand firm" policy on Berlin but then explained what he meant. "If the phrase 'stand firm' means the fixed position that the president ought not examine the realities of the situation, or communicate with Soviet Russia, or take any honorable means to prevent the commencement of hostilities which might expand into a third world war, I disagree," he told colleagues. "And I disagree unequivocally with those who, using the term 'stand firm,' consider it appeasement if any attempt is made by members of Congress or by the president to discuss Berlin except in dogmatic or belligerent terms."[11]

In March, 1962, after Moscow had resumed atmospheric testing of nuclear weapons and it was reported that President Kennedy would do the same, Cooper voiced support for such action. But he added, "We should continue our efforts to reach a true and enforceable agreement with the Soviet Union.... It is argued by some that negotiations are futile, and there is much in the record to support this view. But our free system of government is based on concepts different from those of the Soviet Union – on ethical and religious principles. Even though we may resume atomic tests, and under the circumstances I believe it necessary, we owe it to the people of the world and our principles to continue our efforts to reach agreement with the Soviet Union."[12]

These were remarkable comments, coming as they did at what in hindsight can be seen as the very height of the Cold War. Cooper, perhaps because of his broad experience in international affairs – and in particular in dealing with foreign statesmen – showed a faith in diplomacy quite uncharacteristic of his countrymen. Americans had never been wholly comfortable in the murky world of European-style diplomacy, with its emphasis on pragmatic give-and-take leading to imperfect solutions, and the failed appeasement of Hitler at Munich in 1938 and postwar division of Europe made many doubly suspicious of compromising with adversaries.

Diplomacy indeed held almost no place in the containment policy that emerged after 1945. Since the Soviets were perceived to be fanatics, alien to Western traditions, talking to them was essentially pointless. Since they

---

[11] Ibid, pp. 92–93.
[12] Ibid, p. 93.

also were bent on exporting their system and imposing it on unwilling peoples, the United States, as the leader of the free world, had a moral obligation to stop them. Perceptive observers like Walter Lippmann and George Kennan saw already in 1947, with the enunciation in that year of the Truman Doctrine, the possibility that there was but a short step between this containment policy and an indiscriminate globalism which could compel the U.S. to intervene militarily on behalf of weak puppet states in remote areas of the world. Both men understood that the mere possession of great national power, such as America enjoyed after 1945, would make it hard for leaders to resist projecting that power far and wide and intervening in the affairs of others.

Cooper understood it as well. From an early point he advocated a containment policy that was discriminating, that could distinguish between vital and peripheral interests, and he voiced periodic fears about the tendency of American statesmen to extend too far the nation's limited resources. Thanks in large part to his tenure in India, he also came to appreciate how distorting and confining a strictly bipolar conception of world affairs could be; nationalism, he realized, would usually be a stronger force than any political ideology, which meant that many newly emerging nations would strive for neutrality rather than choose sides in the superpower confrontation.

Which brings us to Vietnam. As American involvement in South Vietnam grew during the John F. Kennedy administration, Cooper became steadily more concerned about the prospects there – about the chances of defeating the insurgency and the likelihood of getting a Saigon government possessing broad popular support. He supported the policy of providing aid and assistance to the Saigon government, but he warned against a large-scale U.S. intervention and urged the Kennedy administration to seek a negotiated settlement. As tensions mounted following the November, 1963, assassination of South Vietnamese leader Ngo Dinh Diem, Cooper grew more restive, especially after reports flooded Washington that the mass of South Vietnamese were weary of fighting and wanted an end to the war. In April, 1964, he urged the Johnson administration to make a serious attempt at negotiation. The prospects for a satisfactory settlement might not be great, he conceded, but the military outlook was worse. The following month, after Johnson asked Congress for $125 million in new funds for South Vietnam, the senator declared: "If the Vietnamese will not fight, I personally cannot see how we can hold our position in that country. Considering our obligations, we should give them a chance, but if they will not fight, I cannot see how we can bear this burden of men, money, and assistance in Southeast Asia." Unless the picture improved soon, he concluded, the United States should seek the reconvening of the 1954 Geneva Conference.[13]

Lyndon Johnson was having his own doubts about the war in this period, but he was not the slightest bit interested in pursuing early negotiations leading to an American disengagement. The vast internal record leaves little doubt on this score. Immediately upon assuming the presidency in November, 1963, he had vowed to stick it out in Vietnam, and the determination had not slackened six months later. A reconvened Geneva Conference, he told Georgia Democrat Richard Russell in late May, "ain't no solution at all."[14] In early August, in response to alleged North Vietnamese attacks on American ships in the Gulf of Tonkin, LBJ ordered a large-scale air attack on targets in North Vietnam. It was the first direct military confrontation between the United States and North Vietnam, and it brought the war to the forefront of Congress's agenda for the first time in a decade. The reason: the administration accompanied the bombings with a request for a Congressional resolution granting Johnson the authority to take whatever steps deemed necessary to defend U.S. interest in Indochina.[15]

The resolution passed both houses of Congress with near-unanimous support, but with much more grumbling and reticence among lawmakers than is generally recalled. In the Senate debate, in particular, expressions of misgivings were frequent, as even a cursory examination of the Congressional Record makes clear. Cooper spoke for many when he cautioned on the Senate floor against a deepened U.S. involvement in the war. The president, he said, "has with respect to our action in South Vietnam, a certain maneuverability, and avenues of negotiation which should be assiduously used, however they may be received." Cooper questioned the importance of Southeast Asia to U.S. interests, and the extent of American military power, "We are committed in Europe and believe our chief

---

[13] Cooper comments to WAVE-TV in Louisville, May 24, 1964, Senatorial series II, box 570, papers of John Sherman Cooper, University of Kentucky, Lexington, KY (hereafter cited as Cooper papers).

[14] On Johnson's opposition to negotiations in this period, see Fredrik Logevall, *Choosing War: The Lost Chance for Peace and the Escalation of War in Vietnam* (Berkeley: University of California Press, 1999).

[15] On the events in the Gulf, see Edwin E. Moïse, *Tonkin Gulf and the Escalation of the Vietnam War* (Chapel Hill, NC: University of North Carolina Press, 1996). On the Congressional debate, an essential source is William Conrad Gibbons, *The U.S. Government and the Vietnam War: Executive and Legislative Roles and Relationships,* 4 vols. (Princeton: Princeton University Press, 1984–1996), vol. 2, pp. 280–342.

interest is in the Western Hemisphere and Europe. In the Pacific we are committed to the defense of Formosa, Korea, Japan, and the Philippines. I do not know how widely we can spread our resources and our men in the military forces."[16]

In an oft-cited exchange with Senate Foreign Relations Committee chairman J. William Fulbright – whose assignment from Johnson was to assure overwhelming passage of the resolution in the Senate – Cooper asked prescient questions about the powers it granted the president to make war:

Cooper: Are we now giving the President advance authority to take whatever action he may deem necessary respecting South Vietnam and its defense, or with respect to the defense of any other country included in the [Southeast Asian Treaty Organization] treaty?
Fulbright: I think that is correct.
Cooper: Then, looking ahead, if the President decided that it was necessary to use such force as could lead into war, we will give that authority by this resolution?
Fulbright: That is the way I would interpret it.[17]

Cooper expected to get these answers, and he worried greatly about them. The Senate's constitutional role in the making of war and peace was being challenged, he believed. Yet he was not prepared to vote against the resolution. He shared many of the same concerns as the only two senators who did in the end vote no – Oregon Democrat Wayne Morse and Alaska Democrat Ernest Gruening – but not their willingness to defy the president at a time when American servicemen were in harm's way. Morse and Gruening were political mavericks; Cooper, though an independent thinker, was not. And to be sure, Johnson's position was difficult to attack. He had asked Congress to approve an action he had already taken, and members felt compelled to go along. The flag of the country was involved. The administration had skillfully cultivated a crisis atmosphere which seemed to leave little time for debate. Cooper opted to keep a low profile and hope for the best. He professed to believe that Lyndon Johnson was a man of peace, a man who would prevent the conflict from escalating into a large-scale war.

His restiveness deepened in late 1964, as South Vietnam descended into politicomilitary chaos and a Vietcong victory appeared imminent. In January, 1965, while Republican leaders were calling for a policy of persevering in Vietnam regardless of cost, Cooper joined with several

---

[16] *Congressional Record*, vol. 110, p. 17833.
[17] Gibbons, *US Government* II, pp. 325–326.

senior Democrats in calling for a reexamination of American policy and in predicting a full-scale Senate debate on the matter. "If these people in South Vietnam will not stand and fight," he told journalists, "I don't see how we can stay there."[18] White House officials worried about the Kentuckian's capacity to influence thinking on Capitol Hill – hence the reference to him in one internal memo as a bellwether who could bring others along with him on the war. On Johnson's orders, senior administration officials worked hard behind the scenes to head off or at least delay a Senate debate, with evident success – the debate would not occur until mid-February and would be a limited affair.[19]

In late March, after the crucial decisions to commence sustained bombing of North Vietnam and to dispatch the first ground forces to the South, Cooper stepped up his effort to bring about a political solution to the war – and to make the Senate a player in the policymaking. On March 25, he joined with Javits in calling for negotiations for a settlement, without pre-conditions on either side. Cooper affirmed his support for Johnson's policy of backing South Vietnam but said the administration had to show more flexibility on the subject of diplomacy. "I do not believe that we can reach negotiations by imposing as a prerequisite that the Communists cease their intervention, rightful as our position is," he told his colleagues. "For then we stand in confrontation, with a position of unconditional surrender and with the possibility of war as the only arbiter." The same day, Cooper introduced a resolution calling on Senate leaders to arrange for a full briefing of all senators by Secretary of State Dean Rusk and Secretary of Defense Robert McNamara on developments in Vietnam.[20]

Senate Majority Leader Mike Mansfield, who shared the essentials of Cooper's position on the war, promised Cooper he would do all he could to facilitate such a flow of information to senators. Perhaps he did, but in the weeks and months that followed neither Mansfield nor other top Democratic senators, nor Cooper himself, were prepared to fully confront the Johnson administration over Vietnam. They were prescient in foreseeing problems in any attempt to Americanize the war and sensible in urging a more flexible American negotiating position, but they weakened their case by at the same time praising Johnson as a man of peace and affirming the need to continue to provide assistance to the Saigon regime. Too many of them were reticent to say what they really believed: that Vietnam was

---

[18] *New York Times*, January 7, 1965.
[19] Logevall, *Choosing War*, chapters 10–11.
[20] *Washington Post*, March 26, 1965; *Congressional Record*, vol. 111.

not worth the price of a major war, that even the "loss" of South Vietnam would not have serious implications for American security; that a face-saving negotiated settlement was the best that could be hoped for. White House officials, all too aware of the widespread concerns on Capitol Hill – and especially in the Senate – were relieved when no full-scale and far-reaching debate on the war ever occurred in the first half of 1965.

Still, an important point remains: John Sherman Cooper's opposition to an American war in Vietnam was fully formed well in advance of the key decisions of early 1965. As the build-up of American military involvement gained pace in late 1965 and into 1966 he continued – almost alone among Republicans – to urge a political solution. His conviction that the military option could never succeed strengthened when he visited South Vietnam in late 1965 and again in early 1966. In January, as the Johnson administration made clear it planned to resume bombing North Vietnam after a weeks-long pause, Cooper registered strong opposition and urged Johnson to continue to search for peace. He made the plea during an Oval Office meeting with the president on the morning of January 26. LBJ would give no assurances, and that afternoon Cooper went to the floor of the Senate and made his most impassioned speech yet. "Negotiations, not escalation, should be the dominant theme of our activity now," he declared. The process could start with a cease-fire supervised and enforced by the United Nations and lasting from three to five years, after which there would be national elections as called for in the 1954 Geneva Agreement.[21]

Cooper added that the Vietcong had to be included in any negotiations, "because it is obvious that neither negotiations nor a settlement are possible without their inclusion." Above all, he declared, reaching the heart of his message, the Americanization of the war was a mistake that must not be allowed to continue:

This is essentially a political and not a military conflict. It is a battle in Vietnam for the hearts and minds of the Vietnamese. It must be limited to Vietnam, and

---

[21] *Washington Post*, January 27, 1966; *Congressional Record*, vol. 112, pp. 1246–1247. See also Cooper's statement of January 10, 1966, in Speech series, box 905, Cooper papers. On January 30, Cooper appeared on the television show *Opinion in the Capitol* and said: "Distasteful as it is, the Vietcong are the main fighters – they are doing the bulk of the fighting. They are supplied, without question, by North Vietnam, and by both men and supplies and with weapons from China. But they are the backbone of the fighting in Vietnam and if we ever reach negotiations they will have to be included." Transcript, January 30, 1966, Speech series, box 905, Cooper papers.

be fought by the Vietnamese if we are to have any realistic hope of an acceptable settlement.... It is crucial that the war in Vietnam not be allowed to escalate further. Now is the time to make every conscientious effort to de-escalate the conflict. For in escalation there is no practical hope of achieving our aims in that unfortunate country and the very real possibility of an Asian wide war in which America would waste her resources and young men in a slaughter that could achieve nothing but these desperate conditions of chaos ideal for the spread of communism.[22]

It was a powerful appeal, but it failed to stir the administration. The bombing resumed, and the build-up of American military personnel continued. Behind the scenes, however, Cooper's quiet advocacy was gaining attention, much as the White House feared it might. In April, 1966, after Cooper declared publicly that the United States had long since fulfilled any obligation to the Saigon regime that it might have had and that it would be foolish to fight on behalf of a people who would not fight for themselves, the *New York Times* called Cooper a man "whose views command respect on both sides of the aisle." The paper spoke of the growing misgivings in the Senate and speculated that the moderate and sober Cooper could pull many fence-sitting lawmakers to his side.[23]

The *Times* hinted that a big Senate debate was in the offing, but it never materialized that spring, or in the summer or fall. When a debate did take place the following year, in May, 1967, columnist James "Scotty" Reston saw little hope that it could have much impact on policy. Lawmakers were despairing, Reston wrote, sensing no way to stop the rising violence. "It is not merely that Senators feel helpless to change the present course of the war, but the fear that the President has set in motion a train of action that he cannot wholly control." Reston singled out Cooper as one who still sought to gain a peaceful settlement before it was too late, and the senator was indeed among the most vocal dissenters in either party. He continued in the spring and summer of 1967 to hammer away on the need for a fundamental reevaluation in policy. In a not atypical speech in July he declared: "Escalation thus far has only brought about the loss of lives and a tremendous drain in resources for the United States, and even greater losses for North Vietnam and for the peasant masses caught between the warring armies. Our escalations have been matched and there are no signs that the will of North Vietnam

---

[22] Gibbons, *U.S. Government* III, p. 139.
[23] On Cooper's April speech and the *New York Times* quote, see Press Release for April 18–22, 1966, Senatorial series II, box 597, Cooper papers.

has been weakened." Plainly, the search and destroy tactics in the South and the saturation bombing of the North had not brought the enemy to his knees, Cooper argued; because they were unlikely ever to do so, the only sensible answer was to initiate a bombing halt and actively seek negotiations.[24]

The speech caught the attention of syndicated columnist Stewart Alsop, a long-time hawk on Vietnam. At a meeting with LBJ in the White House, Alsop mentioned the speech and said he was impressed by it. Perhaps the administration ought to do as the Kentuckian suggested and initiate a bombing halt, if only to persuade friends at home and abroad that the United States was sincere in its desire for a negotiated settlement. LBJ replied that Cooper was "a very fine man" but one who lacked the complete picture. No evidence existed that Hanoi sought negotiations, Johnson said. On the contrary, the communists would use a bombing pause to improve their combat position so they could kill more Americans. "Maybe some day, I'm gonna have to kill ... some more of those marines on the DMZ, just to prove we want peace, but I'm not going to do it now."[25]

It was hardly an encouraging presidential attitude for those seeking imaginative ways to bring about negotiations and a deescalation of the war. Johnson was no more interested than he had ever been. Cooper appeared ready to concede as much. In mid-December, shortly before the end of the congressional session, he gave a speech that received prominent attention in the press. According to the *New York Times*, the speech was notable for the fact that it signaled a shift in emphasis among Senate dissenters, away from the need for negotiations and toward merely heading off further escalation. Cooper spoke of "growing pessimism" about the possibility of a negotiated settlement – the escalating violence had caused both sides to dig in too deeply – and said any last shred of hope for peace talks depended on the administration resisting an extension of the war. Cooper knew such an expansion was under consideration – he had been appointed to the Senate Foreign Relations Committee at the start of 1967 and was aware that the administration contemplated a move against enemy sanctuaries in Laos and Cambodia. Don't do it, was Cooper's warning. He had been urged to make the speech by senators on both sides of

---

[24] *New York Times*, May 18, 1967; Speech Notes, July 11, 1967, Senatorial series II, box 633, Cooper papers. See also Robert Mann, *A Grand Delusion: America's Descent into Vietnam* (New York: Basic Books, 2001), p. 543.

[25] Robert W. Merry, *Taking on the World: Joseph and Stewart Alsop – Guardians of the American Century* (New York: Viking, 1996), pp. 452–453.

the aisle, and he won praise for his comments from Mansfield, Fulbright, Javits, and others.[26]

It was a frustrating period for Cooper. His dissatisfaction went deep. He questioned the whole direction of U.S. national security policy. "Of American foreign policy," aide William Miller would later say regarding the 1967–68 period, "Senator Cooper felt that it had slipped into a void. He thought our world purposes had become tarnished and demeaned – in terms of our generous national nature, a terrible loss."[27] In an address at Ball State University in Indiana in October, 1967, Cooper spoke philosophically about America's role in the world, about the limited utility of the Containment Policy in the present global situation, about the "difficult test of national maturity" that the nation faced. But though the speech ranged over a whole range of global trouble spots and impending policy decisions, Vietnam hung heavy overhead throughout:

I believe that our policy in the future must recognize that in the long run we cannot prescribe the shape of the government and societies of [the] newly independent countries, for the peoples of these countries will have their revolution – whether peaceful or violent – and determine their own future. We can take comfort from the fact that their desire to be independent from our domination and from the domination of any country ought to lead them to resist the blandishments of the Soviet Union and China. Upon this rock Communist aggression, whether open or subversive, may break.

We should recognize and understand the policies of other countries, as we would like them to understand ours. The approach of each nation to world problems is conditioned by what each regards as essential to its own national well-being. We must recognize also the limitations on our ability to influence the form of their governments, their societies and culture. We can help through effective economic assistance and the expansion of trade. We can support the instruments and institutions of international law and order. We can give an example at home. We hope that these emerging people will choose firmly democratic values. But in the long run the choice will be theirs.[28]

The momentous developments of early 1968, beginning with the Tet Offensive in January and ending with Lyndon Johnson's March 31 speech to the nation – in which he called for negotiations with North Vietnam and declared he would not run for reelection – caused Cooper and other Congressional dissenters to hope that an end to the war might be possible

---

[26] *New York Times*, December 16, 1967.
[27] Quoted in Schulman, *Cooper*, p. 96.
[28] Speech at Ball State University, October 3, 1967, Speech series, box 906, Cooper papers.

after all. Their hopes rose with the subsequent start of negotiations in Paris, but before long began to fade. Cooper became frustrated by the lack of progress in Paris, and by the vacillation and lack of urgency which characterized LBJ's approach to the problem. (From Paris, William Miller wrote Cooper in the autumn that the U.S. negotiating team there was "disappointed in the President's performance," certain that he had thrown away promising opportunities for an agreement.)[29]

In addition, the emergence of Richard Nixon as the front-runner for the GOP presidential nomination distressed Cooper. He had come out early for Nelson Rockefeller, telling the press in the fall of 1967 that Rockefeller was the best man for the job, both in terms of domestic policy and foreign affairs.[30] Nixon was a hawk on Vietnam, and Cooper doubted that the former vice president would be prepared to bring the war to a swift end. When Rockefeller faded as a contender, Cooper tried to push the candidacy of his Kentucky colleague, Senator Thruston Morton, a moderate who had recently come to share Cooper's opposition to the war. Morton, however, declined to run.

Little wonder that when Nixon took the nomination and squeaked by Hubert Humphrey for the presidency, he could not count on John Sherman Cooper as a close ally. And indeed, the two clashed early on several policy issues, beginning with the debate over the proposed Anti-Ballistic Missile System (ABM). Cooper had opposed the system from the start, virtually alone among his colleagues, but by early 1969 opposition was growing. Some lawmakers objected to it on economic and technical grounds, some shared Cooper's conviction that the program would do little but spur an intensified U.S.–Soviet nuclear rivalry. For Vietnam doves the vote over ABM funding had important symbolic meaning, because at issue were competing versions of foreign policy and also Congress's role in making it. Nixon ordered aides to work as hard as necessary to secure a victory. "Make sure that all our guys are there" to vote, he instructed one of them, Bryce Harlow. "Don't let anyone go to the bathroom until it's all over."[31]

The pressure tactics worked. On August 6, an amendment to halt all spending for ABM deployment failed by a 51–50 vote, with Vice-President

[29] Miller to Cooper, November 26, 1968, Senatorial series II, box 481, Cooper papers.
[30] See William Greider, "Cooper: Rockefeller Best for '68," *Louisville Courier-Journal*, Nov. 15, 1967.
[31] Quoted in Ashby and Gramer, *Fighting the Odds*, p. 290.

Spiro Agnew casting the tie-breaker. But although the ABM confrontation underlined the difficulty of taking on the administration over foreign policy issues, Senate doves nevertheless found it instructive. The battle had taught them lessons on organization and strategy, and in the course of 1969 discussions took place on working together in a similar fashion to contain the Vietnam War. At one point a group of them met in Majority Leader Mike Mansfield's office. Cooper was there, along with New York Republican Javits and Aiken of Vermont, as well as Democrats Frank Church of Idaho, Stuart Symington of Missouri, Phil Hart of Michigan, and a few others. According to William Miller, the lawmakers avoided specifics but reached agreement on a key proposition: if the war in Southeast Asia could not be stopped, at least one could work for the next best thing – to keep it contained. Subsequently, by carefully choosing issues, and by highlighting the Senate's constitutional obligations regarding foreign policy, the doves could hope to start squeezing the war, working at its margins in order to compress it. In this context, the ABM battle suggested some real possibilities. With hard work and a little luck, it might be possible to increase antiwar sentiment on Capitol Hill and thereby shrink the war.[32]

John Sherman Cooper became a key player in this effort, pushing from 1969 to 1972 a series of amendments aimed at curbing further U.S. military involvement in Southeast Asia. His partner for much of this campaign was Frank Church, the Idaho Democrat. At first glance they were an unlikely pair, representing different parties and different regions of the country, even different generations – Church was not yet born when Cooper graduated from Yale in 1923. Where Cooper was a wooden orator, Church excelled at public speaking. As a youth in 1941 he had been the national winner of the American Legion's annual oratorical competition. In 1960, at age thirty-five, he had electrified the delegates as the surprise keynote speaker at the Democratic National Convention. Church shared Cooper's conviction that American foreign policy had gone astray, that the nation was on the wrong side of history, that successive administrations had lost sight of the principles upon which the United States was founded. Yet like Cooper he was unprepared to advocate an immediate U.S. withdrawal; and like Cooper, he believed that, whatever Congress might do, Nixon should be left sufficient flexibility to protect American soldiers already in Indochina.[33]

---

[32] Ibid, p. 293.
[33] Schulman, *Cooper*, p. 101.

On December 15, 1969, the Cooper-Church team tasted its first success, with what one study later called "the most notable victory yet in the doves' strategy to contain the Vietnam conflict."[34] That day, the Senate approved their amendment (to a Defense Appropriations act) prohibiting the use of funds for sending American ground forces into Laos or Thailand. The vote was 78–11. Cooper and Church were openly skeptical of Nixon's Vietnamization policy and concerned about the air war in Cambodia and Laos. Here was a way to, at the very least, reassert Congressional prerogatives on foreign policy and perhaps also limit the scope of the war. Cooper had produced the original draft with Mike Mansfield and had wanted to include Cambodia on the list, but Mansfield resisted on the grounds that the neutralist Prince Norodom Sihanouk might be offended.

Mansfield would have reason to regret that decision, for in the coming months Cambodia would move to the center of the debate over the war. In March, 1970, a coup d'état against Sihanouk brought General Lon Nol to power in that country. Disorder engulfed the nation. Rival gangs clashed in the streets, and local Vietnamese were massacred by vigilantes. Though Nixon and his national security adviser Henry Kissinger insisted that the coup surprised them, they moved quickly to bolster the new regime. When Lon Nol pleaded for assistance in mid-April and the administration pledged to provide it, Senate doves registered their alarm. Spurred on by the GOP's Aiken and Majority Leader Mansfield, Cooper and Church decided to expand their amendment of December, 1969, to include a prohibition against U.S. ground troops entering Cambodia. On April, 30, Church discussed the amendment with reporters and warned Nixon not to open "a new front" and jeopardize "his declared policy of de-escalation."[35]

Cooper and Church did not know it, but Nixon had already decided four days earlier to send U.S. troops into Cambodia. "We would go for broke," Nixon wrote in his memoirs. Intent on sending a forceful message to Hanoi, he also wanted to show his domestic critics, including those in the Senate, that he would not be pushed around. The battle lines were drawn – the White House and Senate would again square off over the powers of the presidency and the Congress. Over the next three months, as America shook with renewed protest and violence, the Nixon administration pulled out all the stops to try to defeat the amendment,

[34] Ashby and Gramer, *Fighting the Odds*, p. 299.
[35] *Washington Post*, May 1, 1970.

tapping congressional allies, cabinet members, even organized labor, to work against it.[36]

Cooper and Church did not back down. When Kissinger said the nation should recognize that only the president could take the United States out of war and that this called for a national commitment – "almost an act of love" – Cooper shot back tartly that what was needed was "not an act of love but an act of Congress."[37] Still, after the Senate Foreign Relations Committee voted nine to five on May 11 to add the amendment to the Foreign Military Sales Act – which controlled cash and credit arms sales abroad – Cooper and Church showed a willingness to compromise: to mollify defenders of the administration they altered the amendment to say that it targeted only funds spent after July 1. Nixon would have ample time to get the troops out of Cambodia.

On June 30, 1970, the same day that Richard Nixon indicated that the last of the U.S. troops had left Cambodia, the Senate approved a somewhat revised Cooper-Church amendment, 58–37. After July 1, absent approval from Congress there could be neither funding for U.S. troops in Cambodia, nor military instruction, nor air combat activity in support of the Cambodian government. One of the alterations was a disclaimer of any intention to question the president's constitutional powers to protect the lives of U.S. soldiers. The White House immediately announced that the disclaimer constituted a victory for the president, and various voices in the antiwar movement criticized Cooper and Church for allowing their amendment to be watered down. Journalist I. F. Stone, for example, faulted the Cooper-Church people being too busy splitting "constitutional hairs," and criticized the amendment for, among other things, leaving untouched the air war over Cambodia, except to say that the bombing could not be in "direct" support of the Phnom Penh government.[38]

Stone's criticism was fair. There were holes in the amendment, holes that left Nixon a good deal more maneuverability than the two senators had originally vowed. But the antiwar critics of the amendment would also have to ask themselves whether tougher wording would have had any chance of passage. Stone declared his preference for an amendment sponsored by Democrat George McGovern and Republican Mark Hatfield,

---

[36] The fight over the amendment is ably and thoroughly examined in Ashby and Gramer, *Fighting the Odds*, pp. 304–340. See also Mann, *A Grand Delusion*, pp. 659–667.

[37] Quoted in Schulman, *Cooper*, pp. 101–102.

[38] Stone article of July 13, 1970, reprinted in I. F. Stone, *Polemics and Prophecies, 1967–1970* (New York: Random House, 1970), 138–141.

which would have required the administration to withdraw all U.S. forces from Vietnam by the end of 1971. The McGovern-Hatfield motion failed by a vote of 55–39 on September 1. Cooper felt confident that he and Church had achieved about as much as was politically feasible in the summer of 1970, and that they had taken an important step toward ending U.S. involvement. With Cooper-Church, he was convinced, the Senate had taken aim at the economic life blood of the war – its funding. When the House of Representatives that autumn removed the Cooper-Church Amendment from the final version of the Foreign Military Sales Act, the two lawmakers were undaunted, attaching a modified version of the amendment to a Cambodian supplemental aid package the administration wanted badly. Once again the amendment failed to address the air war – the votes were not there, Church said – but the *Washington Post* still called it "one of the most significant aspects of the 91st Congress. It is the first time in our history that Congress has attempted to limit the deployment of American troops in the course of an ongoing war." William Bundy, in his history of Nixon's foreign policy, would write of Cooper-Church that the administration "did not dare challenge its dictates" regarding policy in Cambodia. Many who had voted against the amendment privately were sympathetic to it, the White House knew. Testing their loyalty to the president would not be wise.[39]

The battle over the amendment had taken its toll on Cooper. He was exhausted, so much so that had to be checked into a hospital briefly to regain his strength. In 1971 Church approached Cooper about seeking a true end-the-war amendment, shaped around Nixon's own oft-declared intentions to extricate the United States from Southeast Asia. Cooper initially demurred, but when Church kept pressing, and when Mansfield and Aiken again agreed to cosponsor, he signed on. Whereas the first Cooper-Church proposals had been aimed at limiting the war, this 1971 version would be oriented toward getting the United States out of it. The amendment went nowhere. Cooper's aide William Miller determined that the votes were not there to pass it, and Cooper himself had doubts

---

[39] *Washington Post,* January 1, 1971, as cited in Ashby and Gramer , *Fighting the Odds,* p. 335; William P. Bundy, *A Tangled Web: The Making of Foreign Policy in the Nixon Presidency* (New York: Hill and Wang, 1998), p. 222. On the constraints on U.S. policy imposed by Cooper-Church, see also Richard C. Thornton, *The Nixon-Kissinger Years: Reshaping America's Foreign Policy* (New York: Paragon House, 1989), p. 95; and John Lehman, *The Executive, Congress, and Foreign Policy: Studies of the Nixon Administration* (New York: Praeger, 1974), pp. 72–73.

about whether Congress could block Nixon's apparent determination to maintain a long-term residual force in Southeast Asia. By the end of the year, the end-the-war amendment was dead.

Cooper believed his days as an antiwar agitator were over. He decided that he would not seek reelection in 1972. Let someone else have a turn, he told acquaintances. But when the air war exploded with new fury in late March, 1972, following a massive North Vietnamese invasion of the South, and when savage fighting continued in weeks thereafter, Cooper felt compelled to reenter the arena. The air attacks outraged him. On July 24, before a nearly empty Senate chamber and with no cosponsor, Cooper proposed a new, stringent amendment to cut off all funding of U.S. forces in Indochina in four months, without conditions. "Good God!" a startled Nixon said to Kissinger after learning of Cooper's intentions. "What does *this* do?"[40] The administration, not about to wait for an answer, rallied its troops for a showdown.

The debate that day was long and bitter. When the Cooper proposal seemed dead, Massachusetts Republican Edward Brooke moved to save it by adding a proviso that all American prisoners of war be returned before the pull-out. Still, feelings ran high. Rhode Island Democrat John O. Pastore called the Cooper proposal "a shadow of shame on the conscience of America" and asked what it would accomplish. Cooper responded: "I say to my dear friend from Rhode Island, you ask what we gain. We gain the end of fighting, the saving of American lives, the foreclosure of more prisoners taken, the end of slaughter of human life.... I want someone to tell me how we are going to get our prisoners back if we keep bombing, shelling, and strafing Vietnam."[41]

Brooke's revised amendment passed easily, 62–33, and Senate doves were jubilant. It marked the first time the upper chamber had passed a mandatory end-the-war amendment. The *New York Times* called it "the strongest, most binding amendment yet passed by the Senate to require the withdrawal of U.S. forces from Vietnam." Remarkably, however, the issue was not settled. The administration, desperate to defeat the proposal, decided to sacrifice its entire military assistance bill rather than have it pass with the end-the-war amendment included. The Senate Democratic leadership obliged, ignoring Frank Church's pleas that the administration would be able later to revive the bill minus the end-the-war amendment.

---

[40] Stephen E. Ambrose, *Nixon: The Triumph of a Politician* (New York: Simon and Schuster, 1989), p. 590.

[41] Schulman, *Cooper*, p. 2.

As the Senate voted 48–42 to quash the military assistance bill, Church lamented that the White House had "snatch[ed] victory from the jaws of defeat." *New York Times* reporter John Finney, meanwhile, sensed that, with the reversal, "much of the energy and organization had gone out of the antiwar effort in the Senate."[42]

Cooper too was disappointed, but he also felt a sense of relief, as though an enormous burden had been removed. "I feel purged inside," he declared. "I've felt strongly about this for a long time. Now it's in the hands of the President. He's the only person who can do anything about ending the war now."[43]

That end was not long in coming – within six months, the Paris Peace Accords would be signed. Cooper and the Senate doves had what they had so long sought, an end to the American intervention in Vietnam. Eight years of bloody warfare were over. No more end-the-war amendments would be needed. Perhaps it was fitting, in this way, that the man perhaps most closely identified with those amendments had now departed the scene. Colleagues and journalists, reflecting on his achievements in office, would remark that no one had done more than John Sherman Cooper during the divisive era of the Vietnam War to reestablish, as one put it, the "delicate balance" between the Senate and the White House is the making of war and peace.

That judgment seems sound. Cooper never sought the limelight, and thus seldom got it; perhaps for that reason he has received little notice in the vast literature on the antiwar opposition. But he was an important figure in that opposition, arguably as important as anyone on Capitol Hill. His determination to strike that delicate balance was in fact the secret to his behind-the-scenes influence, the reason why he earned such respect from colleagues from both parties. Critics in the antiwar movement would fault Cooper for being too quick to compromise, too reticent about constraining the president's powers to wage the war. Perhaps they were right, but John Sherman Cooper fought against the war the best way he knew how. His aversion to America's intervention in Vietnam was deep and heartfelt, and from his beloved Kentucky in early 1973 he could take satisfaction in knowing he had helped to bring it to an end.

---

[42] *New York Times*, July 25, 1972; Ashby and Gramer, *Fighting the Odds*, p. 389.
[43] Schulman, *Cooper*, p. 3.

Friendly Fire

Lyndon Johnson and the Challenge to Containment

H. W. Brands

Great legislators do not make great presidents. In fact, they rarely make presidents of *any* kind. The greatest senators and representatives in American history – Henry Clay, John C. Calhoun, Daniel Webster, Thomas B. Reed, Joseph Cannon, and Sam Rayburn – never reached the White House. Those lawmakers who did get there – starting with James Madison and continuing through George Bush – failed to distinguish themselves at one end or the other of Pennsylvania Avenue, often both.

There is a reason for this. The legislative mentality is not the executive mentality. If anything, the former militates against the latter. The successful legislator is an accommodator, a compromiser, a dealmaker, a person who acknowledges that in a democracy differing viewpoints can be equally valid, by the mere fact that they are held by different citizens, and for that reason must be taken into account. The successful executive, on the other hand, is a leader, a decisionmaker, a buck-stopper, a person who embodies not the least common denominator of the polity but the greatest common multiple. Executives get paid to make hard choices, legislators to prevent hard choices from having to be made.

Lyndon Johnson could have been a great legislator. He had Sam Rayburn for a tutor; more important, he had the right instincts. He delighted in discovering what different people needed from government on a particular issue, and in employing what he discovered to fashion a bill a majority could get behind. The crafting of coalitions was in his blood; on his lips, his favorite Bible passage, from Isaiah, "Come, let us reason together." Had he remained in the Senate, where he rocketed to primacy as Democratic leader in only his first term, he might well have achieved the stature of Clay, Calhoun, or Webster.

But he could not have been a great president. Those legislative instincts did not simply fail to serve him in the Oval Office, they betrayed him. To be sure, in guiding the Great Society through Congress, he proved himself a brilliant political strategist, getting more out of the legislature in less time than even his hero and yardstick, Franklin Roosevelt. But no president ever became great for passing a raft of bills. Roosevelt himself almost certainly would have retired after two terms, and likely slipped into historical semi-obscurity, had World War II not transformed him from legislator-in-chief to commander-in-chief. (It was for such as this, incidentally, that Roosevelt's fifth cousin and uncle-in-law Theodore never forgave Woodrow Wilson: for Wilson's cheating TR out of a chance to be a great wartime president.)

Johnson's war was Vietnam, and because he approached it like a legislator he fumbled it terribly. He split the difference between those individuals and groups that demanded rapid withdrawal, and those that insisted on unleashing the military to get the job done. The *via media*, that golden road to legislative success, ran straight into the quagmire that ultimately consumed Johnson's presidency.

Ironically – or maybe not – some of Johnson's former colleagues in Congress warned him where the middle road was taking him and the country. Mike Mansfield, J. William Fulbright and others of less seniority and stature contended that America's burdens had grown too great for even the single most powerful nation in the world. Wisdom, they said, consisted in judiciously accommodating change rather than reflexively resisting it. Unfortunately for Johnson, and for America, other voices advocated staying the course. Not until too late did the president discover that trying to satisfy both sides was impossible and ultimately disastrous.

The Commitments He Inherited

Johnson became president at a time when two major American commitments were falling due. Perhaps he could have dealt with one on its own; dealing with both was more than he could handle.

The first was America's historical commitment to the principal of human equality. Whether this dated to the Declaration of Independence, the Emancipation Proclamation or something subsequent, by the 1960s the United States was far in arrears on its debt to racial and other forms of equality. To Johnson's credit he made settling the debt the centerpiece of his administration. The Civil Rights Act of 1964 killed Jim Crow; the Voting Rights Act of 1965 buried him; much of the Great Society aimed at compensating his victims, or at least letting them compensate themselves. Johnson's accomplishment in this regard was immense; no president save Lincoln did as much. The political toll was hardly less than the accomplishment: as Johnson foretold, the embrace of civil rights cost the Democratic party the South and gave the Republicans – the party of the first emancipation – a new lease on life.

The second American commitment was shorter-lived; perhaps for this reason Johnson was justified in billing it second. In 1947 Harry Truman pledged the United States to the defense of free peoples resisting communist aggression; in 1949 Truman formalized the pledge as it pertained to Western Europe; in 1950 he extrapolated it to East Asia. Dwight Eisenhower continued the committing, expanding existing alliances and establishing new ones until the United States was bound to the survival of noncommunist governments on every inhabited continent and in every time zone.

But the world in which these American security commitments were initially given was not the same world in which American leaders were called on to honor them. The United States in the mid-1960s was stronger militarily and economically than it had ever been; but so was much of the rest of the world, and relative to its adversaries and allies the United States had slipped since the end of the Second World War. The Soviet Union possessed a formidable nuclear arsenal that, if not the equal of America's, was frightening enough to put severe limits on what American leaders could contemplate. China had nuclear weapons too, and by Beijing's professions was not afraid to use them. Japan, a basket case at war's end and an American ward until the early 1950s, was well on its way to capturing much of the East Asia coprosperity sphere it had been denied in 1941. On the other side of the world, West Germany was stronger economically than Hitler's reich had been at the height of the Nazi nightmare. Although indisposed to make military might out of that money-muscle, Bonn increasingly influenced the terms on which *American* military power was deployed and paid for in Europe. The most obvious source of Bonn's influence was a large and growing balance-of-payments surplus with America. France was less wealthy but more prickly than Germany; Charles de Gaulle's sense of Gallic grandeur, his successful pursuit of nuclear weapons, and his penchant for personal diplomacy made Paris almost an independent broker in international affairs. Britain had lost an empire and not yet found a niche; although it still valued its special relationship with Washington, London by the year had less of what had made that relationship special for America.

In nearly every part of the world, Lyndon Johnson was called on to honor commitments made by his predecessors. American power might have covered all those commitments during the heyday of American hegemony in the late 1940s and 1950s – or it might not have: Johnson's predecessors luckily left office before being required to redeem most of their promises. American power could *not* cover them all during the 1960s; Johnson unluckily was holding the bag when the burden it contained grew too heavy for America to bear.

The Ghost of TR

The trouble started in Latin America. In fact it started before Johnson succeeded Kennedy, and indeed before Kennedy succeeded Eisenhower. When Fidel Castro seized power in Cuba in 1959 he gave a severe shake to the status quo of the region over which U.S. hegemony had lasted longest. Eisenhower declared economic war on Castro and prepared paramilitary operations. Kennedy kept the embargo and put the paramilitary in motion; when the latter failed at the Bay of Pigs he resorted to clandestine efforts of a more personal nature. But the assassination attempts failed also, and Castro survived to become the catalyst of the Cuban missile crisis of October 1962. The outcome of the crisis spared the world a nuclear war without solving America's Castro problem. In certain respects it made that problem worse, for by swearing off the invasion of Cuba the U.S. government essentially guaranteed Castro's continued grip on power.

Consequently the most Johnson could hope for was containment: a Caribbean counterpart to the policy practiced against the Soviet Union since Stalin's day. Not only did he hope for it, he practiced it energetically. In January, 1964, riots broke out in Panama. The trigger for the riots was the raising of an American flag in front of a high school in the Canal Zone, an act that contravened an agreement between the United States and Panama on the always touchy subject of whose flag flew where. The powder for the riots was the semi-colonial relationship that had existed between the United States and Panama since 1903, when Theodore Roosevelt had strong-armed Panama from Colombia and negotiated – almost dictated – terms of the treaties that allowed the United States to construct and operate the Panama Canal. Some Panamanians had resented the treaties at the time, but as the price for Panama's independence the treaties did not provoke inordinate contemporary protest. During the next half-century, however, the resentment grew; Panama's president during the

1964 riots, Roberto Chiari, exploited this resentment to demand revision of the treaty structure.

Johnson was reluctant to oblige. The Panama Canal was nine-tenths of what made the Caribbean critical to the United States. (It wasn't lost on Latin Americans, though it was on many U.S. Americans, that while U.S. troops during the decades after 1903 tromped all over the region north of the Canal – that is, athwart or adjacent to the shipping lanes between Panama and the United States – Washington paid only cursory heed to what went on beyond the Canal.) The Panama treaties gave the United States control of the Canal; anything that threatened that control threatened a vital U.S. interest.

The second reason for Johnson's reluctance was that Castro seemed to be behind the Panamanian unrest. Wallace Stuart of the U.S. embassy in Panama City described a leader of the rioters as a "known Communist";[1] Thomas Mann, the assistant secretary of state for Latin America, warned of "Castro agents" hard at work in Panama;[2] military intelligence at the U.S. Southern Command in the Canal Zone ascribed much of the violence to a "pro-Castro, violently anti–U.S. revolutionary group" that was trying to instigate a "Castro-type revolution in Panama.[3]

Administration officials were not alone in seeing the hand of Fidel behind the Panamanian unrest. In the Senate – which of course would have to ratify any revision of the Panama treaties – Castro came under heavy fire. New York Republican Kenneth Keating (whose concern for Cuba had helped alert the Kennedy administration to the Russian missiles only a little over a year earlier), blamed "Castro-Communist agents" for the rioting. "How long will we continue to face the Cuba problem inadequately and ineffectively?" demanded Keating. "How long will we continue to wait until a major crisis occurs?"[4] Keating's New York Republican colleague, Jacob Javits, took much the same line, placing the Panama problem at the feet of "Castroites and other Communist leaders."[5] Richard Russell, Democratic chairman of the Armed Services Committee, privately told Johnson, "If there's any one thing that is essential to the economic life

---

[1] Stuart to Department of State, January 10, 1964, box 1, NSC History File, Lyndon Baines Johnson Library, Austin. This episode and some of the others described in this essay are examined in H. W. Brands, *The Wages of Globalism: Lyndon Johnson and the Limits of American Power* (Oxford Univ. Press: New York, 1995).

[2] Mann to Dean Rusk, January 11, 1964, box 1, NSC History file, Johnson Library.

[3] Ibid., USCICNSO to Joint Chiefs of Staff, January 16, 1964.

[4] *Congressional Record*, January 14, 1964, 379–80.

[5] *Congressional Record*, January 31, 1964, 1472.

as well as the defense of every nation in the hemisphere, it is the Panama Canal. We can't risk having it sabotaged or taken over by any Communist group. There's no question in my mind but that that is Castro's chief aim there."[6]

Certain other congressional leaders saw something more complicated occurring in Panama. Democrat Mike Mansfield of Montana, who held Johnson's old post as Senate majority leader, urged the president to re-member what counted in Panama. "We have only one fundamental in-terest to protect the present situation," Mansfield said. "We have got to insure untroubled and adequate water-passage through Central America." Castro had not created the pressure for change in Panama, nor elsewhere in Latin America, although he certainly exploited such pressure. "The pressure comes primarily from the inside, from the decay and antiquation of the social structures of various Latin American countries. Even if we desired to do so, we could not, as a practical matter, stop the pressure for change. But we may have something constructive to contribute to the form and pace of the change if we play our cards carefully and wisely." Mansfield went on to caution Johnson against "boxing ourselves in at home through the fanning of our own emotions by crediting Castro and Communism too heavily for a difficulty which existed long before either had any significance in this Hemisphere and which will undoubtedly con-tinue to plague us after both cease to have much meaning."[7]

In this case, Johnson chose to follow the moderate advice of Mansfield. He called on the Organization of American States to help defuse the cri-sis, and while rejecting Chiari's demand to "negotiate" a new treaty, he agreed to "discuss" revision. He sent a special envoy south to begin the discussions. Chiari accepted the emissary, and the crisis passed.

The Big Stick Redux

Part of Johnson's equanimity regarding Panama resulted from the pres-ence of American military forces on the ground in the heart of that country. Students might riot and Panama's president fulminate, but if things got ugly the Southern Command could simply get tough.

---

[6] Russell telephone conversation with Johnson, January 10, 1964, transcribed in *Taking Charge: The Johnson White House Tapes, 1963–1964*, edited by Michael R. Beschloss (Simon and Schuster: New York, 1997), p. 156.

[7] Mansfield to Johnson, January 31, 1964, box 1, Memos to the president file, Johnson Library.

The outcome of trouble in the Dominican Republic was less clearly foreseen. During the first months of 1965 the confusion that had afflicted that country since the assassination of Rafael Trujillo in 1961 veered in the direction of revolution. Or so it seemed to officials of the Johnson administration, still on the lookout for Castroist subversion. W. Tapley Bennett, the U.S. ambassador in Santo Domingo, observed poetically, "Little foxes, some of them Red, are chewing the grapes."[8] The Central Intelligence Agency was less literary and more direct: "The revolutionary movement is being controlled by the Communists."[9] Subsequently Director William Raborn asserted that the CIA had made "positive identification of three ring-leaders of the rebels as Castro-trained agents."[10]

The senators and representatives Johnson invited to the White House for a briefing were not inclined to challenge this view. Democratic House speaker John McCormack wondered aloud, "Can we afford another Castro situation?" Republican Everett Dirksen of Illinois said his friends in Miami were telling him Castro was making "a concerted effort to take over the Dominican Republic." The president, Dirksen added, must "take into account the factor of Castro."

Johnson did take Castro into account, and when the fighting reached a stage where the rebels seemed to have a chance to seize the city, the president ordered in the U.S. marines. He initially couched the intervention in terms of a temporary mission "to protect American lives,"[11] but within forty-eight hours the objective had been upgraded to safeguarding Dominican sovereignty. Although Johnson did not mention Castro by name, his meaning was clear when he declared, "There are signs that people trained outside the Dominican Republic are seeking to gain control."[12] Within another two days he became clearer still. Summarizing events in Santo Domingo, Johnson explained that at a crucial moment "the revolutionary movement took a tragic turn. Communist leaders, many of them trained in Cuba, seeing a chance to increase disorder, to gain a foothold, joined the revolution. They took increasing control. And what began as a popular democratic revolution, committed

---

[8] Quoted in Rowland Evans and Robert Novak, *Lyndon B. Johnson: The Exercise of Power* (New American Library: New York, 1966), p. 513.

[9] CIA cable, April 26, 1965, box 4, NSC history file, Johnson Library.

[10] Minutes of meeting with congressional leadership, April 28, 1965, box 1, meeting notes file, Johnson Library.

[11] Johnson address, April 28, 1965, *Public Papers of the Presidents*.

[12] Johnson address, April 30, 1965, *Public Papers*.

to democracy and social justice, very shortly moved and was taken over and really seized and placed into the hands of a band of Communist conspirators."[13]

Unfortunately for Johnson, the evidence supporting such statements was rather flimsy, and as reporters began picking it apart skeptics wondered whether the president had not overreacted. Not the most strident, but almost certainly the most influential, of the critics was J. William Fulbright, Democratic chairman of the Senate Foreign Relations Committee. Johnson and Fulbright had never gotten along, certainly not since Johnson had thrust himself forward for Democratic Senate leader after the 1952 election, at a time when Fulbright thought the party required someone more liberal. George Ball, who knew both men quite well, described the Texan and the Arkansan as simply "incompatible." Ball went on to say, only half-jokingly, that "one of Bill Fulbright's great disabilities was that he read books. Nobody in the Senate should read books."[14] Johnson did not read books – nor did he appoint Fulbright to the position Fulbright evidently coveted. Johnson explained: "Fulbright has never found any president who didn't appoint him secretary of state to be satisfactory."[15]

Whatever the personal element, the tension between Johnson and Fulbright did not become a public issue until the Dominican intervention of 1965. At first Fulbright backed the president. "I support you fully," he told Johnson at a White House meeting a few days after the marines went in.[16] But as the thinness of the administration's rationale grew apparent, Fulbright began to think he had been played for a fool. In September, 1965, he gave a speech in which he essentially accused the president and his advisers of lying – of making statements characterized "by a lack of candor and by misinformation." Moreover, the basis for American intervention – the argument that the revolution in the Dominican Republic was Castro-inspired – missed the point of what was happening in that country. "In their apprehension lest the Dominican Republic become another Cuba, some of our officials seem to have forgotten that virtually all reform movements attract some Communist support." By acting as though all Latin American reformers were Communists, the Johnson administration was going far to guarantee that they *would be* communists. "We

---

[13] Johnson address, May 2, 1965, *Department of State Bulletin*, May 17, 1965.

[14] George Ball oral history interview, July 9, 1971, Johnson Library.

[15] Notes of meeting with Bob Thompson, August 21, 1967, box 2, meeting notes file, Johnson Library.

[16] Notes of meeting, May 2, 1965, box 13, office files of the president, Johnson Library.

have lent credence to the idea that the United States is the enemy of social revolution in Latin America and that the only choice Latin Americans have is between communism and reaction." Such a policy could only fail. "There is no doubt of the choice that honest and patriotic Latin Americans will make: they will choose communism, not because they want it but because U.S. policy will have foreclosed all other avenues of social revolution and, indeed, all other possibilities except the perpetuation of rule by military juntas and economic oligarchies."[17]

Where the Cold War Began

Johnson could congratulate himself on the outcome of the Dominican intervention, which culminated in 1966 elections that installed the non-threatening Joaquin Balaguer as president. Yet the loss of the trust of Fulbright – who as Democratic chairman of the Foreign Relations Committee should have been the Democratic president's strongest foreign-policy supporter on Capitol Hill – portended additional defections on other issues.

During the months the marines remained in Santo Domingo a particularly pressing issue involved the commitment of longest standing in U.S. Cold War policy. With reason, Americans in the mid-1960s felt they had done much for Western Europe. American soldiers had twice rescued Europe from its murderous folly; American dollars had rebuilt Europe during the years of the Marshall Plan; American promises and nuclear weapons had safeguarded Europe since the creation of NATO. It would have been unusual for Americans during Johnson's presidency not to feel as though Europe owed something to the United States – if not gratitude, then at least cooperation.

But the Europeans appeared to be going out of their way to be difficult. The French were the worst. President Charles de Gaulle had an agenda seemingly designed to provoke the United States. De Gaulle insisted on an independent nuclear arsenal for France at a time when American leaders were doing their best to prevent proliferation of the big bombs. He extended diplomatic recognition to Communist China when Washington was trying to isolate the communist regime there. He reduced French participation in NATO and rebuffed British membership in the Common Market when the United States hoped for greater unity among its European allies.

---

[17] *Congressional Record*, Sept. 15, 1965, pp. 23855–61.

According to Charles Bohlen, the U.S. ambassador in Paris, the difficulties with France were not simply side effects of divergent views regarding the world. Washington's relations with France were difficult because de Gaulle wanted them that way. "He undoubtedly feels that too close a relationship between a relatively small country (which he bitterly recognizes to be the case in regard to France) and the U.S. could lead only to an actual derogation of the weaker country's sovereignty" Bohlen observed.[18] C. Douglas Dillon, the treasury secretary and a longtime de Gaulle watcher, interpreted the general's actions slightly differently but came to a similar conclusion. De Gaulle's policies, Dillon said, were "largely based on his messianic belief in the glory and importance of France and thus are not subject to reasoned argument."[19]

Johnson took the view that de Gaulle would do what he would do, regardless of what the United States did. "De Gaulle's going to recognize China," he told Richard Russell, chairman of the Senate Armed Services Committee, in January, 1964. "And the question comes whether *I* ought to protest it rather strongly or whether I ought to let the government protest it. Our disposition is just to let the government protest it. He'll pay no attention." Russell concurred: "I wouldn't go too strong on it, Mr. President. He ain't going to pay much attention to it; it would look bad when he goes ahead. We've really got no control over their foreign policy." Johnson agreed, wearily: "That's right. None whatever."[20]

Johnson marked out a nonconfrontational line. "I keep mum," he told a group of French reporters. "If you hear something nasty about de Gaulle, it has not come from me or anybody in the White House. I told everybody in the government to be polite to President de Gaulle. Just tip your hat and say, 'Thank you, General.' "[21]

Johnson held to this line even in response to de Gaulle's most provocative action. In March, 1966, the French president informed Johnson and other NATO leaders that France was withdrawing from the alliance's unified military command, and that NATO forces would be required to leave France. Against the advice of his closest associates, including Secretary of State Dean Rusk, Johnson refused to be provoked. Taking de Gaulle's action "more in sorrow than in anger," Johnson

---

[18] Bohlen memo, December 13, 1963, box 169, country file, Johnson Library.
[19] Dillon memo, undated (December 1965–January 1966), box 6, memos to the president file, Johnson Library.
[20] Johnson telephone conversation with Russell, January 15, 1964, *Taking Charge*, p. 162.
[21] Quoted in Edward Weintal and Charles Bartlett, *Facing the Brink* (Scribner: New York, 1967), p. 105.

declared, "We look forward to the day when unity of action in the Western family is fully reestablished and our common interests and aspirations are again expressed through institutions which command universal support among us."[22] More colloquially, he told Defense Secretary Robert McNamara, who would have to direct America's part of the NATO pull-out from France: "When a man asks you to leave his house, you don't argue. You get your hat and go."[23]

Johnson's reaction reflected more than his sense of Southern decorum; it also reflected his fear that by getting into a public argument – "pissing match," was his precise term[24] – he would simply inflame anti-European feelings in the United States. Johnson was old enough to remember the isolationism of the 1930s, when Americans had determined to let Europe go to ruin in its own way, and then been forced to retrieve the ruination. The 1960s were not the 1930s, as Johnson fully understood; but shrewd politician that he was, he also understood that politics was local, and Europe was far away. When he assumed the presidency in 1963, NATO was not yet fifteen years old; the commitment of U.S. troops to Europe was younger still. To take for granted continued American support for a strong presence in Europe might prove a serious error.

Already there were rumblings for retrenchment. A few months after de Gaulle served NATO's eviction notice, the entire membership of the Senate Democratic Policy Committee cosponsored a resolution advising the president that a "substantial reduction" could be made to U.S. troop deployments in Europe without jeopardizing the security of the Atlantic alliance. The resolution remarked two basic developments in international affairs that made such a reduction prudent: first, the fact that the means of the other members of the alliance to defend themselves had "significantly improved since the original United States deployment"; and, second, that current levels of troop deployment exacerbated "the fiscal and monetary problems of the United States."[25]

Mike Mansfield spoke for the sponsors. "Western Europe has long since rehabilitated itself after the devastation of World War II," the majority leader said. "It is now a thriving and dynamic region of greatly expanded economic and political, and potential military, capacity." Yet

---

[22] Johnson speech, April 4, 1966, *Public Papers*; Johnson speech transcript, June 16, 1966, box 7, memos to the president file, Johnson Library.

[23] Lyndon Baines Johnson, *The Vantage Point: Perspectives of the Presidency* (Holt, Rinehart, Winston: New York, 1971), 305.

[24] George Ball oral history interview, July 9, 1971, Johnson Library.

[25] *Congressional Record*, August 31, 1966, p. 21442.

American policy for Europe appeared premised on the notion, currently at least a decade out of date, that Europe was still "weakened, exhausted, and incapable of an equitable defense effort of its own." Had America no other responsibilities, this mistake might not be fatal. But the present level of forces in Europe was "very costly both in tax dollars and in dollar exchange to the people of the United States," a circumstance "especially undesirable at a time of balance-of-payments difficulties and enormous and growing military costs." Mansfield did not advocate anything approaching a complete withdrawal from Europe; yet in the spirit of the 1951 Senate resolution advising President Truman on the appropriate level of troop strength in Europe, fifteen years later he offered similar advice. In 1951 the national interest had dictated sending troops to Europe; in 1966 it dictated bringing some of the troops home.[26]

Other senators joined Mansfield. Stephen Young of Ohio declared, "Ten years ago, this nation had almost $22 billion in gold reserves. Today we have $13 billion." France – "the chief beneficiary of the outflow of gold from our country" – had just tossed out the 75,000 U.S. troops stationed there. The administration proposed moving them elsewhere in Europe. "We ought to bring them all home." Young reached way back to World War I to point out the unpaid debts from that war; since World War II France had received $9 billion in U.S. aid, Italy $6 billion, West Germany $5 billion. What did the United States have to show for its generosity – now that it could use some help in such places as Vietnam? "These nations, which have become rich and prosperous, show anything but enthusiasm about coming to our aid and assisting us in Vietnam. Not one has sent even one soldier to South Vietnam."[27]

Wayne Morse saw another reason for cutting back in Europe. The danger of World War III hung over every squabble between the United States and the Soviet Union. "And that danger is increased as long as we continue to maintain heavy contingents of American military forces abroad." The troops in Europe were said to be preserving and promoting peace. The Oregon Democrat was not convinced. "We cannot win peace with bullets."

Johnson wished he could ignore critics like Morse. "Morse is just undependable and erratic as he can be," the president told John McCormack during a moment of exasperation.[28] At another time he explained to

---

[26] Ibid.

[27] Ibid., p. 21448.

[28] Johnson telephone conversation with McCormack, August 7, 1964, *Taking Charge*, p. 508.

Hubert Humphrey that he had left the Senate for the vice-presidency for reasons of health: "I didn't want to fall on my face and be dead there on the floor of the Senate some morning rasslin' with Wayne Morse."[29] Yet the president recognized that Morse represented a segment of American public opinion no president could lightly disregard.

"I don't agree with Morse and all he says," Johnson told Richard Russell, in a conversation that focused on Asia but applied more generally.

"No, neither do I," Russell replied. "But he's voicing the sentiment of a hell of a lot of people."

"I'm afraid that's right," Johnson acknowledged.[30]

Johnson understood that once the Senate opened the issue of U.S. troops in Europe, the entire fabric of assumptions on which the American alliance system was based might start to unravel. "Between now and 1969 we face dark and dangerous ground," he told John McCloy, referring to the date when the NATO treaty would face renewal. "Romney is running all over the country with his shirttails out. Nixon is taking his overseas trips. Bobby Kennedy is all over the place. I've got the liberals beating me on one side, the Southerners on the other. I have to try to maintain a position where we can hold a position that the real majority wants. But it's hard."[31]

Hard, but in this case not impossible. Even as support swelled behind the Mansfield amendment (with the number of sponsors topping two score), Johnson managed to finesse the Europe problem. The president sent McCloy, the former high commissioner to Germany and bipartisan all-purpose fixer, to negotiate a deal with Britain and Germany that eventually alleviated the balance-of-payments problem and placed roughly one division and three aircraft wings on rotation between bases in the United States and Germany. American boys came home, but, as the State Department press release delineating the arrangement averred, the troops remained "fully committed to NATO."[32]

Where the Dike Gave Way

Finesse sufficed in Europe but failed utterly in Vietnam. Johnson inherited from John Kennedy a commitment in Indochina that was on its way to becoming a war. The commitment was one of the messiest in the American history of the Cold War, starting with Harry Truman's decision to appease

[29] Ibid., Johnson telephone conversation with Humphrey, August 14, 1964, p. 515.
[30] Ibid., Johnson telephone conversation with Russell, May 27, 1964, p. 365.
[31] Memo for the record, March 2, 1967, box 18, Francis Bator papers, Johnson Library.
[32] Department of State release, May 2, 1967, box 51, NSC history file, Johnson Library.

the NATO-necessary French (or so they seemed at the time) by allowing Paris to divert U.S. aid to France's quixotic quest to reestablish its Indochinese empire. The commitment deepened when the outbreak of the Korean War appeared to portend a major communist thrust in Asia. Neither of Truman's decisions had much to do with Vietnam per se; each reflected a vague feeling that the United States must do something to stop the spread of communism wherever that spread happened to occur.

At Geneva in 1954, the United States took still more responsibility for Vietnam by godfathering the division of the country into a communist northern zone and a noncommunist south. Yet the Eisenhower administration declined to make clear its intentions for Vietnam; it refused to endorse the Geneva accords even as it warned other powers not to tamper with them. Shortly thereafter it sponsored the creation of the Southeast Asian Treaty Organization, which was patently intended to defend South Vietnam against communist aggression but which lacked (out of respect for the Geneva accords) the key element in that defense, South Vietnam itself.

For much of Kennedy's presidency Laos appeared more threatened than Vietnam, and when Kennedy brokered a neutralist solution to the civil war in Laos, Southeast Asia watchers hoped for at least a few nights of undisturbed slumber.

Only in the summer of 1963 did developments in Vietnam reach a critical pass, and then in a manner that characteristically increased the American stake in Vietnam without commensurately increasing American leverage. The Kennedy administration's support for the coup that overthrew and murdered Ngo Dinh Diem left Washington morally and politically responsible for Diem's successors; but the fact that the support was covert, combined with the fact that what the United States was nominally supporting in Vietnam was self-determination, meant that Washington could not dictate terms to the generals now in charge.

No one had asked Lyndon Johnson, then vice president, what he thought of getting rid of Diem; he later decided it was one of the worst things Washington ever did. "We could have kept Diem," he told his Tuesday lunch group barely a year after the coup. "Should we get another one?"[33]

Yet if Johnson inherited a misbegotten commitment to South Vietnam, he wasn't unaware of its clouded pedigree. At each uncertain step on the path to the swamp, critics warned against going further. In 1949 a State

[33] Notes of meeting, December 1, 1964, box 1, McGeorge Bundy papers, Johnson Library.

Department official questioned U.S. support for France's Bao Dai solution by asserting that in view of the former emperor's "very dubious chances of succeeding," to support him would be to "follow blindly down a dead-end alley, expending our limited resources – in money and most particularly in prestige – in a fight which would be hopeless."[34] During the 1950s noted political scientist Hans Morgenthau – among many others – lambasted the Eisenhower administration for conflating nationalism with communism in Indochina and throughout Asia, and for attempting military solutions to problems best addressed politically. "The ideological cannonade, as it were, soars far above the advancing enemy, and military pacts, far from stopping him, actually help him to advance."[35] John Kennedy himself expressed reservations about the very commitment he was reinforcing in Vietnam. "The troops will march in; the bands will play; the crowds will cheer," he told Arthur Schlesinger. "And in four days everyone will have forgotten. It's like taking a drink. The effect wears off, and you have to take another."[36]

The criticism continued after the weight of Vietnam settled upon Johnson's shoulders. Although much of such criticism he could disregard as emanating from people with no special knowledge of the region and no particular influence in the making of U.S. foreign policy, the counsel of Mike Mansfield fell into quite the opposite category. A longtime student of Asian affairs, Mansfield knew as much about Indochina as most of the Johnson administration's experts; as Senate majority leader he would have commanded the attention of any president, let alone one of his own party and a predecessor in that legislative post.

Johnson had been president barely two weeks when Mansfield sent him a letter urging a change of course in Vietnam. Lately de Gaulle had been advocating a neutralization scheme for Vietnam along the lines of that which had been devised for Laos the previous year; Mansfield thought this a good plan. The Diem government had been unable to halt the insurgency of the Vietcong; what made Johnson think Diem's successors would have any better luck? Preserving the noncommunist character of South Vietnam might be a worthy goal, but the question became: at what cost? And the cost was almost certain to be great. "What national interests

[34] Quoted in Gary R. Hess, *Vietnam and the United States: Origins and Legacy of War* (Boston, 1990), p. 39.

[35] Quoted in H. W. Brands, *What America Owes the World: The Struggle for the Soul of Foreign Policy* (Cambridge Univ. Press: New York, 1998), p. 179.

[36] Quoted in George C. Herring, *America's Longest War: The United States and Vietnam, 1950–1975*, 2nd. ed. (Knopf: New York, 1986), p. 83.

in Asia would steel the American people for the massive costs of an ever-deepening involvement of that kind?" the majority leader asked.[37]

Mansfield was back with similar advice the following month, and the month after that. Some of Johnson's top advisers were recommending a major increase in American activity in Vietnam. Mansfield thought such a route precisely wrong. "A deeper military plunge is not a real alternative. Apart from the absence of sufficient national interest to justify it to our own people, there is no reason to assume it will settle the question. More likely than not it will simply enlarge the morass in which we are already on the verge of indefinite entrapment." To the surprise of neither Mansfield nor other skeptical observers of Vietnam politics, the post-Diem regime had proved unstable; a new group of officers, led by Nguyen Khanh, staged a fresh coup in January, 1964. "It is far from certain that this military coup will be the last," Mansfield warned Johnson. "On the contrary, it is likely to be only the second in a series, as military leaders, released from all civilian restraint, jockey for control of the power which resides in United States aid." There was no telling where it would end. "This process of coup upon coup may be expected to become increasingly divorced from any real concern with the needs of the Vietnamese people. If the people do not go over actively to the Viet Cong, they will at least care very little about resisting them, let alone crusading against them. Indeed, the bulk of the Vietnamese people, as well as the lower ranks of the armed forces, may already be in this frame of mind." Under the circumstances, the president must consider very carefully any step that increased still further American responsibility for the fate of South Vietnam. "We are close to the point of no return."[38]

Mansfield's "point of no return" was a figure of political speech, as he himself doubtless knew. What made Vietnam so agonizing for Johnson was that there *was* no such point. For the United States, the Vietnam War was a discretionary conflict; never during the fighting were such vital American interests at stake as to preclude all questioning of continued American involvement. No equivalent of Pearl Harbor galvanized American resolve in a way that made victory seem essential to an overwhelming majority of American citizens.

The nearest approximation to Pearl Harbor was the incident in the Gulf of Tonkin in the summer of 1964 that supplied the closest thing to a

---

[37] Mansfield to Johnson, December 7, 1963, box 1, memos to the president file, Johnson Library.
[38] Ibid., Mansfield to Johnson, January 6 and February 1, 1964.

declaration of war any president sought during the years of U.S. involvement. Johnson didn't fabricate the first attack on the *Maddox* off the coast of North Vietnam, and if he responded hastily to reports of a second attack, he wasn't alone. But he *did* mislead Congress and the American public about the circumstances under which U.S. vessels were operating in the Tonkin Gulf, and he presented his Gulf of Tonkin resolution to Congress in a manner he knew the lawmakers would be unable to resist. Johnson had been in the House of Representatives at the time of Pearl Harbor, and in the Senate when North Korea attacked South Korea in 1950. He understood that in an emergency, especially one in which the executive held a monopoly on crucial information, Congress would have no alternative to giving the president what he said he needed to protect American forces and American interests. In August, 1964, Congress followed Johnson's script, and he got his resolution with but two dissenting votes.

But if Johnson was *acting* like an executive, he was *thinking* like a legislator. Even as he led the United States into war, he was far more concerned with his legislative agenda. His great triumph of the summer of 1964 was not passage of the Gulf of Tonkin Resolution, the legislative equivalent of a slam-dunk, but approval of the Civil Rights Act, for which he had to scrap and claw. He spoke strikingly in terms commonly reserved for national security, when he recalled his approach to the battle for civil rights: "A President cannot ask the Congress to take a risk he will not take himself. He must be the combat general in the front lines, constantly exposing his flanks. I gave this fight everything I had in prestige, power, and commitment."[39]

This was a fair description of Johnson's strategy on civil rights; it was precisely the strategy he did *not* apply regarding Vietnam. The point of the Tonkin resolution was not to win the war in Vietnam but to quiet his critics in America. Senator and Republican presidential candidate Barry Goldwater was demanding a more forceful policy in Vietnam; the Tonkin resolution would show that Lyndon Johnson was no pushover. But Johnson had no desire really to *wage* war. In a telephone conversation with Olin Johnston of South Carolina, the Democratic senator said he had been asked if he would vote for Johnson come fall. A month after the signing of the Civil Rights Act, which was anathema across much of the South, this was no casual question.

"I said yes," Johnston told the president. "I'm for keeping us out of war and I'm voting for Lyndon Johnson."

[39] Johnson, *Vantage Point*, pp. 158–159.

Johnson replied, "Well, I don't know whether I can do that. I'm going to do my best, Olin."

Johnston elaborated: "The reason I said that – you are going to find in my state and in the South these mothers and people are *afraid of war*."

"They sure are."

"And we've got to stress that point down my way in order to get votes."

"We sure had, my friend."[40]

Through the autumn of 1964 Johnson stuck to his middle road: between the Goldwater hawks who wanted to hammer North Vietnam and maybe China too, and the mothers of South Carolina who feared a wider war. As a campaign strategy it succeeded brilliantly, propelling Johnson to a landslide victory.

But as a strategy for conducting a war, it failed miserably. The first year of Johnson's own term as president produced two fateful decisions for Vietnam: his approval of a sustained bombing campaign against North Vietnam, and his authorization of the dispatch of 100,000 additional troops to Vietnam. Between them, the bombing and the escalation on the ground made Vietnam's war America's war, with casualties and other costs to match.

These decisions placed Johnson in the select group of American presidents who have led their country into war. But far from adopting the role of forceful wartime leader, he continued to concentrate on domestic legislation. He resented the war as potentially robbing him of the dream he had been nurturing for thirty years: the dream of bettering the lives of ordinary Americans. "I was determined to keep the war from shattering that dream," he told Doris Kearns, "which meant I simply had no choice but to keep my foreign policy in the wings. I knew the Congress as well as I know Lady Bird, and I knew that the day it exploded into a major debate on the war, that day would be the beginning of the end of the Great Society."[41]

The day Johnson dreaded arrived a few weeks into 1966. William Fulbright's dissent the previous September on the Dominican intervention had by now transmuted into a fundamental difference over the conduct of American foreign affairs. The policy of containment, the Foreign Relations chairman contended, had become a hubristic attempt to impose

---

[40] Johnson telephone conversation with Olin Johnston, August 4, 1964, *Taking Charge*, p. 501.

[41] Quoted in Doris Kearns Goodwin, *Lyndon Johnson and the American Dream*, (New American Library: New York, 1991), pp. 282–283.

a Pax Americana on the world. Nowhere was the hubris greater than in Vietnam, and nowhere the cost to America – in lives, treasure and good name – likely to be greater. When Congress convened at the beginning of 1966, Fulbright called a full-dress hearing on the war.

The central witness for the administration was Dean Rusk. His argument was simple. The United States had pledged itself to defend South Vietnam; if the United States reneged, the entire policy of containment would be at risk. "The integrity of our commitments is absolutely essential to the preservation of peace right around the globe."[42]

Fulbright's fellow skeptics grilled Rusk. Wayne Morse stated bluntly: "I disagree with practically every major premise not only contained in his prepared statement but in his discussion."[43] Joseph Clark of Pennsylvania decried the bombing of North Vietnam as futile and dangerous. "Personally," he said, "I am scared to death we are on our way to a nuclear World War III."[44] Claiborne Pell of Rhode Island wondered to what purpose the United States was pounding North Vietnam. Suppose the best: a total defeat of the North. "The vacuum would be filled in by the Chinese forces."[45] Minnesota's Eugene McCarthy reminded Rusk of the distinguished American generals who had warned against a war in Asia. Was Rusk overruling them? Idaho's Frank Church challenged Rusk's characterization of the conflict as an international war. Asserting that the struggle was essentially between Vietnamese, Church declared, "When I went to school that was a civil war."[46] Stuart Symington, a principal advocate of retrenchment in Europe, linked the war in Vietnam to the rest of America's defense burden: "How long do you think the United States can be almost the only financier of freedom and at the same time the defender of freedom?"[47]

Fulbright had the last word. "You deny that there is a Pax Americana," he told Rusk, "but the fact is we have troops in Europe, Korea, Vietnam, and the Dominican Republic. We have military missions in half the nations of the world." The United States was acting as though it possessed the right to dictate the future of Vietnam. The Vietnamese people were

---

[42] *Supplemental Foreign Assistance, Fiscal Year 1966 – Vietnam: Hearings Before the Committee on Foreign Relations, United States Senate, 89th Congress, 2nd session,* January 28; February 4, 8, 10, 17, and 18, 1966 (Washington, 1966), pp. 2–3.

[43] Ibid., p. 10.

[44] Ibid., pp. 26–27.

[45] Ibid., p. 32.

[46] Ibid., pp. 46–47.

[47] Ibid., p. 23.

disputing this right. Who could blame them? "We are obviously intruders from their point of view. We represent the old Western imperialism in their eyes." Fulbright rejected Rusk's contention that American prestige would suffer irreparably upon a withdrawal from Vietnam. The Soviets had not suffered excessively after the Cuban missile crisis. "For a week, maybe, people said they had had a rebuff, and within a month everyone was complimenting them for having contributed to the maintenance of peace." The United States should take note. Rather than waste many thousands of lives and vast amounts of money, the United States should seek a negotiated settlement. "This country is quite strong enough to engage in a compromise without losing its standing in the world and without losing its prestige as a great nation."[48]

Targeting Doves

The legislator in Lyndon Johnson accepted criticism as part of the business of lawmaking. Squeaky wheels got oil; noisy congressmen got pork. But the wartime chief executive interpreted public criticism of the war effort as unpatriotic, potentially seditious. And when it came from a fellow Democrat like Fulbright it was all the more infuriating. Congressman Johnson would never have dreamed of openly criticizing Franklin Roosevelt's handling of World War II. If he *had* felt obliged to differ on some point – and he did not – he would have done so quietly, in the privacy of the White House. To go public could only have undermined American morale and heartened America's enemies. Johnson expected similar consideration when his turn came to guide the country's fortunes during war.

Johnson did all he could to stifle Fulbright's dissent. The president crossed party lines to encourage Everett Dirksen, the prowar leader of Senate Republicans, to keep Fulbright from holding his hearings during regular Senate hours. When this failed (Fulbright countered by threatening to move to television prime time) Johnson tried to preempt Fulbright's hearings by holding a summit conference in Honolulu with South Vietnamese leaders. The official White House explanation – that Washington and Saigon needed to coordinate policies – fooled no one. National security assistant McGeorge Bundy, who first learned of the conference when Johnson announced it to reporters, later conceded that

[48] Ibid., pp. 666–669.

it was "a big farrago meant to take the spotlight off the hearings."[49] At Honolulu, South Vietnamese Prime Minister Nguyen Cao Ky praised the president's resolve in terms strikingly at odds with those emanating from the hearings; Johnson accepted the praise with a comment that the United States and South Vietnam must not be discouraged by "special pleaders who counsel retreat in Vietnam."[50]

Beyond public view, Johnson took other actions to discredit the doves. He instructed J. Edgar Hoover's Federal Bureau of Investigation to examine comments made at the Fulbright hearings to determine whether they reflected the communist party line. He also ordered Hoover to track communist diplomats in the United States to see if they were rendezvousing with antiwar members of Congress.[51]

Johnson was angry at the doves; he was also perplexed. At a White House meeting he voiced genuine puzzlement as to "why Americans who dissent can't do their dissenting in private." He felt himself ahistorically plagued. "Once we are committed to a program of action, there has never been public dissent. You have to go back to the Civil War to find this public dissent." Luckily, those who really counted – the soldiers in Vietnam – did not share the views of the foolish few. "Our men understand why we are in Vietnam, even if senators can't."[52]

The Fulbright hearings afforded a respectability to the antiwar movement it formerly had lacked, and Johnson grew increasingly worried. "This thing is assuming dangerous proportions, dividing the country and giving our enemies the wrong idea of the will of this country to fight," he told his wife Lady Bird."[53]

In the months that followed, Johnson intensified his campaign against dissent. Visiting Australia, one of the few countries actively backing the United States in Vietnam, he delivered an address telling the world not to misinterpret the complaints of a vocal minority. "Don't be misled, as the Kaiser was, or Hitler was, by a few irrelevant speeches," he said. The American people were solidly behind the effort to save South Vietnam. "So don't misjudge our speeches in the Senate."[54]

[49] Randall Bennett Woods, *Fulbright: A Biography* (Cambridge Univ. Press: New York, 1995), p. 403.

[50] Ibid., p. 404.

[51] Robert Dallek, *Lyndon Johnson and His Times, 1961–1973* (New York, 1998), p. 352.

[52] Ibid., p. 356.

[53] Melvin Small, *Johnson, Nixon, and the Doves* (Rutgers University Press: New Brunswick, N.J., 1988), p. 81.

[54] Ibid., p. 86.

Yet one by one, mainstream political leaders deserted the administration. When Democratic congressman Thomas P. O'Neill sent a letter to his Massachusetts constituents explaining that he could no longer support the war, an irate Johnson called him in. "Tip, what kind of a son of a bitch are you?" he demanded. "I expect something like this from those assholes like Bill Ryan [of New York]. . . . But you? You're one of my own." After Johnson calmed down somewhat, he changed his tone. He urged O'Neill to give the administration time. "Don't go running to the press or telling everybody your views on the war. You're the first member of the Democratic establishment to oppose me on this, and I don't want you to start the snowball rolling."[55]

The Beginning of the End of the Cold War

But the snowball simply gained momentum. On March 31, 1968, following the Tet Offensive, Johnson essentially surrendered to the doves on Vietnam. And in doing so, he implicitly conceded the heart of the argument Fulbright, Mansfield, and the other critics of American overextension had been making about U.S. foreign policy in general.

Johnson's halt of most of the bombing and his call for negotiations to terminate the war signaled that containment, as practiced by a generation of Cold War presidents, had run its course. From inception in 1947, containment had been essentially open-ended: the United States would defend almost any country beset by communism, and would devote whatever resources were necessary to such defense. Harry Truman's advisers had warned him against this kind of carte blanche, but in the interest of generating popular support for the new policy, and in the flush of America's postwar military and economic superiority over all challengers, the benefits seemed to outweigh the costs. The costs grew more rapidly than the benefits, though, and by the time Johnson took office a fundamental reassessment of containment was in order.

Johnson's critics caught on sooner than he did. When Mansfield called for compromise with Panama and retrenchment in Europe, when Fulbright, denounced the administration's obsession with communism in the Dominican Republic and with U.S. prestige in Vietnam, when Morse and the others assailed the premises of American involvement in Southeast Asia, they exhibited an appreciation that, whatever validity containment

[55] Dallek, 485–486.

might have had in the late 1940s or early 1950s, by the mid-1960s it was obsolescent, counterproductive and dangerous.

An executive personality in the White House might have disagreed with the critics of containment: over the costs and benefits of this intervention or that, over the slope of the comparative curve down which American power was sliding, over precise nature of the continuing communist challenge. But such a personality would have recognized the need to grapple with this fundamental issue of American security, and to make decisions accordingly.

By contrast, Johnson's legislative personality sought to avoid the issue. Preferring domestic affairs to foreign, Johnson hoped to put off potentially divisive debate on world affairs lest it disrupt his reform agenda. He accommodated Chiari in Panama, agreeing to talk about treaty revision. (The talk lasted until the late 1970s.) He sent marines to the Dominican Republic to prevent that country's becoming a second Cuba and thereby poisoning American politics. He cut a deal with Germany and Britain that short-circuited the campaign for retrenchment. On Vietnam, he tried to solve the problem of hawks versus doves the way he had always solved such contentious debates in the Senate: by giving each side enough of what it wanted so that both sides would come back to the table for the next round.

Johnson's approach did little lasting damage in Panama, the Dominican Republic or Europe; but in Vietnam it produced a war that claimed more than 50,000 American lives (and many times that number of Vietnamese lives). It also forced precisely the kind of decision Johnson had been trying to avoid. Mansfield, Fulbright, and the others had been saying that open-ended containment was unsustainable; sooner or later America would have to decide what was essential in American foreign policy and what merely discretionary. Johnson was finally compelled to agree. Only at the last moment did the executive supplant the legislator – and then too late to save the executive. Nor did the transfer of power serve to save containment, which was formally jettisoned by Richard Nixon, a president who, for all his faults, at least possessed a true executive temperament.

Richard Nixon, Congress, and the War in Vietnam, 1969-1974

Robert D. Schulzinger

Domestic divisions over the war in Vietnam helped Richard M. Nixon win the presidency in 1968. Paradoxically, continuing discord over the course of American policy in Vietnam contributed to Nixon's disgrace and downfall in 1974. During the five and a half years of his presidency, Nixon ignored, abused, and fought with members of the Democratic-controlled Congress on a variety of domestic and international issues. The competition was especially intense on the subject of Vietnam, and it deepened as time went on. Nixon and Henry Kissinger, his national security adviser (and, from September 1973, his Secretary of State) enjoyed wide congressional support for their policy of détente with the Soviet Union and opening relations with the People's Republic of China.

But Congressional endorsement of Nixon's conduct of U.S. foreign relations did not extend to the war in Vietnam. Nixon's policy toward the world other than Vietnam seemed fresh and forward looking in 1969. His efforts in Vietnam, however, appeared to many in the general public and in Congress a continuation of the past. In 1969, most Americans were eager for the war to end. Nixon enjoyed a year-long "honeymoon" on Vietnam, but the U.S. expansion of the war in Cambodia in April, 1970, ignited some of the loudest protests of the war. After Cambodia, more and more members of both houses came to distrust Nixon deeply. They made their displeasure known by introducing and sometimes passing a variety of resolutions and laws limiting the president's authority to carry on the war. Congressional desire to reassert the legislature's warmaking power culminated in the passage of the War Powers Resolution over Nixon's veto in November, 1973. Congress passed the War Powers Resolution in the midst of some of the most tumultuous events of the unfolding Watergate scandal. It did so largely because a majority of the members concluded that during the Vietnam war presidents had illegitimately accumulated power over the nation's foreign affairs.

Congressional assertiveness in foreign affairs represented a sea change in the deference lawmakers had accorded presidents during the Cold War years. The change from Congressional acquiescence in a President's actions abroad to demands for codetermination in foreign policy deeply offended Nixon and Kissinger. Both had come of age politically during the rise of the United States to global power after 1940 when the president's importance in foreign policy had grown. The development of the nuclear rivalry between the United States and the Soviet Union had made the president even more important in foreign policy. In Nixon's and Kissinger's view, only the president had the information, political authority and ability to act quickly to conduct foreign affairs. They believed that members of Congress and the permanent foreign affairs bureaucracy pursued narrow personal or parochial agendas. No one but the president's intimate circle could be trusted to advance a wider, national interest. The president and national security adviser believed that the public too lacked the information, judgment, or patience to decide the most important issues of war and peace. Every four years the electorate could express their confidence in or disapproval of an administration's foreign policy. Between elections, however, they were supposed to acquiesce in a president's foreign policy. In office, Nixon and Kissinger became even more committed to maintaining tight control over foreign affairs. The public responded enthusiastically to the drama of developing détente with the Soviet Union and opening relations with the People's Republic of China. No such applause greeted the administration's actions in Vietnam, much to Nixon's and Kissinger's dismay. Their resistance to congressional participation in foreign policy-making during the first years of the administration helped bring about the very result they wanted least – energetic congressional oversight of the nation's foreign relations.[1]

The year 1968 was one of the most tumultuous in American political history, and the presidential and congressional elections of that year produced unusual results. Richard Nixon, the Republican candidate, won with about 44 percent of the popular vote, while the Democrats retained control of both houses of Congress. Not since 1840 had a president entered the White House with the opposition party in control of

---

[1] Robert D. Schulzinger, *A Time for War: The United States and Vietnam, 1941–1975*, (New York, 1997), pp. 287–300.

the national legislature. After 1968, congressional Democrats no longer felt torn between loyalty to a president of their own political party, Lyndon B. Johnson, and growing antiwar sentiment among traditional Democratic party constituencies. As the Nixon administration developed, more and more Democrats who had backed Johnson's conduct of the war, came to oppose Nixon's prosecution of it.

In addition, the President antagonized some members of Congress, both Democrats and Republicans, who might otherwise have endorsed the substance of his foreign policy. Nixon and Kissinger kept the tightest possible control over foreign affairs. They had little use for the permanent apparatus of foreign affairs officials, and none at all for members of Congress who might want a say in foreign affairs. They made their contempt known, and their disregard for Congressional prerogatives set in motion the most significant efforts at the assertion of Congressional codetermination of foreign policy of the post-World War II era.

Congress gave Nixon a chance to end the Vietnam war in the first few months of his term. This four or five month honeymoon, did not prevent members of Congress from asking for a new direction in the course of U.S. foreign relations. By the late spring and summer of 1969, skeptics, and outright opponents of the war, began asking uncomfortable questions about the extent of U.S. military involvement overseas. Democratic Senator Stuart Symington of Missouri chaired a subcommittee of the Senate Committee in Foreign Relations investigating the scope of American commitments abroad. Senator J. William Fulbright, the chair of the full committee, determined to give the new administration some leeway to end the war through negotiations, specifically excluded Vietnam from the Symington's subcommittee.[2]

The Symington subcommittee, however, touched on Vietnam indirectly by investigating U.S. military assistance to Laos. Members of the subcommittee assailed first the Johnson and now the Nixon administration for conducting a "secret war" next door to Vietnam. As hearings opened, Symington announced that he had become "convinced that the secrecy surrounding our relations with that country has gone on too long."[3] Symington's characterization of the war in Laos as secret or clandestine signaled a major shift in congressional attitudes toward the president's authority. Officials of the Johnson administration had told key congressional

---

[2] Randall Bennet Woods, *J. William Fulbright, Vietnam, and the Search for a Cold War Foreign Policy* (New York, 1998), p. 188.
[3] *Washington Post*, October 20, 1969, p. A1.

leaders about what the United States was doing in Laos and had asked them not to make public the extent to which the CIA and U.S. Army Special Forces were conducting raids on the Ho Chi Minh trail in Laos. But the Symington committee believed that both presidents Johnson and Nixon were maneuvering to secure congressional acquiescence in the early stages of another open-ended commitment similar to the growing involvement of the United States in Vietnam in the early 1960s. Symington's committee hired two energetic investigative reporters, Walter Pincus and Roland Paul, who traveled widely in Southeast Asia and Europe detailing the depth of U.S. involvement in Laos. The White House grew alarmed. Kissinger complained to White House chief of staff H.R. Haldeman about what he called "the Symington hearings problem." Nixon's principal lieutenants were worried that Pincus and Paul "have been scooping up secret data all over the world and leaking it to [the] press... building [a] big administration case." The administration, citing executive privilege, declined to testify publicly about Laos before the Symington subcommittee.[4]

The administration did present its case in executive session. Secretary of State William Rogers addressed a closed-door meeting of the entire Foreign Relations Committee on October 30. Upon leaving the hearing room, he told the press that Congress was well aware of what the United States had been doing in Laos since the Geneva agreement of 1962. Fulbright denied that Congress had been involved. In an attempt to refute Fulbright the State Department released a list of the many times the executive had held briefings for members of Congress about what the United States was doing in Laos. In the same vein, CIA announced that it had conducted briefings for sixty-seven members of the Senate regarding U.S. operations in Laos from 1963 until 1970.[5]

The Nixon administration decided that the best way to deal with the Symington committee was to give it as little publicity as possible and hope that the issue of Laos would fade from public view. In late 1969, the House and Senate adopted an amendment to the military appropriations bill banning the use of funds for U.S. military units or advisers in Laos. The Nixon administration accepted the amendment, not wanting to call attention to what the United States had done and continued to do in Laos. The Senate also adopted a resolution asserting that a national commitment of

---

4 H. R. Haldeman, *The Haldeman Diaries: Inside the Nixon White House*, (G. P. Putnam's sons: New York, 1994), p. 91.
5 John Lehman, *The Executive, Congress and Foreign Policy: Studies of the Nixon Administration*, (Praeger: New York, 1974, 1976), p. 129.

U.S. armed forces overseas could come "only from affirmative action taken by the executive and legislative branches of the United States government a treaty, statute or concurrent resolution of both Houses of Congress specifically providing for such a commitment."[6]

By both actions Congress served notice that it was prepared to use the power of the purse and its constitutional prerogatives to regain some control over national decisions to use force. Moreover, the Symington subcommittee's investigations into U.S. commitments to Laos eventually forced the White House into public explanations concerning U.S. activities in the kingdom. The administration denied that the United States had violated the 1962 Geneva accord or that there were any U.S. ground combat troops in Laos. It was forced to admit, however, that there were 1,040 U.S. personnel in Laos, either working directly for the U.S. government or for contractors. The administration also revealed that the United States was flying combat missions over Laos in an effort to slow the flow of supplies down the Ho Chi Minh trail.[7]

The Nixon administration's decision to send U.S. forces into Cambodia to destroy the headquarters of the PLAFVN in 1970 ignited a firestorm of Congressional opposition. In March the United States had supported Cambodian General Lon Nol's coup d'etat against Prince Norodom Sihanouk. Once in power Lon Nol and the American MACV in Saigon urged Washington to send forces into Cambodia to root out Communist positions there. In April, the Senate Foreign Relations Committee suspected that something was afoot in Cambodia and urged the Nixon administration to go slow. Secretary of State William Rogers faced hostile questions from Senators Frank Church (D-ID) and John Sherman Cooper (R-KY) about whether the United States intended to supply arms to Lon Nol. They warned Rogers against any U.S. military action in Cambodia. The senators pledged to use the Congressional power of the purse to deny funds for any U.S. operations in the kingdom.

Kissinger also provided Congress with the vaguest sorts of briefing on the administration's intentions toward Cambodia. On April 24, six days before the United States Army led the ARVN into Cambodia, Kissinger met with Mississippi Democratic Senator John Stennis, chair of the Armed Services Committee. Carefully choosing his words, Kissinger told Stennis,

---

[6] William Bundy, *A Tangled Web: The Making of Foreign Policy in the Nixon Presidency*, (Hill and Wang: New York, 1998), p. 71. Thomas M. Franck and Edward Weisband, *Foreign Policy by Congress* (Oxford University Press: New York, 1979), p. 68.

[7] Lehman, pp. 145–146.

that a "U.S. supported incursion into Cambodia" was needed to assure the success of Vietnamization. While Kissinger was talking to Stennis, President Nixon, by prearrangement with Kissinger, called the senator and asked for his approval of the incursion. Stennis gave his assent, but he probably did not believe that the words "U.S. supported" meant that the United States would actually commit its own forces to the operation.[8] Over the next week, while the administration made final preparations for a U.S. led operation in Cambodia, Nixon administration officials neglected to inform members of Congress that the operation was going to include U.S. troops.

On April 29, 32,000 U.S. infantrymen entered the Parrot's Beak area of Cambodia to destroy the headquarters of the Vietcong. The next evening, April 30, Nixon went on national television with a speech justifying the incursion. He claimed that American credibility was at stake. The United States acted to avoid being perceived as a "pitiful, helpless giant." The incursion would buy protection for the ARVN while the program of Vietnamization went into effect. The President explained that he had kept Congress in the dark about the plans for the operation to assure secrecy. As he prepared for his speech, Nixon frequently called Haldeman for ideas about how to keep Congress in line. The President wanted to block any Congressional limits on the Cambodian operation. He told Haldeman to "be sure we kill or deflect the Reid Amendment [prepared by New York Democratic Representative Ogden Reid] that would stop efforts in Cambodia."[9]

In the wake of the incursion, college campuses erupted in antiwar protests. The next day, May 1, Nixon, poured gasoline on the flames when he referred to the campus demonstrators as "bums." On Sunday, May 3, the governor of Ohio ordered units of his state's National Guard to patrol Kent State University, the site of a weekend of antiwar demonstrations. The next day the Guard broke up a rally called to demand that all military personnel leave the campus. As the demonstrators fled the tear gas, guardsmen opened fire, killing four and wounding eight. Outraged at the killings, tens of thousands of college students traveled to Washington to demonstrate against the war. They held vigils at the Lincoln Memorial, the Washington Monument, and the White House. They crowded into congressional offices, demanding that lawmakers end the war.[10]

[8] Bundy, p. 152.
[9] Haldeman, pp. 157–158.
[10] Bundy, pp. 154–157.

In May and June, Congress moved across a wide front to reassert its authority over U.S. activities in Indochina. Republican Senator Cooper joined Democratic Senator Church to introduce an amendment to the military assistance bill cutting off funds for the operation in Cambodia. The administration used a variety of tactics to delay the enactment of the Cooper-Church amendment. Nixon's political adviser Murray Chotiner advised Kissinger to stress that Cooper-Church amendment prohibited assistance only "to Cambodia." The administration's position, however, was "we are not giving assistance to Cambodia, but are fighting the Vietnamese *in* Cambodia as part of the Vietnamese conflict." Jeb Magruder on Haldeman's staff advised taking the public relations offensive. He planned a massive July 4 rally led by the evangelist Billy Graham to support the president's Vietnam policies. The president should meet publicly with "hard hats" (construction laborers who were outspoken in their support of the Cambodia operation) and conservative religious leaders. He advocated "petition and recall movements" against senators who had spoken out against the Cambodian invasion. He suggested distribution of a 1961 *Cornell Law Quarterly* article in which Senator Fulbright had supported an expansive use of presidential authority in foreign affairs.[11]

Nixon also tried more conventional methods of conciliation and legislative delay to vitiate the Cooper-Church amendment and other Congressional curbs on the President's ability to wage war in Indochina. In the midst of the national fury over Kent State, the President promised on May 8, that U.S. forces would leave Cambodia by June 30. The White House worked with Senate and House Republicans to make certain that the Cooper-Church amendment did not come to a vote before that deadline. Senator Hugh Scott, the minority leader, advised the White House that the amendment would pass the Senate, but that the minority Republicans could delay consideration through June. Republicans added language to the Cooper-Church amendment denying that it impugned "the constitutional power of the President and commander in chief." The delays and changes in language worked for the White House. The Senate approved an altered version of the amendment on June 30, the day U.S. forces withdrew from Cambodia.

The scene then shifted to the House of Representatives. The lower house had been more supportive of both President Johnson's and Nixon's

---

[11] Murray Chotiner to Henry Kissinger, May 4, 1970. Jeb Magruder to H. R. Haldeman, May 21, 1970. Thomas C. Korologos Files. Nixon presidential materials project, National Archives II, College Park, Maryland.

war policy, and it maintained that deference throughout 1970 and early 1971. On June 6, the House turned down the Reid amendment by an overwhelming vote of 321–32. The House rejected the Cooper-Church amendment in July. A House-Senate conference debated the amendment for the next six months, and it was not enacted. In January, 1971, Congress passed a military appropriations bill containing a version of the Cooper-Church amendment. The amendment was worded in such a way as to indicate congressional support for what Nixon was doing: "In line with the expressed intention of the United States none of the funds appropriated pursuant to this ... act may be used to finance the introduction of United States ground combat troops into Cambodia." The bill's two senate sponsors agreed to a key modification – U.S. combat air action would be permitted if it was directed against North Vietnamese supply or forces buildup in Cambodia. Since the Nixon administration no longer had ground forces in Cambodia at that time, Congress, in effect, gave the president the free hand he wanted.[12]

The Cambodian invasion created momentum for several other measures to assert congressional authority over the power to wage war in Indochina. Senators Mark Hayfield, an Oregon Republican, and George McGovern, a South Dakota Democrat, sponsored a resolution to cut off all funds for waging the war in Vietnam by the end of 1970. Senator Jacob Javits, a moderate Republican from New York, who had been largely supportive of the conduct of the war, introduced legislation to define better Congress's role in declaring and prosecuting foreign wars. Finally, a bipartisan push arose to repeal the Gulf of Tonkin Resolution. The Nixon administration strongly opposed the first two efforts. Somewhat paradoxically, given its commitment to the widest possible presidential autonomy in foreign affairs, the administration supported the drive to repeal the Tonkin Gulf resolution. The contradiction was more apparent, than real, however. The Nixon administration based its backing for a repeal of the Tonkin Gulf Resolution on the grounds that a President, as commander-in-chief of the armed forces, needed *no* Congressional authorization for the use of force.

The McGovern-Hatfield resolution gathered twenty-three co-sponsors in the Senate, but it never stood a chance. The Senate defeated it by a vote of 55–39 on September 1, 1970. The next year, the Senate again turned

---

[12] Lehman, pp. 56–57, John Hart Ely, *War and Responsibility: Constitutional Lessons of Vietnam and Its Aftermath*, (Princeton University Press: Princeton, 1993), p. 38. See also Bundy, pp. 160–161, 224.

down McGovern-Hatfield 55–42 on June 16, 1971. The next day the House also defeated the resolution by a vote of 237–147.[13] No less a figure than Fulbright, a long-time critic of presidential actions in Vietnam urged McGovern to modify the terms. Kissinger told Fulbright that Nixon would interpret McGovern-Hatfield as undermining his authority. He would lash out at Congressional doves for giving comfort to Hanoi. Kissinger, as was his custom when dealing with opponents of the war, implied that he shared their concerns, but he had to tread carefully around Nixon. Although Fulbright strongly dissented from Johnson's and Nixon's conduct of the Vietnam, the chairman of the foreign relations committee was largely supportive of Kissinger's efforts to lower tension with the Soviet Union. Fulbright had other, constitutional or political, reasons to be suspicious of the McGovern-Hatfield resolution. Their legislation imposed Congressional restrictions on the President's use of armed force in Vietnam. Fulbright and other Congressional doves had believed since about 1966 that the president had gone into Vietnam without congressional authorization. He feared that Nixon would use Hatfield-McGovern actually to *augment* his power. The president would claim authority to send troops unless congress specifically forbade it. He would argue that "the President can do whatever he pleases – anything goes, that is, unless it is explicitly prohibited."[14]

Congress never passed Hatfield-McGovern, but the War Powers resolution and the repeal of the Tonkin Gulf resolution did become law. Javits' War Powers resolution became law in 1973, and Congress repealed Tonkin Gulf in January 1971. By the end of the Johnson administration the Tonkin Gulf incident had become controversial on both factual and constitutional grounds. Serious doubts arose that North Vietnamese vessels had fired on U.S. naval destroyers on August 4, 1964, as the Johnson administration had claimed. Even if the North Vietnamese had attacked the U.S. navy, there was substantial evidence that the United States had provoked the North Vietnamese by conducting offensive military operations within their territorial waters. Constitutionally, many Senators doubted that the Tonkin Gulf Resolution of 1964 granted the president the sort of open-ended authority to escalate the war to the degree he had in 1966 and 1967. Dissenters who voted for the Resolution in 1964 argued in 1967 and 1968, that they had authorized only a retailaition

[13] Ely, p. 33.

[14] Woods, pp. 228–229. See also Jeffrey Kimball, *Nixon's Vietnam War* (University Press of Kansas: Lawrence, Kansas, 1998), pp. 243–244.

against the attacks in the Tonkin Gulf, not a major ground war in Asia.

During the last two years of his term Johnson had explored the possibility of replacing the Tonkin Gulf resolution with another Congressional declaration of support of his policies. By that time, however, skepticism had grown, and the Johnson administration did not press the issue. For its part, the Nixon administration did not refer to the Tonkin Gulf resolution in justifying its actions in the Vietnam war. Indeed, when Nixon was asked for the legal justification of the incursion into Cambodia, he asserted "the right of the President of the United States under the Constitution to protect the lives of American men."[15]

At the beginning of the Nixon administration, Charles Matthias, a moderate Republican from Maryland, moved to repeal the Tonkin Gulf resolution an the grounds that it was no longer relevant to the current conduct of American foreign policy. The Nixon administration, asserting the prerogative of the commander-in-chief to order U.S. forces into combat, said it was up to Congress. The Foreign Relations Committee formally repealed Tonkin Gulf just before the Cambodia invasion, but the uproar over Cambodia eclipsed interest in the Tonkin Gulf repeal. In June, the White House and Senate Republicans used a series of parliamentary maneuvers to fashion the repeal of the Tonkin Gulf resolution to their liking. Republican Robert Dole of Kansas, a stalwart supporter of the Nixon administration's policies in Vietnam and Cambodia introduced the repeal. He and Senator Hugh Scott, the Republican Senate minority leader, argued that the resolution had long been called meaningless by Vietnam doves. They voted for repeal to show that President Nixon needed no Congressional authority to conduct a war. The entire Senate voted to repeal Tonkin by a vote of 81–10 on June 24, 1970. Six months later the House followed suit.[16]

All the participants – the president, Congressional doves and Congressional supporters of the president's conduct of the Vietnam war – had reasons to be both encouraged and apprehensive about the results. In the short term, the Nixon administration had altered the nature of both the Cooper-Church amendment and the repeal of the Tonkin Gulf resolution to its benefit. In early 1971, the president still seemed to have wide latitude in conducting the war in Vietnam. But the aftermath of the Cambodian incursion had emboldened Congress to become more

---

[15] Bundy, pp. 162–63.
[16] *Ibid.*, pp. 162–163, 223, Woods, pp. 226–227.

assertive in supervising the use of force than at any time before in the cold war era.

The focus of Presidential-Congressional conflict over the Vietnam war shifted away from legislation to electoral politics in 1971 and 1972. During these years Nixon's and Kissinger's foreign policy reputation soared. The two men succeeded in diverting attention away from the apparently endless U.S. war in Vietnam toward improved relations with the Soviet Union and the People's Republic of China. Nixon and Kissinger hoped greater warmth toward the Soviet Union and China might lead to a diplomatic resolution of the Vietnam war. Those hopes never bore fruit, but the thaw in the Cold War brought benefits of its own. The Vietnam war mattered less once the president and the national security adviser relaxed tensions with the major communist nations.

Détente captured the public in 1971 and 1972. In the spring of 1971, Kissinger and Soviet Ambassador to the U.S. Anatoly Dobrynin announced that their two nations would sign an arms control treaty within a year. Détente seemed to proceed, even in the face of the ongoing war in Vietnam. At the same time, something dramatic was taking place in relations between the United States and the PRC. The PRC hosted a visiting American table-tennis team in the spring and invited journalists in the summer. Unknown to the public at this time, the Nixon administration pursued a diplomatic initiative with the PRC as well. In July, these remarkable contacts became public with the announcement that Kissinger had visited Beijing to prepare the way for Nixon to travel to China in 1972. Nixon's trip to China in February, 1972, wiped away every other foreign policy story. The television pictures of President and Mrs. Nixon at the Great Wall and of Nixon raising his glass to Chou Enlai were unlike anything Americans had seen since the end of World War II. Members of congress opposed to Nixon's conduct of the Vietnam war, lauded what they characterized as his courage and vision in opening relations with the PRC.[17]

Dovish members of Congress damned Nixon's Vietnam policy while applauding his efforts at relaxing tensions with the Soviet Union. This ambivalence reached its climax in May, 1972, when the United States simultaneously attacked North Vietnam and moved closer to the Soviet Union. The Nixon administration responded to the North Vietnamese spring offensive of 1972 by bombing Hanoi and mining the harbor of Haiphong. The bombing campaign, code-named Operation Linebacker,

[17] Haldeman, pp. 416–422, Bundy, pp. 303–307, Schulzinger, pp. 277–283.

began in early May, three weeks before Nixon was scheduled to meet Soviet Communist Party General Secretary Leonid Brezhnev in Moscow. Editorialists, members of Congress and even Kissinger worried that the Soviets would cancel the summit in outrage over the attacks on an ostensible ally. They did not – to Kissinger's relief, Nixon's satisfaction, and Congressional doves' amazement. The summit, like Nixon's visit to China, validated Nixon's claim as a master of foreign policy. In both places old communist adversaries welcomed the venerable anticommunist.[18] Nixon's initiatives with China and the Soviet Union in the first half of 1972 seemed to confirm the diminished importance of the war in Vietnam for U.S. foreign policy. Since 1966 congressional critics of U.S. war policy had claimed that Washington's involvement in faraway Vietnam was sapping the nation's ability to conduct an effective foreign policy in more vital regions of the world. Nixon's and Kissinger's opening to China and détente with the Soviet Union undermined that argument. Other developments also converged to lower public anger over Vietnam. No one was drafted in the second half of 1972. The Nixon administration reduced the number of troops to under 60,000 by the summer as well. Continuing negotiations between Kissinger and Le Du Tho also in Paris created optimism. To many Americans, a settlement seemed to be in sight in the summer of 1972.

That was not the view, however, of Senator George McGovern of South Dakota, by June the favorite for the Democratic nomination for President in 1972. McGovern, the most outspoken critic of Nixon's Vietnam policy among the Democratic candidates, argued that negotiations with the North should concentrate on ending the war and returning U.S. troops home. McGovern argued that the United States had long ago fulfilled any obligations it might have had to preserving the viability of the government of the Republic of Vietnam's President Nguyen Van Thieu.

Nixon pounced on McGovern's willingness to let Thieu fall. He ordered staff member Patrick Buchanan, his most fire-breathing publicist, to write a speech labeling McGovern "a sincere dedicated radical." Nixon wanted to "lock [McGovern] into his positions." McGovern had promised to travel to Hanoi and settle the Vietnam war in 90 days. Nixon wanted the public to think "it doesn't take 90 days to surrender."[19] Nixon encouraged leaks to the press that the United States and Hanoi were making progress in their talks. McGovern, on the other hand, would not

---

[18] Haldeman, pp. 451–458, Kimball, pp. 311–318.
[19] Haldeman, pp. 469–470.

negotiate with Hanoi, the president declared – he would yield.[20] Nixon's friend Charles Rebozo informed the President of the success he had with Cuban Americans in denouncing McGovern's willingness to compromise with Hanoi. "I just talk about amnesty. [McGovern's proposal to forgive draft offenders], bugging out of Vietnam. . . . I never mention McGovern's name. But . . . everybody gets up afterwards and says: That sonofabitch, McGovern."[21]

After the Democrats nominated McGovern in July, the senator's campaign almost collapsed. He withdrew his support for his choice for vice-president, Missouri Senator Thomas Eagleton, after Eagleton acknowledged having received electroshock treatment for depression. Several prominent Democrats turned down McGovern's invitation to join the ticket. Finally, Sargent Shriver, the former director of the Peace Corps and the Office of Economic Opportunity, agreed to run as McGovern's vice-presidential candidate. In addition, McGovern lagged far behind Nixon in campaign funds. Public opinion polls consistently showed Nixon between 20 and 30 percentage points ahead of McGovern in the late summer.

In these circumstances, Nixon resisted Kissinger's admonition to speed the process of negotiations by making concessions to the North. Instead, the president continued to portray McGovern as an advocate of surrender, a stratagem that certainly seemed to be working. Charles Colson delighted Nixon, telling him that hecklers were shouting at McGovern: "Why are you giving amnesty to traitors?" On a walk through a midwestern factory a worker told McGovern "you're giving up the country; you're surrendering, and let's bomb the hell out of them." Startled, McGovern asked if the man really believed that such a course would bring the American prisoners home earlier. The man replied "Right, we should bomb the hell out of them a lot more. . . . Nixon wants to show them we have a power over here and we're not just a flunky second rate country." Colson reported that the employee told a television interviewer that he agree with Nixon's handling of the war and thought McGovern favored surrender. "Oh, God," Colson exulted "he just cut the hell out of" McGovern.[22]

In mid-October a breakthrough finally occurred in the Paris negotiations. Key provisions included a cease-fire in place, the return of prisoners of war, the withdrawal of U.S. troops, a continued presence of North

[20] Kimball, p. 329.
[21] Stanley Kutler, ed., Abuse of Power: The New Nixon Tapes, (New York, 1997), p. 61.
[22] *Ibid.*, p. 153.

Vietnamese troops in the South, and recognition of the legitimacy of the government of the Republic of Vietnam. As had happened in the last days of the 1968 election, President Thieu erupted in fury at the terms of the agreement. He believed that agreeing to keep North Vietnamese troops in the South sounded the death knell of his authority. But in 1968, Thieu could delay the agreement the Johnson administration had made with Hanoi in the hopes of swinging the election to Nixon. Now, as Haldeman observed, the current agreement "is the best Thieu is ever going to get, and unlike '68, when Thieu screwed Johnson, he had Nixon as an alternative. Now he has McGovern."[23]

On October 26, 1972, Kissinger announced that he and Le Duc Tho had reached a tentative agreement in Paris and "peace is at hand" in Vietnam. Nixon's initial reaction to Kissinger's briefing was irritation that the national security adviser had stolen the limelight. The president also rebuked Kissinger for not hammering McGovern for conducting what Nixon called a "peace by surrender forum." Nixon believed that the contrast between his "peace with honor" formulation and McGovern's eagerness to withdraw U.S. forces from the war represented his strongest electoral asset. Nixon told Haldeman that his campaign had to stress that Nixon "has achieved his goals in the settlement: the return of POWs, the cease-fire and no Communist government." Nixon wanted to contrast his toughness with McGovern's weakness. According to Nixon, the Democratic Senator would "leave the POWs there, pull a unilateral withdrawal and disarm the South Vietnamese, and provide for a Communist takeover." Nixon also perceived electoral advantage in claiming to have been serenely above the political fray. He urged his staff to "make the point that we've been working on this all down the line, and that there's no concern with the election, our concern is to get it nailed down."[24]

However self-serving, Nixon's tactic of appearing above electioneering paid off. The incumbent overwhelmed the challenger on election day. The public's support for Nixon's foreign policy accomplishments seemed impervious to signs that the war in Vietnam had not been settled. The President won a landslide victory despite the disintegration of the tentative agreement Kissinger an Le Duc Tho reached in October. Nixon was wrong when he predicted that Thieu had no choice but to acquiesce in the arrangement out of fear of a McGovern win. The Democrat was so far behind, that the South Vietnamese correctly reasoned he had little chance.

[23] Kimball, p. 340.
[24] Haldeman, p. 525.

Nor did the public respond to McGovern's complaints against the President's deceptions. McGovern claimed that Kissinger and Le Duc Tho had not reached an agreement. He charged that the Watergate break-in in June was a grave matter. Voters did not seem concerned. Instead, many thought McGovern was making desperate, last-minute accusations.

War and peace in Vietnam dominate public consciousness in the ten weeks between the election of 1972 and Nixon's second inaugural of January, 1973. In November and December the United States put political pressure on South Vietnam to accept the agreement. Deputy national security adviser Alexander Haig told President Thieu that the United States intended to reach an agreement with North Vietnam with or without the South's assent. Should Thieu agree, Haig promised billions of dollars in military aid and renewed American bombing if the North broke the cease-fire. If the South still refused, the United States would go ahead anyway. On December 18, Nixon ordered massive strategic bombing of North Vietnam. Wave after wave of B-52s inflicted the heaviest damage of the war on the capital of Hanoi and the port city of Haiphong. Nixon directed this Christmas bombing, as it was quickly labeled (officially code-named Linebacker II) at the political leadership in both North and South Vietnam. He wanted to drive the North back to the negotiating table in Paris and convince the South that the United States was serious about resuming the bombing of the North after a peace agreement was signed.[25]

Nixon stopped the bombing at the beginning of January, and negotiations quickly resumed. By the time of the inaugural on January 20, 1973, Kissinger and Le Duc Tho had worked out terms of an agreement similar to the one they had arranged in October. An immediate cease-fire would be followed within sixty days by the return of prisoners of war held by each side. The United States would then remove the last of its military personnel from the South. The North's troops would remain in the South, but Hanoi promised not to take advantage of the armistice by adding to its forces below the demilitarized zone. President Thieu would remain in office as chief executive, but a committee of national reconciliation, including representatives of the National Liberation Front, would attempt to broaden the government of the Republic of Vietnam. An International Control Commission would supervise various provisions of the agreement. Nixon also made secret pledges to both Vietnams. He offered over $3 billion in reconstruction assistance to the North (although he carefully hedged his promise with the admonition that Congress held

[25] Bundy, pp. 353–362.

the purse strings.) The United States would continue to arm the Army of the Republic of Vietnam, and he added that the United States would bomb the North once more in the DRV attacked the South. On January 23, Kissinger and Le Duc Tho initialed the agreements, and on January 27, Secretary of State William Rogers and Le Duc Tho signed them.[26]

An exuberant public reaction in the United States deeply gratified the White House staff. The press office informed Nixon that "there is great admiration for the President which seems to grow as we move farther from Washington." Most newspaper editorials praised "the fact of the cease-fire with little concern for the terms." The Linebacker II bombing appeared to many editorialists to have finally brought the DRV to an agreement. The *Denver Post* called the Paris agreements "a tribute to the skill and statesmanship of Henry Kissinger and the determination, spirit and persistence of President Nixon." An Alabama newspaper praised Nixon and Kissinger for their "risk taking, doggedness and high diplomatic skill." Nothing brought deeper satisfaction to Nixon and his lieutenants than the favorable contrast commentators drew between the President's apparent toughness and what they characterized as the weakness of Congressional critics of the war. The *Birmingham News* lauded the "patient, long suffering efforts of the administration.... They represent, in fact, a much better bargain than Sen. George McGovern or other 'dove' critics were willing to settle for." A California radio station joined in the mockery of the Congressional critics: "Their predictions were wrong and [Nixon's] actions were correct."[27]

And yet much of the public's onfidence in Nixon's and Kissinger's diplomatic acheivement was misplaced. The Paris accords were riddled with ambiguities and unfinished business. Nowhere were the agreements less satisfactory than in their references to Laos and Cambodia. These two neighbors of Vietnam were not included in the original cease-fire and the Paris accords contained only vague promises that the parties would work for an end to the fighting there. Most of the Ho Chi Minh trail went through Laos or Cambodia, and the DRV continued to supply its forces in the South through the trail. A cease-fire briefly took place in Laos, but it quickly broke down. By March, the United States had resumed bombing of the Ho Chi Minh trail in both countries. In the four months after the

---

[26] *Ibid.*, pp. 365–68.
[27] Herbert Klein to president, February 13, 1973. box 27, Vietnam 2/3. Ron Zeigler files. White House special files, Staff members' office files, Nixon presidential materials project, National Archives II.

Paris accords, the United States dropped eighty-thousand tons of bombs on Cambodia alone.[28]

By the spring of 1973 the political atmosphere in Washington had changed abruptly. The euphoria over the Paris accords had evaporated, and Nixon's popularity plunged as the investigation of the Watergate scandal intensified. The return of the last American prisoners of war on March 27, removed the final reason the public had to be concerned about the war in Indochina. Congress, back in session, reflected this widespread weariness, even disgust with the fighting in Indochina.[29]

From March through June 1973, Congress successfully challenged the Nixon administration's ability to wage an aerial war in Laos and Cambodia. This effort to end the bombing in states bordering Vietnam proved to be the most successful legislative initiative to limit presidential warmaking power of the entire Vietnam war era. In March Senators Frank Church of Idaho, a Democrat, and Frank Case of New Jersey, a Republican, both long-time opponents of the U.S. war in Vietnam, introduced legislation cutting off appropriations for the bombing of Cambodia. Unlike earlier restrictions, which had been the handiwork of Congressional doves, longtime supporters of the war joined the call to end U.S. participation in the fighting. The House Democratic caucus, customarily more supportive of the war than their counterparts in the Senate, backed a cutoff of all U.S. military action throughout Indochina. Republican Senator Milton Young of South Dakota, one of Congress's staunchest supporters of the Nixon administration's Vietnam policy, observed "we have got our prisoners of war out with honor, and what's the point of supporting a government that has no will to fight and is corrupt?" Arkansas Democratic Senator John McCllelan, who had been as supportive of the U.S. war effort in Vietnam as the other Arkansas Senator, J. William Fulbright, had been critical of it, concurred that the risk of having new prisoners of war was too high. "I have chosen," he said "to risk the consequences of stopping the bombing. At the end of June, as the public's horror at the daily revelations of the Senate Watergate hearings grew, the Nixon administration conceded. Republican House leader Gerald Ford, told his colleagues that the president would accept a law halting U.S. military operations in Laos and Cambodia after August 15. On June 29, both houses of Congress adopted a bill with the August 15 cut-off date, and a weakened President Nixon signed it. Senator McGovern found vindication in

---

[28] Bundy, p. 385.
[29] Schulzinger, pp. 307–312.

the law and called June 29, 1973, "the happiest day of my life." Thomas Franck and Edward Wiesband, two scholars who wrote one of the first and one of the best accounts of congressional efforts to control foreign policy labeled the date "the Bastille Day of the congressional revolution." June 29 was the day on which "the president of the United States acknowledged the right of Congress to end U.S. military involvement in Indochina and promised to stop bombing Cambodia."[30]

The five months from July through November, 1973, was one of the most tumultuous periods in United States political and diplomatic history. As the Watergate scandal washed over Nixon, Kissinger took over as Secretary of State. A war in the Middle East between Israel on one side and Egypt and Syria on the other brought the United States and the Soviet Union to the brink of hostilities and initiated a world-wide economic slump.

In the midst of these traumas, Congress extended its authority over the use of military force. In July, both house both houses adopted versions of the War Powers resolution Senator Javits had introduced in 1970. In October, a House-Senate conference committee fashioned a final resolution under which the president had to notify Congress within sixty days of sending U.S. forces into combat or harm's way. Once the president notified Congress, a sixty day clock began to tick. Unless Congress agreed within those sixty days to approve the sending of the troops, the president had to begin withdrawing them. All of the forces had to be out of harm's way thirty days after the expiration of the first sixty day limit. Both houses of Congress approved the War Powers Act in mid-October. The measure cleared the Senate with an overwhelming majority, but the margin in the House of Representatives was three votes short of the two-thirds needed to override Nixon's veto of the measure. A series of international and domestic shocks occurred immediately after Nixon's veto, severely weakening the President's public standing. The Middle East War preoccupied Nixon and Kissinger. At the same time they had to deal with worsening relations with the Soviet Union. The President fired Archibald Cox, the special counsel he had appointed in the spring to investigate Watergate. The public exploded in fury at Nixon's firing of Cox, and thousands of people demanded that Congress impeach the President. In this atmosphere, Congress overrode Nixon's veto of the War Powers Act on November 7, 1973.[31]

---

[30] Franck and Wiesband, pp. 13–21, Ely, pp. 39–41.
[31] Bundy, pp. 398–399, Ely, p. 41, Franck and Wiesband, pp. 68–70.

So ended the five-year-long battle between President Nixon and Congress over the authority to commit American military forces to fight abroad. At the time it appeared as if Congress had taken back the war-making power. The events of the next twenty-five years, however, demonstrated that presidents retained wide latitude in committing U.S. forces to combat. The lesson of the conflict between the Nixon administration and Congress over the Vietnam war proved to be complex and ambiguous. Nixon entered office in 1969 with inconsiderable public support, or at least acquiescence, in his attempt to end the Vietnam war on terms he deemed acceptable. For about a year his diplomatic and military tactics retained public backing. As time went on, however, Nixon and Kissinger squandered their original goodwill. Many members of Congress came to resent what they considered to be presidential high handedness and deception. Lawmakers' antagonism toward the White House translated into a series of restrictions on the president. These efforts, in turn, only deepened Nixon's hostility toward Congressional dissenters from his Vietnam policy, and a chasm developed between the executive and legislature over the determination of U.S. foreign policy.

Index

Cooper-Church Amendment, 135
  impacts of, 133, 148
  passage of, 115, 137, 137n39, 169,
    214, 254–6
  revision of, 197–9, 288–9, 291
  second, 138–42
corporate liberalism, 56
corporations, 142, 148, 218–19,
    223–4
corruption, 4, 56
Costa Rica, 66
coups, 6, 130, 144
  covert operations and, 144–7, 272
  Lon Nol and, 286
  military, 4, 67–8, 70, 274
  in Saigon, 187
  against Sihanouk, 254
  in South Vietnam, 185
  support for, 272
Cox, Archibald, 299
crimes, penalties for, 4
Cuba, 17, 65
  intervention in, 123, 225–6
  Missile Crisis, 36, 37, 38, 98–9,
    208, 262, 278
  as protectorate of United States, 19
  resolutions on, 187
cultural diversity, 40
culture, 1, 2, 38. *See also* intercultural
    exchange
  global, 40
  political, 3, 215, 216n35, 227
  in Southeast Asia, 11
customs receiverships, 27–8

Dakota Wesleyan University, 87, 92
Daschle, Tom, 118n89
de Gaulle, Charles, 186, 211, 261,
    267–9, 273
deaths, 6. *See also* massacres
  number of, 9, 107, 109, 112, 201,
    212
DeBenedetti, Charles, 28, 115n83

Decade of Development, 97
Declaration of Independence, 260
decolonization, 14, 31, 33, 39, 40
deescalation, 111, 138
defense procurement authorization,
    199
defense projects, 63
Demilitarized Zone (DMZ), 9, 250,
    296
democracy, 4, 55, 57, 60
  v. autocracy, 24
  communism v., 49
  dictatorships v., 87n9
Democratic National Conventions,
    108, 122, 253
Democratic Republic of Vietnam
    (DRV), 3–4
Democrats, 6, 92
  peacemaking and, 43, 284
  policies of, 44, 237, 242
demonstrations, 4, 39, 198, 287
  peace, 112–15, 114n78, 185
Depressions, 20, 86, 90, 94, 220
desegregation, 112, 156
despotism, 148
détente, 282, 283, 292
Dewey, John, 29
Dewey, Thomas, 43, 44
dictatorships, 87n9, 107
  support for, 66, 70, 72, 117, 146,
    167, 208, 225–6
Diem, Ngo Dinh
  assassination of, 185, 187, 244,
    272
  Food for Peace and, 103
  rule by, 3–4, 151, 183–4, 208, 273
  support for, 70, 173, 177, 179–80,
    204, 226
Dien Bien Phu, 3, 36, 178, 207, 240–1
Dillon, Douglas, 268
diplomacy, 7, 42–5
  containment and, 243–4
  culture v. politics and, 1